ACQUISITION AND PERFORMANCE OF COGNITIVE SKILLS

Wiley Series
Human Performance and Cognition

**Acquisition and Performance
of Cognitive Skills**
*Edited by Ann M. Colley
and John R. Beech*

Further titles in preparation

ACQUISITION AND PERFORMANCE OF COGNITIVE SKILLS

Edited by

Ann M. Colley and John R. Beech
University of Leicester

JOHN WILEY & SONS

Chichester · New York · Brisbane · Toronto · Singapore

Library of Congress Cataloging in Publication Data:
Acquisition and performance of cognitive skills/edited by Ann M.
Colley and John R. Beech.
    p. cm.—(Wiley series in human performance and cognition)
Bibliography: p.
Includes indexes.
ISBN 0 471 91461 4
    1. Cognition. I. Colley, Ann M. II. Beech, John R.
III. Series.
BF311.A27   1989   88-34579
153—dc19   CIP

British Library Cataloguing in Publication Data
Acquisition and performance of cognitive
  skills.—(Wiley series in human performance
  and cognition)
  1. Man. Cognitive development.
  I. Colley, Ann M. II. Beech, John R.
  153.4

  ISBN 0 471 91461 4

Typeset by Acorn Bookwork, Salisbury
Printed and bound in Great Britain by Anchor Press Ltd, Tiptree

Contents

Series preface

This Series of studies began as a systematic attempt to provide clear explanations of the main issues affecting human performance, based on a broad range of experimental research. Earlier books in the Series dealt with such topics as the analysis of human skills, the effects of sleep and biological rhythms, the impact of stress and fatigue on human behaviour, the sustaining of attention during vigilance performance, the effects of noise on efficiency, the changes resulting from aging, and sex differences in performance. In each of these volumes, however, it became evident that it was necessary to take account of the cognitive processes that determine the overt expression of human performance variables. In fact, the first volume of the Series, on Human Skills, concluded that the relevant type of skill theory had 'all the elements of a contemporary cognitive model' and predicted that 'after following a separate course for several decades, skills research should now be ready for renewed integration with the remainder of experimental psychology.'

The predicted integration is now virtually complete, and finds expressions in the present, extended Series on Human Performance and Cognition. One advantage of the change in title is to give explicit recognition to what was hitherto implicit, thus acknowledging the part played by cognitive processes in human performance. However, the change in title is not merely one of nomenclature. Rather, it provides an opportunity to prepare books on a much wider range of topics, running from cognitive science to cognitive ergonomics. It is intended that the extended Series will include issues such as human-computer interaction, risk-taking and error, the practical contribution of human memory, and the psychology of speech and language. At the same time, the Series will preserve those features that have made for its present measure of success.

As before, most of the books take the form of edited volumes. However, it should be noted that these volumes are not haphazard collections of papers. Rather, they should be viewed as systematically organized texts which have the advantages of multiple authorship. Writing a monograph is often regarded as the more difficult assignment, but producing an edited volume presents a considerable challenge. On one hand, it provides an opportunity to bring to bear a concentration of expertise that is otherwise unattainable; on the other hand, the multiplicity of contributors carries with it the risk that the overall result may be lacking in coherence. Here, every effort has been made to counter the potential disadvantages attendant on using the edited format while preserving the positive advantages of drawing on special knowledge. The chapters have been specifically commissioned in accordance with an integrated plan for each volume, information about chapter contents has been circulated among the contributors to ensure cohesion, and editorial control has extended to the level of difficulty as well as to the format of each text. These books have thus been designed to combine readability with high standards of scholarship, providing substantial content while emphasizing the explanation of that content.

The present volume has the distinction of inaugurating the extended Series. It integrates performance and cognition in a manner thoroughly in accordance with the new designation. It contains perhaps more theory than many of the prior volumes—production or connectionist models, cognitive growth theory, the adaptive control of thought, the schema, limited capacity versus multiprocessing, the arousal concept—but the theoretical issues are directly related to the very practical problems of comprehending, computing, remembering and moving. The coverage of this volume is commendably broad, addressing major sources of performance variation in addition to cognitive acquisition processes, but the authors have maintained a high level of expository skill throughout the enterprise. Hence, the book more than adequately satisfies the overall objectives of both the original, and the new, Series of studies.

Dennis Holding
University of Louisville

Preface

As we write this we wonder whether it will ever be read by anyone. If you are with us so far, the answer to our question is 'yes'. In performing this act of reading (and we hope that we are not making you too self-conscious to continue), a complex system is operating to decode symbols and convert to meaning. This is a skill which has taken many years to acquire and is one of many we acquire and perform over a lifetime. The beautifully packaged volume by Wiley which you are holding contains within it an examination of the acquisition of cognitive skills in a variety of different settings: problem-solving, reading, computing, and motor skills. These are all areas in which there have been substantial advances in our understanding of underlying mechanisms and are the current focus of much research activity. They therefore can be seen as representative of a much broader field. There are also chapters on acquisition in a wider sense which focus on the development of cognitive skills and on training skilled performance. After dealing with acquisition, the emphasis changes to studying variations in performance. The first of these chapters examines a method for examining exceptional memorial performance, the next discusses issues of the allocation of resources when undergoing multiple tasks. The final chapters focus on ageing, stress and diurnal variations in relation to skilled performance.

Our enthusiasm for this volume derived, in part, from our decision to organize the International Conference on Skilled Behaviour in Sussex, April 1987, under the auspices of the Cognitive Section of the British Psychological Section. Discussion with colleagues before and during this conference heightened our awareness of the way in which advances in cognitive psychology have a bearing on our approach to the learning of cognitive tasks. We are very grateful to Dennis Holding for his guidance, to our colleagues on the cognitive section committee and to all those who gave us help and encouragement during the compilation of the present volume. We are especially grateful to Wendy Hudlass of Wiley for all her help and good humour. To end as we began, now that you have reached so far, you are obviously the sort of reader who reads prefaces of books to the bitter end. We can assure you that what is to follow makes much better reading.

Ann M. Colley and *John R. Beech*
Leicester, June 1988

List of contributors

John Annett — Dept. of Psychology, University of Warwick, Coventry CV4 7AL, UK

P. Arnold — Dept. of Psychology, Murdoch University, Murdoch, Western Australia 6150, Australia

Paul J. Barber — Dept. of Psychology, Birkbeck College, Malet St, London WC1E 7HX, UK

John R. Beech — Dept. of Psychology, University of Leicester, Leicester LE1 7RH, UK

Ann M. Colley — Dept. of Psychology, University of Leicester, Leicester LE1 7RH, UK

Mark Elsom-Cook — Institute of Educational Technology, The Open University, Walton Hall, Milton Keynes MK7 6AA, UK

K. Anders Ericsson — Dept. of Psychology, University of Colorado, Muenzinger Psychology Building, Campus Box 345, Boulder, Colorado 80309-0345, USA

K. J. Gilhooly — Dept. of Psychology, University of Aberdeen, King's College, Old Aberdeen AB9 2UB, UK

A. J. K. Green — Dept. of Psychology, University of Aberdeen, King's College, Old Aberdeen AB9 2UB, UK

L. R. Hartley — Dept. of Psychology, Murdoch University, Murdoch, Western Australia 6150, Australia

D. Morrison — Dept. of Psychology, Murdoch University, Murdoch, Western Australia 6150, Australia

William L. Oliver — Dept. of Psychology, University of Colorado, Muenzinger Psychology Building, Campus Box 345, Boulder, Colorado 80309-0345, USA

Timothy A. Salthouse — School of Psychology, Georgia Institute of Technology, Atlanta, Georgia 30332, USA

Julie B. Sincoff   Dept. of Psychology, Yale University, PO Box 11A,
                        Yale Station, New Haven, Connecticut 06520-7447,
                        USA

Andrew Smith   MRC Perceptual and Cognitive Performance Unit,
                        Laboratory of Experimental Psychology, University
                        of Sussex, Brighton, Sussex BN1 9QG, UK

Robert J. Sternberg   Dept. of Psychology, Yale University, PO Box 11A,
                        Yale Station, New Haven, Connecticut 06520-7447,
                        USA

Chapter 1

Acquiring and performing cognitive skills

Ann M. Colley and John R. Beech

INTRODUCTION

... skill lies in the use of capacities efficiently and effectively as the result of practice and experience. (Welford, 1976, p. 14)

Researchers and laypeople alike would agree that activities are said to be skilled when the performance of them has reached a level where it appears to be effortless, where it is almost always accurate and where additional practice makes little apparent improvement. Fitts and Posner (1967) have proposed additional characteristics: skilled performance is organized spatially (if it has a motor component) and temporally; is goal-directed, and uses feedback for error correction unless there is insufficient time for detection and correction to take place.

Until relatively recently most studies of skilled performance focused on perceptual motor skills. Other kinds of activity which met the criteria outlined above were mostly neglected by investigators looking at learning mechanisms. One particular area of neglect has been that of cognitive or intellectual tasks which were studied both in applied educational contexts and in expert-novice comparisons in the laboratory but the mechanisms underlying their acquisition were not, until recently, studied from the perspective of trying to integrate theories and models with the skills literature in general. Welford (1976) identifies three types of skill which correspond to stages in information processing models of serial processing. Perceptual skills code and interpret incoming sensory information. Motor skills execute skilled movement

Acquisition and Performance of Cognitive Skills. Edited by A. M. Colley and J. R. Beech

efficiently but are reliant on appropriate links between sensory input and action routines. Intellectual skills link perception and action and are concerned with translating perceptual input into a skilled response by using appropriate descisions. Welford concludes that the majority of the most important skills fall into the last category. Why, then, have these intellectual skills received relatively little attention until the last decade? One reason for this may well be that much of their performance is invisible. The skilled problem-solver or mathematician produces a solution. In contrast, the skilled pianist produces a prolonged sequence of hand, finger and foot movements which are clearly visible and are outside the expertise of most of the spectators, in addition to a highly complex pattern of sound. Of course this is not the only reason why the area of cognitive skill developed only relatively recently. The interest in perceptual motor skills which arose in the 1950s and 1960s resulted from sponsorship by industrial and military sources interested in developing and improving weapon and radar systems which had been invented or improved during and after the Second World War. Essential to the design of these, was an understanding of the physical and mental capacities of the individuals operating them, and of the best way to train operators. Indeed, much of the contemporary literature on training is based firmly on research conducted at this time (see Annett's chapter).

The more recent emphasis on cognitive skills has arisen from the increasing use and power of computers. It is unlikely that many useful theoretical advances could be made in this area without the use of computer simulation. Measuring a weapons operator's ability to track a target, or a radar operator's ability to track an aeroplane on an oscilloscope is relatively easy to do using laboratory analogues. Studying how a chess master makes a decision to make a particular move, or how a consultant physician makes a diagnosis of a patient's ailments is more problematic. One methodology, which has gained in popularity since the publication in Ericsson and Simon's book in 1984, uses protocol analysis in which the investigator uses protocols as the basis for inferences about underlying cognitive processes. Ericsson and Oliver in Chapter 8 describe this methodology and how it can be used in the study of memory skills, particularly in exceptional cases. The growth of artificial intelligence has opened up new possibilities for the testing of theoretical ideas. Its influence can be seen in research on problem-solving and on computing. The chapters by Gilhooly and Green and by Elsom-Cook summarize the state of research in their respective fields, and Elsom-Cook argues strongly for the advantages of using simulations to study performance and to make predictions about behaviour.

Cognitive skills involve the effective and efficient translation of information into a response. To accomplish this, it is necessary to interpret the information in terms of current knowledge and to have procedures available to enact the steps necessary to make the translation. The same is true of any problem-solving task, and Anderson (1982) expresses the view that skill acquisition is synonymous with problem-solving. Acquisition of a cognitive skill involves the acquisition of a set of domain-specific rules which allow the solution of a particular problem. The end result of cognitive processing is a decision or a solution. In either case a problem has been solved. Even a fairly universal skill such as reading can be viewed in this way (see Beech's chapter). The framework offered by Van Dijk and Kintsch (1983) for understanding discourse comprehension assumes that the comprehension process consists of a hierarchy of strategies which perform various levels of analysis on written material.

Dimensions of variation among cognitive skills

A large number of the tasks which we perform can be described as cognitive skills. Four of these are discussed in some detail in later chapters: reading, problem-solving, computing, and also motor skills, many of which, Colley argues, have a substantial cognitive component. A mutually exclusive typology of cognitive skills is not possible, since cognitive tasks vary on a number of different dimensions all of which are relevant to the way in which they are learned. We outline some of these below.

(1) Simple-Complex: a simple task, such as a choice reaction time, requires a decision defined by procedural steps. A complex task, such as air traffic control, requires the integration of large amounts of information and a complex set of underlying rules to guide performance. Schneider (1985) points out that practice on simple tasks, such as remembering a phone number, makes perfect, but this is not necessarily true of more complex tasks. It is often the case that learners practise for many hours and do not improve their performance because they have failed to structure the task appropriately. Although the mechanisms underlying simple and complex tasks may be found to be similar, prescriptions for training must take into account the nature of the skill being learned.

(2) Divergent-Convergent: this is the traditional distinction between cognitive tasks which apply well-defined rules to find a single acceptable solution, such as applying a statistical test, and those which result in a novel product within a given domain. This product may be also have to fulfil criteria of being acceptable aesthetically, such as in writing a novel. Aesthetic evaluations are rule-based but use less well-defined and more individualized criteria than more formalized judgements of correctness. In order to produce a solution to meet these evaluations a considerable amount of domain-related knowledge is necessary, and learning this is a significant part of the acquisition process. Many complex tasks have both divergent and convergent elements, for

example, an architect must apply principles of basic engineering and building technology in producing a novel design for a building, which also has aesthetic appeal.

(3) Algorithmic-Heuristic: in algorithmic skills, the performer uses a set sequence of steps to arrive at a solution. An example would be where a car mechanic follows instructions in a manual to dismantle the air filter from an engine. In heuristic skills the performer works from knowledge of underlying principles to produce a solution, as in playing chess. Different kinds of information need to be presented during acquisition to reflect these two strategies.

(4) Inductive-Deductive: in deductive skills, such as solving a crossword clue, the performer works forward from evidence to solution. In inductive skills, inferences are made from particular instances to similar situations so that the solution is highly likely but not necessarily true. An example would be of a consultant physician attempting to make a diagnosis, based upon experience, of a patient presenting with a set of atypical symptoms.

(5) Open-Closed: this dimension was first proposed by Poulton (1957) to distinguish between performance in a predictable (closed) environment and performance in an unpredictable (open) environment. Writing takes place within a closed environment, whereas the decisions made while driving take place in a more open environment. Gilhooly and Green discuss adversarial and non-adversarial problem-solving in their chapter and this distinction relates closely to this dimension. In adversarial tasks, the presence of an opponent (such as in playing GO or chess) increases the unpredictability of the performing environment. The learner must acquire rules about performing the task itself and, in addition, must take into account the way in which the environment is likely to vary in establishing additional rules about the appropriateness of certain actions.

(6) Universal-Specialized: some cognitive skills, such as reading, are acquired by almost everyone, and to a high level of competence. Others, such as computer programming, are learned by relatively few, and even fewer still acquire a high level of competence. This may be partly a function of the universality of teaching and large amounts of practice, but it may also be the case that certain tasks are easier to acquire because the basic abilities required are possessed by the majority of individuals.

Acquisition and performance

The dimensions outlined above illustrate the importance of considering the nature of a task in making prescriptions about the way in which acquisition should proceed. This does not mean that a generalized theory of performance can not be established, simply that the way in which a learner structures a task, the amount of domain-related information available and the way in which the procedural rules are presented to the learner are of significance for training individual skills.

A generalized theory of acquisition must take into account the way in which performance changes during acquisition. One important change is in terms of the apparent use of attentional resources. Early in acquisition, only a small amount of the available information can be attended to, while later on, the performer can accomplish the task easily and apparently has capacity to spare. With sufficient practice, under certain circumstances, two complex tasks can be performed simultaneously. Barber's chapter discusses the implications of this dual task performance for attentional theory. Some investigators (e.g. Schneider and Fisk, 1983; Schneider and Shiffrin, 1977; Shiffrin and Dumais, 1981) have proposed a two-process theory of attention to account for these changes. Early in acquisition, processing is *controlled*, that is, it uses general processing capacity, it is also slow, effortful, generally serial, under intentional control and involves awareness. Later in practice, apparently effortless performance results from *automatic* processing, which is fast, parallel, obligatory, does not involve awareness and has low demands on processing capacity. These two-process theories have been criticized for the lack of internal consistency of the definitions they give (e.g. Cheng, 1985; Phillips and Hughes, 1988). The notion of automatic processing has been described as circular (e.g. Allport, 1980); its presence is inferred from the type of performance that it is invoked to explain. It is probable that several mechanisms underlie the changes in attentional deployment that the controlled-automatic dichotomy describes (Colley and Beech, 1988) , but no current theoretical framework deals with these in a completely satisfactory way.

Speed of performance across a wide range of tasks (motor and cognitive) changes in a characteristic way with practice: large increases in speed occur initially, then performance stabilizes and increases only slightly in speed over a long period. This relationship can be described by a power law: the logarithm of the time to complete a response is a linear function of the logarithm of the number of trials (Newell and Rosenbloom, 1981, discuss this law in some detail). Neves and Anderson (1981) have demonstrated that the law describes the learning of solutions to geometry proofs and have interpreted it within the framework offered by ACT* (Anderson, 1982; see below).

So far we have considered acquisition rather than performance but, of course, the two are intimately related. Performance of a skill varies as a function of a number of factors. Perhaps the most important of these is the amount of practice that a learner has had, but other factors interact with this.

The most notable of these are developmental stage (see the chapter by Sincoff and Sternberg) and individual/environmental factors such as circadian rhythms (see Smith's chapter) and the presence or absence of various stressors (see the chapter by Hartley, Morrison and Arnold). Understanding the way in which these factors interact provides clues to the nature of underlying mechanisms as well as being of considerable practical importance.

RECENT APPROACHES TO SKILL ACQUISITION

In this section we shall briefly outline two areas of theoretical development which seem to us to have important implications for understanding cognitive skill acquisition and performance. Two productions systems theories will be presented. Production systems consist of rules for executing procedures which have an 'if . . . then . . .' form, i.e. if a set of conditions is satisfied, then an operation or operations will be executed. Anderson's ACT* theory, discussed first, has an advantage over many other similar theories, of a clear focus on the mechanisms of learning. Its influence within the literature is evident in several of the chapters in this volume. Hunt and Lansman's Production Activation Model focuses on the distinction between controlled and automatic processing, so has the potential to explain the differences in the way that attentional resources are deployed at different stages of acquisition.

The second area which will be discussed is connectionism, which, although it does not make explicit prescriptions concerning skill acquisition, nevertheless provides a clear theoretical basis for understanding skill.

Production systems approaches

Anderson's ACT* theory

Anderson (1982) has provided a framework for understanding observations made previously by Fitts (1964) on the development of skill. Fitts outlined three main stages: the cognitive stage, in which the learner makes an initial approximation to the skill, based upon background knowledge, observation or instruction; the associative stage, in which performance is refined through the elimination of errors; and the autonomous stage, in which skilled performance is well-established but still continues to improve, albeit very gradually.

Anderson bases his framework on his ACT production system. Three types of memory are distinguished in ACT. Declarative memory contains factual information in a propositional network. Procedural memory contains the procedural steps required to accomplish tasks in *productions*, which are production rules. Working memory is a blackboard for the transfer of information between declarative and procedural memory, and for the intake and rehearsal of information from the environment. Anderson's theory has two main stages. The *declarative stage* is similar to Fitts' cognitive stage, while the *procedural stage* is equivalent to Fitts' autonomous stage. Anderson regards Fitts' associative stage as a transition between assembling facts about skill and enacting and refining procedures. He calls this process of converting facts into procedures *knowledge compilation*.

In the declarative stage, knowledge about how to perform a skill is assembled from declarative memory, and from instruction or guidance, into working memory. General problem-solving procedures then turn this declarative knowledge into productions. As Anderson (1982) points out, instruction rarely specifies a procedure for the performance of a skill. The learner must establish a procedure using existing strategies, or *weak problem-solving methods*. These are very general strategies such as, for example, the use of analogy with a similar problem or working backward from a solution. Analogy is a particularly widely used strategy. Anderson illustrates the way in which students learning geometry use worked examples as a basis for solving unfamiliar problems. Rumelhart and Norman (1981) discuss the way in which procedures incorporating task knowledge (schemata in their theoretical framework) are created or extended by analogy. They also discuss the features of a good analogy from a pedagogic perspective: it should be from an area familiar to the learner and within which he or she can reason well, its domain should be similar to that of the new task, and the same operations should be appropriate or inappropriate in both domains.

Knowledge compilation has two subprocesses of *composition* and *proceduralization*. Composition collapses successive productions into a single production which has the same effect. Proceduralization removes clauses in the condition of a production that require matching from long-term memory via working memory. Compilation is a gradual process which allows for errors in procedural information to be corrected over practice. In the procedural stage of acquisition productions are *tuned*, that is, made more appropriate and efficient for the task in hand. Subprocesses of tuning are first, *generalization*, in which common aspects of specific productions are used to create a more widely applicable production which can then be used in novel situations; second, *discrimination*, which restricts the use of productions to instances where they are successful; third, *strengthening*, where productions are strengthened with repeated application so that the time taken to apply them diminishes. Strengthening produces speedup in the performance of simple tasks such as choice reaction times. Speedup in complex tasks results from strengthening and algorithmic improvement, which is the reduction in the number of productions required through composition, generalization and discrimination.

Anderson's theory exploits the advantages of having both declarative and procedural representations (Neves and Anderson, 1981). Having a declarative representation allows for the changing of procedures to suit prevailing circumstances. Procedural representation provides methods of accomplishing tasks with slightly different requirements by allowing different variables to be entered into productions, but knowledge represented in this way cannot be accessed for inspection.

Hunt and Lansman's Production Activation Model

Hunt and Lansman (1986) produced a production systems model which does not separate declarative and procedural information but which attempts to integrate findings on changes in the use of attentional resources over skill acquisition with those on problem-solving. Hunt and Lansman propose that productions can be triggered either by spreading activation between them or by matching their condition with information in working memory, which acts as a blackboard for the transfer of information between productions or its acquisition from the environment. This allows a distinction to be drawn between automatic and controlled processing in a similar way to that of the two-process theories of attention mentioned earlier. Controlled processing involves the use of working memory. An initial match is made between information in the environment and the conditions of a production rule in long-term memory. When a match is found, the condition is transferred to working memory, then the production is enacted. Automatic processing takes place via the spread of activation between productions. Hunt and Lansman have produced successful computer simulations of various tasks including choice reaction times, divided attention tasks and the Stroop test.

Hunt and Lansman point out that the empirical consequences of the difference between their model and ACT* in terms of the lack of separation of declarative and procedural memory in their Production Activation Model are unclear. The only means of testing such models and distinguishing between them is in terms of the success of computer simulations in replicating a wide range of robust findings in the literature, and more of such simulations are clearly required. One advantage that Hunt and Lansman's model does have over ACT* is in the sharp distinction it draws between controlled and automatic processing. ACT* is based very firmly in the problem-solving domain and has not given full consideration to attentional phenomena, although in ACT* the features of automatization are seen as being solved by proceduralization (Anderson, 1983). Given the earlier discussion of two-process theories of attention, it seems reasonable not to put too much emphasis on explaining a distinction between automatic and controlled processing which is in reality, not absolute. One advantage the ACT* has over the Production Activation Model, however, lies in its focus on skill acquisition. It is not clear how the Production Activation Model deals with skill acquisition, and particularly how the transition from controlled to automatic processing occurs for well-learned tasks.

Connectionist approaches

The study of cognition gathered momentum from the 1960s using the analogy between the programming operations in the computer and cognitive processing. The processing of information was considered to operate in discrete stages, usually in a serial sequence (e.g. Sternberg, 1966). More recently, a new framework has emerged which is more concerned with modelling cognitive architecture, rather than modelling the programming taking place within the hard wiring of the conventional computer. Previously, some cognitive psychologists had argued that their main focus was on the nature of the programs operating within cognition, while the nature of the 'wiring' was more the province of the neuropsychologist. In the new connectionism the modeller develops *networks* of *connections* between *units* which can give the appearance of a model which is actually simulating neuronal networks, and indeed some modellers have explicitly set out to do this (e.g. Gluck and Thompson, 1987). However, this is not the primary intention of most modellers, at least for the present (McClelland, 1988). In this section we shall describe connectionism and how it can be relevant to explaining how skills develop. We shall then briefly consider the connectionist position in relation to the type of symptoms and deterioration sustained by brain damage. Issues raised by these considerations are whether skills are organized within modules and whether all skill operations can be accounted for in terms of the connectionist framework.

Connectionism

McClelland, Rumelhart and Hinton (1986) and Phillips (1988) have briefly outlined the various strands of development leading to the present connectionist approach in cognitive psychology. In the early 1980s and slightly earlier the first cognitive connectionist models began to appear independently of each other. For example, one of us proposed a network model to account for the phenomenon of visual image scanning, proposing that the increase in reaction time as a function of distance scanned across an image could be accounted for by a model involving triggering signals, domino-fashion, across an array of elements representing an image (Beech, 1979a, b); Feldman (1981) proposed what he called a 'connectionist' model of visual memory; an edited book by Hinton and Anderson (1981) highlighted the importance of neural net models for cognitive psychologists; McClelland and Rumelhart

(1981) produced a connectionist model of word recognition; and by 1986 two influential edited volumes had appeared by McClelland and Rumelhart (McClelland and Rumelhart, 1986; Rumelhart and McClelland, 1986a).

A crucial property of the network within the connectionist model is the nature of the individual units. These are 'simple processing devices which take on activation values based on a weighted sum of the inputs from the environment and from other units' (McClelland, 1988). In other words, these units are capable of, for instance, computing the relative importance of a set of inputs. The role of these units varies considerably. A unit might be the representation of a single word in the lexicon, and there could also be units to represent letters and features of letters (e.g. McClelland and Rumelhart, 1981). On the other hand, a conceptualization within cognition might entail a particular pattern of activation over a large network of units (e.g. Beech, 1979a, b).

To illustrate how a weighting system might work, consider the model of Paap, Newsome, McDonald and Schvaneveldt (1982). In this model of word recognition a confusion matrix was used which had been obtained by giving subjects brief visual presentations of individual letters and noting their errors. Paap *et al.* thus derived a set of probabilities for visually presented letters when confused with all possible alternative letters. A lexicon was also stored with the visual confusion matrix in the program to represent the visual lexicon of the reader. In the simulation, single words were 'presented' to the program. All the words in the lexicon were activated on this presentation in accordance with their corresponding probability values in the confusion matrix. Then the geometrical mean was taken (by multiplying the probabilities together and dividing by the number of letters) for each word in the lexicon. This had the effect of attenuating any word which contained letters with a value close to zero. In other words, if a word in the lexicon contained a letter visually very dissimilar (e.g. *M* vs *O*), this would dramatically reduce the geometrical mean for that particular word entry. However, a word visually similar to the presented word (e.g. *PORE* vs *PORK*) would have a reasonably high geometrical mean. It can be seen that this model involves a detailed simultaneous activation of all the words in the lexicon with each unit representing a word being involved in computational activity. Such models are often referred to as modelling parallel distributed processes or simply PDP models. The actual simulation of a PDP model on a conventional computer involves computing activation levels for each word in a serial manner, which is a time-consuming process. Until adequate parallel computer architectures are developed (and accompanying programming languages), these simulations can not take place in real time. Nevertheless, they do provide new ways of looking at experimental phenomena which had not hitherto been contemplated.

Connectionist accounts of skill acquisition

Two examples of applications of connectionism to acquiring a skill will now be considered. The first example is by Gluck and Bower (1988) who have proposed a connectionist account of students learning to make a diagnosis based on descriptions of medical symptoms of patients, using the Rescorla–Wagner model of associative learning (Rescorla and Wagner, 1972; Wagner and Rescorla, 1972). The Gluck and Bower model involves a network with the input units or nodes representing the medical symptoms (e.g. bleeding gums).

Before going further it should be noted that connectionist accounts frequently use linear algebra to describe their models. In many cases this enables components of a vector to be represented in n-dimensional space, where n is the number of components. In the case of the basic Gluck–Bower model, a vector represents the patient, p, who has four binary components corresponding to the medical symptoms. Each patient has either of two diseases. The model operates by being given a series of symptoms for each patient and informing it which disease is operating. The model multiplies the activation of each symptom x_{pj}, with its corresponding weight w_j and then sums these values across all symptoms, in this case, four. This results in the output for the patient, o_p, which is the degree to which that disease is preferred over disease 2, as shown in equation 1:

$$o_p - \sum_{k=1}^{n} x_{pk}w_k \tag{1}$$

Then a change in the value of the weight is calculated which is equivalent to learning about the relationship of the symptoms to the disease. This uses the delta rule, or the Windrow–Hoff rule (Sutton and Barto, 1981), in which the extent of what is learned is proportional to the *difference* (this is the delta part) between the level of actual activation and the target level of activation. This is expressed in equation 2, in which λ_p is the desired disease output, o_p is the calculated output derived from equation 1 and β is the learning rate:

$$\Delta w_j = \beta(\lambda_p - o_p)x_{pj} \tag{2}$$

The result of this function is to produce a learning rate which is negatively accelerated reaching asymptote at a rate determined by the magnitude of β. The constant β must be small, otherwise there will be exaggerated oscillations in the weight changes.

One important aspect common to both the Rescorla–Wagner model and the simulation model of Paap *et al.* (in which the geometrical mean was used) is the use of products to provide a *gating* mechanism. When there is a multiplicative connection this means that one unit is capable of gating the other or several other units, because as mentioned before, if one has a value of zero, this means that the other members are effectively blocked as well. If some weights have a value of unity, they are effectively neutralized and if they are positive but below one, they reduce output according to their value. The state of being positive or negative will also be important; for instance, one negative value will have an inhibitory effect on overall output.

There are several other cases where PDP models have been used to give an account of skill development. One further example to be described here is that of the development of skilled typing. The connectionist model of Rumelhart and Norman (1982) proposed that on reading a word within a sequence, a unit corresponding to that word is activated which in turn activates individual units representing component letters of the word. The activation of the first letter unit to be typed within the word inhibits the rest of the units, the second unit inhibits the remainder, and so on. The end result is the activation of the units in descending order in relation to their serial position. Hand position for each letter-press is relatively unchanged if the letter is on the home row, but can move if the top or bottom rows need to be reached. But the extent of this movement is modified by the activation levels of other units which need to be typed, with the succeeding letter unit to the current letter unit exerting the greatest activation in the context of the overall activation of the remaining letters. One important aspect to note about this model, which has been quite good at predicting inter-keystroke time, is that it proposes that typing is not a serial process in which each letter unit is activated in succession. The role of a central executive function, in the sense of a serial conscious process initiating behaviour, is reduced in this model because important processing functions, involving the computation of weighting levels, are distributed within the operating system. The chapter on motor skills discusses this issue further.

Connectionism and brain damage

The impact of neurological damage on behaviour is of considerable interest for those interested in skill development. In many cases damage can result in the impairment and sometimes the complete disappearance of skills which had previously been acquired. Some connectionists make the strong claim that their PDP approach can provide an account of these effects in a way that other theories are unable to do. Given that brain damage appears to eliminate whole categories of subskills in certain cases, this suggests that whole specialized modules have been eliminated. However, modularity is not a feature of connectionism. This issue is explored briefly and will also be germaine to the chapter on processing resources by Paul Barber and to Beech's chapter which proposes that the development of component subskills is an important feature of learning to read.

Rumelhart and McClelland (1986b), advocating the connectionist position, concede that there are *regions* of specialized brain activity, particularly for lower levels of processing, but generally speaking patients usually experience *graceful degradation* in performance corresponding to deterioration in increasing numbers of neurological units. This is because in neurological structures there is a considerable amount of redundancy, in the same way as in connectionist models. Alzheimer's Disease is a particularly good example of this phenomenon. This position contrasts with the serial cognitive models of the past in which the elimination of one stage of processing would result in a hypothesized catastrophic deterioration in performance, analogous to the performance in the conventional computer in which one error in the program can make the remainder of the operations meaningless.

Hinton, McClelland and Rumelhart (1986) described a connectionist model of learning to read which produced semantic errors (e.g. responding 'apricot' when presented with *peach*) similar to the kinds of errors produced by deep dyslexic patients. This is an interesting result because the acquired dyslexias usually produce quite distinctive symptoms often suggestive of a loss of distinctive modules or specialized functions (e.g. Marshall, 1987). But the connectionist view of Rumelhart and McClelland does not account for different specialities and yet their model is operating in a way approximating that of a deep dyslexic (at least, in one aspect). On this point Phillips (1988), perhaps reading more into their position than is intended, imputes that 'No attempt is made to indicate possible roles for the modules. . . . It grossly undervalues the evidence obtained by other approaches, such as neuropsychology' (p. 396). A middle course is that subsystems could each operate in a connectionist manner. The model described by Hinton, McClelland and Rumelhart produced the symptoms of a deep rather than a surface dyslexic because one layer of the system was concerned with semantic representation. If there had been a grapheme-phoneme conversion layer of units no doubt errors would have been generated more analogous to one of the symptoms of the surface dyslexic. Phillips suggests that modules with different types of specialities will need different kinds of properties. This is a view reinforced by Fodor and Pylyshyn (1988) who are also critical of the connectionist acounts, but in a more radical way. It is not surprising that there are critics, especially as the connectionist view has been expressed in somewhat extreme terms. Nevertheless, as far as skill acquisition is concerned, the approach promises some interesting advances.

CONCLUSIONS

In this introductory chapter we have outlined some general issues concerning cognitive skill acquisition and performance, many of which will be elaborated upon in more detail in the chapters that follow. Two major conclusions can be drawn from the preceding discussion. First, that cognitive psychology is, at last, placing some emphasis on mechanisms of learning. Not only do advances in cognitive psychology suggest new ways of describing these mechanisms, but also, as Langley and Simon (1981) conclude 'Learning theory . . . [has] a central role to play in formulating parsimonious, nearly invariant laws of cognition' (p. 378), since stage of learning is one of the major determinants of performance. Second, that artificial intelligence methodology is central to advances in this area, and complements the more traditional laboratory-based experimentation as well as the more ecologically valid use of protocol analysis to understand cognitive skills in the environment in which they are performed.

REFERENCES

Allport, D. A. (1980). Attention and performance, in G. L. Claxton (ed.), *Cognitive Psychology: New Directions*. London: Routledge.

Anderson, J. R. (1982). Acquisition of cognitive skill, *Psychological Review*, **89**, 369–406.

Anderson, J. R. (1983). *The Architecture of Cognition*. Cambridge, MA: Harvard University.

Beech, J. R. (1979a). Scanning visual images: implication for the representation of space, *Perception*, **8**, 621–628.

Beech, J. R. (1979b). A chronometric study of the scanning of visual representations. D. Phil. thesis submitted to the New University of Ulster.

Cheng, P. W. (1985). Restructuring versus automaticity: Alternative accounts of skill acquisition, *Psychological Review*, **92**, 414–423.

Colley, A. M. & Beech, J. R. (1988). Discussion: Changing representations of skill, in A. M. Colley & J. R. Beech (eds), *Cognition and Action in Skilled Behaviour*. Amsterdam: North-Holland.

Ericsson, K. A. & Simon, H. A. (1984). *Protocol Analysis*. Cambridge, MA: MIT/Bradford.

Feldman, J. A. (1981). A connectionist model of visual memory, in G. E. Hinton & J. A. Anderson (eds), *Parallel Models of Associative Memory*. Hillsdale, NJ: Erlbaum.

Fitts, P. M. (1964). Perceptual-motor skill learning, in A. W. Melton (ed.), *Categories of Human Learning*. New York: Academic Press.

Fitts, P. M. & Posner, M. I. (1967). *Human Performance*. Belmont, CA: Brooks/Cole.

Fodor, J. A. & Pylyshyn, Z. W. (1988). Connectionism and cognitive architecture: A critical analysis, *Cognition*, **28**, 3–71.

Gluck, M. A. & Bower, G. H. (1988). Evaluating an adaptive network model of human learning, *Journal of Memory and Learning*, **27**, 166–195.

Gluck, M. A. & Thompson, R. F. (1987). Modeling the neural substrates of associative learning and memory: A computational approach, *Psychological Review*, **94**, 176–191.

Hinton, G. E. & Anderson, J. A. (1981). *Parallel Models of Associative Memory*. Hillsdale, N.J.: Erlbaum.

Hinton, G. E., McClelland, J. L. & Rumelhart, D. E. (1986). Distributed representations, in D. E. Rumelhart & J. L. McClelland (eds), *Parallel Distributed Processing: Explorations in the Microstructure of Cognition (vol. 1 Foundations)*. Cambridge, MA: MIT Press.
Hunt, E. & Lansman, M. (1986). Unified model of attention and problem solving, *Psychological Review*, **93**, 446–461.
Langley, P.E. & Simon, H. A. (1981). The central role of learning in cognition, in J. R. Anderson (ed.), *Cognitive Skills and their Acquisition*. Hillsdale, NJ: Erlbaum.
Marshall, J. (1987). The cultural and biological context of written languages, in J. R. Beech & A. M. Colley (eds), *Cognitive Approaches to Reading*. Chichester: Wiley.
McClelland, J. L. (1988). Connectionist models and psychological evidence, *Journal of Memory and Language*, **27**, 107–123.
McClelland, J. L. & Rumelhart, D. E. (1981). An interactive activation model of context effects in letter perception: Part 1. An account of basic findings, *Psychological Review*, **88**, 375–407.
McClelland, J. L. & Rumelhart, D. E. (1986). *Parallel Distributed Processing: Explorations in the Microstructure of Cognition (vol. 2 Psychological and Biological Models)*. Cambridge, MA: MIT Press.
McClelland, J. L., Rumelhart, D. E. & Hinton, G. E. (1986). The appeal of parallel distributed processing, in D. E. Rumelhart & J. L. McClelland (eds), *Parallel Distributed Processing: Explorations in the Microstructure of Cognition* (vol. I). Cambridge, MA: MIT Press.
Neves, D. M. & Anderson, J. R. (1981). Knowledge compilation: mechanisms for the automatization of cognitive skills, in J. R. Anderson (ed.), *Cognitive Skills and their Acquisition*. Hillsdale, NJ: Erlbaum.
Newell, A. & Rosenbloom, P. (1981). Mechanisms of skill acquisition and the law of practice, in J. R. Anderson (ed.), *Cognitive Skills and their Acquisition*. Hillsdale, NJ: Erlbaum.
Paap, K.R., Newsome, S. L., McDonald, J. E. & Schvaneveldt, R. W. (1982). An activation-verification model for letter and word recognition: The word-superiority effect, *Psychological Review*, **89**, 573–594.
Phillips, J. & Hughes, B. (1988). Internal consistency of the concept of automaticity, in A. M. Colley & J. R. Beech (eds), *Cognition and Action in Skilled Behaviour*. Amsterdam: North-Holland.
Phillips, W. A. (1988). Brainy minds, *Quarterly Journal of Experimental Psychology*, **40A**, 389–405.
Poulton, E. C. (1957). On prediction in skilled movements, *Psychological Bulletin*, **54**, 467–478.
Rescorla, R.A. & Wagner, A. R. (1972). A theory of Pavlovian conditioning: Variations in the effectiveness of reinforcement and nonreinforcement following prior inhibitory conditioning, in A. H. Black & W. F. Prokasy (eds), *Classical Conditioning: II. Current Research and Theory*. New York: Appleton–Century–Crofts.
Rumelhart, D.E. & McClelland, J. L. (1986a). *Parallel Distributed Processing: Explorations in the Microstructure of Cognition. (vol. 1 Foundations)*. Cambridge, MA: MIT Press.
Rumelhart, D. E. & McClelland, J. L. (1986b). PDP models and general issues in cognitive science, in D. E. Rumelhart & J. L. McClelland (eds), *Parallel Distributed Processing: Explorations in the Microstructure of Cognition (vol. 1 Foundations)*. Cambridge, MA: MIT Press.

Rumelhart, D. E. & Norman, D. A. (1981). Analogical processes in learning, in J. R. Anderson (ed.), *Cognitive Skills and their Acquisition*. Hillsdale, NJ: Erlbaum.

Rumelhart, D. E. & Norman, D. A. (1982). Simulating a typist: A study of skilled cognitive-motor performance, *Cognitive Science*, **6**, 1–36.

Schneider, W. (1985). Training high-performance skills: fallacies and guidelines, *Human Factors*, **27**, 285–300.

Schneider, W. & Fisk, A. D. (1983). Attention theory and mechanisms for skilled performance, in R. A. Magill (ed.), *Memory and Control of Action*. Amsterdam: North-Holland.

Schneider, W. & Shiffrin, R. M. (1977). Controlled and automatic information processing: I. Detection, search, and attention, *Psychological Review*, **84**, 1–66.

Shiffrin, R. M. & Dumais, S. T. (1981). The development of automatism, in J. R. Anderson (ed.), *Cognitive Skills and their Acquisition*. Hillsdale, NJ: Erlbaum.

Sternberg, S. (1966). High-speed scanning in human memory *Science*, **153**, 652–654.

Sutton, R. S. & Barto, A. G. (1981). Toward a modern theory of adaptive networks: Expectations and prediction, *Psychological Review*, **88**, 135–170.

Van Dijk, T. A. & Kintsch, W. (1983). *Strategies of Discourse Comprehension*. New York: Academic Press.

Wagner, A. R. & Rescorla, R.A. (1972). Inhibition in Pavlovian conditioning: applications of a theory, in R. A. Boakes & S. Halliday (eds). *Inhibition and Learning*. New York: Academic Press.

Welford, A. T. (1976). *Skilled Performance: Perceptual and Motor Skills*. Glenview, I11: Scott Foresman.

ACQUISITION OF COGNITIVE SKILLS

Chapter 2

The development of cognitive skills: an examination of recent theories

Julie B. Sincoff and Robert J. Sternberg

For most children, observing an event or transformation is not enough to satisfy their curiosity of the world. They want to know not only what happens in the world around them, but also how or why it happens. Thus, children want to know why the sun sets at night or how clouds produce rain. Psychologists studying children's cognitive development face the same problem. For some psychologists, it is enough to identify what states children pass through as they develop intellectually. For many others, especially many recent theorists and researchers, the more fundamental question is how children pass from one state or level to another. These psychologists, then, aim to identify the processes, or mechanisms, through which cognitive growth proceeds.

Although interest in developmental mechanisms dates back to Piaget, almost all of the research conducted by Piaget and his successors was designed to provide detailed descriptions of the states differentiating children's thought at various ages or levels of development, rather than detailed specifications of the mechanisms responsible for development. Recent methodological and conceptual advances in related disciplines such as information-processing psychology, however, have again directed attention to the importance of investigating the mechanisms responsible for cognitive change. Theories of cognitive growth, especially over the last few years, have certainly progressed since Piaget, with theorists such as Case, Fischer, Klahr, Siegler, Sternberg, Keil, and Carey introducing partial models of cognitive development. Given

Acquisition and Performance of Cognitive Skills. Edited by A. M. Colley and J. R. Beech
© 1989 John Wiley & Sons Ltd

this proliferation of models, an examination of the models and the considerations they raise may sharpen our understanding of the development of cognitive abilities and may underscore the directions the field should take in the near future.

The present examination of cognitive-developmental theories is divided into three main sections. First, an overview and evaluation of the theoretical backdrop provided by Jean Piaget, Lev Vygotsky, and Heinz Werner will be provided. Clearly, these three theorists have been particularly influential in shaping the ideas of current writers; to varying degrees, each has been concerned with the mechanisms underlying cognitive growth. Second, following this backdrop, the new models will be described and evaluated according to how they address six pertinent theoretical considerations raised by several areas of psychology and social science. These six considerations—the roles of stages, processes, knowledge, individual differences, contexts, and constraints in cognitive growth—represent important themes linking contemporary developmental and information-processing psychology. In addition, they reveal the influences of sociology, anthropology, and evolutionary biology upon psychological inquiry. Each consideration will be discussed individually. Finally, suggestions for integrating various parts of the models and recommendations for future theorizing will be offered. Through the integration of the most promising parts of the existing theories, it is hoped that more complete models of cognitive growth will be constructed and that the gaps in our understanding of the development of children's thinking will be highlighted and ultimately reduced.

THE THEORETICAL BACKDROP

Piaget's approach

Within developmental and cognitive psychology, Piaget's stage theory of intellectual development has been enormously influential in guiding theory and research. A biologist by training, Piaget combined his interest in epistemology with his gift for skilfully observing children, especially their errors on intellectual tasks, to examine the structure and function of intellectual activity. Believing that the structure of intelligence changes with age, he divided intellectual development from infancy to adolescence into four qualitatively discrete stages—the sensorimotor stage (birth to approximately age 2), the pre-operational stage (age 2 to 7), the concrete operational stage (age 7 to 12), and the formal operational stage (age 12 through adulthood). Each stage reflects a different internal structure brought about by the reorganization and extension of the immediately preceding stage. According to Piaget, these four stages are universal and occur in an invariant sequential order in all children.

(For detailed descriptions of Piaget's stages, the reader is referred to Flavell, 1963; Ginsburg and Opper, 1979; Piaget, 1970, 1976.) Piaget viewed the child as a young scientist solving problems; development progresses as the child manipulates his or her environment and actively works toward increasingly rational, logical, and abstract modes of thought.

Clearly, Piaget acknowledged the importance of maturation and the child's experiences in his or her physical and social environments. More importantly, though, the child's own internal activities and self-regulatory processes play an especially crucial role in his theory of intellectual development (Piaget, 1970). The function of intelligence, Piaget believed, is to assist the child in adapting to the environment. Movement from one stage of intellectual development to another results from the child's actively working toward adaptation through the process of equilibration. As proposed by Piaget, equilibration involves three phases. At first, the child's mode of thought is adequate for confronting and adapting to the challenges of his or her environment; the child is thus in a state of equilibrium. During periods of stage transition, however, disequilibrium arises from shortcomings in the child's mode of thought as new challenges, for which the child's current cognitive level is no longer adequate, are encountered. The child consequently attempts to restore equilibrium through two processes—assimilation, or modification of the enviroment to fit his or her existing cognitive structures, and especially accommodation, or changing his or her structures to fit relevant aspects of the new environment. Together, assimilation and accommodation result in a more sophisticated level of thought that corrects the deficiencies of the old one, propelling the child to the next stage of development and restoring equilibrium.

Although Piaget was concerned primarily with the structure of intelligence rather than with actual thought processes, he did recognize the importance of mechanisms of development, and thus he attempted to explicate them. Indeed, his equilibration model was proposed to explain how structural change from one stage to another occurs, as well as how competence with specific reasoning and other intellectual tasks improves.

Vygotsky's contribution

Vygotsky's contribution to cognitive-developmental theory is widely recognized, yet Vygotsky probably would not consider himself a developmental psychologist. His theoretical and methodological orientation revolved around the concepts of development and historical change; he did not, however, seem to distinguish between developmental psychology and basic psychological inquiry (John-Steiner and Souberman, 1978).

Although Vygotsky was familiar with only the first two of Piaget's books, the two theorists had several points in common. Like Piaget, Vygotsky viewed the child as an active organism working to overcome impediments to problem-solving. Also like Piaget, he relied heavily on skilful observations of children to understand their intellectual functioning. He studied cognitive growth by creating obstacles or providing alternative routes to task completion, observing children as they grappled with the obstacles or aids during problem-solving. He placed difficult tasks before his subjects in order to trace the development of new skills. He recognized the importance of play, as did Piaget, and argued that play creates opportunities for children to try new behaviours, thus facilitating their own development. Finally, Vygotsky as well as Piaget proposed a stage theory with a spiral model of development. According to Vygotsky (1978), development 'proceeds here not in a circle but in a spiral, passing through the same point at each new revolution while advancing to a higher level' (p. 56).

Despite these similarities, Vygotsky and Piaget differed strongly on several major points. Piaget's mechanism of cognitive growth was equilibration; Vygotsky's mechanism was internalization. For Vygotsky, not only does language reflect thought, but thought comes into existence through language. In other words, Vygotsky believed that children internalize their speech; the child's words to adults become the child's words to him- or herself—that is, his or her thought. Accordingly, a second difference between Vygotsky and Piaget is that Vygotsky believed development proceeds from the social context to the individual rather than from the individual to the social environment. For Vygotsky, it is the process of internalizing social activity such as language that leads to development. Finally, Vygotsky and Piaget both emphasized the role of experience in cognitive development, yet Vygotsky alone stressed the crucial role played by the child's environment or culture. Piaget asserted that his developmental stages apply universally; development proceeds through the same sequence of stages in all children. For Vygotsky, however, such universality is impossible because development reflects the dynamic relations between the child and his or her particular environment or culture, which varies among individuals as well as across time for the same individual.

Certainly, Vygotsky's theoretical insights add much to cognitive-developmental theory. Two insights in particular, though, seem especially relevant today. First, Vygotsky went beyond Piaget in assigning a planning function to speech, anticipating the interest and attention paid to metacognitive skills and development by current theorists and researchers. As noted above, Vygotsky proposed that development from earlier to later stages results from the internalization of culturally-produced sign systems (i.e. speech, writing, number systems). Describing the role of speech in development, he writes:

> The crucial change occurs as follows: At an early stage speech accompanies the child's actions and reflects the vicissitudes of problem solving in a disrupted and

chaotic form. At a later stage speech moves more and more toward the starting point of the process, so that it comes to precede action. It functions then as an aid to a plan that has been conceived but not yet realized in behavior. (1978, pp. 27–28)

Stating the point more strongly, he adds:

Now speech guides, determines, and dominates the course of action; the planning function of speech comes into being in addition to the already existing function of language to reflect the external world. (1978, p. 28)

Second, although some of Piaget's ideas have since been enthusiastically applied to educational settings, Vygotsky himself directly addressed the crucial importance of instruction for facilitating cognitive growth. Indeed, he viewed intelligence as a capacity to benefit from instruction (Bruner, 1962) and proposed that learning creates a 'zone of proximal development' during which psychologists and educators can best study and understand the course of intellectual development (Vygotsky, 1978). According to Vygotsky:

When it was first shown that the capability of children with equal levels of mental development to learn under a teacher's guidance varied to a high degree, it became apparent that those children were not mentally the same age and that the subsequent course of their learning would obviously be different. . . . [The zone of proximal development] is the distance between the actual developmental level as determined by independent problem solving and the level of potential development as determined through problem solving under adult guidance or in collaboration with more capable peers. (1978, p. 86)

Clearly, in addition to advancing cognitive-developmental theory and methodology, Vygotsky's contributions, especially his concept of the zone of proximal development, offer important educational applications.

Werner's theory

Werner's approach to the development of mental capacities represents a third major influence on the works of contemporary cognitive-developmental theorists and researchers. Like Piaget, Werner based his theory on general principles of biology. Whereas Piaget asserted that the function of intelligence—adaptation—is no different from the function of other biological capacities, Werner argued that the mechanisms of cognitive growth—differentiation and hierarchization—are no different from the mechanisms responsible for the development of the nervous system and other biological forms.

Werner believed that cognitive growth results not from the processes of equilibration or internalization, but rather from (i) the increasing differentiation and specialization of mental capacities and abilities, and (ii) the increasing hierarchization, or ordering, grouping, and subordination, of capacities and abilities. For Werner, then, cognitive development does not progress through a sequence of stages. Instead, development proceeds as new capacities emerge and separate from older, more general capacities. Werner's conception of development, indeed, resembles a tree, with finer and finer branches growing out of older ones (see Garrett, 1946, for another example of a differentiation approach to cognitive growth).

Importantly, this difference in the overall structure of intellectual development leads to another theoretical distinction between Werner and traditional stage theorists such as Piaget and Vygotsky. In stage theories of development, once a child reaches a certain level of functioning, he or she does not revert to modes of thought characteristic of previous levels. Werner, on the other hand, asserted that previous modes of thought are accessible even after differentiation of abilities occurs. According to Werner (1948, p. 216), in many instances the lower level 'develops as an integral part of a more complex organization in which the higher process dominates the lower'.

Werner applied his differentiation mechanism to many realms of development. He believed differentiation underlies not only the growth of the child's specific intellectual skills and abilities, but also the development of the child's personality. Thus, he asserted, for example, that the 'basic process underlying individuation is the increase in distance between ego and world, the growing differentiation between person and society as interdependent, yet fundamentally discrete, organisms' (1948, p. 452). In his investigations of children's development, Werner exploited the comparative method. He found similarities in the development of cognition and personality. Likewise, whereas Vygotsky continually distinguished the adaptive capabilities of humans from those of apes and lower animals, Werner found many similarities in the mental life of children, of individuals from certain primitive societies, and of individuals with certain types of psychotic disorders. Throughout his work, he stressed two themes: the value of comparision and the necessity for elucidating the mechanisms of development.

From Piaget, Vygotsky, and Werner to a wealth of recent theories

Before addressing the weaknesses that led current theorists and researchers to respond with new or modified theories of their own, several strengths of Piaget's, Vygotsky's, and Werner's theories of development should be acknowledged. First, both Piaget and Vygotsky introduced a variety of ingenious materials—Piaget's tasks and Vygotsky's use of obstacles and external aids—that researchers today still employ in their experiments. Piaget and Vygotsky, indeed, contributed a rich data base as well as the materials used to construct the data base. Similarly, Werner's use of the comparative method has shaped the nature of some contemporary cross-cultural research, and his theoretical approach has been applied to areas of psychological inquiry other than intellectual development (for example, see Zigler and Glick's [1986] developmental approach to adult psychopathology). Second, as Siegler (1986a) points out, Piaget asked the right questions even if his theory fails to provide totally satisfactory answers to them. The same can be said of Vygotsky and Werner, for all three theorists sought to explicate the capacities possessed by infants or young children, those possessed by older children, and the processes responsible for the transitions from earlier to later capacities. Third, although theories positing qualitatively distinct stages or branching structures may not capture the true nature of all cognitive change, Piaget's, Vygotsky's, and Werner's theories clearly demonstrate the heuristic value of conceptualizing development as a series of stages or as a proliferation of branches. Such guiding principles help researchers select the appropriate tasks and subject populations (i.e. particular age groups) for answering specific research questions. They also provide models of development that can be easily visualized, conceived, and communicated. Fourth, Piaget's emphasis on the experience of the individual and Vygotsky's emphasis on the individual's experience and cultural environment broaden the scope of developmental inquiry to include not only the child, but also the social and cultural contexts in which development occurs. Current writers must not neglect these important theoretical considerations in their own models of development.

On the other hand, current writers should attempt to correct some of the deficiencies or limitations of Piaget's, Vygotsky's, and Werner's theories. One of the major problems with Piaget's theory is that his findings are difficult to replicate, especially with respect to the ages at which children first master specific tasks or reason in specific ways. In general, replication of Piaget's findings is difficult for two reasons. First, his clinical interview procedure for discovering how children think and reason encourages variability in the questions posed, and in the answers obtained, from experiment to experiment as well as from researcher to researcher. Second, Piaget's stringent criteria for success on particular tasks has led several investigators to impose considerably less strict criteria for success on the same tasks. For instance, Piaget required not only that the child correctly judge the answer to a conservation task, but also that he or she correctly justify that answer; Brainerd (1977), conversely, argued that a correct judgement alone is the best criterion for success on conservation tasks. Researchers such as Brainerd, placing fewer demands upon the child, thus find that children master certain constructs at earlier ages than those identified by Piaget. (For an interesting debate on the appropriate criteria for attributing egocentricity to young children, see Borke, 1971, 1972, and Chandler and Greenspan, 1972.)

In addition to replicability, another problem with Piaget's theory is that it fails to account for the phenomenon of horizontal décalage, or children's differing understanding and acquisition rates of related concepts such as conservation of number, volume, and weight (Siegler, 1986a). Stage theories like Piaget's rest on the assumption that the mode of thought characteristic of any particular stage applies across many tasks and problems. A concrete-operational child, then, should demonstrate the ability to conserve quantity on a wide range of tasks from age 7 or 8 on; the same child, of course, should fail to generate hypotheses or to reason abstractly on a similarly wide range of problems. Although some unity in children's thinking does indeed exist, such consistency does not always characterize children's cognitive growth. For example, most children demonstrate the ability to conserve (a) number at approximately age 6, (b) solid quantities at approximately age 8, and (c) weight at about age 10 (Elkind, 1961). Piaget emphasized unities in children's reasoning, and although he acknowledged the phenomenon of horizontal décalage, he did not attempt to explain why it happens. One possible explanation, and another criticism of Piaget's approach, is that his experiments confounded the presence or absence of domain-specific knowledge with the acquisition of higher order concepts (Carey, 1985a). In this case, the ability to conserve number, volume, and weight would depend not only on conservation skills *per se*, but also on the child's real-world knowledge of the properties of number, volume, and weight, respectively; the child's growing knowledge base, not necessarily his or her ability to conserve, may account for the developmental progression.

Piaget's lack of concern for inconsistencies in children's acquisition rates parallels his lack of attention to individual differences in the development of cognitive abilities. With few exceptions, he was interested in general, universal patterns of development rather than in the intellectual differences among children of the same age that so intrigued psychometricians and information-processing psychologists. Certainly, Piaget's theory is one of cognitive competence rather than performance (Piaget, 1976; Sternberg and Powell, 1983). Current models of cognitive growth should attempt to capture the nature of the child's performance on specific tasks as well as his or her underlying competence on those tasks.

In the realms of performance and individual differences, Vygotsky's theory fares better than Piaget's. Vygotsky's emphasis on the child's specific interactions with others in his or her environment and on each child's zone of proximal development underscores his recognition of the importance of individual differences in theories of development. However, whereas Piaget's findings are difficult to replicate, many of Vygotsky's ideas are difficult to operationalize and test. Vygotsky's influence among Western psychologists is considerably more recent than Piaget's. Thus, in the West, Vygotsky's theory has not spurred nearly as much research as has Piaget's, although Western psychologists are now attempting to evaluate Vygotsky's contributions empirically. (See, for example, Rogoff and Wertsch's [1984] edited volume dedicated to refining and operationalizing Vygotsky's concept of the zone of proximal development in the conduct of empirical research.) Many of Vygotsky's core concepts, although intuitively plausible to some psychologists, are difficult to define in a way that facilitates their systematic investigation. This definitional problem is especially true of Vygotsky's important developmental mechanism, internalization. According to Vygotsky (1978, pp. 56–57) the process of internalization involves a series of transformations: (i) operations initially representing external activities are reconstructed so that they begin to occur internally; and (ii) processes between people (interpersonal) are transformed into processes that occur inside the child (intrapersonal), with these transformations resulting from a long series of developmental events and experiences. Vygotsky admits that 'the barest outline of this process [of internalization] is known' (1978, p. 57), yet his description of internalization makes it exceptionally difficult to delineate the process through research, much less to test and evaluate it empirically.

Clearly, Piaget's, Vygotsky's, and Werner's mechanisms of development are vague. Werner's differentiation and hierarchization mechanisms, Vygotsky's internalization process, and Piaget's equilibration model—all inadequately defined and difficult to operationalize—cry out for expansion, modification, or replacement. Indeed, Klahr (1982) underscores this point when he asks:

> For 40 years now, we have had assimilation and accommodation, the mysterious and shadowy forces of equilibration, the 'Batman and Robin' of the developmental processes. What are they? How do they operate? Why is it that after all this time, we know no more about them than when they first sprang upon the scene? (p. 80)

Spurred by Piaget's, Vygotsky's, and Werner's relative inattention to precise specifications of developmental processes, several current theorists have recently published alternatives—sometimes modifications, sometimes replacements—to these reigning theories, attempting to explicate more clearly and definitively the nature and mechanisms of cognitive growth. In particular, Robbie Case (1984, 1985) has presented a neo-Piagetian model of development influenced by the related fields of information processing and computer simulation. Kurt Fischer (1980; Fischer and Pipp, 1984) has proposed a stage theory of skill learning in which the child's thinking develops through the activation of five transformation rules. David Klahr (1984; Klahr and Wallace, 1976) uses self-modifying production systems and other information-processing concepts to explain cognitive growth, especially the acquisition of such Piagetian constructs as conservation. Similarly, Robert Siegler (1984, 1986a) has proposed an information-processing account of the development of Piagetian and other intellectual skills, although he stresses the importance of encoding and strategy implementation rather than of production systems. Robert Sternberg (1984, 1985), influenced by the fields of information processing and human abilities, has offered a three-part theory of intelligence and its development, emphasizing the relations among the child's internal information-processing components, his or her experience, and his or her environment. Finally, Frank Keil (1981, 1984), influenced by the works of Chomsky and Fodor, and Susan Carey (1985a, 1985b) emphasize the crucial importance of domain-specific knowledge structures and representations. Keil asserts that development proceeds via general, all-purpose cognitive processes that restructure specific knowledge, whereas Carey, unconcerned with processes, argues that cognitive development consists of the emergence of new knowledge structures from the reorganization and expansion of older ones. Certainly, these writers are not the only contemporary theorists concerned with cognitive development, although the present discussion will focus on their models because each has written extensively about cognitive growth within the past several years, and each confronts at least a subset of the major issues facing the field today.

In the next section, the models presented by these seven theorists will be classified and discussed according to how they address, or fail to address, six pertinent theoretical considerations raised by several areas of psychology and social science. Indeed, the purpose of the present review is to elucidate the themes and considerations raised by recent advances in cognitive-developmental theory and research rather than simply to explain the details of each model. First, as noted previously, stages have traditionally represented the organizing principle of theories of cognitive growth and have served several heuristic functions. Are the new models stage theories, or do they offer some other guiding principle, such as Werner's branches, for characterizing children's thinking? Second, advances in information-processing psychology have drawn attention to the importance of explicating the processes underlying cognitive change. What kinds of processes do the new theories propose to account for cognitive growth? Third, children's knowledge structures and representations have long been a focus of traditional cognitive-developmental theories as well as of information-processing psychology. Does knowledge play a role in the new theories of development? If so, what role does it play? Fourth, psychometricians and information-processing psychologists have provided a large body of literature documenting and analysing individual differences in cognitive performance. Do the new theories address, or attempt to explain, individual differences in the acquisition and performance of cognitive skills? Fifth, work in several areas has underscored the value of studying development within a contextual framework. Vygotsky considered the influence of the child's social environment, and anthropologists have always studied behaviour within its specific cultural context. What role, if any, does context play in the new theories of development? How do the child's experiences and social or cultural environment influence his or her development? Finally, traditional cognitive-developmental theories, information-processing psychology, and evolutionary biology have all posited various constraints on human behaviour and development. Do the new theories posit constraints on cognitive growth? If so, what kinds of constraints do they propose? Are the constraints viable? As the models presented by Case, Fischer, Klahr, Siegler, Sternberg, Keil, and Carey are described and evaluated, the reader is encouraged to keep in mind the following questions. Are the new theories compatible with the bulk of the existing developmental literature? Do the theories generate interesting empirical research, even if they cannot be falsified directly through research? Do the theories lead to practical implications or guidelines for education? In the next section, these questions, where appropriate, will be addressed.

CURRENT THEORIES OF COGNITIVE GROWTH

The organizing principle of development

In the course of specifying the structure of children's thinking and the processes underlying structural change, cognitive-developmental theorists also indicate, either explicitly or implicitly, the organization of the changes that occur as children develop. Stages represent the traditional organizing principle of cognitive growth, although other guiding principles have recently been proposed.

In general, stage theories imply four characteristics of structural change (Kohlberg, 1969). First, stages imply qualitatively discrete modes of thought at different age levels. Second, the qualitatively discrete modes of thought form an invariant sequence in the course of development. Third, the modes of thought characteristic of any particular stage are related and together form a structured whole. Finally, the stages are hierarchical; more advanced stages reintegrate, and ultimately displace, the modes of thought found at lower levels. Certainly, Piaget and Vygotsky were true stage theorists. Case and Fischer, each adopting a neo-Piagetian approach to the study of intellectual development, also offer stage theories of cognitive change.

Indeed, Case and Fischer are 'Piagetian' because they assume children's thinking develops in stages. They are 'neo' because they offer different structures and processes from those proposed by Piaget. Although Case's stages are similar to Piaget's, they are not identical. Case (1985) proposes four stages that unfold from infancy to adolescence: the sensorimotor stage (birth to age 18 months), the relational stage (age 18 months to 5 years), the dimensional stage (age 5 to 11), and the vectorial, or abstract-dimensional, stage (age 11 to 18 or 19). The mental activity of infants in the sensorimotor stage revolves around perception and physical action. The modes of thought characteristic of young children in the relational stage centre on the relations between, and eventually among, events. Children in the dimensional stage focus on the various dimensions of concrete objects, such as weight or number, whereas adolescents in the vectorial stage focus on more abstract, second-order dimensions. For example, to solve an analogy, an adolescent must find a higher-order dimension, or vector, that links the lower-order dimensions in the analogy, allowing the adolescent to compare the lower-order dimensions on a more abstract plane. Case asserts that children pass through the same sequence of stages and substages across many content domains and that they do so at the same rate and during the same age range. Thus, Case formulates his stages to correct the problem of horizontal décalage that plagued Piaget.

Case further proposes that within each stage, development progresses through four substages in which the child must simultaneously operate on one, two, three, or four representational units, respectively. Different types of representational units characterize different stages, and stage transitions occur as problems whose representations originally required four units are re-represented using only one unit from the next cognitive level.

Case applies a relatively global level of analysis to the study of children's representations; in general, he asks how children represent problems and how they act on their representations to solve the problems. A sensorimotor child, for example, might represent thunder as a loud noise (sensory) and might act on this representation by crawling or walking to his or her mother (motor). It is at this level that Case demonstrates consistencies in children's reasoning across a wide variety of tasks. Although he reveals the utility of such global levels of analysis for eliminating horizontal décalage, he may also find similarities among operations that are not truly comparable, thus exaggerating the degree of horizontal regularity (Siegler, 1986b). Another problem with Case's global analytic level is that the operations unique to each stage are difficult to pinpoint and describe. The operations characteristic of Case's stages are clearly similar to those of Piaget; yet, given the general level Case employs to examine children's representations, it seems difficult to state exatly what sensorimotor, relational, dimensional, and vectorial operations are without recourse to Piaget's theory. Finally, Case does not clearly indicate why re-representation occurs only after four representational units have been consolidated (Siegler, 1986b). He does not explain why four, rather than three or five, is the magic number.

Fischer (Fischer and Pipp, 1984) departs from Piaget and Case by offering ten qualitatively distinct levels of cognitive skill that are hierarchically organized and closely tied to age: a single sensorimotor set, a sensorimotor mapping, a sensorimotor system, a system of sensorimotor systems or single representational set, a representational mapping, a representational system, a system of representational systems or single abstract set, an abstract mapping, an abstract system, and a system of abstract systems or single principle (for a general description of these skill levels, the reader is referred to Fischer and Pipp, 1984). Empirically, spurts in optimal task performance reveal the emergence of new levels. Theoretically, the child's optimal skill level limits his or her information-processing capacities and keeps him or her at a given level of functioning. Development proceeds through the activation of a transformation rule that propels the child to the next stage, thus setting a new optimal skill level. Fischer believes optimal levels merely set the upper limit on the child's skills and abilities; he believes performance varies widely below that limit. This assertion thus represents another significant departure from Case and Piaget, as well as a strength of Fischer's theory. For Case and Piaget, higher stages displace lower ones. For Fischer, however, higher levels do not necessarily displace lower ones, although because they yield optimal performance, in some instances the child may be more likely to operate at such levels than at lower ones.

There are two general problems with Fischer's stage theory of development. First, a theory that postulates ten qualitatively distinct levels of cognitive skill is certainly not parsimonious. Second, although Fischer has studied other abilities, he illustrates his stages primarily by examining a child's skills as he or she plays with dolls (Fischer and Pipp, 1984; Watson and Fischer, 1977, 1980). For example, a child operating at the level of a single representational set can treat the doll as a doctor, making the doll put on a doctor's coat or write a prescription. A child operating at the level of representational mapping can coordinate two related behavioural roles to create a social role, such as making a doctor doll and a patient doll interact in stereotypical ways, whereas a child performing at the representational system level can make two dolls enact two overlapping social roles simultaneously. That is, the child can make one doll act as both doctor and husband to a second doll; the second doll, of course, acts as the first doll's patient and wife. Although Fischer's stages seem appropriate for these instances of pretend play, they may not be appropriate for performance in other domains. As Flavell (1984, p. 202) emphasizes, it is difficult to comprehend the 'precise, domain-invariant, essential meaning of a "system of representational systems, equivalent to a single abstract set"'. Without this understanding, problems arise in applying Fischer's skill levels to domains other than pretend play.

Aside from Case and Fisher, none of the other theorists are stage theorists. Carey's model of cognitive growth implies the same branching organization as Werner's approach. According to Carey, development progresses as increasingly specialized and accurate theories of the world arise from one or two general theories. That is, the child initially possesses only naïve theories of mechanics and psychology; as the child develops, later theories of psychology, mechanics, matter, biology, religion, economics, history, government, and so on grow out of the two naive theories (Carey, 1985b). Because Carey believes only about a dozen theories emerge in the course of development, her branching tree is a small one.

Continuous cycles or feedback loops represent a third organizing principle that characterizes development in several recent theories. This guiding principle is apparently becoming increasingly popular in information-processing accounts of cognitive growth. In such cycles or feedback loops, progress in structure or process x leads to progress in structure or process y, which in turn leads to further progress in x, and the cycle continues repeatedly. Siegler (1986a), for example, supports this view of cognitive change. Siegler believes that children's predictive knowledge of the world and their encoding of features in their environment begin at the same level. Then, children start encoding features they previously missed, and their improved encoding allows them to learn increasingly sophisticated rules, advancing their knowledge of the world. Their greater knowledge, in turn, forms the basis for even more sophisticated encoding, and at this point, the cycle starts again. A child learning to distinguish cats from dogs provides a concrete example of the cyclic nature of cognitive change. A child who distinguishes cats from dogs solely on the basis of size will make many classification errors. As the child begins to encode other features, such as differences in the animals' sounds or the shapes of their ears, the child learns to distinguish cats from dogs more accurately. This increased knowledge, in turn, frees the child to encode additional distinguishing characteristics—the positions of the animals' eyes and so on—leading once again to increasingly accurate and sophisticated rules.

Like Siegler, Sternberg also characterizes development in terms of continuous cycles and feedback loops. The relation between the child's knowledge base and his or her knowledge-acquisition processes (Sternberg, 1984, 1985) is the same as the relation between the child's predictive knowledge and his or her encoding (Siegler, 1986a). According to Sternberg, the knowledge-acquisition processes create a steadily developing knowledge base; the developing knowledge base, in turn, permits increasingly sophisticated forms of acquisition, and the cycle continues. Sternberg further proposes a similar relation between the child's metacognitive processes and the processes responsible for task execution. Continuous feedback loops between the two types of processes facilitate cognitive growth. Sternberg believes that the metacognitive processes responsible for planning and evaluating performance communicate relevant information to the processes responsible for task execution. Feedback from the performance processes to the metacognitive processes about the success or failure of task execution leads to improved planning and evaluation. The improved planning results in improved performance, and the cycle is repeated.

Organizing principles of cognitive growth—stages, branches, feedback loops—allow the nature of development to be visualized and communicated as easily and efficiently as possible. The ultimate test of any guiding principle, however, is how well it captures the true nature of development, or how well it reflects the developmental literature. In general, the success of stages in capturing the nature of children's thinking depends upon the level of analysis employed. Sometimes relatively global levels of analysis are more likely to yield stage-like characteristics (e.g. Case, 1985); sometimes relatively molecular levels are more likely to do so (e.g. Siegler, 1986c). The recent movement away from stage theories to branching models of development and to feedback loops highlights the limitations of stages as well as the desirability of finding a suitable replacement.

Processes

Certainly, understanding cognitive growth requires specifying the processes, or mechanisms, through which children's thinking develops. Information-processing psychologists have traditionally recognized two kinds of processes: executive and non-executive. Executive processes, anticipated in the developmental literature by Vygotsky's planning function of speech, are those involved in planning, monitoring, and evaluating performance on intellectual tasks. Indeed, the terms 'metacognitive' and 'executive' are often used interchangeably. Non-executive processes, on the other hand, are those involved in performance, in actually solving problems and tasks. Complete models of cognitive development require both kinds of processes. Table 2.1 summarizes each theorist's position regarding executive and non-executive processing, along with his or her positions on the other five theoretical considerations raised in the present discussion.

Executive processing

The executive processes proposed by recent theorists to account for cognitive growth differ from one model to another, although in each model the processes serve a similar function—they guide problem-solving and intellectual activity by helping to plan, monitor, and evaluate performance on cognitive tasks. Robbie Case (1984, 1985) argues that children's ability to assemble increasingly sophisticated executive control structures underlies most of their cognitive change. According to Case, executive control structures consist of three interrelated parts: a representation of the problem situation, a representation of the problem objective, and a representation of the problem strategy. A non-conserving child's executive control structure for liquid conservation tasks, then, might encompass the following representations: (i) in representing the problem situation, the child might note the

Table 2.1 Summary of the theorists' positions.

Theorist	Organizing principle of development	Change processes	Knowledge	Individual differences	Contextual considerations	Constraints on development
Case	Stages	Executive: Hierarchical integration of executive control structures, with automatization increasing operational efficiency of short-term storage space Non-executive: Four within-stage transition rules (substitution, focusing, compounding, differentiation); One between-stage rule (inter-coordination)	Executive control structures are procedural knowledge	In rate of executive development	Culture plays an increasing role in stage transition as the child develops	Organismic: Age-related; Operational efficiency of short-term storage space
Fischer	Stages		No particular emphasis	In developmental paths for specific skills	Environmental influences, such as practice, instruction, support	Organismic: Age-related; Optimal skill level
Klahr	Time-line analysis	Non-executive: Generalization (regularity detection), redundancy elimination, elaboration of transformational classes	Generalization processes reflect specific content domains	Result from different experiences	Emphasizes role of experience	Not addressed

Siegler	Continuous cycles	Executive: Associative model of strategy construction. Nonexecutive: Encoding facilitates construction of rules	Helps determine what change processes accomplish	Variability mechanism in evolutionary analogy; motivational variables (prior interest and reactions to negative experiences)	Selection pressures in evolutionary analogy; Emphasizes social context of development	Not addressed
Sternberg	Continuous cycles and feedback loops	Executive: Metacomponents and componential feedback. Nonexecutive: Performance components; Automatization	Steadily developing knowledge base; Knowledge-acquisition components	Stem from many sources, especially from responses to novelty (motivational and information-extraction variables)	Experiential continuum from novelty to full automatization; Contextual subtheory stresses adaptation to environment	Organismic: Functional capacity of working memory; Domain-related: Novelty
Keil	Depends on particular content domain under consideration	Unspecified simple general learning procedures	Very important – dynamics of change depend on knowledge structure	Not addressed	Not addressed	Domain-related: Some content domains are more natural to acquire than others
Carey	Branches	Not addressed	Very important – emphasizes acquisition and reorganization of new knowledge; Posits major restructuring in which new theories emerge from older ones	Not addressed	Not addressed	Domain-related: Limited knowledge

presence of two different-sized beakers of coloured water; (ii) in representing the problem objective, the child might realize that he or she must decide which beaker, if either, contains more water; and (3) in representing the problem strategy, or procedure for accomplishing the problem objective based on the information in the problem situation, the child might decide to pick the beaker with the higher water level. Because the representations of the problem situation, objective, and strategy each contain only one unit, such an executive control structure illustrates the mode of thought characteristic of a child in the first substage of a cognitive level. The control structures of a child in the second, third, or fourth substage contain, respectively, two, three, or four units of each type of representation.

As noted previously, Case proposes that stage transitions result from problem re-representation, or the hierarchical integration of executive control structures. That is, problems that originally required four representational units later require only one unit from the next cognitive stage. According to Case, two types of capacities produce movement from one level to another. First, Case believes that children are born with a set of general processing capacities that allow them to set goals and to construct, evaluate, and practise problem-solving strategies designed to achieve specific goals. Such innate processing capacities contribute substantially to cognitive change, although their use is often limited by a second type of capacity, the child's short-term storage space. If the child possesses the memory capacity required for hierarchical integration, stage transition occurs; otherwise, cognitive growth must await prerequisite changes in the child's short-term storage space. Case proposes that increases in short-term storage space are due not to increases in the absolute size of memory capacity, but rather to the increasing operational efficiency of memory capacity. That is, although the size of the child's total storage space does not expand with age, the proportion of the child's total space that must be devoted to solving particular problems decreases as he or she grows older. According to Case, operational efficiency results from (i) automatization, or the increasing efficiency of processing produced by extensive practice, and (ii) biological maturation, particularly neurological myelinization.

In short, Case believes cognitive growth progresses as executive control structures become hierarchically integrated through the child's innate processing capacities and especially through the increasing operational efficiency of his or her short-term storage space. Case's ideas about myelinization, although plausible, are highly speculative, and his assertion that children are born possessing certain processing capacities—those relevant for setting goals and for formulating, evaluating, and practising strategies—also invites debate. However, his model of cognitive growth has generated many intriguing empirical observations and analyses of children's intellectual development and has provided promising educational applications as well (Siegler, 1986b).

Indeed, his global level of analysis, in addition to revealing unities in children's thought in diverse domains, has important implications for instruction in school classrooms. Case's theory underscores the utility of helping children learn by helping them specify the exact nature of the problem situation, set realistic problem objectives, and formulate effective strategies. For example, children may be taught to solve unconventional multiplication problems (e.g. $3 \times \_\_ = 12$ rather than $3 \times 4 = \_\_$) by helping them identify and practise the most efficient strategy for task completion and by discouraging their use of comparatively inefficient strategies. Educational applications clearly increase the value of models of cognitive growth, and thus Case's model deserves the continued attention of cognitive-developmental and educational psychologists.

Whereas Case's theory revolves around executive control structures, Robert Sternberg's (1984, 1985) model of intelligence and intellectual development posits three kinds of components, or information-processing units: metacomponents, performance components, and knowledge-acquisition components. Of these three kinds, only the metacomponents fulfil executive processing functions. Sternberg (1984, pp. 165–166) identifies nine types of metacomponential processing. A child completing an intellectual task must (i) determine the nature of the problem under consideration, (ii) select the appropriate performance components for solving the problem, and (iii) select a strategy for combining performance components in an optimal way. The child must also (iv) select one or more representations for the information crucial to problem solution, and, given a limited amount of time for task completion, must (v) decide how to allocate his or her processing resources. Finally, the child must (vi) monitor his or her performance, (vii) interpret feedback about the effectiveness of his or her efforts, (viii) decide how to act upon positive or negative feedback, and ultimately (ix) modify his or her performance in response to the feedback.

According to Sternberg, cognitive growth depends heavily upon the metacomponents. The metacomponents, capable of monitoring their own effectiveness, may learn from their failures and successes and may thus continually refine their own functioning. Also, the hypothesized feedback loops among performance, knowledge-acquisition, and metacomponents provide additional information, further facilitating performance and intellectual growth.

Sternberg's model of cognitive change, especially his emphasis on metacomponential processing, accounts for many of the consistent findings in the cognitive-developmental literature. Many studies, for instance, conclude that as children grow older and as novices become experts, they spend relatively more time planning the solutions to problems and relatively less time actually solving them (e.g. Chi, Glaser, and Rees, 1982; Larkin, McDermott, Simon, and Simon, 1980). Thus, older, more cognitively advanced children dedicate relatively more time to executive processing than younger, less cognitively competent children, underscoring the appropriateness of Sternberg's emphasis on metacomponential processing and development. On the other hand, Sternberg's theory summarizes the findings of previous research more than it generates new empirical observations; indeed, Sternberg draws support for his theory primarily from studies conducted prior to its formalization rather than from studies designed to test its predictions after it was formalized. Another problem with Sternberg's model is that the metacomponents, although crucial to intelligence and intellectual development, defy precise operational definition (Carrol, 1986), thus hindering their empirical utility.

Like Sternberg and Case, Robert Siegler represents a third voice stressing the importance of strategy construction in cognitive development. Through his analyses of children's strategy choice for solving arithmetic problems (Siegler, 1986c; Siegler and Shrager, 1984), he concludes that both performance and development progress as children rely more on retrieval strategies and less on backup strategies such as counting or using their fingers as aids to problem-solving, resulting in greater accuracy and faster reaction times. Siegler argues that the increasing strength of associations linking specific arithmetic problems with various possible answers underlies shifts from backup strategies to retrieval strategies. He further asserts that pre-existing associations, the particular numbers in the arithmetic problems, and the frequency of exposure to each problem all lead to greater associative strength. Although the proper evaluation of Siegler's associative model awaits further work in this area, his approach does appear promising for producing new predictions about the role of strategy construction in cognitive development, as well as about unities in children's executive processing across domains. Clearly, strategies play key roles in the models of Case, Sternberg, and Siegler; the systems within which strategies operate, however, differ among the three theories.

Non-executive processing

In addition to executive processing, Sternberg and Siegler also stress the role of non-executive processing in the development of children's thinking. Sternberg's (1985) non-executive, or performance, components include encoding components, combination and comparison components, and a response component. New information is perceived and stored in working memory through the encoding components. The information is then organized and compared with older information through the combination and comparison components. Finally, an answer to a given problem or task is provided by the response component. Although Sternberg argues that metacomponential processing exerts a greater and more fundamental influence on development than non-executive processing, he also believes that the automatization of executive and non-executive processing produces some cognitive growth. As children gain experience with certain kinds of problems and tasks, their processing becomes less controlled and more automated, improving their performance and facilitating their intellectual growth (LaBerge and Samuels, 1974; Schneider and Shiffrin, 1977; Shiffrin and Schneider, 1977).

By arguing that encoding directly influences learning, Siegler (1986a), also emphasizes its role in producing cognitive change. According to Siegler, children's increasingly effective encoding of meaningful information allows them to construct increasingly elaborate rules for operating in their environment. Siegler defines encoding more broadly than does Sternberg. He uses the term to refer to the interpretation and organization as well as the perception and storage of information, and he offers an intriguing account of the ways in which encoding and combination processes may lead to cognitive growth. Likening psychological development to biological evolution, he suggests that variation and selection pressures propel children toward increasingly sophisticated cognitive functioning (Siegler, 1984). Feedback from individuals in the child's environment, such as the child's parents and teachers, provides selection pressures. Changes in the child's encoding of features in his or her environment, on the other hand, produce cognitive variations. As long as the child's encoding produces acceptable outcomes, his or her processing continues unchanged. When the child's encoding repeatedly fails to produce such outcomes, however, he or she starts to (i) encode additional features and (ii) include new features in the rules he or she constructs to guide his or her behaviour and performance.

Neither Steinberg nor Siegler explains how encoding takes place. However, consistent trends in the developmental literature justify the importance they assign to encoding and related processes. Many studies indicate that children become increasingly exhaustive in their processing of information as they grow older (e.g. Brown and DeLoache, 1978; Sternberg and Nigro, 1980). In other words, with increasing age children seem to encode and to consider using more and more of the information available in a given problem. Through their inclusion of encoding and combination processes in their models of intellectual growth, Sternberg and Siegler account for this trend.

Siegler (1986a) concentrates on encoding in his own model of development, although he acknowledges the role of automatization in producing cognitive change. In this way, his views reflect the contributions of Case and Sternberg. Similarly, Siegler also acknowledges the role of generalization in effecting cognitive growth, and here his views reflect those of David Klahr. For Klahr (1984; Klahr and Wallace, 1976), children's thinking develops as they generalize information and experience, detecting regularities and eliminating redundancies in their processing. Klahr studies children's thinking partly by examining their processing and performance on Piagetian number-conservation tasks. He believes that a child's experiences (information about the situation, the child's response, and the outcome of the child's actions) are recorded on an internal time line. In number-conservation tasks, for example, a child's time line may include the following information: the child saw a row of marbles, counted them, and determined that there were six marbles in the row. The child then saw another person compress the marbles, counted them again, and determined once more that there were six in the row. The child develops intellectually by (i) generalizing information, or detecting regularities in the experiences recorded on the time line, (ii) making information processing more efficient by eliminating redundant steps in the time line, and (iii) elaborating transformational classes. The child's regularity detection in number-conservation experiences may take three forms. The child may generalize over objects (e.g. marbles or cookies), over quantitative symbols (e.g. six marbles or eight marbles), and over transformations (e.g. the compression or expansion of a row of marbles). The child's redundancy elimination processes improve efficiency by locating and then removing unnecessary processing steps. Thus, in number-conservation tasks, a child eventually stops counting marbles following compression or expansion, realizing that such procedures leave the number of marbles in the row unchanged. Finally, the child elaborates his or her knowledge of transformational classes (that is, the types of transformations that increase the number of marbles in a row, decrease the number, or leave the quantity unchanged), ultimately acquiring the ability to conserve.

To capture the nature of the development of skills such as conservation, Klahr constructs self-modifying production systems, or computer simulations capable of developing in response to new experiences. Few self-modifying production systems of children's cognitive growth have actually been written, however, and Klahr's model, like Sternberg's, seems more useful for explaining the results of earlier research than for generating new predictions and findings (Siegler, 1986a). The major strength of Klahr's approach is the detail inherent in self-modifying computer simulations; indeed, Klahr's conception of generalization represents one of the most precise, explicit mechanisms of intellectual change that has been proposed to date (Siegler, 1986a).

Finally, like Klahr, Kurt Fischer (1980; Fischer and Pipp, 1984) also asserts that generalization plays a role in producing cognitive change, although whereas Klahr assigns a major role to generalization processes, Fischer assigns a much smaller role to the mechanism. Fischer proposes five transformation rules; four of these rules, substitution, focusing, compounding, and discrimination, specify how children develop within a given level, and the fifth rule, intercoordination, indicates how children progress from one skill level to another. Fischer believes that the process of substitution, or the generalization of a skill mastered in the context of one particular task to other, highly similar tasks, fosters within-level development. An example from children's pretend play illustrates this process. A child originally making a doctor doll interact with a female patient applies this same skill as he or she begins to make the doctor doll interact with a male patient; the child simply substitutes the male patient for the female patient. Second, through the process of focusing, a child combines two related skills by using them in succession. For example, a child first makes a doctor doll interact with a patient doll and then shifts to an interaction between a nurse doll and a patient doll, leaving the doctor doll out of the second play episode. Third, by compounding related skills, a child combines two similar skills to form a single, more complex skill. That is, by compounding, a child makes a nurse and doctor doll jointly examine a patient doll. Fourth, Fischer asserts that the process of differentiation fosters within-level development. Thus, Fischer's developmental mechanisms overlap with Werner's mechanisms as well as with Klahr's, although again Fischer assigns a relatively weaker role to the mechanism. According to Fischer, the process of differentiation accompanies the other transformation rules and involves separating a skill into its distinct components so that each component becomes more clearly defined. Through differentiation, then, a child demonstrating the compounded skill of making a doctor and nurse doll jointly examine a patient doll separates this three-way interaction into its constituent two-way interactions (i.e. interactions between doctor/patient, nurse/patient, and doctor/nurse), resulting in the greater clarification and elaboration of these constituent interactions and roles.

Lastly, Fischer proposes that the process of intercoordination propels a child previously functioning at one skill level to the next cognitive stage. His description of how intercoordination works, however, seems especially vague:

> At the beginning of the process, the child has two well-formed skills at a given level. The two skills function separately from each other until some object or event in the world induces the child to relate the two skills. If at this point the child is capable of the next developmental level, he or she will unravel the relationship between the two skills, gradually intercoordinating them. This unraveling will include a series of microdevelopmental steps involving the other transformations, and it will culminate in the intercoordination. (Fischer and Pipp, 1984, p.65)

The vagueness of Fischer's stage transition process—the same theoretical inadequacy that characterizes Piaget's and Vygotsky's mechanisms—clearly limits its empirical utility. Indeed, until Fischer defines intercoordination more precisely, its value as a possible developmental mechanism cannot be ascertained through research.

The various mechanisms of cognitive growth proposed by Case, Sternberg, Siegler, Klahr, and Fischer show that a consensus in psychologists' conceptions of developmental mechanisms is unlikely to be realized in the near future; as Flavell (1984, p. 190) points out, 'Truth is not yet at hand!' The works of these theorists do reveal progress since the theories of Piaget,

Vygotsky, and Werner, however. Developmental mechanisms now include important distinctions between two types of processing—executive and non-executive—and in some models, especially Klahr's, considerable progress has been made in specifying exactly how the mechanisms of development operate.

Knowledge

Most recent cognitive-developmental theorists assume that knowledge plays an important, although supplementary, role in cognitive growth. In their own models of development, Klahr, Siegler, Case, and Sternberg all concentrate on specifying the mechanisms responsible for intellectual change. Klahr (1984), however, indicates that understanding transition processes requires considering the particular types of information available for processing; his proposed generalization mechanisms account for the acquisition of conservation skills but not necessarily for the acquisition of other types of abilities. Siegler (1986a) indicates that children's prior knowledge helps determine what the change processes accomplish—that is, what features they encode or what strategies they construct—in particular situations. Case (1985), conceptualizing executive control structures as procedural knowledge, assumes that advances in procedural and declarative knowledge each stem from advances in the other, although he fails to test this claim empirically.

Compared to Klahr, Siegler, and Case, Sternberg (1985) expands the role of knowledge in his model of development. He asserts that the child's steadily developing knowledge base contributes to his or her intellectual growth, and he proposes three knowledge-acquisition components designed to account for such increases in the knowledge base. First, the child must selectively encode incoming information, discriminating relevant from irrelevant information and allowing only the relevant information to receive further processing. Second, the child must selectively combine the encoded information, forming an integrated, interpretable whole. Third, the child must selectively compare the newly encoded and combined information to older information already stored in memory, noting relations between the new and old acquisitions. For example, when reading a mystery novel, a child attempting to solve the mystery must discriminate relevant from misleading clues, combine the relevant clues in meaningful ways to highlight particular suspects, and relate the information incriminating the suspects to his or her previous knowledge about the types of characters and situations depicted in mystery novels. Of course, the child's previous knowledge guides the first two processes as well as the third process; not only do the comparisons the child makes depend on previous knowledge, but the clues encoded and the integrations constructed also depend upon previous understanding of murder mysteries.

Sternberg believes that when the processes of selective encoding, selective combination, and selective comparison are extended to novel tasks and situations, they account for children's insights in addition to their acquisitions of new knowledge. Furthermore, Sternberg believes that superior selective encoding, combination, and comparison skills exercised in novel tasks and situations—that is, insightful thinking—distinguish intellectually gifted from non-gifted children (Davidson and Sternberg, 1984; Sternberg and Davidson, 1982, 1983). In a series of experiments, Davidson and Sternberg (1984) showed that superior selective encoding, combination, and comparison skills do indeed distinguish the performance of gifted and non-gifted children on mathematical insight problems (e.g. 'Water lilies double in area every 24 hours. At the beginning of the summer there is 1 water lily on a lake. It takes 60 days for the lake to become covered with water lilies. On what day is the lake half-covered?'). The researchers also showed that pre-cuing relevant information and providing appropriate integrations facilitates the perform-ance of non-gifted subjects more than it does the performance of gifted subjects. Similarly, providing additional selective comparison information aids non-gifted children more than gifted children. These findings support the researchers' views of the role of insight in intellectual giftedness. Whereas non-gifted subjects have trouble achieving the insights necessary for problem solution and thus benefit from pre-cuing, the gifted subjects are more likely to have the insights without pre-cuing. Consequently, the gifted subjects derive fewer benefits from having the relevant information and integrations pointed out to thcm.

Clearly, two important implications arise from Sternberg's proposed know-ledge-acquisition processes. First, Sternberg demonstrates that mechanisms designed to explain normal intellectual development may also underlie excep-tional intelligence. Second, his knowledge-acquisition processes have educa-tional applications, for they suggest that children's insight skills may be facilitated through pre-cuing and training.

Unlike Klahr, Siegler, Case, and Sternberg, Frank Keil and Susan Carey examine changes in children's knowledge structures and representations rather than the processes underlying structural change. According to Keil (1984, p. 83), 'the actual dynamics of change—the causal developmental factors, the precipitating states, and the like—depend primarily on the structure of what is known and on how that knowledge is to be used in the world.' He argues for an approach to cognitive-developmental theorizing in which the investigator first examines the structure of domain-specific know-ledge and only then makes inferences about how transitions in these domains occur. Interestingly, Klahr apparently adopts this approach. His developmen-tal mechanisms explain how children acquire conservation skills; they do not explain how all cognitive growth proceeds.

Keil asserts that a limited set of relatively simple general learning processes, such as differentiation, transform the structure of domain-specific knowledge, thus creating cognitive growth. To support this claim, and to show that the nature of the information transformed is more important than the transformation processes themselves, Keil (1984) examines several areas of developmental research, including studies of the characteristic-to-defining shift. The developmental literature reveals a consistent trend in children's thinking away from characteristic features of a concept toward the concept's defining features. For example, whereas younger children define 'father' by considering age and characteristic behavioural dispositions, older children define 'father' by considering social and kinship definitions. Keil notes, however, that this shift 'occurs at different times for different concepts, suggesting that it is determined primarily by the structures of the concepts themselves rather than by a general transition from instance-bound knowledge to more rule-governed knowledge' (1984, p. 89). Recently, Ritter and Keil (see Keil, 1984) gave children several terms from various semantic fields (e.g. kinship terms such as uncle, aunt, and cousin and cooking terms such as boil, bake, and fry) and found that the characteristic-to-defining shift for the different semantic fields occurs at different ages, even though the shift occurs at approximately the same time for the terms within each field.

Aside from mentioning differentiation, Keil fails to specify what the simple transition processes in different conceptual domains might be, thus limiting the utility of his model and rendering his arguments relatively abstract and difficult to follow. Carey, similarly, realizes that knowledge reorganization must ultimately be explained through one or more kinds of processes, although she does not indicate what forms these processes might take. Indeed, Carey (1985b) is even less explicit about possible mechanisms than Keil; she does, however, offer an exceptionally detailed, carefully worked out description of how children's knowledge of biology emerges from their naïve understanding of human nature and animal behaviour. Carey's research indicates that pre-school children compare animate and inanimate objects to people in order to determine whether or not the objects possess certain animal properties. She traces the development of children's thinking about animals and living things from age 4 to 10 and shows, through her research, how older children's concepts of 'animal' and 'living thing' eventually become sufficiently accurate and abstract to form the basis for a rudimentary theory of biology. Clearly, for Carey, cognitive development entails a major restructuring of knowledge domains, with new theories of particular conceptual categories arising out of older, more diffuse theories.

Carey's model of cognitive growth provides a viable framework for examining structural change in various conceptual categories. Her theory also offers a framework for reinterpreting some of the findings of earlier researchers. For example, Piaget's conclusions regarding childhood animism may be challenged by Carey's work on children's theories of biology; childhood animism may stem not from the child's faulty causal reasoning, but rather from his or her lack of biological knowledge (Carey, 1985a).

The recent models of intellectual development included in the present discussion differ sharply in their relative emphases, with some models emphasizing process over knowledge, some stressing knowledge over process, and some recognizing the crucial roles played by both. Certainly, the developmental literature demands a careful consideration of both process and knowledge in theories of intellectual growth. In addition, theories specifying the interrelations between developmental mechanisms and children's knowledge may have valuable educational applications, highlighting once again the utility of considering knowledge structures as well as the processes responsible for structural change.

Individual differences

In order to portray children's information processing and knowledge acquisition as accurately as possible, current models of cognitive growth must specify how individual differences among children arise. Certainly, intellectual performance varies from child to child; the rate or course of intellectual development may also differ from one child to another.

Case (1985) believes that biological and experiential or cultural factors produce two types of individual differences. First, differences in the growth rate of children's short-term storage space and in the efficiency of their general processing capacities lead to differences in the rate of children's general executive development. Second, children differ from each other in the rate of their executive development on certain domain-specific tasks. Thus, Case, like Piaget and most other traditional stage theorists, believes that the rate of development, not its course, varies among children.

Fischer (Fischer and Pipp, 1984) and Klahr (1984), on the other hand, believe that the course of development may indeed differ from one child to another, although these theorists argue that the mechanisms underlying cognitive change are the same for all children. Fischer proposes that skill acquisition always involves biological (e.g. the child's brain size and brain wave patterns) and environmental (e.g. the degrees of practice, instruction, and support the child receives) influences. According to Fischer, then, the developmental paths for specific skills vary from child to child even though the transformation rules remain the same. Klahr, similarly, assumes that because children's experiences differ, the time lines recording their experiences also vary from one child to another. Each child develops through generalization, yet the course of each child's intellectual developent depends upon the particular experiences preserved on his or her time line.

Individual differences in Siegler's (1984, 1986a) model of cognitive growth arise from two sources. First, the variability mechanism presented in his evolutionary account of cognitive change produces variation among children. Second, motivational variables—the child's interest in certain kinds of problems and tasks and his or her reactions to negative experiences—also lead to performance differences. Because prior interest facilitates both attention and memory (Renninger and Wozniak, 1985), differences in children's interests in particular problems or tasks may lead to later differences in their knowledge about those problems or tasks. That is, a child who is interested in kittens or other pets may watch the animals for longer periods of time and may remember more about the animals than a child who is less interested. In Siegler's terms, the interested child may encode more features about kittens than the less interested child, leading to greater knowledge of, and more sophisticated rules for, animal behaviour. In addition to variations in interest, differences in children's reactions to failure likewise lead to differences in intellectual performance. Whereas some children attribute failure to their lack of ability, others attribute negative outcomes to their lack of effort (Dweck and Goetz, 1978). These latter children, by trying harder to succeed on the tasks or problems that produced the failure experiences, may encode more features than the former children, again resulting in the construction of more sophisticated rules.

Finally, although Sternberg's model contains many sources of individual differences, he emphasizes that variations in children's responses to novelty create a relatively stable source of individual differences throughout childhood and adulthood (Berg and Sternberg, 1985a). Like Siegler, Sternberg argues that children's motivational state—specifically their interest in, and preference for, novel tasks and stimuli—produce individual differences in intellectual functioning. Children who are willing to experience novel tasks and situations increase their opportunities for learning about those tasks or situations. Also, children's differing capacities for dealing with novelty, particularly their capacities for processing and acquiring novel information, influence their performance on intellectual tasks. Differences in children's abilities to encode, combine, and compare novel information distinguish gifted from non-gifted individuals (Davidson and Sternberg, 1984). Similarly, differences in children's capacities for elaborating novel information spontaneously in order to facilitate memory of that information distinguishes academically successful elementary school students from less successful students (Franks *et al.* 1982).

Certainly, complete theories of cognitive development require explanations of individual differences in development and performance. The potential for educational applications further increases the value of individual difference models. Although several studies from the developmental literature support Siegler's and Sternberg's models, additional research is needed to clarify and evaluate the different stances advocated by recent theorists of cognitive growth.

Contextual considerations

Clearly, a child forms only a small part of the society or culture in which he or she lives. Vygotsky considered the child's social and cultural contexts in his theory of development by arguing that the internalization of social behaviours and culturally-produced sign systems underlies intellectual growth. Like Vygotsky, several recent theorists also incorporate contextual factors into their models of development, considering not only the child but also the contexts in which change and growth occur. The contextual factors influencing development may be divided into two categories: the child's experiences and his or her environment. Each child's experiences, his or her daily activities and the consequences of those activities, are unique; on the other hand, each child shares his or her social and cultural environments with other children, specifically with certain subpopulations of children. Thus, one child may enjoy reading mystery novels, whereas another child may enjoy reading poetry. These children will have different experiences, even though they may share the same environment. That is, they both may live in a society that values and rewards literacy, encouraging reading. Other children, of course, may live in a different environment, such as a society that values athletic skill and physical grace over intellectual abilities like reading (see Heath, 1983, for a fascinating discussion of the effects of different socialization patterns on children's language development in two southeastern United States communities). Generally, recent models of cognitive growth have not been particularly sensitive to contextual considerations, although some progress has been made in recognizing their importance.

Experience

Two recent theorists, Klahr and Sternberg, stress the impact of the child's experiences on his or her intellectual development. As previously mentioned, Klahr believes children develop by generalizing the experiences recorded on their time lines. A child who reads mystery novels will have a different time line from a child who reads poetry, and thus the courses of their development may differ as well.

Sternberg incorporates the child's experiences into his model of cognitive growth in a more complex way than Klahr. Sternberg's (1985) 'Triarchic Theory of Human Intelligence' actually encompasses three subtheories: (i) a componential subtheory that specifies how the individual's metacomponential, performance, and knowledge-acquisition processes operate (this subtheory was discussed in the preceding sections); (ii) a contextual subtheory that relates the mental life of the individual to his or her environment (this subtheory will be discussed below); and (iii) an experiential subtheory that relates the individual's mental life to his or her experiences. In his experiential subtheory, Sternberg proposes that information processing operates along an experiential continuum. At one end of the continuum, the individual has no experience with certain tasks and situations; the task and situations are truly novel. At the other end of the continuum, however, the individual has extensive experience and practice with the tasks and situations, and thus his or her information processing is fully automatized. Because Sternberg believes the automatization of information processing spurs cognitive growth, the child's experiences play an important role in his or her development. A child who reads mystery novels may learn to encode and combine relevant clues more rapidly and effectively than a child who reads poetry. A poetry reader, on the other hand, may learn to interpret symbolism by comparing the symbols embedded in poems to his or her previous knowledge of humans and their world more rapidly and skilfully than a mystery reader.

Sternberg's conception of an experiential continuum over which information processing develops has important implications for intellectual measurement and assessment. Sternberg believes that differences in children's abilities to deal with novelty and to automatize information processing distinguish more intelligent children from less intelligent children. Intelligence tests, then, should assess children's performance on tasks that are relatively novel or that are in the process of becoming automatized. Sometimes different tasks are necessary to assess children's responses to novelty and their automatization of executive and non-executive processing. Other times the same tasks may be used to assess both. According to Sternberg (1984, p. 180), 'a given task or situation may continue to provide apt measurement of intelligence over practice, but in different ways at different points in time: early on in the person's experience, the ability to deal with novelty is assessed; later, the ability to automatize information processing is assessed.'

Environment

In his contextual subtheory of intelligence, Sternberg ties information processing to the particular environments in which it occurs. He views intellectual functioning as 'mental activity directed toward purposive adaptation to, and selection and shaping of, real-world environments relevant to one's life' (Sternberg, 1985, p. 45). Thus, different environments produce different adaptational requirements and ultimately different forms of mental activity. For example, mental activity essential for successful adaptation to school may differ substantially from the activity encouraged in the child's home environment. Whereas teachers may value clear, concise, truthful prose, parents and siblings may encourage verbose, imaginative tall tales (Heath, 1983). Often, however, it is not the intellectual abilities themselves, but rather their relative importances, that differ from one environment to another.

Certainly, environmental influences are important not only when considering the child's level of intelligence, but also when considering his or her intellectual development. The environments to which an individual must adapt change as the individual grows older. Children must adapt to home and school, young adults must adapt to new careers and to new kinds of relationships (e.g. marriage and parenthood), and older adults must adapt to retirement and possibly to the deaths of their spouse and friends (see Baltes, Dittmann-Kohli, and Dixon, 1984, and Berg and Sternberg, 1985b, for a discussion of adaptation and related contextual considerations in adult intellectual development). Indeed, the changing conditions to which an individual must adapt over the course of his or her life are elegantly captured by Erikson (1968) in his stage theory of psychosocial development. Contextual theorists like Sternberg argue that mental activity changes along with psychosocial issues and environmental factors, fostering adaptation to different circumstances at various points in the life cycle.

Sternberg argues that social and cultural influences play a crucial role in cognition and thus merit inclusion in models of intelligence and intellectual growth. Although environmental considerations are certainly necessary, contextual approaches to human abilities and to cognitive change are often vague. Sternberg's contextual subtheory is more prescriptive than descriptive. It provides a framework for studying cognitive growth and advocates using the framework in empirical and theoretical work; it does not, however, provide detailed descriptions of the contextual factors relevant for understanding the mental activity of various populations, nor does it provide explanations of how specific contextual factors guide cognition. In addition to vagueness, questionable empirical utility represents a second, related limitation of contextual frameworks such as Sternberg's. Unless specific predictions and operationalizations are made, contextual models cannot be falsified through research.

Sternberg shares his emphasis on adaptation with Piaget, for both theorists claim that intelligence fosters adaptation to the environment. Several other recent theorists, on the other hand, consider contextual factors in development without invoking adaptation as the reason for their influence. Fischer (Fischer and Pipp, 1984), for example, simply states that a child's skills always reflect the environment as well as the child's inherent biological characteristics. Instruction and social support, indeed, represent two environmental factors that may vary from one society or culture to another. Case (1985) notes that culture plays an increasingly important role in stage transition, and in the abilities mastered at successive stages, as progressively higher levels are achieved. Finally, Siegler identifies three ways in which the child's environment helps determine the nature of his or her mental activity. Siegler writes:

> Children's thinking develops within a social context. Parents, peers, teachers, and the overall society influence what children think about, as well as how and why they come to think in particular ways. (1986a, p. 368)

Thus, Siegler believes the environment influences the specific skills children master, their methods of learning, and their motivations for thinking and learning. Empirical research supports these beliefs. First, Japanese children trained to use abacuses to solve arithmetic problems become unusually skilled at performing complicated mental arithmetic calculations (Stigler, 1984) and at remembering strings of numbers (Hatano and Osawa, 1983); children from cultures lacking abacuses fail to achieve such quantitative proficiency. Second, certain African societies discourage children from asking questions, whereas most Western societies encourage this activity, creating cultural differences in how children acquire information (Greenfield and Lave, 1982). Third, feedback from teachers and parents affects children's motivations for learning. Whereas teachers often criticize girls' performance by focusing on their deficient intellectual abilities, they criticize boys' performance by faulting their behaviour, effort, and neatness as well as their inherent ability, thus weakening the girls' motivations—but not the boys'—for persevering on certain tasks (Dweck and Licht, 1980).

Clearly, the developmental literature underscores the impact of environmental factors on children's thinking and development. Current theories of cognitive growth, however, must go beyond simply pointing out the necessity of considering contextual influences. They must pinpoint precisely the contextual factors affecting development and the ways in which those factors alter mental activity. In short, they must generate specific predictions that can be tested empirically and supported or rejected through research.

Constraints on development

The idea of constraints on development originates from the work of Keil (1981), who first used the term to refer to limitations in children's thinking brought about by particular content domains. The idea of constraints is certainly intriguing, and theories of cognitive growth that specify the constraints limiting children's cognitive competence and performance may have important educational applications. Recent models of intellectual development suggest two general categories of constraints: organismic and domain-related. Organismic constraints refer to limitations imposed by the child's inherent biological characteristics. Two types of organismic contraints, age-related and cognitive, will be considered in the present discussion. Domain-related constraints, on the other hand, refer to limitations imposed by the particular content areas the child seeks to master.

Organismic constraints

Stage theorists, by linking the child's cognitive abilities to specific age ranges, impose age-related constraints on development. A child of any given age encounters processing limitations that constrain his or her cognitive capacities. The limitations decrease or weaken as the child grows older, producing corresponding increases in his or her capabilities. Case and Fischer, like Piaget and Vygotsky before them, tie processing limitations to chronological age and propose that such age-related limitations constrain the rate and nature of development from infancy to adolescence.

For both theorists, though, cognitive constraints underlie the age-related limitations. Case argues that the operational efficiency of the child's short-term storage space creates age-related processing limitations. As the child grows older, his or her short-term memory becomes increasingly efficient, allowing the child to think and learn in increasingly sophisticated ways. Similarly, Sternberg (Davidson and Sternberg, 1985) believes that the functional capacity of the child's working memory mediates the child's intellectual competence and thus performance, although unlike Case, Sternberg does not tie this limitation to the child's chronological age. For Fischer, finally, age-related constraints reflect the child's optimal level, or the upper limit on the types of skills a child of any given age can construct.

The developmental literature supports the idea of organismic constraints on development in two ways. First, the rate and nature of cognitive growth during adulthood is not nearly as impressive as the rate and nature of intellectual change during childhood and adolescence (see Flavell, 1984, for a discussion of this point), underscoring the heuristic value of some sort of age-related constraint. Case and Fischer clearly distinguish cognitive growth in childhood from growth in adulthood. The other recent theorists, however, fail to make such a distinction, even though the distinction is warranted by the developmental literature. Second, converging evidence indicates that the functional capacity, although not necessarily the absolute size, of the child's working or short-term memory increases with age (e.g. Case, 1974; Chi, 1976; Pascual-Leone, 1970). Converging evidence also indicates that the functional capacity of working memory mediates performance on a wide variety of tasks (e.g. Brainerd, 1981; Bryant and Trabasso, 1971; Daneman and Carpenter, 1980). Certainly, the developmental literature reveals memory constraints on development and cognition, justifying, perhaps even necessitating, their inclusion in models of cognitive growth.

Domain-related constraints

Whereas stage theorists and theorists concerned with cognitive processes posit organismic constraints on development, theorists concerned with knowledge emphasize domain-related limitations. Sternberg, for example, asserts that novelty introduces domain-related constraints. Thus, a child may be quite skilled at solving certain kinds of arithmetic (e.g. multiplication or division) problems, yet may fail to understand fractions the first time he or she encounters them. With practice, of course, the child's information processing becomes automatized, and the domain-related constraints created by novelty disappear. For Carey (1985b), similarly, limited knowledge in specific domains constrains cognitive skill and development; indeed, cognitive growth consists of overcoming such constraints through the continual acquisition and reorganization of knowledge.

Sternberg and Carey believe that limited knowledge and experience temporarily constrain development in certain content domains. Keil (1981, 1984), however, believes that particular content areas constrain cognition in more pervasive, all-encompassing ways. Keil views the child as a biological organism shaped by evolution to find some content domains easier to master than others. According to Keil (1984, p. 94), 'the notion of constrained faculties views humans less as all-purpose learning machines and more as biological organisms that have, through the course of evolution, developed specialized "mental organs" that are used to deal with different aspects of their physical and mental worlds (cf. Fodor, 1972).' Thus Keil argues not that limited knowledge constrains development until the limitations are overcome through the acquisition of additional knowledge, but rather that children are destined to find certain domains more natural to acquire than others, maximizing their skills and development in the natural domains and hindering their growth in the unnatural domains. Certainly, developmental research and everyday observations of children support Sternberg's and Carey's interpretation of domain-related constraints. Conversely, although Keil's interpretation seems plausible as well as intriguing, he weakens his stance by failing to distinguish the domains children find natural from those they find unnatural.

As the preceding discussion shows, the recent models of cognitive growth proposed by Case, Fischer, Klahr, Siegler, Sternberg, Keil, and Carey are comprehensive yet incomplete. Many considerations—the role of stages or other organizing principles of development, executive and non-executive processes, knowledge, individual differences, the child's experiences and environment, and constraints on development—warrant inclusion in theories of intellectual change. In the next section, selected parts of these recent theories will be combined, forming an integrative model of cognitive growth sensitive to the interrelations among the considerations.

INTEGRATION AND CONCLUSIONS

For many writers, the problem of cognitive growth is complex, and complete theories of cognitive change must encompass not only the six considerations discussed in the preceding section, but also the realms of motivation and social cognition (Flavell, 1984, 1985). Indeed, the incompleteness that still characterizes current theories should not be regarded as a major criticism of the field; rather, it should be accepted as the nature of the beast (see Kessen, 1984, p. 14, for a discussion of the 'essential incompleteness' inherent in the works of developmental psychologists). Given that all of these considerations are necessary for a comprehensive understanding of cognitive growth, the next step thus requires explicating the nature of the interrelations among the considerations. In contrast to the preceding section, which addresses the six theoretical considerations in isolation by examining several different approaches to each, the present section outlines a heuristic model for integrating the ideas raised previously. The model is illustrated in Figure 2.1.

Of course, the model proposed in Figure 2.1 represents only one of several possible ways of capturing the interrelations among the considerations. Other models could be offered—indeed, other considerations could be included—although Figure 2.1 seems particularly suitable for summarizing the ideas presented earlier. According to Figure 2.1, interactions between the child's information processing and his or her experiences lead to the continual acquisition and reorganization of knowledge. Thus, the child's experiences—his or her participation in everyday life events—and the child's information processing—broadly, his or her interpretations of such events—are both crucial to knowledge acquisition and hence cognitive growth. The child's knowledge base itself is crucial for continued cognitive change. Indeed, Figure 2.1 is represented as a Venn diagram, emphasizing the interactions among the child's information processing, experiences, and knowledge.

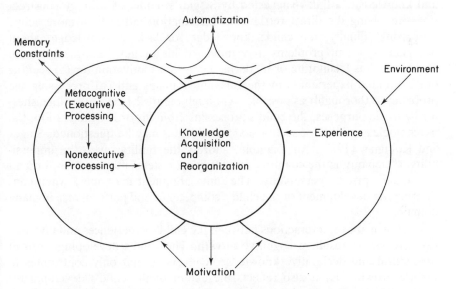

Figure 2.1. A heuristic model for integrating the theoretical considerations necessary for understanding cognitive growth.

Consider the role of processing first. As Figure 2.1 indicates, intellectual development requires executive and non-executive processes. Through planning, monitoring, and evaluating performance, the child's metacognitive processes govern his or her non-executive processes, which in turn allow the acquisition and reorganization of procedural and declarative knowledge. The developing knowledge structures themselves provide the basis for improved metacognitive processing, forming an important feedback loop. Throughout development, working memory constraints influence, and are in turn modified by, the child's information processing. That is, the usable capacity of the child's short-term storage space partially determines the extent and nature of his or her processing; yet the relation between memory constraints and processing is reciprocal, with increasingly efficient processing easing the demands placed on memory and reducing the severity of the constraint. Automatization contributes to the increasing operational efficiency of working memory and results from the interaction between the child's processing and his or her repeated experiences with specific types of problems. With practice, then, the child's processing becomes faster and more efficient.

Now consider the role of experience. The child's cultural and social environment partially determines his or her experiences, both the nature of the experiences themselves and the value the child places on them. Of course, the child must process his or her experiences in order for them to influence knowledge acquisition and reorganization. Eventually, though, the automatization of processing may lead to a more direct link between experience and knowledge, a link—suggested by Siegler's model of strategy construction—involving the direct retrieval of information rather than more active processing. Finally, the child's knowledge, or lack of knowledge, about particular types of problems may influence his or her feelings about the problems, thus facilitating or hindering his or her motivation for (a) seeking out continued experiences in the relevant domains and (b) processing the problems as thoroughly as possible. Although Figure 2.1 clearly distinguishes, for heuristic purposes, the child's processing from his or her motivation, the psychological validity of such a sharp distinction may be questioned. Singer and Kolligian (1987), for example, address the futility, even the impossibility, of separating the cognitive and affective systems that together form an individual's private personality. The same argument may apply when considering the development of the child's competence and performance in many domains.

As shown above, interactions between the child's experiences and information processing result in cognitive growth. The child's developing store of procedural and declarative knowledge, conversely, not only contributes to further growth, but it also reflects the extent of the child's development. Figure 2.1 posits several feedback loops (e.g. the loops involving (a) knowledge and processing and (b) knowledge, motivation, and experience) that ultimately create increasingly sophisticated knowledge structures. The ultimate product of cognitive growth, then, is the continual branching of knowledge that occurs as procedural and declarative knowledge in diverse domains is acquired and organized. Clearly, branching models of cognitive growth are supported by the developmental literature. Carey traces the emergence and reorganization of children's biological (Carey, 1985b) and physical knowledge (Smith, Carey, and Wiser, 1985). Psychometric studies of abilities show that intellectual skills become more distinct, or less highly correlated, as children grow older. Similarly, studies of children's social cognition and affective development reveal branching organizations; Demos (1974), for example, concludes that as children grow older, they become increasingly capable of making clear distinctions among affect terms. The developmental literature indicates that all parts of the model may be important sources of individual differences among children. Differences in children's experiences, for instance—their educational background, the amount of practice they receive on various types of problems—create corresponding differences in the knowledge base they acquire (Heath, 1983). Likewise, children's varying expertise in metacognitive planning leads to differences in task performance and knowledge acquisition (Brown and DeLoache, 1978). Although the model may be used to conceptualize development in many diverse domains, it seems plausible that biologically given domain-related constraints (the kind proposed by Keil) may dictate the content domains to which the model applies.

FINAL COMMENTS

Although psychologists' understanding of cognitive growth has improved considerably since Piaget, Vygotsky, and Werner first proposed their theories, many avenues remain to be explored. One particularly interesting avenue concerns the dynamic nature of cognitive growth, where dynamic refers to changes in the relative importance or influence of developmental mechanisms over time. Just as development is an inherently dynamic process, psychologists' conceptions of the mechanisms underlying intellectual change should be dynamic as well. Developmental mechanisms, indeed, may be differentially important at various points in the individual's life cycle, and research examining the differential importance of various mechanisms over time is clearly needed.

First, consider the dynamic nature of the child's information processing. Research indicates that metacognitive processing may be more important in later childhood than in early childhood, as older children spend relatively more time planning the solutions to problems and relatively less time solving them. Thus, although young children's strategy construction is difficult to study and consequently is not well understood, the developmental literature implies that for young children, non-executive processing may play a comparatively greater role in knowledge acquisition and reorganization, whereas for older children, improved executive processing may contribute heavily to additional advances in the acquisition and reorganization of knowledge. Further research, however, is needed to clarify the role of metacognitive processing in early childhood.

Second, developmental theorists from areas of inquiry other than cognitive growth—for example, psychoanalytic theorists concerned with personality development—suggest that early experiences may play a more critical role in development than later experiences, highlighting the dynamic nature of change over the course of childhood and adolescence. Certainly, ideas about development in other domains may shed light on cognitive growth as well (Flavell, 1984), and it is highly plausible that the child's experiences may be differentially important for intellectual development at different points in time. Repeated experiences and practice with given problems, for instance, are more important during automatization than they are following the automatization of performance. Similarly, experience may play a more important role in cognitive growth before comprehensive knowledge of a particular domain is acquired; that is, the child's experiences may exert a greater influence on how he or she reorganizes knowledge when little is known about the domain than when a considerable knowledge base has already been consolidated.

Finally, the rate and extent of the branching of knowledge, the ultimate products of cognitive growth, may vary at different points in the individual's life cycle. Undoubtedly, development during adulthood differs from development during childhood, and a major cognitive difference between adults and children is that adults know more than children (Carey, 1985a). Thus, the rate and extent of knowledge acquisition and reorganization may be more profound during childhood and adolescence, for it may be during these years that the knowledge structures characteristic of adults are first organized and consolidated. Also, certain life events exposing children and adolescents to vast amounts of information, such as language acquisition, elementary and secondary school, and college, may maximize the branching of knowledge structures during these years. Certainly, the child is impressive. For many psychologists studying the child's evolving capacities and complexities, the psychologists' own appreciation may mirror that of the child discovering the subtleties and richness of his or her world.

REFERENCES

Baltes, P. B., Dittmann-Kohli, F., & Dixon, R. A. (1984). New perspectives on the development of intelligence in adulthood: Toward a dual-process conception and a model of selective optimization with compensation, in P. B. Baltes & O. G. Brim, Jr. (eds), *Life-span Development and Behavior*, vol. 6. New York: Academic Press.

Berg, C. A. & Sternberg, R. J. (1985a). Response to novelty: Continuity versus discontinuity in the developmental course of intelligence, *Advances in Child Development*, **19**, 2–47.

Berg, C. A. & Sternberg, R. J. (1985b). A triarchic theory of intellectual development during adulthood, *Developmental Review*, **5**, 334–370.

Borke, H. (1971). Interpersonal perception of young children: Egocentrism or empathy? *Developmental Psychology*, **5**, 263–269.

Borke, H. (1972). Chandler and Greenspan's 'Ersatz Egocentrism': A rejoinder, *Developmental Psychology*, **7**, 107–109.

Brainerd, C. J. (1977). Response criteria in concept development research, *Child Development*, **48**, 360–366.

Brainerd, C. J. (1981). Working memory and the developmental analysis of probability judgement, *Psychological Review*, **88**, 463–502.

Brown, A. L. & DeLoache, J. S. (1978). Skills, plans, and self-regulation, in R. Siegler (ed.), *Children's Thinking: What Develops?* Hillsdale, NJ: Erlbaum.

Bruner, J. S. (1962). Introduction, in L. S. Vygotsky, *Thought and Language*. Cambridge: MIT Press.

Bryant, P. E. & Trabasso, T. (1971). Transitive inferences and memory in young children, *Nature*, **232**, 456–458.

Carey, S. (1985a). Are children fundamentally different kinds of thinkers and learners than adults? in S. F. Chipman, J. W. Segal, & R. Glaser (eds), *Thinking and Learning Skills: Research and Open Questions*, vol. 2. Hillsdale, NJ: Erlbaum.

Carey, S. (1985b). *Conceptual Change in Childhood*. Cambridge, MA: MIT Press.

Carroll, J. B. (1986). Beyond IQ is cognition, *Contemporary Psychology*, **31**, 325–327.

Case, R. (1974). Mental strategies, mental capacities, and instruction: A neo-Piagetian investigation, *Journal of Experimental Child Psychology*, **18**, 372–397.

Case, R. (1984). The process of stage transition: A neo-Piagetian view, in R. J. Sternberg (ed.), *Mechanisms of Cognitive Development*. New York: W. H. Freeman.

Case, R. (1985). *Intellectual Development: Birth to Adulthood*. Orlando: Academic Press.

Chandler, M. J. & Greenspan, S. (1972). Ersatz egocentrism: A reply to H. Borke, *Developmental Psychology*, **7**, 104–106.

Chi, M. T. H. (1976). Short-term memory limitations in children: Capacity or processing deficits? *Memory and Cognition*, **4**, 559–572.

Chi, M. T. H., Glaser, R., & Rees, E. (1982). Expertise in problem solving, in R. J. Sternberg (ed.), *Advances in the Psychology of Human Intelligence*, vol. 1. Hillsdale, NJ: Erlbaum.

Daneman, M. & Carpenter, P. A. (1980). Individual differences in working memory and reading, *Journal of Verbal Learning and Verbal Behavior*, **19**, 450–466.

Davidson, J. E. & Sternberg, R. J. (1984). The role of insight in intellectual giftedness, *Gifted Child Quarterly*, **28**, 58–64.

Davidson, J. E. & Sternberg, R. J. (1985). Competence and performance in intellectual development, in E. D. Neimark, R. DeLisi, & J. Newman (eds), *Moderators of Competence*, Hillsdale, NJ: Erlbaum.

Demos, E. V. (1974). Children's understanding and use of affect terms. Unpublished doctoral dissertation, Harvard University Graduate School of Education, Cambridge.

Dweck, C. S. & Goetz, T. E. (1978). Attributions and learned helplessness, in J. H.

Harvey, W. Ickles, & R. F. Kidd (eds), *New Directions in Attribution Research*, vol. 2, Hillsdale, NJ: Erlbaum.

Dweck, C. S & Licht, B. G. (1980). Learned helplessness and intellectual achievement, in J. Garber & M. E. P. Seligman (eds), *Human Helplessness: Theory and Applications*, New York: Academic Press.

Elkind, D. (1961). Children's discovery of the conservation of mass, weight, and volume: Piaget replications study II, *Journal of Genetic Psychology*, **98**, 37–46.

Erikson, E. H. (1968). *Identity: Youth and Crisis*. New York: Norton.

Fischer, K. W. (1980). A theory of cognitive development: The control and construction of hierarchies of skills, *Psychological Review*, **87**, 477–531.

Fischer, K. W. & Pipp, S. L. (1984). Processes of cognitive development: Optimal level and skill acquisition, in R. J. Sternberg (ed.), *Mechanisms of Cognitive Development*. New York: W. H. Freeman.

Flavell, J. H. (1963). *The Developmental Psychology of Jean Piaget*. New York: D. Van Nostrand.

Flavell, J. H. (1984). Discussion, in R. J. Sternberg (ed.), *Mechanisms of Cognitive Development*. New York: W. H. Freeman.

Flavell, J. H. (1985). *Cognitive Development* (2nd edn). Englewood Cliffs, NJ: Prentice-Hall.

Fodor, J. (1972). Some reflections on L. S. Vygotsky's 'Thought and Language', *Cognition*, **1**, 83–95.

Franks, J. J., Vye, N. J., Auble, P. M., Mezynski, K. J., Perfetto, G. A., Bransford, J. D., Stein, B. S., & Littlefield, J. (1982). Learning from explicit versus implicit texts, *Journal of Experimental Psychology: General*, **111**, 414–422.

Garrett, H. E. (1946). A developmental theory of intelligence, *American Psychologist*, **1**, 372–378.

Ginsburg, H. & Opper, S. (1979). *Piaget's Theory of Intellectual Development: An Introduction* (2nd edn). Englewood Cliffs, NJ: Prentice-Hall.

Greenfield, P. M. & Lave, J. (1982). Cognitive aspects of informal education, in D. A. Wagner & H. W. Stevenson (eds), *Cultural Perspectives on Child Development*. San Francisco: W. H. Freeman.

Hatano, G. & Osawa, K. (1983). Digit memory of grand experts in abacus-derived mental calculation, *Cognition*, **15**, 95–110.

Heath, S. B. (1983). *Ways with Words*. Cambridge: Cambridge University Press.

John-Steiner, V. & Souberman, E. (1978). Afterword, in L. S. Vygotsky, *Mind in Society: The Development of Higher Psychological Processes*. Cambridge: Harvard University Press.

Keil, F. C. (1981). Constraints on knowledge and cognitive development, *Psychological Review*, **88**, 197–227.

Keil, F. C. (1984). Mechanisms of cognitive development and the structure of knowledge, in R. J. Sternberg (ed.), *Mechanisms of Cognitive Development*, New York: W. H. Freeman.

Kessen, W. (1984). Introduction: The end of the age of development, in R. J. Sternberg (ed.), *Mechanisms of Cognitive Development*, New York: W. H. Freeman.

Klahr, D. (1982). Nonmonotone assessment of monotone development: An information processing analysis, in S. Strauss (ed.), *U-shaped Behavioral Growth*, New York: Academic Press.

Klahr, D. (1984). Transition processes in quantitative development, in R. J. Sternberg (ed.), *Mechanisms of Cognitive Development*. New York: W. H. Freeman.

Klahr, D. & Wallace, J. G. (1976). *Cognitive Development: An Information Processing View*. Hillsdale, NJ: Lawrence Erlbaum.

Kohlberg, L. (1969). Stage and sequence: The cognitive-developmental approach to socialization, in D. Goslin (ed.), *Handbook of Socialization Theory and Research*, Chicago: Rand McNally.

LaBerge, D. & Samuels, J. (1974). Toward a theory of automatic information processing in reading, *Cognitive Psychology*, **6**, 293–323.

Larkin, J., McDermott, J., Simon, D. P., & Simon, H. A. (1980). Expert and novice performance in solving physics problems, *Science*, **208**, 135–1342.

Pascual-Leone, J. (1970). A mathematical model for the transition rule in Piaget's developmental stages, *Acta Psychologica*, **63**, 301–345.

Piaget, J. (1970). Piaget's theory, in P. H. Mussen (ed.), *Carmichael's Manual of Child Psychology* (3rd edn), vol. 1. New York: Wiley.

Piaget, J. (1976). *The Psychology of Intelligence*. Totowa, NJ: Littlefield, Adams.

Renninger, K. A. & Wozniak, R. H. (1985). Effects of interest on attentional shift, recognition, and recall in young children, *Developmental Psychology*, **21**, 624–632.

Rogoff, B. & Wertsch, J. V. (eds) (1984). *Children's Learning in the 'Zone of Proximal Development,'* New Directions for Child Development (No. 23). San Francisco: Jossey-Bass.

Schneider, W. & Shiffrin, R. (1977). Controlled and automated human information processing, I: Detection, search, and attention, *Psychological Review*, **84**, 1–66.

Shiffrin, R. & Schneider, W. (1977). Controlled and automated human information processing, II: Perceptual learning, automatic attending, and a general theory, *Psychological Review*, **84**, 127–190.

Siegler, R. S. (1984). Mechanisms of cognitive growth: Variation and selection, in R. J. Sternberg (ed.), *Mechanisms of Cognitive Development*. New York: W. H. Freeman.

Siegler, R. S. (1986a). *Children's Thinking*. Englewood Cliffs, NJ: Prentice-Hall.

Siegler, R. S. (1986b). A panoramic view of development, *Contemporary Psychology*, **31**, 329–331.

Siegler, R. S. (1986c). Unities across domains in children's strategy choices, in M. Perlmutter (ed.), *Perspectives for Intellectual Development: Minnesota Symposium on Child Development*, vol. 19. Hillsdale, NJ: Erlbaum.

Siegler, R. S. & Shrager, J. (1984). Strategy choices in addition and subtraction: How do children know what to do? in C. Sophian (ed.), *Origins of Cognitive Skills*. Hillsdale, NJ: Erlbaum.

Singer, J. L. & Kolligian, J., Jr (1987). Personality: Developments in the study of private experience, *Annual Review of Psychology*, **38**, 533–574.

Smith, C., Carey, S., & Wiser, M. (1985). On differentiation: A case study of the development of the concepts of size, weight, and density, *Cognition*, **21**, 177–237.

Sternberg, R. J. (1984). Mechanisms of cognitive development: A componential approach, in R. J. Sternberg (ed.), *Mechanisms of Cognitive Development*, New York: W. H. Freeman.

Sternberg, R. J. (1985). *Beyond IQ: A Triarchic Theory of Human Intelligence*. Cambridge: Cambridge University Press.

Sternberg, R. J. & Davidson, J. E. (1982, June). The mind of the puzzler, *Psychology Today*, **16**, 37–44.

Sternberg, R. J. & Davidson, J. E. (1983). Insight in the gifted, *Educational Psychologist*, **18**, 51–57.

Sternberg, R. J. & Nigro, G. (1980). Developmental patterns in the solution of verbal analogies, *Child Development*, **51**, 27–38.

Sternberg, R. J. & Powell, J. S. (1983). The development of intelligence, in P. H. Mussen (series ed.) & J. H. Flavell & E. Markman (volume eds), *Handbook of Child Psychology* (3rd edn), vol. 3. New York: Wiley.

Stigler, J. W. (1984). 'Mental abacus': The effects of abacus training on Chinese children's mental calculation, *Cognitive Psychology*, **16**, 145–176.
Vygotsky, L. S. (1978). *Mind in Society: The Development of Higher Psychological Processes*. Cambridge: Harvard University Press.
Watson, M. W. & Fischer, K. W. (1977). A developmental sequence of agent use in late infancy, *Child Development*, **48**, 828–836.
Watson, M. W. & Fischer, K. W. (1980). Development of social roles in elicited and spontaneous behavior during the preschool years, *Developmental Psychology*, **16**, 483–494.
Werner, H. (1948). *Comparative Psychology of Mental Development*. New York: International Universities Press.
Zigler, E. & Glick, M. (1986). *A Developmental Approach to Adult Psychopathology*. New York: Wiley.

ACKNOWLEDGEMENTS

We thank John Kolligian, Jr. and Janet Davidson for their many thoughtful comments on earlier drafts of this chapter.

Chapter 3

Training skilled performance

John Annett

Learning and training are two sides of the same coin; learning is concerned with the processes underlying the acquisition of skill and training with prescribing optimal methods of instruction and schedules of practice. Training research has typically been task-oriented, concerned with the best methods of teaching skills like flying or golf, but the prescriptions are often heavily influenced by the currently predominant theories of learning. This was seen very clearly in the 1950s and 60s when B.F. Skinner's radical behaviourist view of learning gave rise to the *programmed instruction* movement but current theories of learning are predominately *cognitive* in character and rely on concepts such as *information processing, storage* and *retrieval* derived from information theory and computing.

Training research has a long history. The manipulation of practice conditions, such as the rate of presentation and the length and structure of lists of items to be learned, was an important feature of early investigations of memory by Ebbinghaus (1885). In perceptual-motor skills Bryan and Harter (1897) studying morse telegraphy and Book (1908) investigating typewriting added the notion of a *learning curve* to Ebbinghaus's *curve of forgetting* and drew attention to qualitative features of skill learning, notably the *plateau* where the rate of improvement with practice flattens out for a period before a renewed spurt. The phenomenon of *grouping*, in which the trainee becomes able to integrate simple elements as in transcribing words as wholes rather than one letter at a time, also emerged from this early work.

The problem of *transfer of training* had made an even earlier appearance in some observations on bilateral transfer by Weber in 1844, reported by Fechner in 1850 (Woodworth, 1938). Manipulative skills learned with one hand can be transferred to the other but more generally a skill acquired by

Acquisition and Performance of Cognitive Skills. Edited by A. M. Colley and J. R. Beech
© 1989 John Wiley & Sons Ltd

practice may be transferred to the learning of a new task. The transfer paradigm, in which the effects of prior training are measured in terms of *savings* in training time in acquiring a new skill, provides one of the earliest research paradigms for training research. Swift (1903), for example, demonstrated savings of two-thirds of the practice trials in learning a left-handed ball skill when subjects had prior training with the right hand.

The pace and direction of training research was profoundly affected by the need to train pilots and gunners during the Second World War. In the psychological laboratory simplified versions of these tracking tasks were developed for selection and training purposes. The behaviour of subjects in learning to track presented two main problems, the first being how best to schedule practice, that is to determine the optimal distribution of practice trials and rest pauses. Ammons (1947) saw the relevance of Hull's learning theory, notably the concepts of reactive and conditioned inhibition (Ir and sIr). Repetitive practice, according to the theory, not only strengthens S–R bonds but causes inhibition to build up and this depresses performance. Following a rest the inhibition dissipates, sometimes leading to *reminiscence*, that is better performance immediately following rest than at the end of the previous practice trials. After much research it was agreed (Irion, 1966) that this was a performance effect, temporarily raising or lowering tracking accuracy but leaving learning itself unaffected.

The second important issue was the role of *knowledge of results* (KR). Ground-based gunnery trainers and flight simulators could readily be provided with means of scoring performance and of feeding back this information to the learner. One gunnery trainer, for example, continuously measured the discrepancy between a filmed moving target and the trainee's gunsight and caused a red filter (simulating a hit) to drop over the projector lens whenever the trainee pulled the trigger with the gun correctly aimed. Immediate KR was found to be very beneficial in the short term but performance often deteriorated when KR was withdrawn. These practical findings set in train a line of basic research on variables such as the timing, frequency and information value of knowledge of results which will be discussed later in this chapter.

The growing sophistication of military equipment (especially aircraft) raised the old issue of transfer of training in a new form. Learning to fly on a real aircraft is expensive and dangerous. Ground-based flight simulators provide a partial answer but experienced pilot instructors were initially sceptical of their value since it is difficult to reproduce visual and body motion cues in a totally realistic way. Training psychologists argue that, despite these shortcomings, it is possible to judge a simulator by its *transfer value*, that is by *savings* in flying training hours resulting from practice on simulator. Transfer is still one of the more controversial areas of training research and some recent analyses of the problem from a cognitive view will be presented later in this chapter.

Around 1950 a new analysis of human performance based on analogies with information-processing devices such as computers began to emerge, principally due to the wartime work at Cambridge by a team led by Sir Frederick Bartlett. The main thrust of this work was to do with the effects of stress and fatigue on skilled performance but Annett and Kay (1956, 1957) attempted to reinterpret some of the familiar training problems, such as part-whole learning and knowledge of results in information-processing terms. In the USA Paul Fitts (1961, 1964) proposed an account of skill learning which has influenced training theory ever since. As a former aviation psychologist Fitts addressed the problem of learning complex real-life skills and drew attention to the importance of cognitive processes, such as understanding principles and developing action plans and strategies. The early stages of flight training are characterized by verbal description and analysis of the technique and procedures involved. Fitts was unable to complete the research programme he had outlined but the main part of this chapter is concerned with recent research on these cognitive processes, some of it in the spirit of Fitts' intentions.

The former preoccupation of training psychologists with vehicle control skills probably peaked in the early days of the manned space programme when some of the most sophisticated simulators were built but interest in tracking has declined since computers now do more of the actual flying than human pilots. Pilots and engineers in control of complex systems, such as nuclear power stations, play a more supervisory role, monitoring the progress of the equipment and making occasional interventions to troubleshoot problems in an emergency. Operator training in the 1980s is now more concerned with cognitive than with perceptual-motor skills. There is, however, an important exception which is due to the recent rapid development of research into the psychology of sport and kinesiology. Since the middle 1970s research on bodily control skills from table tennis to skiing has provided not only new tasks but new concepts which derive from movement physiology, especially the work of the Russian physiologist Bernstein (Bernstein, 1967) and from Gibson's (1979) 'ecological' theory of perception.

Training psychology is currently in an interesting stage with new ways of looking at some old questions and some issues previously thought beyond the scope of scientific method are being actively investigated. This chapter is devoted to these more recent developments. Useful historical reviews can be found in Irion (1966) and Adams (1987).

MODES OF TRAINING

Cognitive processes

Since cognitive processes are so obviously important in the acquisition of skill I have attempted to provide a general theoretical framework within which to explore these issues (Annett, 1981, 1983, 1985, 1986). Figure 3.1. illustrates the cognitive processes involved in acquiring a skill and some of their interconnections. Any particular motor performance can be elicited in one of three different ways. A simple act such as raising the right hand may be a direct response to some environmental event, for instance to ward off a blow, or the result of a verbal instruction 'raise your right hand', or in imitation of another individual. Figure 3.1 shows only the latter two classes of stimuli. Similarly, verbal utterances can be a direct response to some non-verbal environmental event or a verbal description of an event or an 'imitation' of a verbal stimulus, as in reading or shadowing spoken text.

Figure 3.1 also indicates that the connections between action and language are two-way. As well as being able, for the most part, to act on verbal instructions we are able to translate perceived (and imagined) actions into words when, for example, giving a running commentary or explaining to someone else how to carry out some task. Both of these are of practical importance in coaching and training but have received rather little systematic attention in the research literature. I refer to this two-way system as the

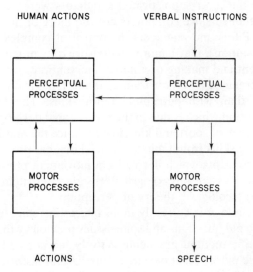

Figure 3.1. Two important classes of events, the actions and verbalizations of other individuals, are analysed by specific perceptual systems. Each perceptual system is intimately linked with a corresponding output system. Imagery, motor or verbal, occurs when the perceptual and motor processes are jointly active (as represented by the vertical bi-directional arrows) in the absence of external inputs or motor output. The action and language systems communicate via the perceptual processes, the action-language bridge represented by the horizontal bi-directional arrows. The figure illustrates the processes and connections believed to be active during imitation, following instructions and imaginary practice.

action-language bridge and the key problem which it poses is what mechanisms mediate the translation between action and language. Figure 3.1 also illustrates another fundamental translation problem, that is the nature of the relation between the *perception* of actions and their *production*. It is on this relationship that imitation must depend. According to James (1890) the 'idea' of a movement is sufficient to elicit it but the link between thought and action is not susceptible to further analysis. It is, of course, possible to contemplate actions without executing them during mental rehearsal but there are nonetheless strong and direct links between perception and action.

Both the action-language bridge and what Prinz (1986) has called the *ideo-motor hyphen* required the postulation of an internal representation of action which is somehow accessible to and modifiable by *both* the perceived actions of others *and* verbal instructions and descriptions. This representational system must be able to access output mechanisms so that perceived action can be imitated and verbal instructions can be obeyed. We can investigate these representations and their interconnections by looking at some of the experimental paradigms described in Figure 3.1, notably imitation, verbal instruction and mental practice.

Imitation and observational learning

There has been a near theoretical vacuum about imitation which has been only partly filled by Piaget's developmental theory (Piaget, 1951, 1953) and Bandura's social learning theory (Bandura, 1971, 1977). The behaviourists rejected observation as a basic learning mechanism in favour of the reinforcement of overt responses and industrial trainers referred somewhat disparagingly to 'Sitting by Nellie' as an inferior training method (Seymour, 1966). Any theory of observational learning, modelling and imitation requires an internal representation of actions which is capable of being dissociated from their actual production. This internal representation must be such that it is modifiable by experience without feedback from the consequences of action on the real world. As a first step in understanding how actions are represented we should consider how actions are perceived. The behaviour of conspecifics constitutes a highly significant category of perceptual events for any social species. The most important cues we pick up from observing leaders, mates and competitors enable us to deduce what their *intentions* are. Whilst social perception is undoubtedly modifiable by experience it is of such biological importance that it is present, at least in a crude form, virtually from birth. Merltzoff and Moore (1977) have demonstrated that 12 to 21-day-old-infants can imitate lip and tongue protrusion, and manual gestures such as waggling the fingers. Just as primitive walking responses are also present at birth but tend to disappear before being replaced eventually by true walking, this primitive imitative response may be only a precursor of mature imitation.

However, its presence at such an early stage of development indicates its importance and suggests the possibility at least of some hard-wired connection between action perception and action production.

Bandura's social learning theory refers to four groups of underlying processes. First we have to account for how and why people attend to others and to aspects of their performance. Second is the question of how the behaviour of the model is encoded in the memory of the imitator. Third is how it is reproduced and the fourth why it is reproduced at all. In what follows I shall focus on the first three questions. In adults we know from the work of Johannson (1973), Cutting and Kozlowski (1977) and Cutting and Proffit (1981, 1982) that only minimal cues are necessary to perceive meaningful human action. A model filmed in dark clothing and a small number of point light sources located on the main body joints (ankles, hips, elbows etc.) is quickly seen by most subjects as an individual whose actions are interpretable (without movement one sees simply a jumble of dots). Individuals can be recognized by their gait (some people are better able to recognize themselves) and it is possible to guess with reasonable accuracy the sex of the model and the weight of any load they may be carrying. It appears we are able to abstract invariants from such impoverished stimuli and these enable us to make socially significant judgements. It is important for humans to be able to infer not only the identity but the *intentions* of the model. Lasher (1981) has presented evidence to suggest that action perception is particularly tuned to the detection of outcomes, that is the significant perceptual unit identifies some kind of end state, goal or intention. Experts in the martial arts and stage conjurors employ tricks designed to deceive the observer as to their intentions.

Sheffield (1961) has suggested some guidelines of what constitutes a good demonstration. Perceiving actions, like perceiving other events, is governed by some general rules of perceptual organization. In performances to be imitated these organizational factors would include 'natural' units and the way in which they are organized into a meaningful act or succession of acts. Both of these features would have to be prominent in a successful demonstration. I have carried out several studies in which subjects were asked to explain how they carried out tasks in which they were relatively skilled (Annett, 1986). The most frequently found statements in answer to 'explain how you take two ends of string and tie them together to make a bow' refer to end states which must be achieved before the next step of the task is undertaken (see Figure 3.2). For example something like 'grasp the two ends of string' is a necessary precursor to the next stage which is 'twist them together'. There is other evidence which suggests that the perceptual units relevant to action are related to outcomes, that is states which are necessary conditions for subsequent actions, and not just arbitrary chunks of movement.

Subject 6
'OK / um create a loop holding it between/ oh round my index finger on both hands/ and tie the bow together/ in a double knot/ creates a bow.'

Subject 8
'Er yes I would pick up the string and slide my hands along one to each end/ er bring the ends up to meet one another/with my right hand I would put the string over the left end/ and then bring it underneath/ and then the piece that I've just brought underneath I would put over the what is now the right hand piece of string/ and fold that over/ and push it through the pull it through loop/ and pull the whole thing tight.'

Subject 11
'Um well I would take both pieces of string between er/ the forefinger and thumb of each hand/ er being right handed I would hold the left hand still/ and take the right hand and pass er/ pass the free end of the string in my right hand over the standing portion of the string in my left hand over and under to produce a a a um/ what would be a 360 degree wrap e/r that would provide the basis for a bow . . . .'

Figure 3.2. Sample protocols. Subjects are asked to explain how to tie a bow. Protocols from subjects 6 and 8 and complete but only the first 10% of subject 11's response is shown.

Bandura's theory does not tell us about the behaviour of the model as such but it is evident that individuals who are required to give demonstrations behave in a characteristic way which often involves slowing down the action and exaggerating critical movements. Individuals who are required to demonstrate how to tie a bow (as opposed to just doing it) not only perform slowly but increase the physical magnitude of significant actions, such as pulling the knot tight (Annett, 1986).

Demonstration is a technique used very frequently in the early stages of training human perceptual motor skills where it is believed to be more efficient in general than pure trial and error learning. This belief is confirmed by the results of a study by Landers (1975) on learning a gymnastic skill, climbing a free-standing (Bachmann) ladder. Some of the learners, 180 11- to 13-year-old girls, were given demonstrations prior to or interspersed with actual practice on this relatively novel task while some did not have demonstrations until after a period of active trial and error practice. The latter group did not learn as effectively as those who were given the prior demonstration but the group given practice interspersed with demonstrations also learned effectively. The results of using video-tape recording in athletic performances have been somewhat equivocal. Scully and Newell (1985) suggest that the significant variable is whether or not 'the topological characteristics of the relative motion of the activity' are available through modelling. The ladder-climbing task used successfully by Landers enables the observer to detect relative motion patterns (as the subjects of Johannson's and Cutting's experiments were able to pick up invariant features of gait). In another task used by Martens, Burwitz and Zuckerman (1976) which consisted of rolling a ball up an incline, the differences between successful and unsuccessful performance are not so obvious from an external viewpoint and here natural demonstrations were not as effective as specially filmed sequences. Some demonstrations can reveal 'how it is done' but there are other tasks where the critical cues are invisible. Mirror drawing might be such a task. The observer who can see the subject struggling to trace a star pattern viewed in a mirror can have little appreciation of how it feels to the subject to cope with mirrored reversal of hand movements. Nonetheless I have found with undergaduate practical classes that experimenters who after testing one subject take over the role of subject themselves do significantly better on the first few trials than the original naïve subjects. What exactly it is they have learned is a matter of speculation but it could be that it is a response strategy such as 'do not try to do what the visual stimulus tells you—try the opposite' or even 'if you get stuck, pause and reconsider your next move'.

What, then, can we say about the internal representation which is formed during observational learning? Bandura (1971, 1977) refers to *symbolic representations* which may be either *imaginal*, that is in the analogue form of visual imagery, or *verbal*, that is coded as verbal equivalents to the actions to be carried out. Bandura and Jeffrey (1973), Bandura, Jeffrey and Bachicha (1974) and Jeffrey (1976) have studied verbal coding and shown that in serial motor tasks, verbal coding can enhance retention. However, gymnastic and other complex bodily skills are difficult to code verbally whilst visual imagery might be of greater value. Gerst (1971) compared the retention of a serial movement task based on learning a series of hand signals with various types of verbal and visual coding and found the former to be more effective as judged by retention tests, but any instruction as to how to code the demonstration information was more effective than none.

In summary it appears we still know relatively little about the processes underlying imitation. The basis for perceiving and reproducing simple actions is present at birth and by adulthood we can extract significant information about actions and intentions from minimal cues. Learners are able to form internal representations of complex actions which may be either visual (analogue) or verbal (symbolic) but we do not know much about these representations. More studies are needed on how trainees extract information from demonstrations, what are the characteristics of effective demonstrations and what types of task benefit most from demonstration. One obvious question is whether imagery ability is correlated with the ability to benefit from demonstrations and observational learning but this remains to be answered by future research.

Verbal processes—knowledge of results

Providing the trainee with knowledge of the results is one of the most common training interventions and one which is generally believed to have a powerful effect on learning. While not necessarily verbal in form (lights, buzzers and graphic displays have all been used) some symbolic representation of the adequacy of the learned response in relation to one or more performance criterion is always involved.

Thorndike (1932) and later Skinner (1957) held that informing the learner that a response was right or wrong is equivalent to providing a reward which reinforces the connection between stimulus and response. This formulation, known as the *Law of Effect*, was contrasted with the *Law of Exercise* which attributes the strengthening of S–R connections to repetition pure and simple. Cognitive psychologists have regarded the law of effect as an unsatisfactory analysis of the function of KR. The arguments have been spelled out in detail by Annett (1969), Adams (1971) and Schmidt (1975), all of whom offer information-processing interpretations. My proposal was that the primary function of KR is corrective, the view also taken by Salmoni, Schmidt and Walter (1984). The Adams and Schmidt theories emphasize the learning of association between response output and criterion-related sensory feedback but the two viewpoints are not incompatible. The classic motor-skill acquisition task is learning to make a discrete movement of a given extent. Much of the research effort on this task has been devoted to variables such as the relative frequency of KR, that is on every trial or some smaller proportion, its timing in relation to both the preceding and the next response, and its accuracy, that is whether it is purely evaluative, such as 'good' or gives more information about the relationship between the response just made and the criterion response, such as 'too long'. This research has been reviewed at considerable length by Bilodeau (1966), Annett (1969) and Newell (1976). KR is much more effective when it provides directional information than when it is purely evaluative, that is only indicates 'good/bad' performance. Annett (1969) proposed that subjects learned the task by applying a simple transformation rule to the information provided in KR coupled with short-term memory of the response to which it relates. This is a simple strategy which can be stated as 'if KR is "correct" than repeat the response; if KR is "too short" then produce a response which is longer (by some arbitrary amount); if KR is "too long" then produce a response which is shorter (by some arbitrary amount)". In this way the learner homes on to an approximately correct response in a few trials. Error reduction is initially rapid but typically falls off as the limits of kinaesthetic discrimination are approached. The shape of this negatively accelerated learning curve and subsequent retention are relatively insensitive to variations in the precision of the KR information (Annett, 1969; Bilodeau, 1952) which lends support to the idea that learning at this stage is primarily due to the use of this simple strategy. The theory does not require any long-term trace of either responses or KR since at each trial the only stored information required is a record of the immediately preceding response and of its associated KR. This is not to say that no longer term traces exist. In this blind positioning task the subject has to learn to attend to internal cues from the movement and to relate them to the externally specified criteria provided in KR. It is the association of these two sets of data (the *response trace* and the *perceptual trace* in Adam's theory or the *schema* in Schmidt's theory) which are presumed to provide a basis for longer term retention and transfer to trials where KR is finally withdrawn. Despite the considerable amount of research on timing and precision we do not know if greater precision of KR is an advantage in extended practice.

KR is also said to have a *motivating* effect. Learners generally like to know if they are making progress and are more likely to give up practising if no feedback is available. Annett (1969) argued that it is misleading to attribute a special energizing quality to KR over and above what might be expected of its informational properties. A simple mechanical feedback system such as a thermostatically controlled boiler, seeks the set point by switching on when the temperature drops and off when the set point is exceeded. It does this simply on the basis of its design as a feedback loop—there is no special ingredient over and above the feedback loop itself and the information fed into it. Human tasks may be similarly described whether they be simple, such as drawing a 4-inch line, or complex such as flying a 'plane, since neither can be accomplished without feedback. To put it succinctly the motivating function of knowledge of results is simply feedback in action.

The timing of KR relative to responses has not been found to be particularly critical (Bilodeau and Bilodeau, 1958). Long delays following KR or prior to the subsequent response can give as effective learning as short intervals. Paradoxically KR which arrives during the course of the action to which it relates can give high levels of performance but poor learning and retention. Studies of military training devices during and shortly after the Second World War (Biel, Brown and Gottsdanker, 1944; Morin and Gagne, 1951; Lincoln 1954; Smode, 1958) showed that devices which gave special signals such as flashing lights or buzzers when the subject was on target during the execution of a response often provided no more than a temporary boost to performance but gave little evidence of long-term learning. As Annett and Kay (1957) pointed out, if KR provides a cue which can be used as a crutch to performance then learning will not necessarily occur. Trainees have to learn to perform with the aid of only that feedback which is intrinsic to the task. This point has been reiterated by Salmoni, Schmidt and Walter (1984) who remind us that the effects of KR can often be different for immediate performance and for longer transfer and retention and that theories of KR must take both into account.

Much of the classic work on KR has been carried out on relatively simple tasks such as line drawing and tracking. Newell (1981) reminds us that in practical settings, including training in sports or complex tasks like flying, variables such as timing and precision take on a different aspect. Immediate KR could disrupt ongoing performance and may have to wait until a debriefing session some time later when the instructor and trainee analyse practice sessions by going through performance records such as video-tape recordings. In complex tasks the criterion performance is also more likely to be defined in terms of some ideal pattern rather than as a single unidimensional variable. Processing detailed KR could place a very considerable information load on the learner but *outcome KR*, that is information about the general standard of performance, is not very helpful in a complex task unless accompanied by some indication of the particular aspects of performance which were at fault.

Lindahl (1945) used tracings of the force pattern applied to the pedal controlling a cutting wheel to demonstrate an efficient cut and to enable trainees to compare their own efforts with a standard pattern. Recently studies by Hatze (1976), Newell and Walter (1981), Newell, Quinn, Sparrow and Walter (1983) and Newell and McGinnis (1985) have shown some of the difficulties in providing complex KR in a way in which it can be useful to the trainee. Symbolic information, such as numbers representing peak force of a response, is less efficient than graphic displays showing the ideal time-force pattern together with the trainee's attempt for comparison. Hatze (1976) had shown that detailed kinematic information (i.e. a representation of the response pattern) was very much more efficient than simple outcome (good/bad) KR.

Video-taped feedback potentially provides even more detailed kinematic KR but the result of field studies have indicated only a moderate degree of success. Both the trainee and the coach face a complex series of problems in interpreting video-tape records. First the coach has to be able to identify correctly aspects of performance which contribute significantly to the overall outcome (e.g. a correct dive or a successful tennis serve); second, the trainee must also be able to see this, and be able to relate it to his own memories of what he was doing or attempting to do at the time; next the trainee (helped by the coach) must formulate a remedial strategy to try out on subsequent trials. We thus come by another route to see the importance of the internal representation of complex behaviour patterns and the level of conscious control discussed in earlier sections of this review.

PRACTICE

The best known generalization in human learning is that practice makes perfect. The repetition of simple motor patterns of the sort involved in routine industrial tasks results in a progressive and apparently continuous reduction in cycle time for as long as practice can be maintained. Plotting cycle time against number of trials generally gives a negatively accelerated learning curve. On closer analysis it appears that the logarithm of cycle time is a linear function of the logarithm of the number of practice trials and this is known as the *log-log linear law of practice* (Crossman, 1959; Newell and Rosenbloom, 1981). Explanations of this basic phenomenon come in a variety of forms. The traditional view is that a process of 'engraining' is involved, that is connections between task elements are facilitated by frequent use. Mackay (1982) has recently proposed a theory along these lines to account for the learning of sequential skills. Another popular theory suggested by Poulton (1957) and elaborated by Pew (1966, 1974) and Schneider and Shiffrin (1985) proposes that practice leads to a progressive change in the level of control from *closed loop*, in which the consequences of each elementary action must be monitored, to *open loop* in which prepared responses are run off and checked only intermittently. Other authors (Crossman, 1959; Annett, 1985) have suggested that practice permits a selective process which progressively eliminates actions which take more time or effort and substitutes cheaper alternatives. Finally Newell and Rosenbloom (1981) propose that component processes become grouped into progressively larger *chunks*, each of which can be processed as a whole. Capacity is limited by the number of chunks to be dealt with and hence the performer is able to do more in less time.

Mental practice

Practice produces both internal and external sensory consequences which are thought to be essential for learning to occur. It is for this reason that *mental practice* (MP), rehearsal of a skill in imagination rather than by overt physical activity, has intrigued training theorists, especially those interested in cognitive processes. Mental practice has often been recommended by sportsmen (Nideffer, 1976; Syer and Connolly, 1984) and has a long, but not entirely respectable history in the experimental literature (for reviews see Corbin, 1972; Feltz and Landers, 1983; Paivio, 1985; Richardson, 1967a, b). There is enough positive evidence to indicate that mental practice can sometimes be almost as effective as overt practice and it is sometimes very much more convenient: Prather (1973) has described the use of imagery as a flight simulator! Almost as many theories have been advanced to account for MP effects as for overt physical practice but the principal varieties include (i) those which attribute the positive effects to motivation enhancement, (ii) those which argue that in mental practice muscular activity is still present, but in a much attenuated form, and finally (iii) theories which attribute to a separable symbolic component of the skill.

The motivation enhancement theory is popular amongst sportsmen and their coaches who often recommend that one should imagine oneself as being successful—a general technique for 'psyching up' morale. While the possibility should not be lightly dismissed the evidence for it is largely anecdotal. Paivio (1985) suggests that any motivational effects are probably secondary, for example imagining success may reduce the negative effects of anxiety or may simply encourage more participation in useful physical practice. The definitive studies on this issue remain to be done.

The theory that mental practice effects are due to subliminal activity in the motor output system reflects the classical behaviourist view of thought processes as suppressed physical activity. Jacobsen (1932) recorded electrical activity in the appropriate muscles during imaginary activities. More recent evidence goes against this theory. First, muscular activity is not always detectable and sometimes involves opposing muscles. Second, mental practice effects can survive conditions in which the muscles are engaged in some different activity from that being imagined. Johnson (1982), in an ingenious set of experiments which exploited a well-known interference effect in short-term motor memory, had subjects first learn to make a simple linear movement of a prescribed extent. Next some subjects were required to make a movement of a different extent (for some twice as long and for others half as long) and then recall the original movement. The effect of this interpolated activity was to induce systematic error in recall of the original movement which was overestimated if subjects had produced longer interpolated movement and underestimated if the interpolated movement had been shorter than the standard. A second group of subjects were instructed to imagine making movements (some longer and some shorter) with their hands resting on the table, while a third group counted backwards during the retention interval. On the retention trials the imaginary movement group made over- and underestimations, just like those who had made real movements, while the counting backwards group showed no systematic bias. In a second experiment the mental conditions were repeated but subjects were also required to carry out secondary tasks during the retention interval. These tasks included making tapping movements either on one spot or between two points separated by some distance and either listening to intermittent sounds or watching flashing lights in a single location or alternating between two separate locations. The bias in recalling the original movement induced by imagining one of a different extent survived the additional load of both the motor (tapping) and the perceptual tasks but only those versions in which the stimulus or the response was confined to a single location. Where two locations were involved the effect of the interpolated imaginary movement was abolished. The experiments thus demonstrate both a clear mental practice effect and that the primary motor system is not involved. The critical element in these experiments was the representation of spatial locations since the effect of mental practice disappeared only when the subject had to perform a spatial task.

Mackay (1981, 1982) has proposed a theory to account for improvements in speed and fluency of serial skills due to either physical or mental practice and has presented some results which show stronger practice effects on speech production from mental than from physical practice. The particular skill was to speak an unfamiliar sentence as fast as possible and in the theory the skill is represented as a set of interconnected mental modes. A high-level node represents the propositional content, or care meaning, of the sentence to be uttered while other (lower level) nodes specify grammatical rules which constrain the order in which the words are uttered. At the lowest level there are nodes which control specific muscles. When a sentence is uttered the node network is activated from the top down, from idea to articulation. However, the upper part of the hierarchy can also be activated from the bottom up by hearing someone else speak the sentence, so the whole representational structure deals with both reception and production. In subvocal speech or silent reading activation is prevented from spreading all the way down to the muscle nodes. When a node is activated it primes other nodes to which it is connected and the node which receives most priming from all sources becomes activated. If it is a muscle node the movement will occur. If an adjective and a noun are both primed by superior content nodes the grammatical sequence node primes the adjective, thus ensuring that it will occur first.

The effect of practice is to strengthen the linkage between nodes which are activated together by facilitating the priming process. The theory is able to make a number of predictions about speech errors (which will not be discussed here) but it also predicts benefits from mental practice. If an unfamiliar sentence which contains unusual links between linguistic elements is practised, the high-level internodal links will be strengthened relatively rapidly. The lower level muscular nodes are so well used that their linkage strength is not much affected by further practice. Mackay is, then, able to predict that the speed with which an unfamiliar sentence can be rehearsed silently will improve with practice faster than overt speech improves with repetition, and so it turns out (Mackay, 1981). I have attempted to replicate this finding in the motor field using knot tying as the sequential task (Annett, 1988a). Subjects are instructed to tie an imaginary bow as fast as possible, marking the beginning and end of each trial by striking a timer. The results are compared with the time taken to tie a real knot over a number of practice trials. It is predicted by the theory that mental bow tying is faster than physical bow tying because fewer nodes must be activated. The actual mean times were 4.5 seconds for the imaginary bow compared with 6.5 seconds for the real bow, but no significant learning was observed. However with a relatively unfamiliar knot, a bowline, 12 trials of mental practice yielded a 24 per cent improvement in speed while physical practice yielded a 30 per cent improvement in speed. This only partially replicates Mackay's results with sentence production. In a second study (Annett, 1988b) skilled and unskilled typists were required to practise mentally or physically meaningful sentences or nonsense letter strings. The two main predictions were (i) that physical practice with meaningful sentences would be relatively more effective for unskilled typists and (ii) that mental practice would be more effective than physical practice for both groups when nonsense material was used but relatively more so for the skilled typists. The main effects of practice trials, typing skill and meaning were all highly significant, as expected, but unskilled typists carried out their mental practice trials faster than physical practice while skilled typists stuck to a uniform rate. However, neither of the specific predictions was confirmed and so this apparently promising theory is still awaiting support with respect to motor skills. The problem of mental practice still awaits a solution but when one is found it should also tell us something about why *any* kind of practice should bring about improvements in performance.

RETENTION AND TRANSFER

Training ideally merges imperceptibly into the full-time practice of a skill but not infrequently there is a definite break between training and performance, between the status of trainee and skilled worker. After a three-day first aid course it may be months or years before the trainee has to put resuscitation skills into practice, and even then the circumstances in which the skill was originally learned may differ in important ways from the context in which it must be applied. Skills may simply be forgotten or may not be effectively deployed because the context in which they are required is different from that in which they were learned. These are the problems of retention and transfer. A training prescription has to be judged not only on the speed and efficiency with which a given performance standard can be achieved but also on how well the skill is retained after long periods without practice and how well the trainee can transfer what has been learned to a different context.

Both retention and transfer are concerned with *savings*, that is economies which can be made in retraining. A classical method of measuring the retention of a skill is to compare the rate at which it can be relearned with the rate at which the original learning took place. Hill (1934, 1957) reported on the retention of typing skill which he had orginally acquired as a research student at Columbia in 1907. After 25 years with no further practice it took him only one day of retraining to achieve the level of skill (in words typed per minute) which he had originally taken 27 days of practice to attain. The classic savings formula expressed the reduction in effort required to relearn the task as a percentage of the original learning effort, in this case $(27-1)/27 \times 100 =$ (just under) 93 per cent, which represents a very substantial saving (or retention of the skill) after 25 years with no practice.

The same idea of savings can be extended to the transfer of previously learned skills in a rather different situation. For example, if it takes 100 hours to train a heavy goods vehicle driver to a specified performance criterion but it takes people who already know how to drive a private car only 50 hours further training to reach the same performance criterion then the transfer value of PC to HGV is 50 per cent. That is, 50 per cent of the HGV training is 'saved' by the initial training. There are other methods of measuring both retention and transfer but the savings methods, which is common to both, is a very convenient way of comparing the efficiency of training techniques.

Retention of skill

As Hill's study shows, perceptual-motor skills can be very well retained after very long periods without overt practice and this contrasts with the picture we have of the retention of verbal material (such as nonsense syllables or random paired associates) declining rapidly over rather short time intervals. It is difficult to make valid comparisons of the retention of different types of skill by any other method than savings because there is no common metric on which we can assess how well any skill has been learned or even how often it has been practised (Annett, 1979). It is easy enough to say how many times a learner has repeated a vocabulary list or some other discrete task but the same question cannot be answered for continuous skills such as tracking where a trial is simply an arbitrary chunk of time. Leavitt and Schlosberg (1944) had subjects learn a 15-item nonsense trigram list by the anticipation method over 10 trials and subjects were then required to practise a motor skill, the pursuit rotor, for ten 30-second trials. They were then recalled (without warning) to relearn both tasks after 1, 7, 28 or 70 days. Over 70 days the savings on the nonsense syllable task were 51.4 per cent and on the pursuit rotor task savings were 75.2 per cent. Even after one day the savings on relearning the motor task were better than on the verbal task, providing support for the generalization that motor skills are better retained than verbal skills. The results of a number of studies agree that motor skills are generally retained for fairly long periods. However, there is some variation in the retention one can expect of skills of various types. Procedural tasks which require the operator to recall a precise sequence of discrete steps seem to be particularly vulnerable to the omission of some responses. For example, Shields, Goldberg and Dressel (1979) found that soldiers could remember how to assemble and fire a gun, but were inclined to forget additional steps such as checking that the backblast area was clear of personnel and resetting the safety catch.

A key question is whether the method of training can affect retention. The evidence reviewed by Annett (1979) suggests that retention is closely related to mastery. Well-retained skills are those which are well-learned or even overlearned (Ammons *et al.* 1958; Krueger, 1929; Luh, 1923). There are other factors which affect retention, including the nature of the material to be mastered, for example, a skill which has been learned, partly forgotten and then relearned is retained better than material which has been learned only once. As long ago as 1897 Jost proposed two 'laws' the second of which was 'if two associations are of equal strength but of different ages, further study has greater value for the older one'. What this means in practice is that every time 'old' material is rehearsed it not only is relearned more easily than it was originally but the rate of subsequent forgetting is also slowed down. Jost based his laws on the results of verbal learning experiments but Annett and Piech (1985) have confirmed that the law seems to hold for perceptual-motor skill learning and retention. A video-game skill in which moving targets were intercepted was learned to a criterion level and half the subjects were given a one-week rest and then relearned to the original level. The second group learned to the same criterion and then had 50 per cent more practice trials. Both groups then relearned the task after a further one-week lay-off. The group which had originally learned the skill two weeks earlier showed 53 per cent savings on final relearning as compared with only 31 per cent savings for the group which had learned the task only once before although both had the same number of practice trials. This result needs confirmation in a wider range of tasks and retention intervals but if it turned out to be generally true it could have important practical implications for retraining and refresher courses. A trainee with any previous experience, even if it had been a long time before, could be expected to make more rapid progress than most beginners.

Transfer of training

Similar issues are raised with respect to transfer. Will trainees with previous experience of similar tasks to that now being learned transfer their existing skill to the new task? The classical theory of transfer is known as the *formal discipline* theory. The basic idea is that when any skill is practised it strengthens the abilities on which it depends. In this way other skills which depend on the same ability will be enhanced, even though they are not directly practised. The formal discipline theory provided a theoretical rationale for educational practices which stressed memorization on the grounds that memory as a general ability would be strengthened. This theory went out of favour after William James (1890) failed to improve his own memory by learning large slabs of poetry, to be replaced by the *identical elements* theory (Thorndike and Woodworth, 1901) which proposed that transfer depended on there being some 'elements' common to the two tasks so that savings in learning the new task could be due to some elements already having been learned. The key question is how to identify these common elements? In behaviourist learning theory the elements common to the two tasks were *stimuli* and *responses*, but Osgood (1949) drew attention to an apparent paradox. It might be expected that transfer would occur when the two tasks contained either stimulus or response elements in common. While this was generally true, whenever two tasks share the same stimulus elements but require different responses *negative transfer* occurs, that is the new task is harder to learn. British and American light switches look almost identical but the switching on action in Britain is typically to press the toggle down while in the USA the opposite is required. It takes a lot of practice to rid oneself of the old habit and this may still recur in moments of stress or inattention (Reason, 1980).

An implication of the identical elements theory is that when the target or transfer task is only very broadly defined the content of the training should include elements most likely to be found in a very broad range of jobs and tasks. In recent years considerable efforts have been made to devise a curriculum for school leavers which will include the most commonly used skills. Pratzner (1978) refers to these as *transferable skills*, Greenan (1986) has a similar list of *generalizable skills*. In Britain the Manpower Services Commission (1985) has produced a list of *core skills* to be taught on Youth Training Schemes. These elementary skills vary from list to list but typically comprise basic mathematical operations, communication skills (including reading and writing, speaking and listening), skills of reasoning and problem-solving as well as perceptual-motor skills. Annett (1987), in reviewing these developments, drew attention to a number of problems. One is how to arrive at an agreed list without going to the enormous cost of analysing the content of a full range of industrial and commercial jobs. Even if this were done the transfer problem would still remain since job elements learned in one context are not always readily transferred to another, apparently because the trainee does not relate the old skill to the new problem. For example, in a recent study of the transfer of measurement skills in engineering apprentices, Fotheringhame (1984) found that there was no transfer from using a micrometer to learning how to use a vernier height gauge, although the two instruments depend on the same measurement principle. Ormerod (1987) has similarly shown disappointingly little transfer between computing tasks which involve similar principles. Learners often note the superficial similarities and differences between tasks without looking for deeper relationships and can be deceived into thinking tasks are similar when they are not.

Metacognition

It is clear that neither of the classic theories of transfer helps us with these problems so Annett and Sparrow (1985) and Annett (1987) have taken some steps towards a new theory of transfer which takes into account the cognitive structures underlying performance. In this theory a skill is seen as a hierarchically organized control structure. At the top of the hierarchy general strategies control the selection of subordinate routines. For example, getting dressed involves subskills such as doing up buttons, but these are subordinate to other routines which determine the order in which clothes are put on and these in turn are controlled by even higher order routines which determine how to dress, that is to keep out the weather, to impress one's friends and so on. Shaffer (1980) has shown very elegantly how these levels of control operate in highly skilled piano playing. It is assumed that any skill is subject to at least two levels of control and that (relatively) low-level cognitive processes are controlled by (relatively) high-level processes which we shall call *meta-cognitive* after Flavell (1976) who introduced the concept of metacognition in the context of learning retardation. Given some material to learn, the normal learner can use one of a number of possible strategies such as mnemonics, repetition and self-testing and so on, and can generally choose a method appropriate to the learning task. Poor learners are found to be deficient in both the knowledge and use of these metacognitive strategies (Brown and Campione, 1986; Downs and Perry, 1986).

A more detailed diagnosis of metacognitive deficiencies has been offered by Feuerstein (see for example Feuerstein, Hoffman, Jense and Rand, 1985). Poor learners are characterized by underdeveloped strategies for gathering and analysing information and in defining the problem. Their actions tend to be impulsive and unplanned. The question is whether metacognitive skills can be taught to those who for whatever original reason are shown to be deficient in metacognitive skills. Brown and Campione (1986), summarizing a substantial body of research, conclude that successful training is possible. The successful techniques include direct instruction in how to generalize from one situation to another, and the use of variety of training materials which will provide opportunities for noting relationships and generalities. Feuerstein's approach is to try to tackle problems such as deficiencies of attention control through specially designed exercises. Typically students are given practice in analysing the content of apparently meaningless stimulus materials, but it in not just the training tasks which are important but the role of the trainer. Feuerstein attributes metacognitive deficiencies to lack of mediation by human teachers. Teachers mediate learning of this kind as much by modelling effective cognitive strategies as by the materials and problems they use. A rather different view stresses self-direction. Training which encourages a passive attitude does not provide the best environment for the development of metacognitive skills and according to the *experiential learning* movement (Kolb, 1984) students should be encouraged to take charge of their own learning.

A review of these developments by Segal, Chipman and Glaser (1985) and Chipman, Segal and Glaser (1985) gives some encouragement to the belief that intervention programmes can raise the level of metacognitive skills but rigorous evaluation studies are rare and the evidence is better described as supportive than conclusive. Moreover there is as yet little direct evidence that those who are successful at acquiring perceptual-motor skills have developed special metacognitive strategies to help them to solve motor problems. However, given the importance of the problem and the growing involvement of cognitive psychologists in applied problems of training this could be a fruitful field for research.

REFERENCES

Adams, J. A. (1971). A closed loop theory of motor learning, *Journal of Motor Behavior*, **3**, 111–150.

Adams, J. A. (1987). Historical review and appraisal of research on the learning, retention and transfer of human motor skills, *Psychological Bulletin*, **101**, 41–74.

Ammons, R. B. (1947). Acquisition of a motor skill: 1 Quantitative analysis and theoretical formulation, *Psychological Review*, **54**, 263–281.

Ammons, R. B., Bloch, E., Neumann, E., Dey, M., Marion, R. & Ammons, C. H. (1958). Long-term retention of perceptual-motor skills, *Journal of Experimental Psychology*, **55**, 318–328.

Annett, J. (1969). *Feedback and Human Behaviour*. Harmondsworth: Penguin.

Annett, J. (1979). Memory for skill, in M. Gruneberg and P. Morris (eds), *Applied Problems in Memory*. London: Academic Press.

Annett, J. (1981). Action, language and imagination. Paper to British Psychological Society, Cognitive Section Conference on Memory, Plymouth.

Annett, J. (1983). Motor learning, a cognitive psychological viewpoint, in H. Rieder, K. Bos, H. Mechling & K. Reischle (eds), *Motorik und Bewegungsforschung*. Schorndorf: Verlag Karl Hofmann.

Annett, J. (1985), Motor learning: a review, in H. Heuer, U. Kleinbeck, & K-H Schmidt (eds), *Motor Behaviour: Programming, Control and Acquisition*. Berlin: Springer Verlag.

Annett, J. (1986). On knowing how to do things, in H. Heuer & C. Fromm (eds), *Generation and Modulation of Action Patterns*. Berlin: Springer Verlag.

Annett, J. (1987). *Training in Transferable Skills*. Report to the Manpower Services Commission. Sheffield: MSC.

Annett, J. (1988a). Motor learning and retention, in M. Gruneberg, P. Morris & R. Sykes (eds), *Practical Aspects of Memory 2*. Chichester: Wiley.

Annett, J. (1988b). Imagery and skill acquisition, in M. Denis, J. Engelkamp & J. T. E. Richardson. (eds), *Cognitive and Neuropsychological Approaches to Mental Imagery*. Martinus Nijhoff, NATO ASI Series.

Annett, J. & Kay, H. (1956). Skilled performance, *Occupational Psychology*, **30**, 112–117.

Annett, J. & Kay, H. (1957). Knowledge of results and skilled performance, *Occupational Psychology*, **31**, 3–15.

Annett, J. & Piech, J. (1985). The retention of a skill following distributed training, *Programmed Learning and Educational Technology*, **22**, 182–186.

Annett, J. & Sparrow, J. (1985). Transfer of training: a review of research and practical implications, *Programmed Learning and Educational Technology*. **22**, 116–124.

Bandura, A. (1971). *Psychological Modeling: Conflicting Theories*. New York: Atherton Press.

Bandura, A. (1977). *Social Learning Theory*. Engelwood Cliffs NJ: Prentice-Hall.
Bandura, A. & Jeffrey, R. (1973). Role of symbolic coding and rehearsal processes in observational learning, *Journal of Personality and Social Psychology*, **26**, 122–130.
Bandura, A., Jeffrey, R. & Bachicha, D. L. (1974). Analysis of memory codes and cumulative rehearsal in observational learning, *Journal of Research in Personality*, **7**, 295–305.
Bernstein, N. (1967). *The Coordination and Regulation of Movements*. Oxford: Pergamon Press.
Biel, W. C., Brown, C. E. & Gottsdanker, R. (1944). The effectiveness of a check sight technique for training 40 mm gun pointers who are using the computing sight M7. *OSRD Report No. 4054*, Applied Psychology Panel, NDRC, Washington DC.
Bilodeau, E. A. (1952). Some effects of various degrees of supplemented information given at two levels of practice upon the acquisition of a complex motor skill. *USAF HRRC Research Bulletin*, 52–15.
Bilodeau, E. A. (1966). *Principles of Skill Acquisition*. New York: Academic Press.
Bilodeau, E. A. & Bilodeau, I. McD. (1958). Variations of temporal intervals among critical events in five studies of knowledge of results, *Journal of Experimental Psychology*, **55**, 603–612.
Book, W. F. (1908). The psychology of skill: with special reference to its acquisition in typewriting, *University of Montana Publications in Psychology*, Bulletin No. 53, Psychological Series No. 1.
Brown, A. L. & Campione, J. C. (1986). Training for transfer: guidelines for promoting flexible use of trained skills, in M. G. Wade (ed.), *Motor Skill Acquisition of the Mentally Handicapped*. Amsterdam: North Holland.
Bryan, W. L. & Harter, N. (1897). Studies in the physiology and psychology of the telegraphic language, *Psychological Review*, **4**, 27–53.
Chipman, S. F., Segal, J. W. & Glaser, R. (1985). *Thinking and Learning Skills: vol. 2. Research and Open Questions*. Hillsdale NJ: Erlbaum.
Corbin, C. B. (1972). Mental practice, in W. D. Morgan (ed.), *Ergogenic Aid and Muscular Performance*. New York: Academic Press.
Crossman, E. R. F. W., (1959), A theory of the acquisition of speed skill, *Ergonomics*, **2**, 153–156.
Cutting, J. E. & Kozlowski, L. T. (1977). Recognising friends by their walk: gait perception without familiarity cues, *Bulletin of the Psychonomic Society*, **9**, 353–356.
Cutting, J. F. & Proffitt, D. R. (1981). Gait perception as an example of how we may perceive events, in Walk, R. D and Pick, H. L (eds.), *Intersensory Perception and Sensory Integration*. New York: Plenum.
Cutting, J. E. & Proffitt, D. R. (1982). The minimum principle and the perception of absolute, common and relative motions, *Cognitive Psychology*, **14**, 211–286.
Downs, S. & Perry, P. (1986). Can trainers learn to take a back seat? *Personnel Management*, March, 42–45.
Ebbinghaus, H. (1885). *Uber das Gedachtnis*. (English translation 1913 by Ruger & Bussenius, *Memory*, New York: Teacher's College Press).
Feltz, D. L. & Landers, D. M. (1983). The effects of mental practice on motor skill learning and performance: a meta analysis, *Journal of Sport Psychology*, **5**, 25–57.
Feuerstein, R., Hoffman, M. B., Jensen, M. R. & Rand, Y. (1985). Instrumental enrichment, an intervention program for structural cognitive modifiability, in Segal, J. W., Chipman, S. F. & Glaser, R. (eds), *Thinking and Learning Skills, vol. 1. Relating Instruction to Research*. Hillsdale NJ: Erlbaum.
Fitts, P. M. (1961). Factors in complex skill training, in R. Glaser (ed.), *Training Research and Education*. Department of Psychology, University of Pittsburgh, Pennsylvania.

Fitts, P. M. (1964). Perceptual-motor skill learning, in A. W. Melton (ed.), *Categories of Human Learning*. New York: Academic Press.

Flavell, J. H. (1976). Metacognitive aspects of problem solving, in L. B. Resnick (ed.), *The Nature of Intelligence*. Hillsdale NJ: Erlbaum.

Fotheringhame, J. (1984), Transfer of training: a field investigation, *Occupational Psychology*, **57**, 239–248.

Gerst, M. S. (1971). Symbolic coding processes in observational learning. *Journal of Personality and Social Psychology*, **19**, 7–17.

Gibson, J. J. (1979). *The Ecological Approach to Visual Perception*. Boston: Houghton-Mifflin.

Greenan, J. P. (1986). Curriculum and assessment in generalisable skills instruction, *Journal for Special Needs Education*, **9**, 3–10.

Hatze, H. (1976). The complete optimisation of a human motion, *Mathematical Biosciences*, **28**, 99–135.

Hill, L. B. (1943). A quarter century of delayed recall, *Pedagogical Seminars, Journal of General Psychology*, **44**, 231–238.

Hill, L. B. (1957). A second quarter century of delayed recall, or relearning at eighty, *Journal of Educational Psychology*, **48**, 65–69.

Irion, A. L. (1966). A brief history of research on the acquisition of skill, in Bilodeau, E. A. (ed.), *Acquisition of Skill*. New York: Academic Press.

Jacobsen, E. (1932). Electrophysiology of mental activities, *American Journal of Psychology*, **44**, 677–694.

James, W. (1890), *Principles of Psychology*. New York: Holt.

Jeffrey, R. W. (1976). The influence of symbolic motor rehearsal in observational learning, *Journal of Research in Personality*, **10**, 116–127.

Johansson, G. (1973). Visual perception of biological motion and a model for its analysis, *Perception and Psychophysics*, **14**, 201–211.

Johnson, P. (1982). The functional equivalence of imagery and movement, *Quarterly Journal of Experimental Psychology*, **34A**, 349–365.

Jost, A. (1897). Die assoziationsfestigkeit in ihrer abhangigkeit von der verteilung der widerholungen, *Zeitschrift fur Psychologie*, **14**, 436–72.

Kolb, D. A. (1984). *Experiential Learning*. Engelwood Cliffs, NJ: Prentice-Hall.

Krueger, W. C. F. (1929). The effect of overlearning on retention, *Journal of Experimental Psychology*, **13**, 152, 163.

Landers, D. M. (1975). Observational learning of a motor skill: Temporal spacing of a demonstration and audience presence, *Journal of Motor Behavior*, **7**, 281–288.

Lasher, M. D. (1981). The cognitive representation of an event involving human motion, *Cognitive Psychology*, **13**, 391–406.

Leavitt, H. J. and Schlosberg, H. (1944). The retention of verbal and motor skills, *Journal of Experimental Psychology*, **34**, 404–417.

Lincoln, R. S. (1954). Learning a rate of movement. *Journal of Experimental Psychology*, **47**, 465–470.

Lindahl, L. G. (1945). Movement analysis as an industrial training method, *Journal of Applied Psychology*, **29**, 420–430.

Luh, C. W. (1923). The conditions of retention, *Psychological Monographs*, **31**, No. 142.

Mackay, D. G. (1981). The problem of rehearsal or mental practice, *Journal of Motor Behavior*, **13**, 274–285.

Mackay, D. G. (1982). The problem of flexibility, fluency and speed-accuracy trade-off in skilled behavior, *Psychological Review*, **89**, 483–506.

Manpower Services Commission (1985). *Core Skills in YTS, Part 2*. Sheffield: MSC.

Martens, R., Burwitz, L. & Zuckerman, J. (1976), Modeling effects on motor performance, *Research Quarterly*, **47**, 277–291.

Meltzoff, A. N. & Moore, M. K. (1977). Imitation of facial and manual gestures, *Science*,**198**, 75–80.

Morin, R. E. & Gagne, R. M. (1951). Pedestal sight manipulation test performance as influenced by variations in type and amount of psychological feedback. *USAF HRRC Research Note* 51–7.

Newell, K. M. (1976). Knowledge of results and motor learning, in J. Keogh & R. S. Hutton (eds), *Exercise and Sport Sciences Reviews*. Santa Barbara: Journal Publishing Affiliates.

Newell, K. M. (1981). Skill learning in D. H. Holding (ed.), *Human Skills*. Chichester: Wiley.

Newell, K. M., & McGinnis, P. M. (1985), Kinematic information for skilled performance, *Human Learning*, **4**, 39–56.

Newell K. M., Quinn, J. T. Jr., Sparrow, W. A., & Walter, C. B. (1983). Kinetic information for learning a simple rapid response, *Human Movement Science*, **2**, 255–270.

Newell, A. & Rosenbloom P. S. (1981). Mechanisms of skill acquisition, and the law of practice, in J. R. Anderson (ed.), *Cognitive Skills and their Acquisition*. Hillsdale NJ: Erlbaum.

Newell, K. M. & Walter, C. B. (1981). Kinematic and kinetic parameters as information feedback in motor skill acquisition, *Journal of Human Movement Studies*, **7**, 235–254.

Nideffer, R. M. (1976). *The Inner Athlete: Mind Plus Muscle for Winning*. New York: Thomas Crowell.

Ormerod, T. C. (1987). Cognitive processes in logic programming. Ph.D. Thesis, Sunderland Polytechnic.

Osgood, C. E. (1949). The similarity paradox in human learning: A resolution, *Psychological Review*, **56**, 132–143.

Paivio, A. (1985). Cognitive and motivational functions of imagery in human performance, *Canadian Journal of Applied Sport Science*, **10**, 22–28.

Pew, R. W. (1966). The acquisition of hierarchical control over the temporal organisation of a skill, *Journal of Experimental Psychology*, **71**, 764–771.

Pew, R. W. (1974). Human perceptual-motor performance, in B. H. Kantowitz (ed.), *Human Information Processing: Tutorials in Performance and Cognition*. Hillsdale NJ: Erlbaum.

Piaget, J. (1951). *Play, Dreams and Imitation in childhood*. London: Routledge & Kegan Paul.

Piaget, J. (1953). *The Origins of Intelligence in the Child*. London: Routledge & Kegan Paul.

Poulton, E. C. (1957). On prediction in skilled movements, *Psychological Bulletin*, **54**, 467–478.

Prather, D. C. (1973). Prompted mental practice as a flight simulator, *Journal of Applied Psychology*, **57**, 353–355.

Pratzner, F. C. (1978). *Occupational adaptability and transferable skills*. National Center for Research In Vocational Education, Ohio State University.

Prinz, W. (1986). Modes of linkage between perception and action, in Prinz, W. & Sanders, A. (eds), *Cognition and Motor Processes*. Berlin: Springer-Verlag.

Reason, J. (1980). Actions not as planned, in R. Stevens & G. Underwood (eds), *Aspects of Consciousness*. London: Academic Press.

Richardson, A. (1967a & b). Mental practice: A review and discussion, *Research Quarterly*, **38**, 95–107 and 263–273.

Salmoni, A. W., Schmidt, R. A. & Walter, C. B. (1984). Knowledge of results and motor learning: A review and critical appraisal, *Psychological Bulletin*, **95**, 355–386.

Schmidt, R. A. (1975). A Schema theory of discrete motor skill learning, *Psychological Review*, **82**, 225–260.

Schneider, W. & Shiffrin, R. (1985). Categorisation (restructuring) and automatisation: two separable factors, *Psychological Review*, **92**, 424–428.

Scully, D. M. & Newell, K. M. (1985). Observational learning and the acquisition of motor skills: towards a visual perception perspective, *Journal of Human Movement Studies*, **11**, 169–186.

Segal, J. W., Chipman, S. F. & Glaser, R. (1985). *Thinking and Learning Skills. vol. 1, Relating Instruction to Research*. Hillsdale NJ: Erlbaum.

Seymour, W. D. (1966). *Industrial Skills*. London: Pitman.

Shaffer, H. (1980). Analysing piano performance. A study of concert pianists, in G. Stelmach & J. Requin (eds), *Tutorials in Motor Behavior*, Amsterdam: North Holland.

Sheffield, F. D. (1961). Theoretical considerations in the learning of complex sequential tasks from demonstration and practice, in A. A. Lumsdaine (ed.), *Student Response in Programmed Instruction*. Washington D.C.: NAS-NRC.

Shields, J., Goldberg, S. L. & Dressel, J. D. (1979). Retention of basic soldiering skills. *US Army Research Institute for the Behavioural and Social Sciences, Research Report* No. 1225.

Skinner, B. F. (1957). *Verbal Behavior*. New York: Appleton-Century.

Smode, A. F. (1958). Learning and performance in a tracking task under two levels of achievement information feedback, *Journal of Experimental Psychology*, **56**, 297–304.

Swift, (1903). *American Journal of Psychology*, **14**, 201–251.

Syer, J. & Connolly, C. (1984). *Sporting Body Sporting Mind: An Athlete's Guide to Mental Training*. Cambridge: Cambridge University Press.

Thorndike, E. L. (1932). *Fundamentals of Learning*. Teachers College, Columbia University.

Thorndike, E. L. & Woodworth, R. S. (1901). The influence of improvement in one mental function upon the efficiency of other functions, *Psychological Review*, **8**, 247–261.

Woodworth, R. S. (1938). *Experimental Psychology*. London: Methuen.

Chapter 4

Learning problem-solving skills

K. J. Gilhooly and A. J. K. Green

INTRODUCTION

In this chapter we will be discussing learning aimed at acquiring and improving problem-solving skills that are either domain-dependent (e.g. chess skill) or domain-independent (e.g. skills underlying measured intelligence). First, let us consider the concept of a 'problem'.

Problems come in an unending variety of forms and any general definition of the term is bound to be rather abstract. However, many years ago the Gestalt psychologist Karl Duncker (1945, p. 2) offered a still serviceable definition when he wrote that 'a problem exists when a living organism has a goal but does not know how this goal is to be reached'. Duncker's definition might be rephrased in cognitive science terms by stating that 'a problem exists when an information processing system has a goal condition which cannot be satisfied without a search process'. Note that a goal condition may or may not signal the existence of a problem. If a solving method can be accessed and applied without search then there is no problem. So, a numerate adult does not find '18/3 = ?' a problem, or even '18729/3 = ?'. On the other hand, to find a good move in a given chess position would normally be a problem requiring search, although its difficulty may vary from solver to solver.

Going beyond Duncker's definition, it may be pointed out that most, perhaps all, problems can be described as having a three-part structure (Reitman, 1965). The three main components are a *starting state*, a *goal condition* and a *set of actions* that can be used to transform the starting state in order to meet the goal. An important attribute of these problem components is the degree to which they are *well-* or *ill-defined* (Reitman, 1965). A

Acquisition and Performance of Cognitive Skills. Edited by A. M. Colley and J. R. Beech
© 1989 John Wiley & Sons Ltd

problem as a whole is well-defined if all its components (i.e. the starting state, the goal state and the actions available) are completely specified. Completely well-defined problems are probably only found in the realms of the formal sciences, and in games and pastimes. In other areas of life, problems tend to be more or less ill-defined in one or more components. In practice, most research in psychology has focused on rather well-defined problem-solving. This is a reasonable initial strategy, since the problem interpretation stage is less 'problematic' with well-defined problems.

A useful distinction has been drawn between *adversary* and *non-adversary* problems (Nilsson, 1971). In non-adversary problems, solvers are faced with non-responsive materials that are not trying to defeat the solvers' purposes. In adversary problems, a rational opponent must be faced who is trying to undo the solver's attempts. Thus, adversary problems have an additional layer of complexity compared to non-adversary problems (Winston, 1984).

Recently, the distinction between *semantically rich* and *semantically impoverished* domains has become increasingly important in problem-solving research. To a large extent, this distinction refers to the solver's view of the problem area. A problem is semantically rich for solvers who bring considerable relevant knowledge to the task. So, if someone had just been introduced to the game of GO, a particular problem in the game would be semantically impoverished for that person, but not for a GO master. Recent research has focused on semantically rich problem areas such as game-playing, physics problems, mathematics problems, political analysis and so on. Such areas are ideally suited for examining the nature of problem-solving skills.

DOMAIN-DEPENDENT PROBLEM-SOLVING SKILLS

In this section we will be considering skill in solving semantically rich problems. Most research on this topic has been cross-sectional and has compared experts and novices on what they know and how they use their knowledge in particular domains. Because it usually takes many years of study to acquire expertise in semantically rich domains, there are no studies that have attempted to trace the development of complete complex skills. Despite the unfortunate paucity of data on the growth of skills in semantically rich problem-solving, various theories have been proposed, sometimes in considerable detail, and will be discussed here.

Historically, adversary problems were the first semantically rich domains to be studied from the point of view of expertise. Subsequently, theory developed in that domain has had a major influence on the analysis of skill in other areas. Accordingly, we will discuss adversary problem-solving first and then go on to discuss non-adversary problem-solving.

Adversary problems: the case of chess

The hallmark of an adversary problem is that the actions of a rational opponent must be considered as well as the solver's own actions. Board games are good sources of well-defined adversary problems and among such games, chess has been a favourite target of investigations by psychologists and artificial intelligence researchers. Chess offers a range of complex problems and, of course, players vary very markedly in skill, which makes it a convenient area in which to examine differences in expertise.

First, some idealized notions of how chess and other game-problems might be solved will be outlined below and then we will consider empirical studies aimed at uncovering how humans might actually play.

Looking ahead in game-trees

In simple games, it is possible to set out all the moves, counter-moves, and counter-counter-moves, and so on, in a diagram that looks like an upside-down tree. At the root of the tree is the starting state of the game. From there all the possible moves of the first player lead to a number of different states of the game; and for each of these states there are moves open to the opponent that lead to still other states and so on. This process continues until states are reached from which no further moves are possible, i.e. states in which the first player has won, the second player has won or a draw exists. If players could look ahead from the starting state and envisage the whole game tree then they could infer the best move to make at each turn by using the 'minimax' procedure. This assumes that each player will always make his or her most rational choice and works backwards from the end-states of the game.

Looking ahead through the whole game-tree and minimaxing therefore seems to provide a perfect strategy for solving adversary problems. The drawback which makes the pure method impossible in practical terms is that games of any interest involve trees of astronomical sizes. For example, the complete game-tree for chess is estimated to contain 10^{120} possible sequences of moves. There are a mere 10^{16} micro-seconds per century to explore these alternatives. Even the fastest supercomputers available today cannot dent this vast search problem. How then do humans and computer programs play reasonable games of chess? Computer chess programs typically look ahead completely to a limited depth and assess the states reached at the limit of look-ahead in terms of their promise. These assessments are then used by a minimax type of procedure to select the best-looking move at each of the program's turns. The best rated programs in terms of performance engage in considerable search, often of millions of possible states in the game-tree before making a final decision (see Clarke, 1988, for a review of computer chess). Humans cannot, of course, search to the same extent. We will now consider theory and data on human chess play.

Human chess play: early studies

A popular method of studying thought processes in problem-solving is to ask the subjects to think aloud as they tackle a representative task. The resulting think-aloud records (or protocols) can then be analysed with a view to extracting underlying processes. De Groot (1965) used this method in his pioneering studies of differences between expert and less skilled players when given the problem of choosing a good move in given chess positions.

In De Groot's study, five Grand Master level players and five less skilled (but quite strong) players were given the same chess position to study and were asked to think aloud as they chose the best move. From the protocols their patterns of looking ahead or 'mental search trees' could be abstracted. The following points emerged from these data. Surprisingly, there were only quite small differences in the quantitative aspects of the search trees of the more and the less skilled groups. Both groups looked ahead to about the same depths (6–7 moves), considered a similar number of possible first moves (4) and in total considered a similar number of possible moves and counter-moves (30–55). Despite the lack of quantitative differences, the more skilled group still chose the moves that were significantly better in terms of their ratings by independent experts.

How then do more skilled players choose better moves with no more search than less skilled players? Evidence suggesting a possible explanation emerged from the chess memory task detailed in the next section.

Chess memory studies

De Groot (1965) tested more and less skilled chess players on their memory for chess positions which were presented for only five seconds. Subjects' reconstructions of such briefly exposed positions, involving 20–24 pieces, varied markedly with skill level in the predictable direction. However, the more skilled players' superiority in the memory task only held up if the arrangement of pieces on the board made 'chess sense'. If randomly arranged positions were used then the skilled players' advantage was lost and all players performed equally poorly.

Chase and Simon (1973a, b) argued that these chess memory data mean that expert players know and recognize patterns that are larger in scope than those known and recognized by novice players. These patterns constitute 'chunks' and about seven such chunks are held in short-term memory irrespective of skill level. However, the experts' chunks are richer than the novices'; they are larger units and therefore permit better recall. Chase and

Simon went on to argue that not just chess memory but chess-playing skill might be determined by the number and richness of chess patterns stored in long-term memory. The idea was that the familiar patterns would be associated with recommendations for action. So when a familiar pattern was identified an associated action possibility would be evoked. This view is known as the *Pattern Recognition hypothesis* of chess skill.

The Pattern Recognition hypothesis was explored in a computer simulation, the Memory Aided Pattern Perceiver (MAPP), reported by Simon and Gilmartin (1973). As a result of observing the performance of the MAPP simulation with different numbers of patterns in its equivalent of long-term memory, Simon and Gilmartin estimated that somewhere around 50,000 patterns would be required to simulate expert-level performance on the chess memory task. If the model is correct then expert players have a similar number of patterns in their repertoire. Recently, Holding (1985, p. 109) has pointed out that the number of patterns required can be reduced considerably if it is assumed that the patterns would still be recognizable if they were shifted a few squares or changed from black to white. On these assumptions, the required number of patterns comes down to the more manageable levels of 500–5000. Learning these numbers of patterns would be quite feasible with extended study.

Difficulties with the Pattern Recognition hypothesis of chess skill

Stated baldly, the Pattern Recognition hypothesis states that chess skill levels depend on memory for familiar chess patterns. The contrary view has been argued by Holding (1985) who suggests that things may well be the other way around, that better recognition and memory for chess patterns depend on skill levels and not *vice versa*. In support of this alternative view, Charness (1981a, b) found that even when skill levels were equal, chess memory performance varied inversely with the age of the performer. Thus, chess memory cannot be the sole determinant of chess skill. While Charness's studies showed memory differences without skill differences, Holding and Reynolds (1982) found skill differences without memory differences. In their study, subjects varying in skill level were asked to choose what they considered the best move in chess positions in which the pieces had been randomly arranged. There was a clear increase in the quality of the moves chosen by the subjects as their chess skill ratings increased. However, in a memory test, there was the usual non-effect of skill rating on recall of the random positions.

These studies, showing a dissociation between chess memory and chess skill, imply that the Pattern Recognition hypothesis of chess skill is no longer tenable. Rather than chess skill being determined by chess memory it seems that chess memory is a side-effect of chess skill. In accord with this view, Pfau and Murphy (1988) found in a study of 60 players that rated chess skill was only weakly predicted by chess memory performance ($r = 0.44$ with criterion) but was well predicted by a 75-item chess knowledge test ($r = 0.70$ with the criterion). Thus, general chess knowledge, rather than memory for specific patterns, seems to be the critical factor in chess skill.

Non-adversary problems

We begin this section on non-adversary problem-solving by examining research in the domains of physics, mathematics and political science. Findings are discussed in terms of the quantitative and qualitative differences in performance between experts and novices. We then go on to describe and evaluate recent models of expertise acquisition referring to findings from empirical studies of human learning and computer simulations of learning.

Physics

Physics is a formal domain, meaning that it includes a set of principles logically sufficient to solve physics problems. The difficulty in solving physics problems lies in selecting which principles to apply rather than in the application of principles to generate an equation. How do skilled physicists select useful principles to apply to problems? The advantage of experts may lie in the way principles are stored and accessed from memory. In addition, if problem categories which guide solutions exist, they may give an indication of the way the problem has been represented. One technique used to assess a student's understanding of problems is to ask the student to sort or categorize problems according to their similarity. Evidence exists from related domains such as algebra (Hinsley, Hayes and Simon, 1978), suggesting that solvers represent problems by category and that these categories might direct problem-solving. Chi, Glaser and Rees (1982) asked advanced PhD and undergraduate students to sort physics problems on the basis of similarities in how they would solve them, without actually solving them. Their results gave no evidence for *quantitative* differences between the two skill groups, such as number of categories, number of largest categories or time to categorize, showing that novices were not limited by their capacity to discriminate problems as rapidly as experts. However, *qualitative* differences were apparent in the nature of the categories into which novices and experts sorted the problems. Novices grouped together problems noticeably similar in *surface structure*, i.e. objects and key words referred to in the problem, or a physical configuration involving the interaction of several object components (e.g. a block on an inclined plane).

In contrast, experts did not sort on the basis of similarity in surface structure. Instead, their categories reflected sortings on the basis of *deep structure*, or major physics principles, such as 'Conservation of Energy'.

Indeed, the basis for their categorization could only be appreciated by a physicist. This suggests that knowledge useful for a particular problem is indexed when the problem is categorized as a specific type. These categories probably correspond to problem schemata or 'packets' of knowledge that can be used to solve a particular type of problem.

Part of the skill of expert physicists, then, lies in their ability to categorize a problem appropriately. This ability must depend upon the presence of large-scale units for solving problems. Larkin (1978) set out to examine this by asking two experts and one novice to think aloud while solving textbook physics problems. Hypothesized chunks were constructed by Larkin and physicist colleagues such that each chunk contained one fundamental principle together with those subsidiary principles commonly applied with the fundamental principle. Larkin found that the pairs of equations generated by experts with intervening times of 10 seconds or less were typically 'same chunk' pairs. Those with intervening times of 15 seconds or more tended to be 'different chunk' pairs. In contrast, the novices data fit well the random distribution curve, suggesting that principles were accessed individually.

The finding was not replicated by Chi et al. (1982), who used the same analysis. If anything, their results indicated that the opposite was true, as novices seemed to have generated a greater number of relations in close succession. Unless the discrepancy can be resolved, it cannot be concluded that storage of equations in the knowledge base differs between experts and novices. It may be the case that Chi's novices generated clusters of equations as a result of a problem-solving strategy rather than structure in the knowledge base. If this is the case, it may be useful to repeat the experiment in a problem-free context.

What are the processes through which skilled solvers select useful principles? Larkin (1978) addresses this question, again through the analysis of think-aloud protocols produced by expert physicists as they solved a problem. Rather than examine the experiment in detail, we shall instead refer to the finding that experts seem to engage in a qualitative analysis of the problem prior to generating equations. By 'qualitative analysis' is meant a planning phase involving the generation of inferences essential to solve a problem. It seems that this planning lays the foundation for the successful selection of chunks of principles appropriate to solution. Chi et al. (1982) found that novices also carry out a qualitative analysis of a problem. However, the difference between experts and novices lies in the *quality* of inferences, as novices often fail to draw the necessary inferences.

A good test for the ideas discussed in this section lies in their application. In the same paper, Larkin attempted to teach novices directly the knowledge structures and processes used by experts. A training group received instructions on how to apply principles in chunks and how to elaborate qualitative features relevant to these chunks. A control group received training in systematically applying principles to generate equations. Despite there being only five subjects in each group, the special training group performed significantly better than the control group. Such a finding suggests that one potentially effective means of teaching physics problem-solving may be to use models of the structures and processes employed by experts. Clearly it is necessary to determine whether such a finding can be replicated. Also of interest are questions of individual differences. Do some students profit more from instruction than others?

We have considered differences between experts and novices in the knowledge base, but have not yet examined differences in strategies employed by solvers differing in level of expertise. Larkin, McDermott, Simon and Simon (1980) have shown that novices use a 'working backwards' strategy while experts use a 'working forwards' strategy when solving physics problems. Specifically, novices solve a problem using a näive representation which provides little guidance in selecting principles for application. Thus novices fall back on a rather primitive means-end analysis which involves working backward from the unknown to the givens, gradually eliminating differences between the written equations and an equation that would provide the desired answer. Experts, however, work forward from the givens to the goal, giving the impression that they have the solution procedure available as one large equation or 'large functional unit' as Larkin (1979) describes it. Thus problem-solving is primarily search-driven for the novice and schema-driven for the expert.

Mathematical problem-solving

Previous research in physics suggests that the ability to categorize a problem correctly facilitates the problem-solving process. The correct perception of a problem seems to cue access to a 'problem schema' which suggests a straightforward, stereotypical solution method. At the other extreme an incorrect perception can send the solver up a blind alley. Problem perception, then, is clearly an important component of problem-solving performance. Of interest are the changes that occur in perception with skill acquisition. Specifically, if researchers can identify the critical changes, then mathematical training may capitalize on this and enhance problem-solving performance. We refer here to an experiment with just this goal in mind by Schoenfeld and Herrmann (1982).

The study replicated previous findings that novices sort problems on the basis of surface structure and experts sort on the basis of deep structure. Results also showed that after a month-long course in mathematical problem-solving, an experimental group of subjects subsequently sorted problems significantly more often on the basis of their deep structure than did a control group who had received training in computer programming. This shows that the course, which focused on general mathematical problem-solving heuristics, enhanced performance of the experimental group. One problem with the study lies in the fact that the pre-test and post-test problems were matched for mathematical content. Because of this, it is difficult to determine whether the improvement in performance was 'tied' to the context in which training occurred or whether performance might have generalized to less similar problems. This question of transfer of performance is central to the issue of teaching thinking skills and is discussed in later sections.

Political science problem-solving

Political science problems differ from physics and mathematical problems in that they are typically ill-structured. By this we mean that the goal is often vaguely stated, candidate operators may vary and often there is no agreed-upon solution. Given these additional considerations, how do individuals learn to solve such ill-defined problems and to what extent does the political science expert resemble the physics expert?

We shall refer to a study carried out by Voss, Greene, Post and Penner (1983) who employed think-aloud protocols obtained from expert and novice solvers. The problem facing the subjects was to suggest how to increase crop production in the Soviet Union. One interesting feature of this study was that the researchers also collected protocols from non-expert experts, i.e. individuals expert in political science but not in the domain-area of the Soviet Union and individuals expert in a completely different domain, namely chemistry. This design helps to 'unconfound' some expert-novice differences by attempting to distinguish general world knowledge and general problem-solving strategies from domain-specific knowledge and domain-related strategies. The former may be acquired from a number of sources while the latter are assumed to be acquired within the domain via experiences which provide opportunities to utilize and organize the information.

The results showed that experts on the Soviet Union tended to do a review of the problem from which a representation was built. This may correspond to the qualitative analysis carried out by physics experts. The nature of their solutions was to find one general solution to the problem, such as 'greater capital investment in agriculture', which would also solve a number of subordinate problems. The proposal of a general solution was followed by extensive exploration of the ramifications of the solution and by supportive argumentation. Social scientists unfamiliar with the field of the Soviet Union tended to fall back on general knowledge of political science but did utilize domain-related strategies. Chemists, however, lacked *both* the data base and domain-related strategies and performed at the same level as novices. Of course, the absence of the data base may have precluded use of strategies, and so it cannot be concluded that the chemists simply lacked the relevant strategies. Thus, experience within a domain provides for the acquisition of knowledge and domain-related strategies, which may be content-independent, such as problem conversion, or content-dependent, such as historical analysis.

Voss *et al.* conclude first that learning within the domain involves the development of networks providing information about relations among concepts and facts. Second, the individual acquires knowledge of the inter-dependencies that exist within a domain, which facilitates argumentation in support of solution. Third, the knowledge base becomes hierarchically organized so that some problems, such as lack of fertilizer, become subordinate to a more abstract problem, such as lack of capital investment. In general terms, Voss *et al.* conclude that the political science expert is like the chess master, since experience provides for the development of recognizable 'patterns'. Unlike physics where 'exposing learners to selected, special cases' (Larkin 1979, p. 112) may be crucial, exposure to a *variety* of problem types seems important in political science.

MODELS OF SKILL ACQUISITION

In the following sections, we describe the principal models of skill acquisition and then evaluate each in terms of the empirical findings already discussed. All four models employ the notion of *production systems*. Productions are sets of condition-action pairs which are essentially rules for action. A simple production rule might be:

IF the traffic lights are at red,
THEN stop the car.

While there are obvious similarities between production systems and stimulus-response theories, production systems incorporate a cognitive element which is the critical difference. By 'cognitive element' is meant that the conditions and actions of a rule can refer to cognitive states and actions. This contrasts with stimulus-response theories which focus on the link between external stimuli and elicited responses.

Adaptive Control of Thought (ACT*)

Given the emphasis on knowledge as central to expertise, we begin by briefly outlining Anderson's (1983) model of skill acquisition (see also Chapter 1). Anderson argues that all incoming knowledge is encoded declaratively as a set of facts, such as 'A = B', 'C = D'. These *declarative encodings* are accessed step by step by a procedure subject to capacity limits and under conscious control. How do experts by-pass the lengthy interpretation phase and arrive at solutions automatically and in few steps? The answer, argues Anderson, lies in the manner in which knowledge is *compiled*. Compiled procedures take the form of productions or condition-action pairs. Basically, whenever a production's conditions are satisfied, its corresponding action can be performed. Two processes are hypothesized to accomplish knowledge compilation. The first of these is *proceduralization*. Proceduralization creates specific productions that eliminate retrieval of information from long-term memory by building that information into the rule. We can illustrate this with an example of the GRAPES (Goal-Restricted Production System) simulation of learning to program in LISP drawn from Anderson, Farrell and Sauers (1984).

P1: IF the goal is to code a relation defined on an argument and there is a LISP function that codes this relation,

THEN use this function with the argument and set as a subgoal to code the argument.

If the second part of the condition matches 'CAR codes the first member of a list', retrieval of the CAR definition can be eliminated by making the production specific to 'First Member' and the function CAR, producing the following proceduralized rule:

P2: IF the goal is to code the first member of a list, THEN use CAR of the list and set as a subgoal to code the list.

Proceduralization leads to direct recognition of the application of CAR, in this case, and also reduces the amount of long-term information that needs to be maintained in working memory.

The second process is termed *composition*. Composition collapses repeated sequences of operations to create a macro production which has the effect of the sequence of productions but speeds up the process considerably. The composed action is the sequence of the two original actions. Composition, then, is an abbreviation process while proceduralization is an automation process.

The final stage involves the refining and tuning of productions by processes of generalization and discrimination. *Generalization* requires that the learner formulates rules which capture what two problems and their solutions have in common, so that the rule can be applied when the learner encounters similar problems in the future. *Discrimination* means that the solver imposes restrictions on productions that are too general and apply in incorrect situations by adding a condition which restricts the range of applicability of a production.

Lewis (1981) objects to composition as the sole means for streamlining productions. He describes the formation of combined operations in the domain of algebra in terms of the conversion of a *two-pass* operation to *one-pass* operation. A two-pass procedure scans once for multiplying out and then again for collecting operators. A one-pass procedure combines both operators, thereby increasing efficiency. Lewis argues that composition of productions cannot develop combined operations, because a one-pass system does not *mimic* a two-pass system, and composition produces accurate mimics. With an infinite string of objects, a two-pass system will never progress beyond the stage of applying the first operation. A one-pass system will eventually produce a state where the final operation has been applied to the first object in a string. In short, composition fails because it cannot consider the *range* of possible inputs.

Anderson acknowledges another route to learning which is the process of *subsumption*. Subsumption involves the development of new problem-solving schemata out of old ones and is described by Anderson as a form of learning with structural understanding. There are two forms—elaborating existing schemata to apply to new situations and building new schemata out of existing schemata. (For a full description, see Anderson, Greeno, Kline and Neves, 1981.)

The idea that skill develops by collapsing together multiple steps into one step is a natural one and predicts practice effects such as Einstellung and automatic speed-up. The tuning operators provide a means by which a working backwards strategy can be converted into a working forwards strategy like that described by Larkin *et al.* (1980). Tuning achieves this by inserting additional tests of applicability into the condition side of a production and by adding inferences to the action side. The step-by-step solution becomes a working forward solution. The theory serves to integrate knowledge acquisition and practice, two central components of learning. However, one problem for the theory is in accounting for differences between faster and slower learners with equivalent experience. That novices show differences in performance has been noted by Thorndyke and Stasz (1980) using a map-learning task. One way to interpret this finding is to hypothesize that a hierarchy of processes exists, one set, the *executive*, directing a second set, the *non-executive*. ACT* makes no distinction between such executive processes and non-executive processes, since production rules are held to handle in a unitary way what is handled in a dual way by executive and non-executive processes in a hierarchical theory. There is no executive, as production rules may create and control other production rules, and even modify themselves. One limitation of Anderson's theory may be its failure to consider the effects of individual learning procedures. Another problem for the theory is that it does not readily account for the invention of *new* actions.

Larkin's ABLE model

In this section, we examine the model of expertise proposed by Larkin (1981). Larkin's approach is to characterize the minimal knowledge a learner might acquire from a textbook and then to propose means by which practice might facilitate the application of primitive knowledge to solve problems. The computer-implemented model, ABLE, consists of BARELY ABLE, the novice model, and MORE ABLE, the expert simulation.

BARELY ABLE becomes MORE ABLE by developing its knowledge as it works through problems. Whenever a principle is successfully applied, a production is stored in long-term memory with a condition linking the principle and the situation it was applied in, and an action which incorporates knowledge that can be generated by that principle. BARELY ABLE searches for principles by means of a general domain-independent strategy, means-end analysis, and engages in a degree of backtracking and interpretation of principles.

The model implies that the procedure for finding the correct equation and the desired quantity becomes automated after execution of the initial production. This avoids backtracking and lengthy interpretation, meaning that learning takes place in one trial. In reality, this is seldom the case—some aspects of learning take place faster than others, which may reflect different learning procedures employed by an individual. A second limitation is that the model cannot link a series of productions into one, as Anderson's model can do. Finally, the model simulates learning. Ideally, one would wish to evaluate the model in the context of a longitudinal study showing the transition from working backwards to working forwards.

Since this is a rather lengthy approach, an alternative might be to focus on a very small subset of problems from the problem domain. This approach was adopted by Sweller, Mawer and Ward (1983) who used a subset of kinematics problems. It was found that after solving many problems, subjects switched from a means-end to a forward-chaining strategy. In addition, Sweller *et al.* manipulated goal specificity in order to examine the degree to which the focus on a goal and its influence on the control of moves affected knowledge acquisition. Results showed that reducing the influence of a goal facilitated the acquisition of expertise as measured by use of a forward-chaining strategy. This means that Larkin's model is insufficient to explain skill acquisition. In practical terms too, if the goal of an exercise is to assist problem-solvers in acquiring knowledge concerning problem structure, means-end analysis may not be maximally efficient. A no-goal procedure should result in more exploration and therefore more knowledge of the problem space than the conventional procedure. Indeed, there is some evidence that exploration-based training promotes the use of analogical reasoning in knowledge transfer and facilitates the induction of abstract schemas (Kamouri, Kamouri and Smith, 1986).

Anzai and Simon's theory of learning by doing

Both Anderson and Larkin emphasize the role of knowledge in skill acquisition. One model which focuses primarily on the development of strategies in problem-solving is that of Anzai and Simon (1979). The study examined the evolution of strategies for solving the Tower of Hanoi puzzle in one subject, focusing on the processes that subjects may use to acquire or transform strategies. During the course of learning to solve the problem, the subject generated four different strategies, each one transformed from and more efficient than the one used on the previous trial. These strategies are described as selective forward search, a goal-peg strategy, a goal-recursion strategy and finally, a pyramid subgoal strategy. Analysis of the think-aloud protocol suggested that information stored in long-term memory during the previous trial provided cues for strategy transformation. In addition, it seemed that four kinds of processes occurred in each episode: applying the current strategy, gathering information that would later be used to modify the strategy, using information gathered in previous episodes and deciding when to terminate a solution attempt.

The subjects' behaviour was modelled first by building a production system. While this did not actually model the learning process, it did elaborate on the strategies. The strategy transformation process itself was very simple, since new strategies were dependent only on the strategies that immediately preceded them. In practice, this would suggest that a learner who employs a relatively ineffective strategy early on is likely to be hampered during the course of learning. Therefore individuals who get off to a sticky start are handicapped, not just initially, but over a considerable part of the learning curve. Such an effect has been noted in observational studies of system use (Hammond and Barnard, 1984). As a second stage, an adaptive production system was built, which used similar processes to their subject in developing increasingly efficient strategies. The system began by learning to avoid bad moves by recognizing that it is inefficient to visit the same state twice and by detecting the similarity between two states. By learning to avoid bad moves, the system could narrow its search and begin to acquire a goal-recursive strategy. So if an individual recognizes a segment of the search path as part of the correct route, then the less desirable and longer alternative routes can be avoided. The goal-recursion strategy depends upon the ability to posit goals. For instance, the system might find that a move from a given state creates a new state from which a desired move can be made, therefore, Goal 1 can be seen as a subgoal to Goal 2. A generalized production that is not tied to a specific state might incorporate as the condition, a series of tests for the legality of a move, instead of specifying a given state. The next strategy implemented was the pyramid subgoal strategy. This was the first instance of a specialized strategy, since it referred to an arrangement of disks and was restricted in its range of application. To create a generalized production, the system simply recognized instances in which a sequence of moves always obtains a given subgoal and forms a production to execute the sequence of moves whenever the subgoal is evoked.

The processes described are all general and therefore not tied to the specific task environment, which is critical for a theory of skill acquisition. Briefly stated, the central notion is that if an individual can solve a problem, the correct solution forms a basis for the construction of new, more efficient productions.

Holland *et al.*'s framework for induction

Holland, Holyoak, Nisbett and Thagard (1986) note that standard production systems, because of their seriality, fail to offer a description of parallel processing which may take place at *subcognitive* level. The emphasis tends to be on what occurs at the *conscious level*. We shall briefly consider a parallel processing framework proposed by Holland *et al.* in the context of learning problem-solving skills. The general view of the cognitive system is similar to that of Kelly (1955) in that the system is held to be goal-seeking and actively engaged in trying to reduce uncertainty about the environment, or make accurate predictions.

The framework takes production rules as the basic building blocks of knowledge. The three types of rule are (i) empirical rules, (ii) inferential rules which modify existing empirical rules, and (iii) system-operating rules which serve performance functions, such as resolving conflict among competing rules, and knowledge modification. In a departure from the more traditional production systems such as ACT*, Holland *et al.* acknowledge that a degree of parallel processing takes place. This means that a number of rules may fire simultaneously but only those whose conditions are matched completely will register. The rules which register then enter a 'strength' competition and those which exceed a threshold value will fire.

Central to the issue of the modification is the problem of apportionment of credit. Ideally, a system should isolate and reward rules contributing to success. Holland *et al.* describe this in terms of the 'bucket brigade' algorithm. This simply means that *all* the rules in a successful sequence receive a portion of credit in turn. Rules outside the successful sequence receive no credit.

The generation of new rules occurs through the application of inferential rules. Two related types of rule modification are *generalization* and *specializa-*

tion. Generalization may proceed from rules or from examples and makes an existing rule more general by eliminating part of its condition while discrimination produces a new rule by associating features found in examples.

Specialization serves to combat the problem of overgeneralization which occurs when the conditions of a rule are met but the outcome is a prediction failure. A new rule is derived from the existing rule by modifying the conditions to be met and substituting the unpredicted outcome as the action of the new rule. Generalization and specialization then serve similar functions to Anderson's (1983) tuning mechanisms of generalization and discrimination.

Rules may also be modified through 'abduction'. Abductive hypotheses are constructed to account for a set of facts or an observation. Since abduction demands a search to find the most appropriate explanatory hypothesis, it is desirable that the learner avoids weak or wrong explanatory hypotheses, and the best way to do this seems to be to use multiple abductions which explain a number of facts.

A further interesting aspect of Holland *et al.*'s framework is their discussion of the recombination of existing rules. They propose that the most useful parts of existing structures may be selected for recombination. In this way, the model can account for the creation of new actions, unlike ACT*. An important proposal is that old rules co-exist with new rules, rather than being replaced. This appears counter-intuitive, but does explain certain inconsistencies, such as the fact that knowledge available in one context is not always available in a different, but appropriate context.

The framework as a whole is ambitious and potentially a useful one in which to examine skill acquisition. There is, however, a need to test some of the many hypotheses generated by the approach. Perhaps the most appealing aspect of the framework is the ease with which it deals with individual differences in learning, and in the goals that people pursue. That people pursue different goals implies that certain rules will be of differential value to different people.

DOMAIN-INDEPENDENT PROBLEM-SOLVING SKILLS: INTELLIGENCE AND CREATIVITY

Can people acquire very broad range problem-solving skills applicable to a wide variety of novel problems? If such domain-independent skills could be effectively taught, might people's measured intelligence be boosted and their creativity be enhanced?

In view of the potential practical importance of domain-independent problem-solving skills it is not surprising that a large number of training programmes have been devised with a view to enhancing such skills. (See Nickerson,

Perkins and Smith, 1985, for a thorough review of this area.) Although many of these programmes have been implemented by enthusiastic teachers at all levels of education, relatively few have been subject to even moderately rigorous evaluations. It may be noted also that the sources of such programmes are extremely diverse and include psychometric theories of intelligence and impairment, theories of creativity, problem-solving theories, and developmental psychology as well as sheer intuitition. The great variety of sources and the unevenness of the evaluations makes it very difficult to compare programmes and to draw comparative conclusions.

In the following sections we will first consider two programmes aimed at developing skills in the mainly 'convergent' types of problems that feature in most standard intelligence tests (these are problems with one correct solution). The programmes concerned, Instrumental Enrichment and Project Intelligence, were chosen for discussion here because they are exceptionally thorough-going and have been well evaluated. Second, we will review two proposals (brainstorming and lateral thinking) for developing skills in 'divergent', or creative, problem-solving. In such problems there is no clearly correct answer and emphasis is placed on producing many alternative solutions from which it is hoped that a good option can be selected. Both brainstorming and lateral thinking have been extensively investigated.

Training to boost intelligence

Instrumental Enrichment

The Instrumental Enrichment Programme was developed over a number of years by Reuven Feuerstein. (The programme is fully described in the book by Feuerstein, Rand, Hoffman and Miller, 1980.) It is based on Feuerstein's views (i) that 'intelligence' resides in cognitive modifiability, (ii) that cognitive modifiability is fostered by specific learning experiences and (iii) that if such experiences are not provided naturally during a person's early life, they can be usefully provided later in a remedial programme. By 'cognitive modifiability' is meant the ability to learn and profit from experience. This ability is itself modifiable through appropriate experiences. The particular types of experience that Feuerstein views as necessary are 'mediated learning experiences' which are brought about by the intervention of a mentor who supplies needed cultural information or explicitly points to aspects of learning and problem-solving skills. Feuerstein's approach grew out of his remedial work with culturally deprived young immigrants to Israel in the 1950s and it has mainly been applied to young people who have suffered varying degrees of cultural deprivation.

The programme aims to improve the individual's self-image as an active generator of knowledge rather than as a passive recipient and to boost motivation for learning and problem-solving. More cognitive goals of the programme include stimulating reflective thinking on successes and failures, and acquiring basic concepts, labels and vocabulary useful for describing and carrying out cognitive tasks. The programme involves largely content-free tasks in order to avoid any 'resistances' the learner may have to particular content areas that may be associated with past failures and in order to focus attention on the cognitive processes involved rather than on the content.

The programme comprises 15 'instruments' which are sets of pencil-and-paper exercises aimed at improving particular cognitive functions. The whole set of instruments provides material for more than three to five one-hour lessons per week for two to three years. The instruments are to be used in conjunction with a teacher who provides the necessary mediated learning experiences. The instruments are tools to help the teacher, and are not themselves seen as remediating. Mediation generally involves pointing out to the students the cognitive processes used in working through the exercises. This presumably increases the subjects' level of metacognitive awareness.

The Instrumental Enrichment Programme has been used quite extensively in many different countries and a number of evaluation studies have been carried out. A very full study by Rand, Tannenbaum and Feuerstein (1979) examined the impact of the programme on 86 Israeli adolescents who were described as disadvantaged. Their school performance was some 3–4 years below average levels for their ages (12–15 years). The experimental subjects received an Instrumental Enrichment programme involving some 200 to 300 hours work over a two-year period. An equivalent group of 78 subjects served as controls and were given a so-called General Enrichment programme, which involved remedial work on school subjects. Performance was compared using Thurstone's Primary Mental Abilities test, a specially devised achievement test (the Project Achievement Battery) and two non-intellectual tests (the Classroom Participation Scale and the Levidal Self-concept Scale).

The results indicated that Instrumental Enrichment produced greater gains on both the cognitive and the non-cognitive tests than did General Enrichment. Also, significant differences in favour of the Instrumental Enrichment group were detected two years after the Programme when the adolescents were tested on enlistment into the Israeli Army. Such demonstrations of long-term effects of remediation are highly desirable but rarely available. Furthermore, the data indicated that the gap between the Instrumental Enrichment group and the General Enrichment group had widened as time elapsed. This is in line with Feuerstein's 'hypothesis of divergent effects' whereby individuals whose cognitive modifiability has been increased will learn more effectively and thus show a cumulative gain in time over controls.

Overall the data reported by Rand et al. (1979) are impressive. Few programmes aimed at improving very broad range problem-solving skills have been assessed so thoroughly over such long time periods. There is, however, a question mark over even these results in that the quality of teaching and teacher motivation may not have been as high in the General Enrichment group as in the Instrumental Enrichment condition. (This is one of a number of pervasive problems in 'evaluating evaluations'.)

Project Intelligence

This project was sponsored by the Venezuelan government as part of a general effort to increase intellectual performance throughout society. The project involved researchers from Harvard, Bolt Beranek and Newman, and the Venezuelan Ministry of Education. The researchers devised a set of materials and methods for teaching general thinking skills at the secondary school level. (Fuller details may be found in Herrnstein, Nickerson, de Sanchez and Swets, 1986.)

The course was aimed at improving performance on a range of tasks requiring close observation and classification, inductive and deductive reasoning, careful use of language, hypothesis generation and testing, problem-solving, creative thinking and decision-making. The skills being trained for were very general and were felt to apply to intellectual performance independently of subject area. The skills concerned seem to match most views of the important components of intelligence. Approximately 100 lessons of 45 minutes each were prepared; each lesson was aimed at a specific skill such as 'using tabular representations', 'representing problem spaces', 'analysing complex decision situations'.

To test the utility of the course, approximately half of the lessons were taught to 12 Seventh Grade classes from three schools in the academic year 1982–83. Twelve matched classes from three other schools in the same year served as controls. The schools concerned served deprived areas of a Venezuelan city. There were 463 subjects in the experimental classes and 432 in the control classes. The experimental classes received project lessons for 45 minutes per day for three to four days a week over the school year. The control classes received their normal curriculum.

A number of tests were administered to both experimental and control group subjects immediately before and after the experimental period. These tests comprised both general ability tests (e.g. Otis–Lennon School Ability Test, General Abilities Test) and some special purpose Target Abilities Tests aimed at assessing the target skills the lessons were planned to teach.

The results indicated that while both control and experimental groups showed significant improvements over the period of the study, the experimental group showed considerably larger gains on all the standard general ability tests than did the controls. As might be expected, the largest relative gain by the experimental group was on the Target Abilities Tests (which were specifically related to the experimental training). The results were clearly promising. However, the effects reported were obtained with immediate post-testing and any longer lasting effects are unknown. Also, the controls were not given any equivalent of the project lessons, so they were not a good 'placebo control' group.

Training in creative thinking

Before discussing training in creative thinking techniques it is necessary to consider what is meant by the term 'creative'. Let us begin by defining creative *products*. Creative products, be they poems, scientific theories, paintings or technological advances, are both novel and acknowledged to be valuable or useful in some way. Whether a product is novel or not is relatively easy to determine, although an element of judgement does enter, in that some products are more obviously related to previous developments than others. Objective measurement of novelty is possible in laboratory settings, since the same task can be given to a large number of people (e.g. 'think of ways of improving a doorknob'), and the degree of novelty of proposed solutions can be readily assessed by counting their frequencies of occurrence. When we turn to the quality of a product, subjective judgement looms larger than in the case of judging novelty. However, in science and technology the criteria for quality are clearer than in the arts. A new theory or gadget can be seen to 'work' if it covers more phenomena with no more assumptions than its predecessors (e.g. Einstein's theory compared to Newton's) or meets the function for which it was devised (e.g. the first telephone). Notoriously, there is usually less agreement about the merits of artistic productions, both at the time of their emergence and over history. Initial reactions may well be negative to artistic products that either depart too far from established styles or, at the other extreme, are too conventional.

It is often felt that a major obstacle to creative work lies in the difficulty of overcoming conventional habit-bound ways of thought. Are there any training schemes that might develop skill in the production of divergent or novel ideas? Numerous proposals have been put forward (see Stein, 1974, 1975) for stimulating the idea production stage of creative thinking. Probably the most famous, and certainly the most researched, method is that known as 'brainstorming' (Osborn, 1953). More recently de Bono (1983) has popularized his 'lateral thinking' methods. Since these two approaches have been very widely adopted in education and business we will outline and evaluate them in the following sections.

Brainstorming: basic results

In the 1940s and 1950s a practical businessman, Alex Osborn, developed a package of recommendations known as the brainstorming method. This was intended mainly for use in group problem-solving and as a means of increasing idea production. The method can be adapted for individual use and is described in Osborn's (1953) book *Applied Imagination*. Brainstorming has been taken up quite widely in a variety of organizations and has also been extensively investigated in laboratory settings.

Osborn adopts the view that problem-solving and creative thinking involve (i) problem formulation, (ii) idea-finding and (iii) evaluation of ideas to find a likely solution. Brainstorming aims at facilitating the middle, idea-finding stage and it can be summarized as involving two main principles and four rules.

Principles.
1. Deferment of judgement.
2. Quantity breeds quality.
Rules.
1. Criticism is ruled out.
2. Free wheeling is welcomed.
3. Quantity wanted.
4. Combination and improvement sought.

The 'deferment of judgement' principle meant that evaluation of ideas was to be postponed until a set period of idea production had elapsed. The untutored thinker will tend to evaluate each idea as it is produced. Osborn suggests that this can be inhibiting and may lead to premature abandonment of ideas that, although not useful in themselves, may lead on to possible solutions. The 'quantity breeds quality' principle states that the more ideas produced, the larger the absolute number of useful ones there are likely to be, even if the proportion is very low. The rules listed above remind 'brainstormers' not to criticize their own ideas or those of others, to free associate to ideas already produced, to aim for quantity and to combine and improve suggestions already generated. The method was originally devised for group use but can be adapted for individual applications. The following questions immediately rise, e.g. does the method lead to better productivity (a) for groups and (b) for individuals?

Numerous studies support the hypothesis that groups using brainstorming produce more ideas than similar groups that work along conventional lines. Brainstorming instructions strongly affect the quantity of ideas produced and although effects on *average* quality are not so evident, reports of more high-quality ideas have been obtained (as would be expected by virtue of a 'quantity effect'). An example study is the following by Meadow, Parnes and Reese (1959). They compared the effects of brainstorming instructions with the effects of instructions that stressed the quality of ideas produced. The tasks set the subjects were to think of as many uses as they could for (i) a broom and (ii) a coathanger. Ideas were rated independently for *uniqueness* (the degree to which the suggested use differed from normal use) and for *value* (social, economic or aesthetic). 'Good' ideas were defined as those rated highly on both uniqueness and value. The results indicated that significantly more good ideas were produced with the brainstorming instructions than with the non-brainstorming instructions.

Favourable results on individual brainstorming have also been reported by Parnes and Meadow (1963). In one study, subjects were individually required to think up possible solutions to problems for 5 minutes. On one problem they operated conventionally, evaluating ideas as they thought of them, on the other problem, they used deferred judgement. The first method produced an average of 2.5 'good' ideas, while the second produced an average of 4.3 'good' ideas.

The brainstorming approach attracted considerable research in the 1960s and 1970s (particularly on the relative benefits of individual vs group brainstorming) but very little recent research seems to have been directed at this method. Overall, the approach seems useful for a range of divergent tasks and appears to be easily learned and applied. However, long-term effects and transfer outside the laboratory do not appear to have been investigated.

Lateral thinking

De Bono (1983) has popularized the notion of lateral thinking and has developed instructional materials aimed at teaching lateral thinking skills. Lateral thinking involves re-representing a problem while 'vertical' thinking involves working within a given problem representation. Vertical thinking is seen as logical, sequential, predictable and habit-bound, while lateral thinking would be characterized by the opposite attributes. The instructional materials are known as the CoRT programme (named after de Bono's Cognitive Research Trust). The programme involves six units each of 63 35-minute lessons. The six units are outlined in de Bono (1983) and may be summarized as follows. CoRT 1, 'Breadth', stresses thinking about problems in many different ways. CoRT 2, 'Organisation', aims at effective control of attention. CoRT 3, 'Interaction', focuses on questions of evidence and arguments. CoRT 4, 'Creativity' provides strategies for producing unusual ideas. CoRT 5, 'Information and Feeling', considers affective factors related to thinking. CoRT 6, 'Action', presents a general framework for tackling problems. De Bono suggests that CoRT 1 should be taught first, after which the other units can be used in any order. Broadly speaking, the CoRT lessons involve 'operators' which are given labels that will, it is hoped, help students retrieve and apply the operations when needed. Sample operations are 'consider all factors' or 'CAF', and 'positive, negative and interesting points', or 'PNI'.

De Bono (1976) reports studies in which students who had undergone CoRT instructions produced more ideas than control groups. This certainly suggests a 'quantity' effect; whether average quality was improved is unclear. Also the test questions were similar to the training material exercises and so the extent of transfer of training is unclear. Edwards and Baldauf (1983) carried out an instructional study using CoRT 1 and found that various measures of quantity and quality of divergent thinking improved after the CoRT 1 course. Transfer to performance in physics was investigated but the design did not permit any clear conclusions; there was no clear indication of a transfer from CoRT 1 to physics performance.

Rather stronger evidence supporting the CoRT programme comes from a Venezuelan study (de Sanchez and Astorga, 1983). Large groups of lower class children received training in a modified version of CoRT for periods of one to three years. Control subjects of similar background did not receive these lessons. Pre- and post-tests with divergent problems similar to those used in training showed significantly larger gains on quantity and quality measure for the experimental group compared to the controls. Further, the relative gains increased with the number of years of training.

The results, particularly those of the Venezuelan study, are encouraging for the CoRT programme. However, questions regarding transfer to dissimilar tasks and long-term effects remain open.

OVERALL DISCUSSION AND CONCLUSIONS

The literature on skill in domain-dependent problem-solving centres implicitly or explicitly on the expert. Findings are described in terms of the domain-specific knowledge and strategies possessed by an expert and yet to be acquired by a novice. To a large extent, the chess expert model has been adopted by researchers working in non-adversary domains and the adoption has been a success overall. However, it now seems that the 'modal' pattern-recognition model is under review in adversary domains, such as chess, but with no parallel review in non-adversary domains. This is critical for two reasons. First, an account of problem-solving skill must be parsimonious. Second, the objective of expert-novice contrasting designs has been to identify the factors which make up 'expertise' in the hope that this will yield an insight into how skills are acquired. If accounts of adversary and non-adversary problem-solving proceed in differing directions, conflicting accounts of expertise and skill acquisition may well ensue.

By employing the expert-novice paradigm, some researchers (e.g. Larkin, 1978) aim to 'aid students in learning to solve problems by teaching them directly the knowledge structures and processes used by experts' (p.456). This may not be the most effective approach. Contrasting group designs do not address the question of how expertise developed in the first place, or what facilitates the acquisition of expertise. One might predict differences in speed of learning amongst novices, but a more interesting finding is that experts of equivalent background, intelligence and experience differ in performance on a programming task (Brooks, 1977). Perhaps research should focus more on individual differences in knowledge acquisition.

It has been suggested that an analysis of the development of expertise in terms of psychological theories of learning may be inadequate. Lesgold *et al.* (1988) argue that developmental psychology may provide a better 'fit' considering the time scales involved, than learning theories in accounting for the development of expertise. They back up this assertion with the finding that complex cognitive skills (such as perceptual-diagnostic skill in radiology) may be non-monotonic, resembling the U-shaped behavioural growth curves often noted in developmental psychology (e.g. Brown, 1973). If this proves to be the case, it will be necessary to carry out longitudinal studies of skill acquision in order to characterize the intermediate stages of learning. Perhaps, then, many studies fail to capture the nature of expertise because the wrong question is addressed using inappropriate methods.

Our second point takes us from the novice to the expert again. Studies that contrast expert with novice performance typically employ problems that a novice can solve, although not always easily, and that are routine for an expert, in that they require little if any search. A full account of problem-solving skill should focus on *both* search- and schema-driven problem-solving in experts, as it does already with novices. As Gick (1986) noted, when confronted with highly complex problems, experts must fall back on search-driven strategies.

Our examination of domain-independent problem-solving skills focused on programmes aimed at developing convergent or divergent problem-solving. The two convergent programmes reviewed (Instrumental Enrichment and Project Intelligence) have met with some success and both assume that intelligence is modifiable to a degree. They also highlight some of the difficulties in reviewing thinking skills programmes. Evaluations are often not as rigorously conducted as they might be. Successes are claimed for programmes which lack long-term evaluation, adequate controls or evidence for transfer. The divergent programmes discussed (brainstorming and lateral thinking) have also met with some apparent success, but again suffer from inadequate evaluations.

To conclude, we note that one of the principal problems for thinking skills programmes, until recently, has been the absence of a comprehensive theory of intelligence. As a result, programmes have largely been concoctions based on intuition, commonsense and fragments of models in developmental an cognitive psychology. The recent triarchic theory of intelligence proposed by

Sternberg (1985) and discussed in this volume provides a framework in which to consider both domain-dependent and domain-independent problem-solving skills. In particular, the componential approach to intelligence is useful for conceptualizing thinking which varies in degree of generality.

REFERENCES

Anderson, J. R. (1983). *The Architecture of Cognition*. Cambridge, MA: Harvard University Press.

Anderson, J. R., Farrell, R., & Saunders, R. (1984). Learning to program in LISP, *Cognitive Science*, **8**, 87–129.

Anderson, J. R., Greeno, J. G., Kline, P. J., & Neves, D. M. (1981). Acquisition of problem solving skill, in J. R. Anderson (ed.), *Cognitive Skills and their Acquisition*. Hillsdale, NJ: Erlbaum.

Anzai, Y. & Simon, H. A. (1979). The theory of learning by doing, *Psychological Review*, **86**, 124–140.

Brown, R. (1973). *A First Language*. Cambridge, MA: Harvard University Press.

Brooks, R. (1977). Towards a theory of cognitive processes in computer programming, *International Journal of Man-Machine Studies*, **9**, 737–751.

Charness, N. (1981a). Search in chess: age and skill differences, *Journal of Experimental Psychology: Human Perception and Performance*, **7**, 467–476.

Charness, N. (1981b). Aging and skilled problem-solving, *Journal of Experimental Psychology: General*, **110**, 21–38.

Chase, W. G. & Simon, H. A. (1973a). Perception in chess, *Cognitive Psychology*, **4**, 55–81.

Chase, W. G. & Simon, H. A. (1973b). The mind's eye in chess, in W. G. Chase (ed.), *Visual Information Processing*. New York: Academic Press, pp. 215–282.

Chi, M. T. H., Glaser, R., & Rees, E. (1982). Expertise in problem solving, in R. J. Sternberg (ed.), *Advances in the Psychology of Human Intelligence*, vol. 1. Hillsdale, NJ: Erlbaum.

Clarke, M. (1988). Adversary problem-solving by machine, in K. J. Gilhooly (ed.), *Human and Machine Problem-solving*. London and New York: Plenum Press.

de Bono, E. (1976). *Teaching Thinking*. London: Temple Smith.

de Bono, E. (1983). The cognitive research trust (CoRT) thinking program, in W. Maxwell (ed.), *Thinking: the Expanding Frontier*. Philadelphia: The Franklin Institute Press.

De Groot, A. D. (1965). *Thought and Choice in Chess*. The Hague: Mouton.

de Sanchez, M. A. & Astorga, M. (1983). *Projecto aprendar a pensar*. Caracas: Ministerio de Educacion.

Duncker, K. (1945). On problem solving, *Psychological Monographs*, **58**, Whole No. 270, 1–113.

Edwards, J. & Baldauf, R. B. (1983). Teaching thinking in secondary science, in W. Maxwell (ed.), *Thinking: the Expanding Frontier*. Philadelphia: The Franklin Institute Press.

Feuerstein, R., Rand, Y., Hoffman, M. & Miller, R. (1980). *Instrumental Enrichment*. Baltimore: University Park Press.

Gick, M. L. (1986). Problem solving strategies, *Educational Psychologist*, **21**, 99–120.

Hammond, N. V. & Barnard, P. J. (1984). Dialogue design: Characteristics of user knowledge, in A. F. Monk (ed.), *Fundamentals of Human–computer Interaction*. London: Academic Press.

Herrnstein, R. J., Nickerson, R. S., de Sanchez, M. L. & Swets, J. A. (1986). Teaching thinking skills, *American Psychologist*, **41**, 1279–1289.

Hinsley, D. A., Hayes, J. R. & Simon, H. A. (1978). From words to equations: meaning and representation in algebra word problems, in P. A. Carpenter and M. A. Just (eds), *Cognitive Processes in Comprehension*. Hillsdale, NJ: Erlbaum.

Holding, P. H. (1985). *The Psychology of Chess Skill*. Hillsdale, NJ: Erlbaum.

Holding, D. H. & Reynolds, J. R. (1982). Recall or evaluation of chess positions as determinants of chess skill, *Memory and Cognition*, **10**, 237–242.

Holland, J. H., Holyoak, K. J., Nisbett, R. E. & Thagard, P. R. (1986). *Induction: Processes of Inference, Learning, and Discovery*. Cambridge, MA: MIT Press.

Kamouri, A. L., Kamouri, J. & Smith, K. H. (1986). Training by exploration: facilitating the transfer of procedural knowledge through analogical reasoning, *International Journal of Man/Machine Studies*, **24**, 171–192.

Kelly, G. C. (1955). *The Psychology of Personal Constructs*, vols. 1 & 2. New York: Norton.

Larkin, J. H. (1978). Problem solving in physics: structure, process, and learning, in J. M. Scandura & C. J. Brainerd (eds), *Structural/process Models of Complex Human Behaviour*. The Netherlands: Sijthoff & Noordhoff.

Larkin, J. H. (1979). Information processing models and science instruction, in J. Lochhead & J. Clement (eds), *Cognitive Process Instruction*. Philadelphia: Franklin Institute Press.

Larkin, J. H. (1981). Enriching formal knowledge: a model for learning to solve textbook physics problems, in J. R. Anderson (ed.), *Cognitive Skills and their Acquisition*. Hillsdale, NJ: Erlbaum.

Larkin, J. H., McDermott, J., Simon, D. P. & Simon, H. A. (1980). Models of competence in solving physics problems, *Cognitive Science*, **4**, 317–345.

Lesgold, A., Rubinson, H., Feltovich, P., Glaser, R., Klopfer, D. & Wang, Y. (1988). Expertise in a Complex Skill: Diagnosing X-ray Pictures, in M. Chi, R. Glaser & M. Farr (eds), *The Nature of Expertise*, Hillsdale, NJ: Erlbaum.

Lewis, C. (1981). Skill in algebra, in J. R. Anderson (ed.), *Cognitive Skills and their Acquisition*. Hillsdale, NJ: Erlbaum.

Meadow, A., Parnes, G. J. & Reese, H. (1959). Influence of brainstorming instructions and problem sequence on a creative problem solving test. *Journal of Applied Psychology*, **43**, 413–416.

Nickerson, R. S., Perkins, D. N. & Smith, E. E. (1985). *The Teaching of Thinking*. Hillsdale, NJ: Erlbaum.

Nilsson, N. J. (1971). *Problem Solving Methods in Artificial Intelligence*. New York: McGraw-Hill.

Osborn, A. S. (1953). *Applied Imagination*. New York: Scribner.

Parnes, G. J. & Meadow, A. (1963). Development of individual creative talent, in C. W. Taylor & F. Baron (eds), *Scientific Creativity: its Recognition and Development*. New York: Wiley.

Pfau, H. D. & Murphy, M. D. (1988). The role of verbal knowledge in chess skill, *American Journal of Psychology*, **101**, 73–86.

Rand, Y., Tannenbaum, A. J. & Feuerstein, R. (1979). Effects of instrumental enrichment on the psychoeducational development of low functioning adolescents, *Journal of Educational Psychology*, **71**, 751–763.

Reitman, W. (1965). *Cognition and Thought*. New York: Wiley.

Schoenfeld, A. H. & Herrmann, D. J. (1982). Problem perception and knowledge structure in expert and novice mathematical problem solvers, *Journal of Experimental Psychology: Learning, Memory, and Cognition*, **8**, 484–494.

Simon, H. A. & Gilmartin, K. (1973). A simulation of memory for chess positions, *Cognitive Psychology*, **8**, 165–190.

Stein, M. (1974–75). *Stimulating Creativity*, vols 1 & 2. New York: Academic Press.

Sternberg, R. J. (1985). *Beyond I.Q: a Triarchic Theory of Human Intelligence*. New York: Cambridge University Press.

Sweller, J., Mawer, R. F., & Ward, M. R. (1983). Development of expertise in mathematical problem solving, *Journal of Experimental Psychology: General*, **112**, 4, 639–661.

Thorndyke, P. W. & Stasz, C. (1980). Individual differences in procedures for knowledge acquisition from maps, *Cognitive Psychology*, **12**, 137–175.

Voss, J. F., Greene, T. R., Post, T. A., & Penner, B. C. (1983). Problem solving skill in the social sciences, in G. Bower (ed.), *The Psychology of Learning and Motivation*, vol. 17. New York: Academic Press.

Winston, P. H. (1984). *Artificial Intelligence*, 2nd edn. Reading, MA: Addison-Wesley.

Chapter 5

The componential approach to learning reading skills

John R. Beech

INTRODUCTION TO THE COMPONENTIAL APPROACH

Children learn to read by gradually acquiring a complex assemblage of skills. These reading skills develop at the same time as other areas of intellectual growth, indeed, the development of reading skills may well encourage development in other intellectual areas as well. But some children, even though their intellectual development proceeds normally and even though they have no gross neurological, sensory or emotional problems and have good socioeconomic opportunity, still have problems in learning this complex assemblage. Why should this be? Many studies have shown an association between particular cognitive tasks and reading ability. This association could be produced as a result of problems in the development of a component or components of reading skill having a deleterious effect on reading development. However, viewed another way, the improved cognitive task performance of good readers could be a reflection of the progress of extra components developed by skilled readers that are not directly connected with the component skills involved with reading. Therefore, the 'impaired component' explanation has to demonstrate that the improved component found in good readers really was responsible, or partially responsible, for improving their reading development and was not a consequence of reading development. This chapter reviews such issues from the perspective of the componential

Acquisition and Performance of Cognitive Skills. Edited by A. M. Colley and J. R. Beech
© 1989 John Wiley & Sons Ltd

approach, and begins by critically examining various components of the reading task.

Sternberg (1977) proposed that a complicated skill can be divided into a set of components, a process which he called 'componential analysis'. In broad terms, the componential approach in this chapter proposes that a normal child with normal intellectual development needs to reach a certain level of attainment in a particular component of reading in order to proceed at the normal rate of reading development. The implication of this proposal is that training in that particular component should improve the general level of reading. But as will be seen, extracting meaning from individual words can be achieved by three contrasting routes which can each be specified in many different ways. This complicates matters further because, supposing a child is experiencing problems using a particular route, what should the training strategy be? Should one train the child's strengths so that reading is improved for the strongest route, possibly at the expense of the others, or should one train the child's weak areas? The componential approach would suggest the latter, especially if a particular weakness were instrumental in retarding reading development.

Considering the componential approach in juxtaposition to the 'reading effect' explanation has other pedagogic implications. Elaborating the reading effect explanation further, the cluster of cognitive deficits associated with reading performance in the poor reader is not considered to be influential in causing the reading problem. Looking elsewhere for the reason for the reading problem, it could be argued that retardation in reading is what one might expect from the normal distribution of performance in the development of many cognitive skills. Since it is unclear why particular children are lagging in reading, perhaps the best way to teach reading involves a general onslaught on training *all* the skills of the children. By analogy, the doctor treats the patient with a range of drugs. By contrast, the componential approach implies that somehow one finds the problem area and the child undergoes training specifically on this task. However, to be realistic, other components of the reading task would not be neglected during the training period. All studies undertaking specific training programmes have done so while the child receives normal classroom teaching. The analogy with the doctor would be that one of the new 'magic bullet' drugs intended for a specific area would be administered.

A final point to make in this introduction to the componential approach is that it could have the 'spread of effect' problem. It may be the case that a component skill is impaired, or at least is lagging in development. But its actual effect is to retard progress in other reading skills at the same time. Thus it might be difficult to differentiate an impaired component problem from a reading effect problem. Other cognitive areas might also be impeded, but they might be impairments unrelated to reading. Consequently, there may be a problem in selecting the area of deficiency. Apart from the negative aspect of the spread of effect problem, there is also the positive side that will be examined later. A training programme on the specific component could produce a generalized improvement in other components.

A detailed model of reading development needs to be elaborated and tested to get a clearer picture of how components might related to one another. There is an implication in this componential model that the development of processes follows in sequence from one to another. A stages notion of reading development perhaps has its limitations (Beech, 1987), but there may be certain limited sequences of development, in which retardation of one process in the sequence retards progress in the rest. In the following sections various components of the reading process are examined in detail. As in the old idea of 'chunking' in memory (Miller, 1956), in which there was the problem of defining a chunk, there is a problem here in defining what we mean by a component of a skill. For the purposes of exposition, fairly large units will be taken, but they can be broken down into subcomponents.

COMPONENTS OF READING DEVELOPMENT

The grapheme-to-phoneme converter

The phonics approach to teaching reading is aimed at developing the grapheme-to-phoneme converter or GPC. Graphemes consist of a letter or letters that represent one phoneme, but identifying graphemic units is not an easy task in some cases. In the phonics method the individual sounds constituting words are emphasized to help the child identify individual words. Such an approach relies on exposing the child to large numbers of regularly spelled words which generate phonemes in a fairly unambiguous manner. Unfortunately, the more frequent the usage of words, the greater the likelihood that there is not a direct correspondence between spellings and sounds, so constructing such texts can be difficult. However, although identification using the GPC might ultimately be slower than an approach that emphasizes a 'whole-word' method, it usually generates the word closest in sound to the actual word. If the word is in a context, this can further narrow down the likely identity of the word. For instance, if the word is *bread* in the following context: *In order to make a sandwich, she cut the bread*, the word *bread*, might generate /brid/ (rhymes with need) and /bred/ (correct pronunciation, but a less frequent connection between grapheme and phoneme) via the GPC, but be finally identified by the context of the sentence.

The GPC involves a number of processes during its development, and retardation in any of these may be responsible for arresting its progress. One subcomponent which has received much attention is that concerned with 'phonemic awareness', that is, the ability to recognize the individual phonemes in a word. This is because, in order for the GPC to operate effectively, the graphemes have to be identified, a phoneme has to be generated for each one and then the phonemes have to be blended. Finally, the phonological code that has been generated has to be identified by the auditory lexicon. To complicate matters, some kind of memory is involved in order to retain information at various points during these processes and, as mentioned before, there can be alternative phonemes generated from the same grapheme.

To return to phonemic awareness, there is much evidence indicating a strong connection between phonemic awareness and reading problems (see Bryant and Goswami, 1987, Wagner and Torgesen, 1987, for recent reviews). A componential approach would query the nature of this relationship. A deficiency in phonemic awareness might be retarding the development of the GPC, which in turn might be affecting overall reading development. On the other hand, the reading effect explanation might suggest that children who develop normally in reading learn that words consist of a limited set of letters with relatively invariant sounds connected to each. Continuously encountering these sorts of connections builds up their knowledge of phonemes in a way unavailable to readers not developing normally for their age. A way to test this, and a method actually carried out by Bradley and Bryant (1983, 1985), is to obtain a group of children lagging behind in phonemic awareness, train them on that particular skill, and then to compare them on their subsequent reading development with a similar group which is given training on an unrelated skill. Apart from running these phonemic training and 'placebo' training groups in this manner, Bradley and Bryant also used a group given no training and another group given training on phonemic awareness and on the connection between letters and their sounds via the use of plastic letters. This last group was given training closest to the likely skills required of a GPC and these children were significantly better at reading by the end of the study relative to the placebo training group. However, although the phonemic awareness group had improved relative to the placebo controls, they had not improved to a significant extent. There were similar differences in spelling, and when tested many years later in 1986 these differential improvements in the children, by now 13 years of age, were still preserved (mentioned briefly in Bradley, 1988).

This study is an illustration of the componential approach. Children were identified at the age of 4 and 5 years of age as being deficient in a skill potentially useful for the development of the GPC. Obviously, as they had not started to learn to read at this age (Bradley and Bryant checked that they could not read), they could not be tested for their level of GPC skill. The plastic letters group were given training to rectify this phonemic deficiency (40 sessions of 15 minutes each spread over two years) as well as rudimentary training in letter-sound connections. Although Bradley and Bryant did not test to see whether there was a specific improvement in the GPC, nevertheless, they found a significant improvement in reading and spelling relative to the placebo training group at the age of 8 or 9 years. The reading tests used were the Schonell, a test of the visual lexicon by reading isolated words which increase in orthographic irregularity with reading age, and the Neale which tests the visual lexicon and the reading of text.

Thus there seems to have been a general improvement in the standard of reading. It would have been interesting to have had data on the relative performance on non-words as an indication of the development of the GPC. This would have confirmed whether the training had produced substantial improvements in the GPC, and whether this had led to a spread of effect across a wide range of reading skills. The inferred connection between improvement in the GPC and a spread of effect improving overall reading is enigmatic. One possibility, suggested by Barron (1981), is that using the GPC makes children attend to the sequencing and positional aspects of the letters in words rather than to more structural aspects such as the word outline. For example, Barr (1974–75), comparing phonics and whole-word readers, noted that the erroneous responses to words of phonics readers were more likely to have letters in common to the actual word (e.g. 'Kate' for *cat*), whereas the initial consonant matched only 7 per cent of the time compared with 28 per cent for whole-word readers. The phonics readers produced words with no matching letters 18 per cent of the time and the whole-word readers 28 per cent. It seems that whole-word readers pay more attention to the initial letter but rather less to the rest of the letters in the words. Thus explicit GPC training probably encourages the coding of more letters in a word. Another possible explanation why GPC training generalizes to overall reading is suggested tentatively by Bryant and Bradley (1985) who propose that backward readers, in particular, normally dissociate their knowledge of the sound pattern of words in the visual lexicon from its visual structure. Their plastic letters group categorized words simultaneously in terms of their shared sounds *and* common appearance (e.g. *cat*, *hat*, *mat*, etc.). These were important connections to make.

A third explanation, suggested by Jorm and Share (1983), is that the GPC may be used as a back-up mechanism should the lexical route fail. The lexical route depends on the capability of retrieving information from the visual lexicon; if the information is irretrievable and a GPC does not function, the means to identification are severely limited. Therefore, having a functioning GPC provides a decoding mechanism, which provides continuity for decoding ongoing text. This in turn provides confidence and practice for the development of the skill of reading.

In another training study, Bradley (1988) selected four groups of children with normal sound categorization skills. Teaching environment, reading, spelling and vocabulary were matched across the groups. There were 28 training sessions lasting for 10 minutes each over a 4-month period beginning in the second school term. One group was equivalent to the plastic letters group of the previously described study in that they were always given training in phonemic awareness and on the sounds of individual letters in the same training session. A second group was given both phonological training and training with plastic letters, but in separate sessions. The third and fourth groups had only phonological or only visual orthographic training, respectively. The children were then tested one month after training, which was eight months after the pre-tests and again at the end of their third year. The first group, taught both strategies in combination, was significantly better at reading on the Neale than the second and third groups, but not significantly better than the fourth group. The advantage of the first group disappeared by the third year. Children with normal phonological skills benefit from training on components of the GPC in the short term in relation to their reading performance, as long as the training also covers the connections between the subcomponents. Direct training on the GPC without phonological training (Group 4) also seems to be useful for word decoding skills but not for comprehension. As noted previously, the longer term effects of such training are apparent in children who are initially deficient in phonological skills (Bradley and Bryant, 1983). It could be that the normal children in the Bradley study might also have demonstrated longer term gains if they had been trained to the same extent. In a further study (mentioned in Bradley, 1988) older backward readers made little progress in reading and spelling using the same design, but those with difficulties in sound categorization made good progress.

These studies overall lend support to the notion that a deficiency in the skill of sound categorization, if rectified by training in phonological and GPC skills, leads to a general improvement in reading. It is hypothesized that this is because such training directly facilitates the operation of the GPC, as long as the training establishes the important connections in the context of the developing GPC (in this case via the use of plastic letters). It is therefore interesting to compare such training studies with the work of Gittelman and Feingold (1983) suggesting that the sound categorization element in phonics teaching may not be so essential. They had two groups of backwards readers with a mean age of 10 years, one of which was given phonics training, and the other placebo training in academic subjects. At the end of training involving four months of visiting a clinic three times a week, the phonics group were on average 12 months ahead in reading compared with the other group. When tested eight months later this improvement persisted. The programme also included whole-word recognition to counteract an overdependence on the possibly laborious operation of the GPC. A phonetics test at the end of treatment demonstrated the greatest gains of all the reading measures but there was a lack of improvement in spelling. On the Rosner test, which analyses auditory analytic skills, both groups improved slightly. This might indicate that training phonemic awareness need not be a key aspect in the training of the GPC. Bradley's study demonstrated an improvement given plastic letters in the absence of phonemic training, while the phonemic training in conjunction with plastic letters training was slightly better, but not significantly so.

The precise role of the developing GPC in relation to other components, such as the developing visual lexicon, is open to question. Beech (1987) has specified ways in which the GPC might develop in conjunction with direct lexical access. Doctor and M. Coltheart (1980) have suggested that the GPC is used to generate a phonological code prior to lexical access, whereas Henderson (1982) and V. Coltheart, Laxon, Keating and Pool (1986) proposed that words are first identified via the visual lexicon and are then transformed by a post-lexical phonological code. V. Coltheart et al. suggested that visual access develops first, followed by the slower development of the GPC, and this is a view shared by Ehri and Wilce (1985). However, this pattern may be just a reflection of the different teaching methods used for subjects in individual studies.

Wagner and Torgesen (1987) have reviewed several studies demonstrating that phonological processing prior to formal education is significantly associated with subsequent reading, holding IQ constant. But they also examined the reading effect hypothesis and found supporting evidence that the process of learning to read facilitates phonological awareness. Remember that the Gittelman and Feingold (1983) study suggests that this is not invariably the case. However, the studies cited by Wagner and Torgesen were as follows. Alegria, Pignot and Morais (1982) examined two groups of 6-year-olds who had undergone four months of either phonics or whole-word training in reading and found that the phonics group were much better than the whole-word group on a phonemic reversal task (58 vs 15 per cent correct). Similarly, Read, Zhang, Nie and Ding (1986) made a comparison between Chinese readers taught in *pinyin*, an alphabetic system, with those taught in the Chinese logographic system. Again, the alphabetic readers had superior phonemic awareness compared with the other group. Perfetti, Beck and Hughes (1981, see Perfetti, 1985) tested children four times during First Grade either by a phonics or whole-word method. For both types of trained reader, ability in sound blending measured on a prior occasion predicted performance on reading non-words, which is a good measure of GPC skill, as mentioned before. They also found that on the third testing the preceding ability on reading non-words predicted subsequent performance on phoneme deletion, which required a more advanced form of phonological development. This suggests that learning to read was facilitating more advanced features of phonemic awareness. Note that these results occur irrespective of the type of training in this particular study. At least we may conclude that there is evidence for bi-directional influences. It seems likely that development of the GPC is facilitated by a reasonable level of phonological awareness, but the process of learning to read also promotes the further development of phonemic awareness. However, in studies such as these it is difficult to know whether or not phonological awareness was explicitly taught as part of the phonics programme. But at least in the Perfetti *et al.* study even the whole-word method produced improved phonemic awareness.

Direct lexical access

The whole-word approach to reading aims to promote the development of a visual lexicon without recourse to the use of an intervening phonological code. It is likely that the majority of normal fluent reading operates this way and this style of reading is encouraged in the early stage by giving the child a limited set of highly frequent words irrespective of their spelling regularity. The acquisition of reading via direct lexical access has not generated as much research interest, even though it is the most widely used teaching method; or at least, it is the predominant method with phonics training gradually introduced at a slightly later stage.

Lesgold, Resnick and Hammond (1985) made a comparison between the whole-word method and a phonics approach in two groups of multiracial children from First to Third Grade. The phonics method trained on word decoding skills as well as comprehension in an individualized manner, whereas the whole-word method was more eclectic and not so individualized. Performance was assessed by means of progress in the development of the visual lexicon at set points in each course. The children taught by the phonics method were rather slower on a test of word-reading latency, especially in the initial stages; furthermore accuracy on this same test was better for the whole-word group, with the difference more exaggerated towards the end of the experiment. Thus children decoding via the GPC were slower and less accurate than those using a strategy of direct access to the visual lexicon. A further problem for the phonics group was that irregular words would generate phonological representations at variance with the correct phonological code for the word. On the other hand, a developed GPC helps the identification of words previously unseen. The direct lexical access reader might apply analogical processes, described in the next section. Thus both these contrasting approaches have positive and negative aspects for the beginning reader.

A detailed study by Seymour and Elder (1986) has been made of a class of beginning readers in a Scottish school in their first year in which phonics teaching was restricted to spelling and writing. Thoughout the year each child was tested on a regular basis in an adjoining room by the presentation of about 20 items each time to give a total of 400 items throughout the year. The word-naming responses and latencies were recorded and, with the exception of one child, it was noticeable that although there was a reasonable level of accuracy on previously taught words, performance on unfamiliar words was very poor. The exceptional subject (PM) had a reading age of 8 years 11 months by the end of the year, and Seymour and Elder proposed that he had spontaneously developed a GPC, and furthermore, that he seemed to acquire new words very easily. Thus he could have been decoding words phonically or it could have been possible that he was actually familiar with the so-called unfamiliar words having encountered them outside school in different contexts.

There were three aspects of the response data examined to check for GPC usage. These were overt signs of lip movements and whispers, generation of non-word responses (neologisms) and regularizations in which irregularly spelled words were pronounced as if converted by the GPC (e.g. /ov/ for *of*). The neologisms and regularizations were highly infrequent for all subjects, even for the subject PM, and phonological mediations were also infrequent; but PM and two other subjects made twenty or more such responses. However, phonological mediation may also be a post-lexical phenomenon. When the children were given phonics teaching in their second year, a large number of neologisms and regularizations appeared. Thus at least these two measures appear to be sensitive to GPC operations.

Seymour and Elder investigated further these children who were developing their reading in the absence of GPC mediation. The response latencies to correctly named words for most of the children increased with word length but none of the latency slopes reached significance. This indicates the absence of a letter-by-letter serial process. Further classification of reading errors revealed that where subjects made an error: (i) it was much more likely that the word would come from a word in the set of words previously taught; (ii) it was likely that the erroneous word had the same length as the presented word and had other visual similarities, especially salient letter features; (iii) other kinds of errors such as episodic, semantic and derivational errors did not seem to be very common.

In another experiment Seymour and Elder distorted the format of the presented words to test whether the children were learning *gestalts*, that is, whole invariant configurations. The three formats, normal zigzag and vertical, are illustrated as follows:

yellow   y$_e$l$_l$o$_w$ y
                                         e
                                         l
                                         l
                                         o
                                         w

They found that only one child was unable to read the distorted words and for the rest there was a wide range of results from some relatively unaffected to others who were drastically impaired. They concluded that the gestalt explanation was disconfirmed and that the operation of the visual lexicon varied in its tolerance of such distortions across subjects. Seymour and Elder found a significant association between subjects' ability to tolerate the distortion and the acquisition of sight vocabulary. However, the effect of IQ was not partialled out in this analysis.

The Seymour and Elder study is unique in offering a fine-grained empirical analysis of developing visual lexicons in the relative absence of a GPC. The componential approach would use this information to devise a training programme to help those children who did not make normal progress. In fact, two children by the end of the year could read, or as Seymour and Elder would put it, 'discriminate', more than 100 words; but six were reading fewer than 40 words. Seymour and Elder viewed the development of the lexicon as involving the continuous refinement of a visual discrimination system. New words are identified on the basis of how they might be discriminated in relation to words already within the visual lexicon which have a similar length and which are possibly coded in terms of only one or two salient letters. It would be interesting to devise an experiment to test children before they learn to read on the principles of such discrimination using pictorial stimuli and then to relate this to the subsequent acquisition of a visual lexicon. If a positive relationship were to be found, this would be the way forward for an experiment analogous to the Bradley and Bryant training experiment, in that those retarded in discrimination skills might be given a special training programme. There have been a few studies in the past giving visual training (Bieger, 1974, 1978; Rosen, 1966, 1968) but these did not produce an improvement in reading. However, the training ought to be oriented specifically to the kinds of discrimination skills required for the developing visual lexicon.

A discussion of lexical processing without phonology is not complete without mentioning the 1985 study by Campbell and Butterworth of a student who had developed a normal visual lexicon seemingly without the development of a GPC. This was discovered when they found that she could not read even the simplest non-words. Thus although the previous section presented evidence of how a normally developing GPC facilitated overall reading development, nevertheless, it is not a *sine qua non* for fluent reading.

Analogical coding

An analogical strategy is employed when a word is identified by retrieving and matching part of the orthographic structure to a similarly spelled word within the visual lexicon. This implies that it is a strategy employed when there is already some information stored in the lexicon. Further implications of the developmental role of this mode of processing are examined by Baron (1977, 1979), Beech (1987), Goswami (1986), Marsh, Desberg and Cooper (1977) and Marsh, Friedman, Desberg and Saterdahl (1981).

Goswami examined the use of analogy by normal children. Each child had six experimental sessions in which real words and non-words were read while the same 'clue' word was present throughout (e.g. 'beak'), but no instruction on potential usage of the clue word was given. The clue word was different for each session. For the children who could read they found an enhancement in accuracy (relative to a previous session reading the words without the presence of the clue word) if the clue word shared the beginning orthographic sequence (e.g. *beak-bean*) or end sequence (e.g. *beak-peak*). This effect occurred for both words and non-words and for both a group of readers with a mean reading age of 6 years and 10 months and for a group with a mean of 7 years and 4 months. By contrast, when the clue word was not analogous (e.g. *beak-rain*) there was no significant enhancement. Furthermore, the end of the word was more influenced by analogy than the beginning.

A further analysis confirmed the lack of change in the use of analogy as a function of reading age, by correlating the extent of enhancement with reading age for both beginning and end analogies. None of the correlations was significant. This finding is at variance with a proposal of Marsh and Desberg (1983) that the use of analogy develops at a later stage. Of course, demonstrating that the young readers are influenced by the clue word in these experimental situations does not imply that analogies are used spontaneously by children in the course of their normal reading. Goswami may be overstating the case to suggest that 'analogy may play an important role in reading development' (p. 80). For example, Barr's beginning whole-word readers, mentioned earlier, made erroneous responses which had a tendency to have an *initial* letter in common with the actual word, relative to the phonics readers, whereas Goswami's experiment would predit a tendency to have the end of the word in common. Thus validation of the use of analogy in a natural setting would be well served by examining reading errors and on present evidence the influence of analogy does not appear to be strong.

However, Goswami's study illustrates that analogy could potentially be used by young readers as a means of enhancing their identification of a word, irrespective of whether the reading style of the child is phonically or lexically oriented. What would be particularly valuable would be the encouragement of the child to make comparisons between words, which should be a further stimulation of the discrimination process. It has been previously suggested that enhancing GPC usage in turn improves overall reading, perhaps because the child is making further and finer discriminations of letters in words in terms of their identity and sequencing. The encouragement of the use of analogy would, among other things, emphasize the orthographic-phonological connections between words. For example, the child would learn that many orthographic patterns can represent different phonological codes (e.g -int—pint or hint).

Comprehension

So far we have concentrated on the decoding skills of individual words. However, ultimately the meaning of the text has to be grasped. Children will not be motivated to sustain their reading if they find great difficulty in extracting such meaning. Frederiksen (1982), an advocate of a componential view of reading, suggested that the components of reading might be grouped into word decoding skills (already described here), discourse analysis and integration. He proposed that the aim of developing reading ability is to become so skilled on each component that they each operate virtually automatically. This would mean that the components can operate in parallel without mutual interference. This point will be examined more critically later. Discourse analysis and integration reflect two levels of comprehension of text. In the former, the relationships between the propositions expressed in the text are formed, in the latter, the reader uses 'top-down' knowledge, such as generating expectancies of what should follow. Frederiksen's three components were operationalized to include pronouncing real words and non-words for word analysis, anaphoric reference for discourse analysis and the influence of a semantic context on word recognition for integrative processes. Performance on these tasks correlated well with performance on general reading ability.

At one stage Perfetti (1977) proposed that some children may have adequate word decoding skills in terms of accuracy, but be slow in identification. This in turn would impede working memory and reduce resources for comprehension. This 'decoding bottleneck' hypothesis would fit in with the predictions of Frederiksen (1982) but there are contradictory findings. For example, on the one hand Fleisher, Jenkins and Pany (1979) found no improvement in comprehension for poor readers trained in rapid decoding, whereas support for the hypothesis comes from Lovett (1987) who compared slow-reading-rate children with normal readers matched on accuracy and found that the rate-disabled readers experienced interference in comprehension.

A study by Yuill and Oakhill (1988) is a direct investigation of Frederiksen's three components. They trained three groups of subjects on rapid decoding skills, standard comprehension exercises or in making high-level inferences. The training periods were quite short (roughly 30 minutes each, seven sessions over 4 weeks) and the subjects were either good or poor comprehenders matched in age and word decoding skill. They found no improvement for the skilled comprehenders, but for the poor comprehenders there was a striking improvement of 17 months, on average, for the inference training group which was a significantly greater improvement than that for the rapid decoding group, but this was not significantly different from a 14 month improvement of the comprehension exercises group. Again, this is a case of a skill deficiency being identified and trained to good effect.

Eye movements

Eye movements and memory for the spatial location of text have a role to play in fluent reading and might be thought of as comprising a component of reading which develops with practice. A regressive saccade while reading text is very often precisely located and is unaffected by the distance required to make the regression (Kennedy and Murray, 1986, reported in Kennedy, 1987). In a study examining eye movements and poor reading Kennedy and Murray (1986) tested three groups of children. Two groups were matched in age (10–11 years) and non-verbal IQ, but differed in reading quality, and the third were younger normal readers but matched in reading with the older poor readers. The task was to read a 10–12 word sentence followed by a 4–5-word question (all on the same line) which was responded to by pressing a button. The sentences contained anaphoric references, in other words, pronouns which were separated some distance from their antecedents. It was found that good readers made a single, long and accurate regressive saccade to locate remote antecedents, whereas the poor readers were less efficient. Most commonly, they read the sentence again from the beginning; less frequently they 'backtracked' making a right-to-left series of fixations. Furthermore, they were also 10 times more likely to respond initially by closing their eyes or giving a series of short blinks. Interestingly, the younger group or normal readers behaved more like the good readers. As the relevant statistical comparisons were all significant, Kennedy (1987) proposed that such differences may be a possible cause of reading failure, particularly as it indicates that poor readers sometimes seem unable to locate crucial information. This may be yet another skill which would be worthwhile training.

ALTERNATIVES TO THE COMPONENTIAL APPROACH

In case the reader might be thinking by this stage that the componential approach can encompass all possible problems in reading it will be instructive to consider some alternative approaches in order to set the componential approach into the appropriate context. It may be noticed that these alternatives can sometimes be difficult to distinguish from the componential approach.

The maturational lag hypothesis

This approach proposes that the intellectual development of the child in particular cognitive areas can be retarding the appropriate development of reading. It emphasizes the interaction between genetic factors and environmental factors and the componential approach, in this context, can be seen as an aspect of this broader picture. The most comprehensive theoretical and experimental work on maturational lag has been produced by Satz and his colleagues (e.g. Satz and van Nostrand, 1973; Satz and Sparrow, 1970). Satz and Sparrow observed similarities between the patterns of problems of children with reading problems and the configuration of problems in adult patients associated with damage to the left angular gyrus (in the posterior part of the parietal lobe). This pattern, known as Gerstmann symptoms (Gerstmann, 1930), includes left-right confusion, dyscalculia, dysgraphia and finger agnosia. Satz and Sparrow noted that the underlying problem of all Gerstmann symptoms is aphasia, thus problems arising in the left hemisphere have associated language impairments. They also pointed out that the angular gyrus is slower to mature, being the last region of the cortex to complete the development of its cells.

Satz and van Nostrand (1973) describe the maturational lag theory as follows: 'The theory postulates that developmental dyslexia is not a unitary syndrome but rather reflects a lag in the maturation of the brain (left hemisphere) which delays differentially those skills which are in primary ascendancy at different chronological ages' (p. 123). An implication of this is that the level of skill of dyslexic children should be similar to that of younger normal children. Viewed in this way, impaired acquisition in reading is seen as being developmentally delayed rather than as the result of some underlying damage. An attempt at this implication was made by Beech and Harding (1984) who tested a group of poor readers and two control groups of normal readers, one matched on reading age, but younger, and the other matched on chronological age. These controls were matched on socioeconomic status and non-verbal IQ. In nearly all tests of phonemic processing and ability in short-term memory, as measured by digit span, the chronological age controls were significantly better than the poor readers, but there was no difference between the poor readers and the younger normal readers. However, these results can also be explained by the reading effect hypothesis: lack of experience in normal reading depressed the development of phonemic processing (and indirectly memory span, see Beech, 1988, for further discussion), which is why the level of phonemic processing was at the same level as the reading age controls.

Rutter (1984), commenting on the notion of maturational lag, has conceded that there is a certain amount of plausibility in the notion that different parts of the brain develop at different rates in different children, in the same way that there is variability in tooth eruption or variability in the age at which a child walks. But there are difficulties with the concept. First, one needs direct measures of brain development, and in addition, an understanding of the relationship between such brain development and the development of functions such as language and reading. However, Prichep, John, Hansook and Kaye (1984) suggest, via the use of 'neurometrics', a way of developing norms of electrical activity of the brain for different phases of development. Rutter's second difficulty was in terms of the nature of development in the area which is lagging behind. For instance, surely one would expect subsequent normal development even though there has been a delay. Furthermore, one would expect that later on, having matured in the essential areas, there would be a process of catching up in reading. But with conventional teaching this is not normally the case. A review by Schonhaut and Satz (1984) noted a grim prognosis for poor readers. For example, in one study (Satz, Taylor, Friel and Fletcher, 1978) only 18 per cent of mildly retarded readers at the end of Second Grade had caught up by Fifth Grade.

The maturational lag framework suggests that there is a 'sensitive period' in which a child is particularly receptive to training on a particular skill. The concept of a sensitive period is actually quite difficult to test experimentally. One needs to demonstrate that a particular type and quantity of training is more effective within a certain range of ages than at other times, or more likely, that efficacy is an inverted-U function of chronological age. Suppose that at a certain chronological age a group of children are tested on a particular skill and only 10 per cent score significantly above chance on this test. The children are then trained, perhaps for 10 weeks, using a standard training programme and at the end of the period 25 per cent of the whole group are above criterion. Further groups of children are tested and trained across a range of older ages. Baseline performance on this test prior to training will improve as a function of mean chronological age for each group. Thus the residue of children not able to reach criterion will decline from 90 per cent for the youngest group as a function of age. The proportion of children from the residue who reach criterion as a result of training will follow an inverted-U as a function of age according to the sensitive period hypothesis. But this may not imply that any child has a period of maximum receptiveness. It could be because the characteristics of the residue of children not reaching criterion will change as a function of age. For example, in terms of the absolute levels of performance on an intelligence test, the intelligence of those in the residue will increase, on average, as a function of age, but probably not at the same rate. Thus a child failing to reach criterion on initial testing in the oldest group would be relatively much poorer on this test in standardized terms relative to his or her peers than on other standardized cognitive tests of other skills. A consequence of this would be that the same training paradigm for different age groups has a differential effect, as training at a particular level may be inappropriate for a particular absolute level of intelligence. There may also be an increasing proportion of children within the residue lagging substantially in overall intellectual development. Another reason for a sensitive period effect could be that the probability of improving spontaneously in the absence of training is likely to be far higher within a particular range of chronological ages, therefore training for such children may not actually be necessary, especially if the training is stretched over a long time period. It should be possible to overcome most of these problems with careful research designs, but this examination of the concept has highlighted its difficulties. On the other hand, to be pragmatic one wants to apply a training programme during the period when it will have the maximum impact. This is a much easier proposition to test experimentally.

Drug-based treatment of reading problems

There is evidence that the nootropic drug piracetam (2-oxo-1 pyrrolidine) can be helpful for dyslexic children. Before examining some of the evidence it should be noted that piracetam is a safe drug which has been used for 21 years and is sold in 86 countries to treat memory and learning difficulties in the elderly. In the large number of trials on children there has been a lack of reported side-effects. For example, two large studies (DiIanni et al., 1985; Wilsher et al., in press) examined safety intensively and found the same incidence of adverse reactions in the placebo group as in the drug group. The total tested were 237 and 245 in the placebo and drug groups, respectively.

It has been suggested that the drug seems to improve verbal processing, but in a way that is not yet understood. For instance, Dimond and Brouwers (1976) found that 14 days of taking piracetam in a double-blind study produced a significant improvement in verbal learning, but not on a pursuit motor task (a bi-lateral task) in students. Connors et al. (1984) have demonstrated changes in event-related potentials in piracetam-treated dyslexic children for verbal material presented to the left hemisphere. Generally speaking, piracetam appears to produce no change in spatial ability, but has an effect by improving verbal memory, naming and coding.

DiIanni et al. (1985) treated 257 dyslexic boys for 12 weeks (at 3.3 gm/day) which resulted in increased reading speed but not in increased reading accuracy; furthermore, digit span scores increased for those with initially poor digit spans. Wilsher et al. (in press) treated 225 dyslexic children (aged 7–12 years) in a double-blind study for 36 weeks (at 3.3 gm/day). Although of average intelligence, these children averaged 3.4 years behind in a prose reading test (the Gray Oral Reading Test). Piracetam produced significant improvements in reading ability and in comprehension relative to the placebo controls. Studies such as these suggest that in severe cases of reading retardation there is a good case for using piracetam. It should be noted that in these piracetam studies the children underwent ordinary schooling in reading. If a programme of training deficient specific skills were to be applied, the improvement in reading might be quite substantial. The effects of the drug appeared to be manifest after 12 weeks and its potency was sustained during the 9-month test period.

Motivational aspects

The motivational aspect of poor reading is difficult to assess, especially in the conventional sense of measuring motivation by applying a psychometric test which is both reliable and valid. However, there seem to be three aspects of reading which suggest that motivation is a potent and underestimated force in reading development. These aspects are that parental influences may be important, that reinforcement programmes seem to be relevant to reading progress and that development in the later stages of reading should be intrinsically motivating if enjoyment can be derived from the material being read.

As any reading investigator notices when visiting schools, there is much evidence for a strong influence of socioeconomic status on reading perform- ance. Furthermore there is good experimental evidence for such an influence (e.g. Cox, 1987). But the difficulty is in establishing whether, if parental involvement is the causal agent, the effect is one of increasing the level of motivation of the children to want to read, or are most children from middle-class backgrounds simply being given extra training in the skill of reading by their parents? Evidence for the motivational element necessary for reading was suggested by the work of Tizard, Schofield and Hewison (1982) demonstrating that the involvement of parents in a programme of listening to children reading was more potent than allocating equivalent extra time for a remedial teacher. Further support is reviewed by Topping and Wolfendale (1985); however, a recent report (Hannon, 1987) suggests that this evidence for the extra efficacy of parents may be difficult to replicate. Hewison and Tizard (1980) and Hannon (1987) found a strong association between the extent to which working-class parents heard their children read at home and the reading attainment of these children. Perhaps on present evidence the main contribution is the extra skill explanation, but further research is needed.

The Gittelman and Feingold experiment, previously described, provides an illustration of the efficacy of reinforcers to motivate reading performance. Their poor readers ranged between 7 to 13 years and were of normal intelligence, but reading lagged in relation to expected reading level, given their individual IQs. Both the experimental and control groups were given remediation with the reinforcement procedure of Staats, Mincke, Goodwin and Landeen (1967). Here are Gittelman and Feingold's comments on the programme:

> The fact that we excluded children with clear behavioral problems may lead to the erroneous impression that the youngsters were eager to cooperate. Quite to the contrary, most were willing victims at best, and obtaining their active involvement was of concern in many cases. The reinforcement made a tremendous difference in obtaining the children's cooperation. This difference does much, in turn, for the morale of the teachers, and it cannot be assumed that progress such as that obtained in this study can be accomplished . . . with less enthusiastic staff. (p. 188)

MORE GENERAL ASPECTS OF THE COMPONENTIAL APPROACH

Lesgold, Resnick and Hammond (1985) draw an analogy between the skill of reading and learning to drive. As is the case for driving, almost everyone should be able to read. However, there are situations when driving becomes difficult, revealing substantial individual differences in driving performance. Similarly, reading for most supposely fluent readers from the normal population does not usually involve reading complex material, so that subjecting them to reading difficult material would again produce a wide variation in performance. Most of driving instruction involves teaching the components of driving, such as being able to operate the controls at the appropriate times and to monitor traffic conditions. Driving is normally taught holistically; subskills are usually taught within the context of other driving skills. Again, in the case of reading, the holistic (or eclectic) approach is normally favoured, but there are certain subskills which do not seem to be completely mastered. The componential approach tries to detect weaknesses and then to strengthen them with an appropriate training programme.

Both reading and driving, and indeed other skills as well, can be considered to pass through the three well-known stages, as defined by Fitts (1964): the cognitive, associative and autonomous stages. The end product should be the development of automatic processes. The componential approach aims to achieve this in all necessary components in order that they may function efficiently. This is brought about by automatic processes operating in parallel, in contrast to non-automatic, or controlled processes which operate serially because they are under conscious control (Schneider and Shiffrin, 1977; Shiffrin and Schneider, 1977). There has been substantial work on automaticity in cognitive processes, with many attempts to define the concept. For example, Jonides, Naveh-Benjamin and Palmer (1985) suggested that automaticity ought to be a concept applied to the component processes involved in a task rather than to the behaviours as a whole. They also proposed that certain theoretical features of component processes should be identified as criteria for establishing automaticity, because relying on experimenters' definitions of automaticity has the danger of relying on subjective judgements of the most appropriate definition to use. Instead, a good model will specify the component processes in a task which in turn generates criteria for determining any changes in processes over the course of development of automaticity.

So far, reading processes have been considered in terms of automaticity being a desirable end product. However, Humphreys (1985) takes the view, in contrast to Frederiksen discussed earlier, that at least as far as comprehension processes are concerned, these require controlled processes and are not therefore automatic. Humphreys sees the evidence for automaticity in word decoding skills as more equivocal, but even in this case he prefers to consider them as more *autonomous* than automatic as they can demand resource capacity in the fluent reader. Autonomy here is taken to mean that a process has the capability of automatic functioning in that it can operate in parallel and be undemanding of processing resources. But unlike an automatic process, it need not have the qualities of being resource-free and parallel.

To return directly to the componential approach, this chapter puts forward the relatively simple proposition that reading skills can be divided into subcomponents and poor readers can be given training in those particular subcomponents that are retarding their progress in reading, in order to improve their reading. Without going into elaborate detail this approach has several aspects or implications which are summarized by the following points in no particular order of priority:

(1) The componential approach in one sense is not falsifiable (in the Popperian tradition) because if one trained a child on a particular skill and there was not a subsequent improvement in reading performance relative to an appropriate control group of children who had experienced a placebo training condition, this would indicate that the particular skill in question was not instrumental in regarding reading. But it would not be a threat to the componential approach as there could be another hitherto undiscovered component skill responsible for retarding reading. However, the approach is useful in highlighting the problem of teasing out reading effects from components causally involved in reading retardation, as elaborated earlier.

(2) The spread of effect phenomenon is both a practical advantage and a theoretical hindrance. Training a component seems to spread benefits in other areas of reading in a way which needs further investigation. On the other hand, reading-disabled children seem to have a number (or spread) of cognitive areas which are problematic, but it is likely that from the theoretical viewpoint only specific areas are causally connected to the reading problem.

(3) The efficacy of training may interact with the maturational development of the child. One implication is that a child may not have matured
in certain cognitive areas in order to learn to read. This is similar to the
concept of 'reading readiness', which has been used since the 1930s and
which has been criticized more recently by several authors (e.g. M.
Coltheart, 1979; Marshall, 1987). Another implication is that there
might be a sensitive period for training. For instance, the adolescent
learning to read may simply be slower to learn than if the same learning
had taken place at an earlier stage of development. Rutter (1984)
suggests that this problem may be compounded with secondary feelings
of failure. The notion of a sensitive period has been discussed and it
was concluded that although it is difficult to test experimentally the
reasons for such sensitivity, it is a simpler matter to discover the best
age range, or the best point of skill development, to apply a particular
test programme.

(4) An implication of the componential approach is that there may be a
sequence of skills that develop in a particular area, or component of
reading. If one skill in the sequence does not develop normally,
subsequent skills cannot develop either. If one conceptualizes these
reading components as modules, this means that there is retardation
within a module. However, it is possible for other modules to develop
normally. For instance, it is possible to develop normal lexical access in
the absence of normal GPC functioning (Campbell and Butterworth,
1985).

(5) Part of the componential approach is reliant on the idea of training a
deficient area. Unfortunately, the process of training is somewhat
lacking in precision, for instance, it can vary with the personality of the
trainer and with the success of the social interaction between teacher
and pupil. When training is ineffective, this may be due to the ineffec-
tiveness of the teacher or to the training programme itself, or simply, it
may have been curtailed too early. One way to overcome the variability
of the human interaction element is to use computers whenever feasible. For instance, Schwartz (1984) presents useful software for training
studies within the context of the componential approach. Another way,
if human interaction has to be used, is to ensure that several teachers
are involved in the training programmes. Unfortunately, this is not
always practicable. Therefore, the few training studies that have been
carried out so far seem to give rather variable results. The situation
might actually be much worse because training studies that do not work
are less likely to get published, not only because of conservatism among
editors about publishing null results, but because of the variety of
reasons which can explain a lack of training effect. This may mean that
a considerable amount of research effort will be required before clear
patterns of results eventually emerge.

REFERENCES

Alegria, J., Pignot, E. & Morais, J. (1982). Phonetic analysis of speech and memory codes in beginning readers, *Memory and Cognition*, **10**, 451–456.

Baron, J. (1977). Mechanisms for pronouncing printed words: use and acquisition, in D. LaBerge & S. J. Samuels (eds), *Basic Processes in Reading: Perception and Comprehension*. Hillsdale: Erlbaum.

Baron, J. (1979). Orthographic and word specific mechanisms in children's reading of words, *Child Development*, **50**, 60–72.

Barr, R. (1974–75). The effect of instruction on pupil reading strategies, *Reading Research Quarterly*, **10**, 555–582.

Barron, R. W. (1981). Development of visual word recognition: a review, in G. E. Mackinnon & T. G. Waller (eds), *Reading Research: Advances in Theory and Practice*, vol. 3. New York: Academic Press.

Beech, J. R. (1987). Early reading development, in J. R. Beech and A. M. Colley (eds), *Cognitive Approaches to Reading*. Chichester: Wiley.

Beech, J. R. (1988). Phonological coding and memory in reading disorders: cause or effect? in M. M. Gruneberg, P. E. Morris & R. N. Sykes (eds), *Practical Aspects of Memory: Current Psychological Research and Issues*. Chichester: Wiley.

Beech, J. R. & Harding, L. M. (1984). Phonemic processing and the backward reader from a developmental lag viewpoint, *Reading Research Quarterly*, **19**, 357–366.

Bieger, E. (1974). Effectiveness of visual perceptual training on reading skills of non-readers: an experimental study, *Perceptual and Motor Skills*, **38** (3, Part 2), 1147–53.

Bieger, E. (1978). Effectiveness of visual training of letters and words on reading skills of non-readers, *Journal of Educational Research*, **71**, 157–161.

Bradley, L. (1988). Making connections in learning to read and to spell, *Applied Cognitive Psychology* (special issue on cognitive psychology and the unskilled reader), **2**, 3–18.

Bradley, L. & Bryant, P. E. (1983.) Categorizing sounds and learning to read: a causal connection, *Nature*, **301**, 419–421.

Bradley, L. & Bryant, P. E. (1985). *Rhyme and Reason and Reading and Spelling*. Ann Arbor: University of Michigan.

Bryant, P. E. & Bradley, L. (1985). *Children's Reading Problems*. Oxford: Blackwell.

Bryant, P. E. and Goswami, U. (1987). Phonological awareness and learning to read, in J. R. Beech & A. M. Colley (eds), *Cognitive Approaches to Reading*. Chichester: Wiley.

Campbell, R. & Butterworth, B. (1985). Phonological dyslexia and dysgraphia in a highly literate subject: a developmental case and associated deficits of phonemic awareness, *Quarterly Journal of Experimental Psychology*, **37A**, 435–475.

Coltheart, M. (1979). When can children learn to read—and when should they be taught? in T. G. Waller & G. E. Mackinnon (eds), *Reading Research: Advances in Theory and Practice*, vol. 1. New York: Academic Press.

Coltheart, V., Laxon, V. J., Keating, G. C. & Pool, M. M. (1986). Direct access and phonological encoding processes in children's reading: effects of word characteristics, *British Journal of Educational Psychology*, **56**, 255–270.

Conners, C. K., Blouin, A. G., Winglee, M., Louge, L., O'Donnell, D. & Smith, A. (1984). Piracetam and event-related potentials in dyslexic children, *Psychopharmacology Bulletin*, **20**, 667–673.

Cox, T. (1987). Slow starters versus long-term backward readers, *British Journal of Educational Psychology*, **57**, 73–86.

DiIanni, M., Wilsher, C. R., Blank, M. S., Connors, C. K., Chase, C. H., Funkenstein, H. H., Helfgott, E., Holmes, J. M., Lougee, L., Maletta, G. J., Milewski, J., Pirozzolo, F. J., Rudel, R. G. & Tallal, P. (1985). The effects of piracetam in children with dyslexia, *Journal of Clinical Psychopharmacology*, **5**, 272–278.

Dimond, S. J. & Brouwers, E. Y. M. (1976). Increase in the power of human memory in normal man through the use of drugs, *Psychopharmacology*, **49**, 307–309.

Doctor, E. A. & Coltheart, M. (1980). Children's use of phonological encoding when reading for meaning, *Memory and Cognition*, **8**, 195–209.

Ehri, L. C. & Wilce, L. S. (1985). Movement into reading: Is the first stage of printed word learning visual or phonetic? *Reading Research Quarterly*, **10**, 163–179.

Fitts, P. M. (1964). Perceptual-motor skill learning, in A. W. Melton (ed.), *Categories of Human Learning*. New York: Academic Press.

Fleisher, L. S., Jenkins, J. R. & Pany, D. (1979). Effects on poor readers' comprehension of training in rapid decoding, *Reading Research Quarterly*, **15**, 30–48.

Frederiksen, J. R. (1982). A componential theory of reading skills and their interactons, in R. J. Sternberg (ed.), *Advances in the Psychology of Human Intelligence*, vol. 1. Hillsdale: Erlbaum.

Gerstmann, J. (1930). Zur symptomatologie der hirnlasionen im ubergangsgebiet der unteren parietal- und mittleren occipitalwindung (das syndrom fingeragnosie, rechts-links-storung, agraphie, akalkulie), *Nervenarzt*, **3**, 691–695.

Gittelman, R. & Feingold, I. (1983). Children with reading disorders: I. Efficacy of reading remediation, *Journal of Child Psychology and Psychiatry*, **24**, 167–191.

Goswami, U. (1986). Children's use of analogy in learning to read: A developmental study, *Journal of Experimental Child Psychology*, **42**, 73–83.

Hannon, P. (1987). A study of the effects of parental involvement in the teaching of reading on children's reading test performance, *British Journal of Educational Psychology*, **57**, 56–72.

Henderson, L. (1982). *Orthography and Word Recognition in Reading*. London: Academic Press.

Hewison, J. & Tizard, J. (1980). Parental involvement and reading attainment, *British Journal of Educational Psychology*, **50**, 209–215.

Humphreys, G. W. (1985). Attention, automaticity, and autonomy in visual word processing, in D. Besner, T. G. Waller & G. E. Mackinnon (eds), *Reading Research: Advances in Theory and Practice*, vol. 5. London: Academic Press.

Jonides, J., Naveh-Benjamin, M. and Palmer, J. (1985). Assessing automaticity, *Acta Psychologica*, **60**, 157–171.

Jorm, A. F. & Share, D. L. (1983). Phonological recoding and reading acquisition, *Applied Pscyholinguistics*, **4**, 103–147.

Kennedy, A. (1987). Eye movements, reading skill and the spatial code, in J. R. Beech & A. M. Colley (eds), *Cognitive Approaches to Reading*. Chichester: Wiley.

Kennedy, A. & Murray, W. S. (1986). On the necessity of eye movements for reading. Paper presented to the International Conference on Cognitive Approaches to Reading, Leicester, April.

Lesgold, A., Resnick, L. B. & Hammond, K. (1985). Learning to read: a longitudinal study of word skill development in two curricula, in G. E. Mackinnon and T. G. Waller (eds), *Reading Research: Advances in Theory and Practice*, vol. 4. London: Academic Press.

Lovett, M. W. (1987). A developmental approach to reading disablility: accuracy and speed criteria of normal and deficient reading skill, *Child Development*, **58**, 234–260.

Marsh, G. & Desberg, P. (1983). The development of strategies in the acquisition of symbolic skills. In D. R. Rogers & J. A. Sloboda (eds), *The Acquisition of Symbolic Skills*. New York: Plenum.

Marsh, G., Desberg, P. & Cooper, J. (1977). Developmental strategies in reading, *Journal of Reading Behavior*, **9**, 391–394.

Marsh, G., Friedman, M. P., Desberg, P. & Saterdahl, K. (1981). Comparison of reading and spelling strategies in normal and reading disabled children, in M. P. Friedman, J. P. Das & N. O'Connor (eds), *Intelligence and Learning*. New York: Plenum.

Marshall, J. C. (1987). The cultural and biological context of written languages: their acquisition, deployment and breakdown, in J. R. Beech & A. M. Colley (eds), *Cognitive Approaches to Reading*. Chichester: Wiley.

Miller, G. A. (1956). The magical number seven, plus or minus two, *Psychological Review*, **63**, 81–97.

Perfetti, C. A. (1977). Language comprehension and fast decoding: some psycholinguistic prerequisities for skilled reading comprehension, in J. Guthrie (ed.), *Cognition, Curriculum and Comprehension*. Newark, Delaware: IRA.

Perfetti, C. A. (1985). *Reading Ability*. New York: Oxford University Press.

Perfetti, C. A., Beck, I. L. & Hughes, C. (1981). Phonemic knowledge and learning to read. Paper presented at the Society for Research in Child Development. Boston, MA.

Prichep, L., John, E. R., Hansook, A. & Kaye, H. (1984). Neurometrics: quantitative evaluation of brain dysfunction in children, in M. Rutter (ed.), *Developmental Neuropsychiatry*. Edinburgh: Churchill Livingstone.

Read, C. Zhang, Y., Nie, H. & Ding, B. (1986). The ability to manipulate speech sounds depends on knowing alphabetic writing, *Cognition*, **24**, 31–44.

Rosen C. L. (1966). an experimental study of visual perceptual training and reading achievement in first grade, *Perceptual and Motor Skills*, **22**, 979–986.

Rosen, C. L. (1968). An investigation of perceptual training and reading achievement in first grade, *American Journal of Optometry*, **45**, 322–332.

Rutter, M. (1984). Issues and prospects in developmental neuropsychiatry, in M. Rutter (ed.), *Developmental Neuropsychiatry*. Edinburgh: Churchill Livingstone.

Satz, P. & van Nostrand, G. K. (1973). Developmental dyslexia: an evaluation of a theory, in P. Satz & J. J. Ross (eds), *The Disabled Learner: Early Detection and Intervention*. Rotterdam: Rotterdam University Press.

Satz, P. & Sparrow, S. S. (1970). Specific developmental dyslexia: a theoretical formulation, in D. J. Bakker & P. Satz (eds), *Specific Reading Disability: Advances in Theory and Method*. Rotterdam: Rotterdam University Press.

Satz, P., Taylor, G., Friel, J. & Fletcher, J. (1978). Some developmental and predictive precursors of reading disabilities: a six year follow-up, in A. L. Benton & D. Pearl (eds), *Dyslexia: an Appraisal of Current Knowledge*. New York: Oxford University Press.

Schneider, W. & Shiffrin, R. M. (1977). Controlled and automatic human information processing: I. Detection, search and attention, *Psychological Review*, **84**, 127–190.

Schonhaut, S. & Satz, P. (1984). Prognosis for children with learning disabilities: a review of follow-up studies, in M. Rutter (ed.), *Developmental Neuropsychiatry*. Edinburgh: Churchill Livingstone.

Schwartz, S. (1984). *Measuring Reading Competence: a Theoretical-prescriptive Approach*. London: Plenum.

Seymour, P. H. K. & Elder, L. (1986). Beginning readers without phonology, *Cognitive Neuropsychology*, **3**, 1–36.

Shiffrin, R. M. & Schneider, W. (1977). Controlled and automatic human information processing: II. Perceptual learning, automatic attending and a general theory, *Psychological Review*, **84**, 127–190.

Staats, A. W., Mincke, K. A., Goodwin, W. & Landeen, J. (1967). Cognitive behavior modification: 'motivated learning' reading treatment with sub-professional therapist-technicians, *Behavioral Research Therapy*, **5**, 283–299.

Sternberg, R. J. (1977). *Intelligence, Information Processing and Analogical Reasoning: the Componential Analysis of Human Abilities*. Hillsdale: Erlbaum.

Tizard, J., Schofield, W. N. & Hewison, J. (1982). Collaboration between teachers and parents in assisting children's reading, *British Journal of Educational Psychology*, **52**, 1–15.

Topping, K. & Wolfendale, S. (eds) (1985). *Parental Involvement in Children's Reading*. London: Croom Helm.

Wagner, R. K. & Torgesen, J. K. (1987). The nature of phonological processing and its causal role in the acquisition of reading skills, *Psychological Bulletin*, **101**, 192–212.

Wilsher, C. R., Bennett, D., Chase, C. H., Conners, C. K., DiIanni, M., Feagans, L., Hanvik, L. J., Helfgott, E., Koplewicz, H., Overby, P., Reader, M. J., Rudel, R. G. & Tallal, P. (in press). Piracetam and dyslexia: effects on reading tests, *Journal of Clinical Psychopharmacology*, **7**.

Yuill, N. & Oakhill, J. (1988). Effects of inference awareness training on poor reading comprehension, *Applied Cognitive Psychology* (special issue on cognitive psychology and the unskilled reader), **2**, 33–45.

Chapter 6

Acquisition of computing skills

Mark Elsom-Cook

INTRODUCTION

Programming computers is a cognitive skill which has only been developed in recent years. The first 'computer' was created in the 1940s, and the first studies of the psychology of programming were conducted in the late 1950s. The nature of programming changes quickly as technological innovations continue to occur. Programming has been studied from a variety of perspectives. This paper seeks to outline the reasons why this skill is worth studying, and also to introduce and justify the use of an artificial intelligence methodology in this area. The paper begins by exploring the reasons for studying programming. It then outlines artificial intelligence (AI) methodology and explains why such a methodology is the most appropriate. Following this discussion, a framework for thinking about learning programming is introduced and some approaches to learning programming are outlined. The next section discusses bugs, which are the manifestation of incorrect attempts to write a program. The final four sections discuss in detail some work within the AI paradigm. These approaches are the overall structure proposed by Taylor (1987), the cognitive modelling of GREATERP (Anderson, 1986), the intention-based approach of PROUST (Johnson, 1986), and the learning-based method of IMPART (Elsom-Cook, 1984).

WHY STUDY PROGRAMMING?

There are two major reasons for studying programming. The first is that a study of computing skills facilitates good teaching by allowing the teacher to

Acquisition and Performance of Cognitive Skills. Edited by A. M. Colley and J. R. Beech

explore the consequences a particular teaching activity may have upon the learner. The second is that programming provides us with a means for exploring the problem-solving processes which humans use, in a domain which is quantifiable. Let us examine this in more detail.

A programming student is typically provided with a specific problem which must be solved. The student will eventually produce a program which is a solution to that problem (we hope). This explicit representation of the solution to the problem, couched in highly formal terms (and constrained by the formal system), is itself of great interest because it allows us to study the student's result without having to make assumptions about the implicit knowledge which the student is using. If we follow the development of the program we find that between the initially stated problem and the final solution there are a number of attempts and partial solutions which represent points in the student's problem-solving process. The fact that these intermediate points have been externalised renders the details of the process of problem-solution partially visible. Many researchers also collect protocols on audio or video tape to facilitate their interpretation of the partial programs.

WHY USE AN ARTIFICIAL INTELLIGENCE METHODOLOGY?

The first attempts to study programming derived from a desire to improve the effectiveness of commercial programming groups. Large teams of people were working on large programs, and it was necessary to ensure that they cooperated, that each person did the part of the task at which they were best, and that any new recruit could fit into the team effectively. These demands led firstly to the application of social psychology methods in studying team programming (see for example, Brooks 1975), and later to the development of batches of psychometric tests for assessing 'programming skill'. This latter field has continued to develop more sophisticated techniques for studying programming (Shneiderman, 1980; Weinberg, 1971).

Studies have focused on issues such as the readability of certain layouts of program, the memory load involved in various programming tasks, and the ways in which individuals store knowledge about programming. There are many empirical studies conducted across large numbers of subjects. Unfortunately, these studies are not very helpful in trying to understand what programmers are like and the activities that they engage in. One reason for this is that there are a great variety of activities which come under the heading of programming. A more significant reason is the importance of individual differences between programmers. People who write software come from a variety of backgrounds and approach the process in a huge number of different ways. These differences outweigh the similarities to such an extent that the only universally applicable outcomes of the empirical studies are so general as to be useless. For example, one study (on which there have been many variations) showed that all programmers find it harder to read programs if the names of the objects in the programs are meaningless (Schneiderman, 1980)!

Another typical study followed the lines of the experiments which showed that chess experts represent the board position differently from novices. Expert and novice programmers were shown a piece of 'program' and subsequently asked to reconstruct it from memory. If the program was simply a jumbled sequence of programming language statements that did nothing, experts and novices found it equally difficult to recall (Adelson, 1981).

Since these studies do not really help us in understanding the cognitive skills involved in writing a program, it is necessary to take a different approach. Detailed studies of individual programmers would seem to be the obvious way to tackle the problem, given the magnitude of individual differences. An AI methodology should allow us to build models of the skills of these individuals, and combine models of individuals to produce more general models of programming skills. Let us explore this proposal in more detail.

An artificial intelligence approach to the study of cognition involves building a computer program which emulates cognitive skills. The programming language provides a formal system within which to specify theories about the cognitive skill being studied. The fact that the program is an executable representation of the theory is important since it allows the theory to be rigorously tested. The computer will only execute the program if the theory is complete (i.e. every required component of the theory is present at some level of detail). The predictions, strengths and weaknesses of the theory are made visible in the behaviour of the machine. The behaviour of the program is a model of the behaviour of humans as predicted by the theory. The program should produce the same behaviour as a human, both in terms of 'correct' behaviour and in terms of typical errors.

To illustrate this idea, let us consider the simple example of memorizing and recalling nonsense syllables. Psychology experiments in this area typically provide subjects with a list of meaningless words to memorize. At a later time, the subjects are asked to recall whether a particular word was in the list. For example, I may ask you to remember 'dit ben yat yom yol', and come back two hours later and say 'Did I ask you to remember yol?'.

Computers have efficient memory systems which never forget things, and which normally organize things being stored into a linear sequence. A typical way to program a computer to remember nonsense syllables is as follows:

Remembering
1: Create a list in which to store the syllables.
2: Whenever a new syllable is encountered, add it to the end of this list.
Recall

1. Start at the beginning of the list and check if the first item is the thing which you are being asked to recall. If it is, say 'yes', otherwise check the next item in the list.

2: If you get to the end of the list and you have not found the item, say 'no'.

This simple model makes some very specific predictions about the process of recall which can be tested against the actual behaviour of real people. For example, it predicts that the subject will always be completely accurate in recalling whether words were on the list. It also predicts that answering a question about the second word on the list will take twice as long as answering a question about the first word, the third word will take three times as long, etc. Finally, it will predict that deciding that a word was not on the list will always take longer than deciding that a word was there. Of course, this is nothing like the recall process in human beings. Humans take almost the same time to retrieve a word, no matter where that word occurred in the list. Deciding that a word is not on the list is faster than deciding that a word is on the list, and there are interactions between the probes (the words which the subject is asked to recall) and the originals. For example, if the list contained 'yol' the subject is more likely to recall (incorrectly) that 'yul' was on the list than if there were no similar words.

A better model of recall of nonsense syllables was developed in a system called EPAM (Feigenbaum, 1963). This system uses a knowledge representation called a discrimination net to store words. Figure 6.1 represents part of such a net. The words are stored as sequences of characters with a unique choice of path for each letter at each point in the net. The word 'yol' corresponds to the path shown darkly. Using this representation, the storage and recall processes are different:

Remembering

1: Starting at START HERE, check if the first letter of the syllable appears on any branch. If it does, go along that branch. If it doesn't, then make a new branch with that letter on it.

2: From the current node, look for a branch with the second letter. If there is one, follow it. If not, create one.

3: From the current node, look for a branch with the third letter. If there is one, follow it. If not, create one.

Recall

1: Start at START HERE and look for a branch with the first letter. If there isn't one say 'NO', otherwise go along that branch.

2: Start at the current node. Look for a branch with the second letter. If there isn't one say 'NO', otherwise go along that branch.

3: Start at the current node. Look for a branch with the third letter. If there isn't one say 'NO', otherwise say 'YES'.

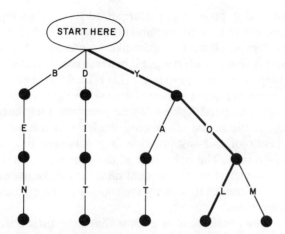

Figure 6.1. A discrimination net containing nonsense syllables.

This representation provides a better model of the way in which people store nonsense syllables in their heads. For example, it predicts that all words will have approximately equal recall times, and that deciding a word is not on the list is faster than deciding that a word is on the list. These predictions are borne out by observation. On the other hand, there are still many things which this model would predict that disagree with actual observations of people. For example, the model does not contain any predictions about the decay of recall ability with time.

In the case of programming, we are trying to build AI programs which attempt to write programs in the same way as humans. This can be confusing to think about—remember that there is a program we produce, which is the AI model, and the programs which that program produces, which are the predictions of that model. Our task is not simply to write programs which can generate correct programs. Our AI model must also generate the same sorts of programming errors (bugs) as humans, and adopt the same sort of strategies in order to repair them.

There are many factors involved in the process of programming. Rather than trying to model the whole process, researchers normally choose a small subset of the tasks. For the purpose of this paper we will adopt a model in which a student is initially presented with a written problem. The 'teacher' believes that the student has the necessary knowledge to find a solution to this problem, but that the problem is making use of skills at the boundary of the pupil's ability.

We will assume a model of the programming process which involves the following stages. Firstly, our student transforms the written representation of the problem into some internal representation which is meaningful by virtue of being expressed in pre-existing internalized terms. The representation is used to retrieve units of knowledge and proceduralized skills which appear to be relevant to the problem. This information is used to break the problem down into subproblems which the pupil believes can be solved in the particular programming language being used. This is likely to involve some restructuring of the problem representation. These subproblems may be regarded as segments of plans or partial plans. These plans are then instantiated using knowledge about the actual statements available in the programming language. The result of this instantiation is a complete program which the computer can execute. The behaviour of the program is unlikely to be that which the student expected. The student must now make use of the feedback provided by the computer to identify the sources of the erroneous behaviour and to eliminate them.

The process described above is a somewhat unrealistic abstraction. Strict top-down methodologies are commonly advocated for programming. A top-down methodology means working from the most general to the most specific level in sequence when solving a problem. In the case of programming this means setting down all the goals before choosing a representation, choosing all the algorithms before writing any code, etc. It is rare to find a programmer (novice or expert) who uses these methods. It is almost never the case that a program (particularly a large one) is written completely before being put into the computer. The program is written in stages so that the individual components can be tested before the whole program is put together. It is also unusual for a programmer to complete the design of the high-level specification before looking at lower level details. An expert will often identify some critical difficulty in writing a program, and will create and test the code for

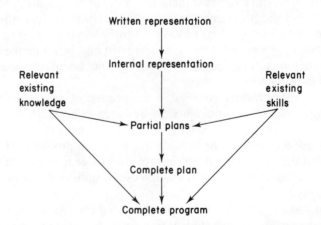

Figure 6.2. A simple model of the programming process.

that part first. When that code has been produced, the rest of the program will be constructed around it.

If we accept the simple model described above, then there are a number of stages in the process of programming which involve widely different skills. Each of these stages brings with it different forms of error which our student can potentially make.

Transforming the written representation into an internal one may lead to a faulty perception of the problem itself (this will be discussed with reference to programming in a later section). The transformation from external to internal representation of the problem has been studied in most depth in physics problem-solving. Priest (1987) and Larkin, Dermott, Simon and Simon (1980) have developed models which describe how an individual confronted with a simple physics problem extracts (or fails to extract) the relevant information to produce a solution. The lessons learnt in this domain are difficult to generalize to programming. The physics domains chosen are based on a small number of equations. Understanding the transformation from external to internal representation becomes much more complex when we are confronted by the range of possible statements in a programming language.

The quality of the internal representation affects the way in which knowledge is retrieved to make partial plans. There are also many other factors involved. For example, if a student has been reading a section of a programming text which deals with a particular function or concept (e.g. conditional statements), the expectation will be that the examples at the end of that section will involve the new concept which has just been introduced. Since the skills of choosing an approach to a programming problem are rarely taught, it is not uncommon for programmers confronted with their first 'real-world' problem to feel lost without such clues. Using knowledge about the details of the langauge to turn these partial plans into a complete plan for the program can run into difficulties if the pupil misunderstands (or is unaware of) certain features of the language. Expecting certain statements to behave differently from their actual behaviour is a common source of error. Even if a complete plan is made, the pupil may still generate errors in transforming that plan into the external code of the solution.

The above process provides a description of an approach to programming which can be applied to many languages, and which is a particular case of a general problem-solving strategy. Although it is being claimed here that there are many cognitive skills which apply to learning to program in any environment, it should also be acknowledged that there are many skills and difficulties encountered by a programmer which are specific to the language being used for implementation. The most commonly studied languages are Lisp, Prolog and Pascal. These languages are more appropriate for study than something like Basic because they are more highly structured and, at least in the case of the first two, have a pure underlying theoretical model. A more practical reason for studying these languages is that since Pascal is the most popular language for computer science, and Lisp and Prolog are the main artificial intelligence programming languages, there is a good supply of human subjects to study. Each of the approaches which we discuss in detail has investigated a different one of these languages. Brief introductions to each language will be given in the appropriate section of the paper.

WAYS TO LEARN PROGRAMMING

It is worth mentioning that the behaviour of the programmers which we study is very strongly determined by the form of the teaching which they received. PROUST (Johnson, 1986) was very effective at detecting programming errors which students made at one university, but when the system was tried at another university with different teaching methods, the success rate of the debugger decreased drastically. It had to be told about a new set of bugs which were due to this new teaching style.   ·

The main dimension of variation in teaching programming is the level of the process on which the most emphasis is placed. The two extreme positions are top-down teaching and bottom-up teaching. A top-down approach teaches people to think about 'real' programming problems from the start— even though they will not initially understand the language well enough to write their solutions. A bottom-up approach teaches the language as an abstract system, and only introduces real problems when the system has been mastered. The former approach is more motivating, and lays emphasis on the issues of selecting a representation for the problem. The latter approach ensures a minimum number of coding bugs, and should support the planning process by making the pupil aware of the limits of the formal system.

Teaching style will influence the learning process in many other ways. Having noted that this is so, we will not consider this influence in any further detail during the rest of the paper. The remaining sections all refer to bugs which are commonly observed in students from many backgrounds.

A TAXONOMY OF PROGRAMMING BUGS

Bugs are the visible effects of some mistake in a program. They correspond to unexpected behaviour of the computer. Bugs are important because they are the manifestation of some deeper error in the programmer's solution to the problem. It is by exploring these errorful cases that we can begin to see the processes which the programmer uses. This section gives examples of bugs in three programming languages; Lisp, Prolog and Pascal. For readers unfamil-

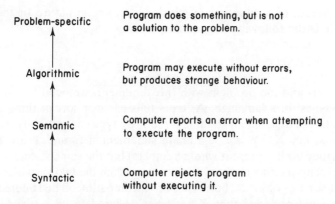

Figure 6.3. Levels at which bugs occur.

iar with any of the languages, brief descriptions can be found at the start of the next three sections.

For the purposes of this paper we will divide the set of bugs which can occur in the programming process into four major categories: syntactic, semantic, algorithmic, and problem-specific. These are illustrated in Figure 6.3. This division into types of bug is not really clear-cut, as will be illustrated below, but it is a useful approximation for thinking about the issues.

Syntactic bugs

Syntactic bugs are visible as incorrect sequences of characters within the program code. These include the misspelling of critical words, references to procedures or variables which do not exist, and omission of trivial delimiters. An obvious example is a misspelled procedure name such as 'plus' in the following Lisp statement:

(plis 3 4)

and an example which is not so obvious, but which affects the program structure, making the program as a whole syntactically incorrect, is the omitted semi-colon in the following Pascal program. This separator should occur after the statement write('hi').

```
program jane;
begin
    write('hi')
    write('jane')
end.
```

An example of a situation in which the syntactic nature of the error is debatable is the following assignment in Pascal:

x:=3

To understand the problem with this statement, we need to introduce the idea of 'types' in a language. A 'type' tells us what sort of thing a variable represents. An assignment statement requires 'type compatibility' between its arguments, i.e. X:=Y is a legitimate statement if X and Y are both type integer (they both represent whole numbers) but the same statement is illegal if Y represents a string of characters, because then the two variables represent different sorts of object. Their types are incompatible. The statement shown above is valid provided that X has been declared to be a variable of type integer elsewhere in the program, but is not valid otherwise. One argument would suggest that the assignment statement has an implied variable declaration elsewhere and to omit it is syntactically wrong. Another argument would be that this statement is independent of the declaration, and cannot be syntactically wrong. If we take this view then we must appeal to the semantics of the statement to account for the error (see, for example Teitelbaum, Reps and Horowitz, 1981). A strict grammar for the language can be written to reflect either model.

Semantic bugs

Semantic bugs, then, are to be regarded as problems which arise due to the misunderstanding of the behaviour of a single expression in the language. The above case illustrates a lack of understanding that the assignment statement involves the concept of types and type compatibility. Perhaps a clearer (and quite common) example of such errors in the typical misconception that the *while* loop is a software interrupt (DuBoulay, personal communication). This is illustrated below:

```
while k <> 'stop' do
   begin
    read(k);
     write ('hello', k)
   end
```

This loop will repeatedly read words and echo them preceded by 'hello' (e.g. 'hello Fiona', 'hello Kate') until the word 'stop' is typed in .The software interrupt model implies that the student believes the loop will magically exit as soon as the test is false (i.e. as soon as the user types 'stop'), whereas in fact the system completes this pass through the loop and exits only if it is at the start of an iteration and the condition is false. A student with this misconception would be surprised that the program types 'Hello stop' before completing. This example can be made clearer with an analogy. Suppose that I go to visit someone and they are out, but expected to return soon. It is a nice day, so I decide to walk round the block and then check if they are in again. I will keep doing this until the person is at home. This could be written in Pascal as

```
while not_home do
    walk_round_block
```

The correct model is that I check if the person is home, then walk round the block, then check if the person is home, etc. In the faulty 'software interrupt' model, the belief is that as soon as the person arrives home, no matter where I am in my walk round the block, I will be magically and instantly transported to their front door.

The use of such analogies as the one given above can also lead to certain semantic errors. Burstein (1985) investigated errors associated with analogical models of variables. To illustrate this consider the following example. It is common to describe a variable as a box with a name on it. The name is the name of the variable, and the contents of the box the value of the variable. This analogy is reasonable for simple assignment statements; assigning the value 3 to X means taking a 3 and putting it in the box marked X. A problem can arise, however. Suppose Y has the value 3 and we use the statement X:=Y. This is interpreted as taking the thing from the box named Y and putting it in the box named X. The problem is that this should leave nothing in the Y box. In fact, after the assignment, the *same thing* (3) is in both boxes. The analogy has broken down.

Algorithmic bugs

Algorithmic bugs arise when a number of statements are used in combination to achieve some goal. These statements constitute a plan for realizing that goal in the programming language. Algorithmic problems are distinct from problem-specific ones in that they arise in combinations of statements which may appear in a variety of contexts, and may even be reified to become commonly used 'cliches' (Shrobe, 1979). Whereas semantic errors are independent of context, something may or may not be an algorithmic error depending on what the programmer is trying to achieve.

We can illustrate the kind of bugs which occur at the algorithmic level with the following example of a simple recursive script. Recursion involves taking a complex problem and breaking it down into subproblems until the problem is so small that it is trivial to solve. The trick is to use the *same* method to break the problem down each time. Consider the following example.

```
(defun name (argument)
  (cond ((stopping-test argument)  stopping-value)
        (t     (build-result (name (simplify argument))) )))
```

This piece of Lisp constitutes a 'plan' for a way to perform recursion. A function 'name' is given an argument. If some stopping-test is true than the function just returns a value, otherwise it uses the function 'build-result' with whatever it gets by calling itself with a simpler argument. By replacing the parts of this plan with actual Lisp functions we can construct a variety of programs which are essentially identical at the algorithmic level, but have different semantic interpretations. Functions to count the length of a list, generate a list of specified length, find the factorial of a given number or sum the integers to a given number are all examples of programs which can be generated in this way.

To ensure that the roles of the components in the plan are clear, let us consider how to count the number of things in a list.

```
(defun count (Lst)
  (cond ((emptyp Lst) 0)
        (add1 (count (remove-one Lst))) )))
```

PLAN	PROGRAM
name	count
argument	Lst
stopping-test	emptyp
stopping-value	0
build-result	add1
simplify	remove-one

Equivalences between the plan and the program

In this case, we say that an empty list has a length 0. Any other list has a length one greater than the same list with one element removed. One critical thing that the programmer should know (apart from the overall structure of this algorithm) is that the relationship between the *stopping-test* and *simplify* function is critical. Repeatedly applying the *simplify* function to the argument MUST eventually result in an argument for which the *stopping-test* is true. Many novices fail to realize this intimate connection and consequently write programs which continue indefinitely. This is not a semantic error, for the student can make this mistake even if she clearly understands the semantics of the individual statements. It is an error caused by a misunderstanding of the interdependence of statements which is a vital part of this algorithm.

Problem-specific bugs

Problem-specific bugs refer to the highest level of analysis—the mapping from an external description of the problem to an internal representation which can be used to guide the search for a solution to the problem. This representation will consist of a set of goals to be satisfied and constraints to be met.

Consider the following problem. 'Write a program which allows the user to type in a number. It prints out the total of all the numbers up to and including that number. For example, if the user types 3, then the program prints 6 (1+2+3). If the user types 4 then the program prints 10 (1+2+3+4), for 5 it prints 15 etc.' The following Pascal program is an attempt at solving this problem.

```
res := 0;
Y := 0;
read(X);
while Y < X do
    begin
        res := res+ Y;
        Y := Y + 1
    end;
write (res)
```

This program will execute, but it prints the wrong numbers. For 3 it prints 3, for 4 it prints 6 and for 5 it prints 10. The error is that it does not match the description in the problem. The program adds all the numbers up to the number which was typed in, but *not including the largest number*. This is a problem-specific error because the program is otherwise perfectly correct.

In the remainder of this paper we will examine four AI models of programming in more detail.

LEARNING 'LISP' AS COGNITIVE SKILL ACQUISITION

Lisp

Lisp is a language used in artificial intelligence research. It has its roots in mathematical function theory. The basic idea behind the language is that each 'command' which the computer understands is a *function* which accepts a number of *arguments* and does something to them in order to return a result called the *value* of the function. In Lisp, a function is held together with its arguments by a pair of brackets. For example,

(PLUS 3 4)

represents the function PLUS applied to arguments 3 and 4. This will return a value of 7. The arguments to functions can be functions themselves, so

(PLUS (TIMES 3 3)
      (TIMES 4 4))

will multiply three by itself, multiply four by itself, and add these two numbers together to get the final value (which is 25 in this case). It is also possible to define new functions from combinations of old ones. This is achieved using the special Lisp function DEFUN, which expects to be given a name for the new function, a list of variables which are the names to be given to the arguments, and a piece of Lisp which uses these variables. As an example, the following code defines a new function 'square' which expects to be given a number and returns a value which is that number multiplied by itself.

(defun square (some-number)
       (times some-number some-number))

If we now ask Lisp to (square 3), it finds our definition of *square*, notes that the variable *some-number* has the value 3, and hence the actual code to execute is (times 3 3). So Lisp returns the value 9.

The GREATERP system

GREATERP (Anderson, 1986) is a tutor for Lisp which embodies a model of the programming process derived from ACT* theory (Anderson, 1983). This theory incorporates a production-rule model of the way in which problem-solving processes develop. The key features of the theory are as follows:

(1) A student reads a textbook and acquires a set of declarative knowledge about the domain she is learning.
(2) When presented with a problem, the student applies general purpose problem-solving strategies to the declarative knowledge to generate a solution.
(3) If particular combinations of declarative knowledge and problem-solving procedures are used frequently, they become combined into a

new piece of procedural knowledge. This is known as *knowledge compilation*.

The project is founded on an empirical study of Lisp learners (Anderson, Farrell and Savers, 1984). In this study, detailed production rules were derived from longitudinal observations of three individuals learning programming from a textbook with no other assistance. The various behaviours which they engaged in (both correct and incorrect) were noted and used to produce a model of the ideal student learning Lisp. Their incorrect behaviour provided the basis for a model of 'bugs'—errorful variations on the ideal student.

This information has been encoded as a production system model within GREATERP. A production system contains a set of independent *if-then* rules. It chains these rules together to produce a sequence of behaviour. This behaviour is a model of what the student is expected to do. There may be multiple rules which can apply at a particular point in this sequence. In this case there is a choice of models. Let us illustrate this with the following three rules.

1: IF the goal is to return a value 1 when the argument is zero
   THEN set a subgoal of testing if the argument is zero
   AND set a subgoal of returning the value 1

2.: IF the goal is to code a test to see if a value is zero
   THEN write down the function *zerop*
   AND set a subgoal of coding the argument to the function

3: IF the goal is to code a test to see if a value is zero
   THEN write down the function *equal*
   AND set a subgoal of coding the value as the first argument
   AND set a subgoal of coding 0 as the second argument

Rule 1 sets a subgoal which either rule 2 or rule 3 may satisfy, so these both correspond to possible models of a particular student. In GREATERP rule 2 is in the ideal student model, while rule 3 is regarded as a bug. The system attempts to model the student by a technique Anderson calls 'model tracing'. This involves following the student through a problem step by step. At each stage, the set of rules which could be applied constitute a set of predictions about which actions the student could perform next. If the student chooses a 'buggy' rule, the system immediately corrects her and continues. For this reason the system cannot build a complete model of an individual with a faulty model of Lisp. To do this would involve knowledge about complex interactions between bugs and about the semantics of Lisp which GREATERP does not have.

Anderson's system avoids syntactic errors by providing an interface which prevents the programmer from generating such errors. It enforces a top-down, left-to-right programming methodology on the student. This means that the system only models the part of the programming process which can be regarded as a translation from the representation to the code. The goal/subgoal hierarchy is assumed to correspond to the plan structure of the problem, and the tutor 'assumes that productions represent the student's intentions, and that the student's subgoals represent the tutor's subgoals' (Anderson, 1986, p. 843). This is a fairly major assumption about the psychological validity of this model.

Despite these limitations, the modelling in GREATERP has been found to be quite effective in this domain (Reiser, Anderson and Farrell, 1985). It has been successfully used as part of the undergraduate teaching programme at Carnegie-Mellon University for several years. The system is used in conjunction with a textbook that introduces concepts and explains about Lisp. The role of the tutor is to monitor the student carrying out the exercises in the book. This combination has proved to be more effective than simply providing the student with a Lisp textbook. It is not as effective as a human teacher, however.

A WIDER VIEW OF NOVICE'S MISUNDERSTANDINGS

Prolog

Prolog is a language based upon first order predicate calculus. A program is a set of assertions and logical rules. This program is used to try to prove various facts. For example, the following is a Prolog program

```
p if true.
q if true.
z if p and q.
```

This set of logical statements says that P is true, that Q is true, and that Z is true provided P and Q are true. We could use this program to prove that Z is true in this particular case. Prolog would achieve this by using the third rule to determine that Z is true if P and Q are true. It then proves that P is true (using the first rule) and that Q is true (using the second rule) and hence concludes that Z is true.

A more realistic example of the power of Prolog can be shown if we introduce *variables* into the language. Variables are associated with predicates (such as p) and allow them to apply to more than one case. Variables are written in upper-case. For example, the following rule says that anyone (ANY) is happy provided that they have a car and can drive.

happy(ANY) if can-drive(ANY) and has-car(ANY).

Let us add some rules about Mark and Kate.

can-drive(kate) if true.
can-drive(mark) if true.
has-car(mark) if true.

In this case, if we ask Prolog to prove *happy(mark)* it will succeed, but if we ask it to prove *happy(kate)* it will fail. In both cases it used the same rule for *happy*, but the variable was applied to different people. Prolog can also tell us about variables for which we do not know the value. If we ask *happy(X)* (i.e. is there anyone who is happy) it will succeed and tell us that $X = mark$.

To do this, Prolog used the rule to try to prove that there was anybody who can-drive. It succeeded, and made *ANY* have the value *kate*. It then tried to prove *has-car(kate)*, but it could not do this. Consequently it tried to find someone other than kate who can-drive. It found *mark*, so it changed *ANY* to have the value *mark*, and tried to prove *has-car(mark)*, which succeeded.

Taylor (1987) has investigated novices learning to program in Prolog. The main contentions of her thesis, however, are more widely applicable to the study of programming. The general issues which she discusses are supported by some detailed empirical studies of Prolog programmers which she has carried out.

The main point of Taylor's work is a suggestion that we should revise the methodology which we choose to study programming. One of the major issues which Taylor raises involves assumptions about existing knowledge. Most approaches to programming ignore the developmental history of the student, and the knowledge brought to the domain. Instead, they focus on detailed models of lower level aspects of the process. Taylor is critical of cognitive modelling work of the form described by Anderson (see previous section). She suggests that we must examine what a novice believes about computers and programming, and what analogies are inappropriately imported from other experiences. Taylor also considers that most studies regard novices as small experts, whereas they are actually quite different and are faced with radically different problems.

Taylor claims that the overriding importation to interaction with a computer is a model of interaction processes between humans. Attempting to fit the computer into such a model immediately leads to difficulties, because there are significant differences between natural languages and formal languages. For our purposes, the most significant of these is that a formal language makes everything explicit whereas natural language relies upon implicit communication to a very high degree. This importation results in a number of high-level misconceptions about programming which Kurland and Pea (1985) refer to as superbugs. Taylor investigated three of these superbugs as applied to Prolog.

(1) Parallelism—in this case we believe that the statements in a programming language do not necessarily have a sequential aspect, but that several statements may be active simultaneously.

(2) Intentionality—this involves assuming that the computer has a structure of goals and intentions, as another human does during an interaction.

(3) Egocentrism—this involves exporting our reasoning processes to someone (or something) else. In conversation we omit much because we assume that the hearer reasons as we do and can infer the appropriate information to fill in the gaps. Doing the same in a programming language means that we expect the computer to understand what we meant, rather than what we wrote.

In the case of Prolog these three superbugs are particularly strong, because they are supported to some extent by the language:

(1) One way to teach Prolog is to emphasize the logical basis which it has and its role as a declarative language. An alternative and less often used approach is to teach directly about the virtual machine. A computer is a real machine which behaves in a particular way. When we use a programming language, we are making the computer behave like some other machine (a Prolog machine, a Lisp machine or whatever). This machine does not exist physically, so we refer to it as a virtual machine. Most teachers choose the logical rather than the machine model of Prolog. It is increasingly clear, however, that experts rely on just such procedural knowledge of Prolog in order to write their programs. Because the declarative view does not emphasize the serial search structure of Prolog, many people believe that it can operate in parallel. This leads to bugs such as proving (or disproving) clauses in unusual orders, dealing with rules before facts, etc.

(2) The goal-directed problem is difficult because Prolog does indeed have goals. Executing a Prolog program corresponds to giving the computer the goal of proving that something is true. From this goal Prolog generates other goals which it attempts to satisfy using the program. These goals are very simple-minded, and have little in common with

human goals. The fact that they exist and are referred to in this terminology leads to confusion, however.

(3) It is not an unreasonable assumption to believe that Prolog can carry out inferences. The Prolog interpreter is just an inference engine. The mistake students make is to assume that it is in any way 'intelligent' or similar to human reasoning. Prolog actually carries out an exhaustive search process in order to prove things, exploring chains of reasoning which are 'obviously' incorrect to a human observer.

The model which Taylor proposes for the programming process lays a far greater emphasis on the task of finding a problem representation than we did in Figure 6.2. In part this is due to the fact that she is studying Prolog, in which much of the problem-solving is done before attempts to encode solutions in the language are made. Taylor emphasizes the fact that the process of writing a program to solve a problem involves a mixture of solving the problem and working out how to map a solution into the language. It is often the case that a particular representation for a problem provides a very direct mapping into the target language when some other representation will leave difficulties. It is for this reason that programming cannot be regarded as a simple process of translation from an informal language to a formal one. What distinguishes an expert from a novice, Taylor claims, is the ability to change the representation of the problem into a form which is amenable to the constraints of the formal system into which it will be encoded. This part of the programming process is not taught explicitly—probably because we do not understand it well enough to teach about it.

The major difficulties with this process lie in certain skills which the expert has but which the novice lacks. These include a lack of knowledge about the process of programming, about possible strategies for problem decomposition and about recognizing the intentions embodied in the initial problem description. In essence, the programmer must 'look ahead' to the algorithmic phase of the process in order to guide the structuring of the internal representation.

Following from these general errors are a number of specific errors which are due to the nature of the particular programming language and the way it has been taught (and learnt). In the case of Prolog many of these difficulties arise from the fact that it is an approximation to a logic programming language, and is often taught as though there is no procedural virtual machine. One of the major consequences of this is that students grasp parts of the declarative model and parts of the procedural model. They fail to realize that the two are separate and this results in a hybrid model which makes all sorts of wrong predictions. For example, students often use a procedural model to describe rules which have a right-hand side and a left-hand side, but have a declarative model of rules which have no right-hand side. The latter rules are often called 'facts', which further confuses the issue. Both these sorts of rule are treated identically by Prolog, but students often believe that Prolog will check facts before rule or vice versa, and cannot establish a consistent link between the representations.

Related to this is the problem of the extra-logical items in Prolog. There are many things which we want a programming language to do (such as opening and closing files or writing information on a screen) for which there is no sensible declarative interpretation. They do not fall within the scope of traditional logic. There are also odd features (such as *repeat* and *cut*) which are only meaningful in terms of the procedural model of Prolog. It is difficult for students to integrate such features with the model of the language which they are attempting to create.

As we discussed earlier, our only clue to the existence of misconceptions is the way in which they manifest themselves in bugs. Most of the bugs which Taylor studied involve the procedural behaviour of Prolog. Novices are often confused about the order in which Prolog proves things, and how it behaves when it cannot prove something. Consider the following program:

all if first and second and third.[1]
first if true.[2]

first if true.[3]
second if true.[4]

If we ask Prolog to prove that *all* is true it first uses rule 1, so it sets proving *first, second, third* (in that order) as subgoals. It can prove *first* trivially using rule 2. *Second* is similarly trivial using rule 4. But there is no rule for *third*, so Prolog cannot prove third. At this point Prolog starts looking for alternative proofs. Most new Prolog programmers have a misunderstanding about what happens here.

One misunderstanding (which accords with our human intuition in this case, since it is 'obvious' that we cannot prove 'all') is known as 'try once and pass'. Essentially we say that, since Prolog failed to prove a subgoal it cannot prove the whole goal ('all') so Prolog must fail. This is the right answer for the wrong reasons.

A second misunderstanding occurs when pupils realize that Prolog does not give up immediately. Prolog actually looks for alternative ways to prove the other goals in case the particular proof which it used for them is preventing it from proving *third*. A bug called 'redo from left' occurs when the pupil believes that what Prolog does next is to go to the leftmost item (*first* in this case) and try to reprove that. In this case the bug would predict that Prolog manages to find a second proof for *first* (using rule 3), and then tries to reprove *second*. It fails to do this so the goal fails. Again we have the right answer for the wrong reasons.

What Prolog actually does is try to reprove the thing it proved most recently. In this case, the failure of *third* leads to an attempt to reprove *second*. This fails, so Prolog attempts to reprove *first*. It manages this using rule 3, so Prolog starts to go forwards again. It manages to prove *second* using rule 4, then tries to prove *third*. When this fails again, it tries to reprove *second* again and fails. Now Prolog tries to reprove *first* for the third time, but it cannot do it since it has used both rules (2 and 3). Consequently *first* fails and, since it is the leftmost goal of *all*, *all* fails.

This is a long and complex way for Prolog to realize that it cannot prove *all*, so it is not surprising that novices find it hard to master. This example also highlights a particular problem about Prolog, which is that all three of the above models expect the program to fail, but for different reasons. This makes distinguishing the models difficult and Prolog students can often hang on to their misconceptions for a considerable length of time.

We can illustrate the difficulty of seeing a Prolog program in a declarative way with the example below (from Taylor, 1987). In this case the 'append' predicate has been written with the standard procedural model in mind. Most people find the alternative declarative behaviours which it permits to be very strange.

In list-processing langauges, the idea of 'append' is an operation on two lists of objects. It is a means of joining the lists together to produce a new list. If we apply this model to Prolog we expect 'append' to be a predicate with three arguments. The first two arguments are given to the predicate (our two lists), and the third argument is a variable. The predicate acts by instantiating the third argument to be a list containing all the elements of the first two lists, e.g.

```
?- append([have, you, seen], [the, cat],RESULT).
RESULT = [have, you, seen, the, cat]
```

This is indeed what 'append' does if we give it two lists. However, since we can choose which arguments should be instantiated and which left to be determined, there are possible behaviours of 'append' in Prolog which do not have a corresponding behaviour in this procedural view. For example, if we were to make the first two arguments into variables and instantiate the third argument to be a list, then the predicate would give us all the possible combinations of lists which could be appended to make that result, e.g.

```
?- append(A, B, [furious, green, ideas]).
A = []   B = [furious, green, ideas]
A = [furious] B = [green, ideas]
A = [furious, green]   B = [ideas]
A = [furious, green, ideas]   B = []
```

This behaviour can be explained consistently and neatly by thinking of 'append' as expressing a relationship between three lists (rather than as a process for turning two into a third). Learning to think about Prolog in this way is not a simple process and, since the procedural model can cover some parts of the language, it is possible for an individual to use the language (according to the procedural approach) without realizing the full power of Prolog.

Taylor has not attempted to produce a program emulating the bug generation behaviour of Prolog programmers (but for an attempt, see Fung, 1987). Taylor's work is based around analysis of individual programmers and detailed empirical studies. In addition to providing a low-level study of Prolog itself (see also Pain and Bundy, 1985), she has attempted to identify a larger framework within which to place the study. Perhaps one of the most important contributions of this work is the attempt to outline this framework. By identifying levels of knowledge about programming and the sorts of error that can be imported at each stage in the cognitive process, Taylor offers a perspective within which to place other programming studies. The work necessarily raises more questions than it answers, therefore. One of the issues which Taylor raises, the nature of programming intentions, has been explored to some extent. One system which investigated this is the subject of the next section.

AN INTENTION-BASED MODEL OF PASCAL PROGRAMMING

Pascal

Pascal is a very popular language used in computer science. It is *procedural*, which means that a program consists of a set of procedures—which are collections of instructions on how to perform certain actions. A procedure may take arguments (like Lisp) but it does not return a value. Instead it acts by directly affecting the values of variables. Such effects are known as side-effects.

For this discussion we only need three features of Pascal—variables, assignment statements and while loops. As in other languages, Pascal has variables which are names that have values associated with them. A difference in Pascal is that variables are 'typed': that is, a name can only have one sort of value. If the name 'freda' once had a value which was an integer, it must always have values which are integers (though of course they can be different integers). Variables obtain values through assignment statements such as FREDA := 5. This associates the value 5 with the name FREDA.

A loop construct in a programming language allows the programmer to repeat some sequence of actions several times. The 'while' loop is one such construct. It allows us to repeatedly carry out an action until some test is true. The format is

'while' test 'do' actions

and an example is

while Y < 5 do begin writeln('hi'); := Y + 1 end

This loop repeatedly prints 'hi' and adds one to Y until Y has the value 5. If Y was initially zero, it will print 'hi' 5 times.

PROUST

PROUST (Johnson, 1986) tackles the planning process in programming. The pupil is assumed to have a number of correct plans and faulty plans in her head. The programming task is to combine these plans into a complete plan which satisfies the original problem specification. The model of programming in PROUST is based upon a large empirical study which collected a vast number of plans and faulty plans. These are put into the system as a knowledge base, and PROUST attempts to analyse the problems in a particular program by comparing it with all the plans it knows.

The major new idea embodied in PROUST is that a program can be described as a set of *intentions* of the programmer. These intentions are used to guide the production of a hierarchy of plans, which eventually lead to actual code in a programming language.

PROUST expects to be provided with a program written by a student, and a set of intentions describing what that program should achieve. These intentions are given to the system by a teacher. PROUST uses this information to build a model of the student in terms of plans and bugs (i.e. faulty plans) which provide a mapping between the intentions and the actual program. The bugs which are needed to produce this model can then be used as input to a program which gives the student advice about the errors which she has made. PROUST achieves this mapping using the process of analysis by synthesis. This involves starting from the intentions and, using a library of plans, building every program which could satisfy those goals. If the program which the student has written is not one of these, then PROUST assumes it must contain errors. At this point it attempts to replace or modify correct plans in the solution using the library of faulty plans. This process continues until PROUST successfully 'explains' the errors or decides that it cannot do so.

The example program below adds up all the numbers which are input until the value 99999 is typed. At this point it prints out the total of the numbers and stops. The specification of intentions in this case is a formal description which is more or less equivalent to the English description which has just been given.

```
program total;

var sum, new: real;

begin
  sum := 0;
  readln(new);
  while new <> 99999 do
    begin
      sum := sum + new;
      readln(new)
    end;
  writeln(sum)
end.
```

We can follow the mapping from intentions to program in Figure 6.4. The intentions are at the top, and moving down the page corresponds to expanding plans in more detail. Actual program code appears in boxes.

The intentions look something like:

1: Read numbers until 99999 encountered.
2. Sum numbers.
3. Print result.

This breaks down into two plans. Intentions 1 and 2 are combined into the plan 'sentinel-controlled-read-and-process-inputs'. This simply means that the program will involve both reading and processing things, and that this activity will continue until some particular situation (the 'sentinel' case) arises. Intention 3 becomes a plan for 'print results'. At the next level of detail, 'sentinel-controlled-read-and-process-inputs' can be divided into two possible approaches. One is 'read-then-process-input', the other is 'read-input' and 'process-then-read-input'. These simply indicate alternative orders in which the reading and processing activities could be performed. Since the particular program which we are illustrating uses the latter model, we will expand that one further. Note that at each point where there is a choice, the tree could be expanded in depth to produce a legitimate program which achieves the intentions in a different way. 'Read-input' can be mapped directly into a read statement in the code. 'Process-then-read-input' can be

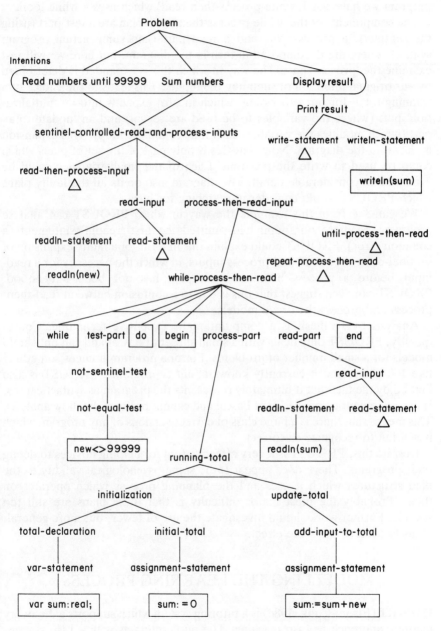

Figure 6.4. Simplified PROUST plan tree.

mapped into any one of three standard loop structures in Pascal. For this program we have used 'while-process-then-read' which uses a while loop.

The components of the 'while-process-then-read' plan are a test-part (using the sentinel), a process part and a read part (and some actual program syntax). These are decomposed in turn in the diagram, but here we will just examine the 'process' part. The way in which this is expanded is determined by our original intention of summing the inputs. This leads to the choice of a 'running-total' for our processing, which in turn expands into an 'initialization' part (where the variables to be used are set up) and an 'update-total' part (which modifies the variables each time round the loop). This expansion is shown in the diagram. Note that this is only part of the set of plans which could be used to write the program. Each of the small triangles could be expanded in considerable detail. The diagram also omits all the faulty plans which PROUST would consider in searching for bugs.

We can see from this example the way in which PROUST can analyse programs. Suppose our pupil had omitted the first 'readln' statement (a common error). PROUST could explain this in terms of a faulty expansion of sentinel-controlled-read-and-process-inputs, in which the necessity for a read-input before a process-then-read-input plan has not been understood. PROUST can even suggest that this is due to a confusion between read-then-process and process-then-read models.

Analysis by synthesis is a computationally expensive technique. Consequently, PROUST only deals with a small subset of Pascal and can only build models for a small number of problems. For one program it needs something like 100 plans, and it currently knows about 5 programs. PROUST is also limited by the fact that it ultimately represents the program as syntactic units. It has no semantic knowledge of Pascal and cannot perform dataflow analysis. This means that there is a large class of correct versions of any program which it will fail to recognize as correct.

Despite this, PROUST is a very effective tool for helping novices to debug their programs. There does appear to be some psychological validity to the plan structures which it uses and the planning process which operates on them. Probably the most major difficulty is that these plans are still too specific. Further work should investigate the use of fewer, but more general, plans to achieve the same effect.

MODELLING THE LEARNING PROCESS

IMPART (Elsom-Cook, 1984) is a tutoring system which supports a discovery learning approach to Lisp teaching. The pupil interacts with a Lisp system, and is expected to learn by generalizing from the behaviour which he or she sees. The system is interesting from the psychological point of view because it attempts to model the learning process of the student. IMPART is restrictive in that it assumes that the pupil initially knows nothing about Lisp, and does not learn anything except from IMPART itself.

To illustrate this modelling process, suppose the pupil is a complete novice who has typed '(QUOTE HELLO)' to the system and has been given the value 'HELLO' in return. It is clearly not possible to know exactly what the pupil learnt from this observation. Instead of trying to make an exact model, IMPART creates a *bounded user model* which puts upper and lower limits on what the student has learnt. It is unlikely (though possible) that the student has learnt nothing from this, and it is highly unlikely that the student has managed to generalize this example sufficiently and in the appropriate way to understand the whole of Lisp. IMPART uses a three-stage process to build the bounded user model.

In this case, the lower bound of the model is simply a description of the observable behaviour. This corresponds to saying that the least the student has learnt is that typing (QUOTE HELLO) gives the result HELLO. To create an upper bound for the model, IMPART applies an algorithm for learning by generalization. In this case, the generalization process produces a description to the effect that the function QUOTE takes any argument and returns that argument unchanged (this happens to be a correct model of QUOTE). If this had not produced a description which established a relationship among all the components of the observation, IMPART would then have applied a set of transformation rules (such as evaluating everything) to try to find such a link.

Given an upper and lower bound, IMPART can predict what the user will expect for other problems dependent upon where their belief lies in this space of possible models. By generating problems and making predictions from the model, IMPART can improve its model of the student until it 'knows' what they learnt.

Moving from a novice to someone with a little experience of Lisp, suppose we have a pupil with some model of QUOTE who now types '(SETQ FREDA (QUOTE HELLO))' and gets the value 'HELLO' as a result. The modelling process is much as before but, since IMPART has a model of the pupil's understanding of QUOTE, the lower bound is no longer simply a description of the observable behaviour. Instead, the model of QUOTE is embedded within the model of SETQ to indicate that the understanding of one depends upon the understanding of the other.

IMPART is interesting from the psychological viewpoint because it tries to model the application of a learning method to the observations which the student can make. The actual learning process which it uses is derived from work on machine learning, and hence is not necessarily like that used by humans. It nevertheless provides an effective base for modelling the outcomes of human learning in the restricted cases which it handles. An interesting extension of this work would be to make the system support multiple psychological models of the learning process. Unfortunately no psychological models of learning have yet been formalized in sufficient detail to make this possible.

SUMMARY

This paper has sought to give an overview of the major directions being taken in the study of computing skills. It has attempted to demonstrate the reasons why programming is an interesting topic of study and to show the appropriateness of an artificial intelligence methodology in this domain. In brief, the claim is that programming provides a domain for studying the problem-solving process in which results of the problem-solving can be described exactly (the program), and artificial intelligence provides us with a means for modelling the processes involved. Work in this area from the perspective of cognitive science is still quite new. The examples given here were intended to show the variety of approaches which can be taken in tackling this area, and to show the broad nature of the problem itself.

REFERENCES

Adelson, B. (1981). Problem solving and the development of abstract categories in programming languages, *Memory and Cognition*, **9**, 422–440.
Anderson, J. R. (1983). *The Architecture of Cognition*. Harvard: Harvard University Press.
Anderson, J. R. (1986). The automated tutoring of introductory programming, *Communications of the AMC*, **29**, 842–850.
Anderson, J. R., Farrell, R. & Savers, R. (1984). Learning to program in LISP, *Cognitive Science*, **8**, 87–129.
Brooks, F. P. (1975). *The Mythical Man-month*. New York: Addison-Wesley.
Burstein, M. (1985). Learning by reasoning from multiple analogies. Unpublished doctoral dissertation. Yale University.
Elsom-Cook, M. T. (1984). Design considerations of an intelligent tutoring system for programming languages. Unpublished PhD Thesis, Warwick University.
Feigenbaum, E. A. (1963). The Simulation of Verbal Learning Behavior, in E. A. Feigenbaum & Feldman (eds), *Computers and Thought*. New York: McGraw-Hill.
Fung, P. F. C. (1987). Novice prolog programmers. CITE technical report. Open University, Milton Keynes.
Johnson, W. L. (1986). *Intention-based Debugging of Novice Programming Errors*. London: Pitman.
Kurland, D. M. & Pea, R. D. (1985). Children's mental models of recursive Logo programs, *Journal of Educational Computing Research*, **1**, 235–243.
Larkin, J. H., Dermott, J., Simon, D. P. T. & Simon, H. A. (1980). Models of competence in physics problem-solving, *Cognitive Science*, **4**, 317–348.

Pain, H. & Bundy, A. (1985). What stories should we tell novice prolog programmers? in R. Hawley (ed.), *Artificial Intelligence Programming Environments.* Chichester: Ellis-Horwood.

Priest, A. (1987). Errors in physics problem-solving. Unpublished PhD Thesis, Open University, Milton Keynes.

Reiser, B. J., Anderson, J. R. & Farrell, R. J. (1985). Dynamic student modelling in an intelligent tutor for Lisp programming, *Proceedings of the Ninth International Joint Conference on Artificial Intelligence*, Los Angeles, pp. 8–14.

Schneiderman, B. (1980). *Software Psychology*. Cambridge, Mass: Winthrop.

Shrobe, H. E. (1979). Dependency directed reasoning for complex program understanding. Unpublished doctoral thesis, MIT.

Taylor, J. (1987). A study of novices programming in PROLOG. Unpublished phD Thesis, Sussex University.

Teitelbaum, T., Reps, T. & Horowitz, S. (1981). The why and wherefore of the Cornell Program Synthesiser, *ACM SIGPLAN notices*, **16**, no. 6.

Weinberg, G. M. (1971). *The Psychology of Computer Programming*. New York: Van Nostrand Reinhold.

Chapter 7

Learning motor skills: integrating cognition and action

Ann M. Colley

This chapter will focus on the learning of motor skills with a particular emphasis on the involvement of cognitive mechanisms in this learning and more generally in the control of movements. In the last decade, traditional notions of the way in which perceptual processes encode information from the environment, and in which such information is used in the planning and control of movement, have been questioned and modified. The ecological or action systems approach to perception and action (e.g. Kugler, Kelso, and Turvey, 1982; Reed, 1982; Turvey, 1977; Turvey and Carello, 1986; Turvey and Kugler, 1984) has stressed the importance of the interaction between the performer and the environment in which a movement occurs, for the control of movement. In its strongest form it defines information, not as that which is processed but as that which is specific to a given action. It denies the presence of internal representations of movements in the form used in cognitive explanations of movement control, for example, as memory traces or schemas (Adams, 1971; Schmidt, 1975). It therefore argues against a significant role for cognitive processes in movement control. As this approach has raised fundamental questions challenging the role of cognition in movement, it will be outlined, and its strengths and limitations discussed, in the first section of this chapter. Drawing on conclusions from this first section, the next section will focus on the question of how movements are planned, and how various stages of planning are represented. Finally, the acquisition of skilled movement will be examined and some attempt will be made to integrate the ecological approach with current cognitive theories.

Acquisition and Performance of Cognitive Skills. Edited by A. M. Colley and J. R. Beech
© 1989 John Wiley & Sons Ltd

THE ECOLOGICAL APPROACH

This approach has been developed from Gibson's ecological theory of direct perception (Gibson, 1979), and the work of Bernstein (1967) who identified some major conceptual problems with cognitive accounts of the control of movement. Traditional views of the control of action have their basis in the information-processing theories of the 1950s and 1960s. They emphasize the role of feedback in modifying ongoing responses, knowledge of results in amending response specifications, and the stored representation of movements in memory traces or schemas, which are used as the basis for movement initiation and correction. On the perceptual side, information from the environment is 'processed', while on the motor side, movements are 'programmed'. Information is only meaningful once it has been processed. The ecological theorists reject this separation of perception and action, and define information as being an integral part of the interaction between an animal and its environment, which is not arbitrary but meaningful in its own right in that it is unique and specific to the activity to which it is relevant:

> Information is optical *structure* generated in a lawful way by environmental structure (for example, surface layout) and by the movements of the animal, both the movements of the body parts relative to its body and the movements of its body as a unit relative to the environment. This optical structure does not resemble the sources that generate it, but is specific to those sources in the sense that it is nomically (lawfully) dependent on them. The claim is that there are laws at the ecological scale that relate optical structure to properties of the environment and action. (Turvey and Kugler, 1984, p. 382)

As this is rather abstract, it is perhaps useful here to give an example. Lee (1980) and Lee and Reddish (1981) have investigated the role of the time-to-contact variable, *tau* (the inverse of the rate of dilation of the retinal image of an object), in gannet diving behaviour. The gannet dives into the water for its prey, and a critical part of the dive requires the wings to be retracted before entry into the water. Given that the dive can be initiated from different heights and from different starting speeds, the problem to be resolved is what triggers wing retraction so that dives are always executed successfully and gracefully. It appears that retraction occurs when tau reaches a certain marginal value. This tau value is a property of the animal-environment interaction which provides *direct* information concerning collision with an oncoming object.

The ecological theorists argue that properties of the environment relevant to action are perceived directly and are not mediated by elaborative processing or representations. The Gibsonian concept of the *affordance* is used to explain how properties of the environment relate to movements (Gibson, 1979). An affordance is an environmental property which permits a certain action, and optical properties specific to an affordance can directly trigger action. For example, Warren (1984) describes how riser height determines whether stairs are climbable and can directly trigger appropriate adjustments in stair-climbing.

The ecological theorists have also questioned traditional views of motor programming, which assumes that a cortical executive specifies impulses to be sent to individual muscles for the enactment of movement. Turvey (1977) outlines three reasons why this view is untenable. First, the action of individual muscles is so closely interrelated that it seems wasteful to command each one individually. The second and third reasons were also outlined by Bernstein (1967). Innervation of a given muscle does not always result in the same movement. The result of innervation varies according to the prior condition of the muscle and its relationship with other muscles. Because the same impulse can produce different movements, and different impulses can produce the same movement, Bernstein argued that there cannot be a direct mapping between impulses and movements. Finally, in order to make even the simplest of movements, the executive would need to address a vast number of degrees of freedom, controlling all of the muscles relevant to the movement.

Because it is unlikely that the executive addresses individual muscles, and because there are close interrelationships between muscles, the ecological theorists propose that the basic units of motor control are collectives of muscles and joints constrained to act in a manner appropriate to a currently active goal. These *coordinative structures* reduce the degrees of freedom of the motor system. The role of the executive is to control the way in which lower centres interact, and it therefore does not need to deal with the detail of the innervation of individual muscles. An *action plan*, a working representation of the movement, is only crudely stated at the highest levels. Detail is provided at lower levels of the nervous system. Turvey (1977) suggests that there is an abstract entity, the *action concept* subserving motor constancy, or the production of a similar response using different groups of muscles (e.g. writing a word on paper with a pen versus spraying it on a wall with a can of paint). It is an operator which can modify and relate coordinative structures, and as such performs an executive function.

Sheridan (1988) has argued that the ecological theorists have treated the motor programme as a 'straw man'. He points out that there is a tradition of neurophysiological work which dates from Flourens in the 1820s, which has transposed muscles and their innervation from one part of the body to another and found that they can fulfil their new function. This is strong evidence against the addressing of individual muscles by an executive, and it is far from new. Sheridan also points out that Keele's (1968) definition of a motor programme as a pre-structured set of commands which specify an entire movement has provided the major focus for criticism. Not every motor control theorist would have adhered to this definition then, and Keele himself modified his position in a later publication to focus on a central representation for movement rather than simply a programme of commands (Keele, 1981).

One of the major implications of the ecological approach concerns the way in which research into motor control and learning is undertaken. The aims of research, according to this view, are twofold: first, research should seek to discover lawful relationships between properties of the environment and movement. As mentioned earlier, lawful perceptual relationships which trigger action have been discovered for stair-climbing (Warren, 1984) and for ball-catching (Todd, 1981). According to the intention of the performer, the perceptual system can behave in different ways, dedicated to the task in hand, which allow lawful relationships to be perceived. Turvey and Carello (1988) describe the perceptual system when it is functioning in this way as a 'smart perceptual instrument'. A similar point is made by Saltzman and Kelso (1983) who propose that during skill acquisition we do not accumulate representations which can then be used in the interpretation of incoming information. Instead we become increasingly attuned to information which is always present. They use Runeson's (1977) terminology to describe this process in terms of learners becoming 'increasingly smarter special purpose devices' (p. 20). Second, research should try to describe the organization of the motor system in physical-biological terms in order to present a picture of how motor problems are solved and the physical-dynamic nature of movement. An example of a physical model of a particular class of movements has been produced by Guiard (1988) who has proposed a kinematic chain model of human asymmetrical bimanual cooperation (such as is involved in swinging a golf club or playing the guitar). This model makes an analogy between two hands and two motors assembled in serial so that the action of one hand precedes and delimits the action of the other. This type of research ignores any contribution of cognitive processing to the tasks it describes:

> rather than figuring out putative brain processes that make the right inferences, the ecological approach promotes the investigation of the form of laws at the ecological scale, the kinds of properties they relate and the design principles of the biological systems that exploit them. (Turvey and Carello, 1986, p. 145)

As a research strategy, it is certainly easier to start with the peripheral motor system and apply known physical laws, or to discover lawful relationships between perception and action. The problem with starting with cognitive processes without detailed knowledge of the biomechanics of movement and the capabilities of the perceptual system, is that one could impute far too much of the control of movement to processes which are relatively inaccessible. This is, in essence, one of the major criticisms of traditional approaches to motor control. However, this strategy has so far said little about how the movement skills it describes are learned, and this is one area in which cognitive involvement is strongly implicated.

CENTRAL REPRESENTATION OF MOVEMENT AND MOVEMENT PLANNING

If there is central representation of movement (and all but the most strident ecological theorist would accept that there is), then what is its role? Turvey (1977) has suggested that there is an action concept which can be applied to coordinative structures, to constrain them to act in a manner which will allow a movement of a particular type to be accomplished. It is clear from the literature on cognitive motor skills (see Colley, 1989, for a review) that a number of levels of representation must be present in the motor programme for many skills. For example, Mackay (1982) has produced a theory of speech production which is based upon the activation of content-specific nodes at a number of levels. A phrase to be spoken is first represented in abstract form and then decomposed into smaller units by the activation of nodes in the *conceptual system*. These units then activate content nodes in the *phonological system* specific to vowel and consonant sounds, and pronunciation features. Finally, nodes in the *muscle movement system* which represent articulatory movement organization are activated. An abstract intention is therefore differentiated into a detailed specification for action. In common with researchers in similar areas, such as Shaffer (1975, 1978, 1980) in his work on typing and musical performance, Mackay draws a distinction between an abstract level of representation which contains a structural specification for movement, and a level of representation for movement commands. These various levels of representation have been referred to as the motor programme in line with Keele's (1971) definition. There is, however, some confusion in the literature concerning definitions of a motor programme. Schmidt (1975) takes a view which appears to be much closer to Keele's earlier definition.

Schmidt's schema theory of motor learning

Schmidt proposed a schema theory of motor learning in order to cope with criticisms of an earlier closed-loop theory of Adams (1971). Adams had proposed that two traces represent each movement in a performer's repertoire—a memory trace for initiating movement and a perceptual trace used to detect and correct error by providing a comparison for feedback. According to Adams these traces develop as a function of feedback and knowledge of results. A number of criticisms were levelled at the theory, including its lack of parsimony (two traces are required for every movement) and potential storage problem, and its implications for stereotyped performance (accurate but *novel* movements would not be possible since traces for their control would not exist). Schmidt, in line with Adams, proposed that two representations are necessary for movement, one which initiates and one which can be used for error detection. However, he proposed that these should take the form of schema rules derived from practice within a class of movements, capable of generating specifications for movements within that class. These schema rules operate after the selection of a generalised motor programme (GMP) which defines the movement class (e.g. throwing overarm), and supply parameters to the programme (force, timing) which determine how it is executed. Shapiro and Schmidt (1982) suggest various possible parameters which might be determined in this way: time, overall force, response size, and muscle selection.

In order to generate a good schema rule, it is clearly desirable to be exposed to a variety of similar movements, rather than to repeated presentations of the same movement, as varied practice will produce a rule which can potentially generalize to a large number of movement instances within a given class. The positive effects of varied practice on the later learning of novel but similar movements have been demonstrated in a number of experiments using a wide variety of different tasks (e.g. Carson and Wiegand, 1979; Wrisberg and Ragsdale, 1979). As Shapiro and Schmidt conclude, however, the viability of schema theory rests on the presence of the GMP. In order to demonstrate the existence of GMPs it is necessary to find invariant movement features which can be recorded across a number of similar movements. Kinematic and biomechanical analyses of movement timing and trajectories, however, have provided only limited evidence for such features (Marteniuk, Mackenzie, and Leavitt, 1988), and research which bears upon how they are learned in the first place is very sparse. Newell and Barclay (1982) suggest that if GMPs are not muscle-specific, then they are simply schemata under a different guise. This view is close to the role Turvey and others envisage for the executive, that is, one of coordinating the interaction between lower centres. This role would be well served by a schema rule.

Schmidt's account of GMPs and schemata which supply the GMPs with appropriate parameters does not necessarily imply a large role for cognitive processes in movement. Marteniuk *et al.* suggest that the best explanation of motor control stresses the cooperation between various parts of the nervous system required to meet the demands both of the performer and of the environment. In order to examine the effect of the demands of the performer on movement control it is necessary to provide evidence that the course of movements is affected by knowledge which can only be acquired indirectly through experience, or by intention.

Evidence for a significant role for planning and intention in motor control

In the case of cognitive motor skills such as typing, writing, etc. which require the translation of symbolic material into a movement response, and in the early stages of skill acquisition, an intention to make a movement of a particular kind will need to be differentiated through cognitive stages before the form of the movement can be determined. What of movements which do not fall into these categories? Marteniuk, MacKenzie, Jeannerod, Athenes, and Dugas (1987) have demonstrated that even relatively simple reaching and grasping movements are affected by previous knowledge and by differing movement intentions. In one study, subjects reached for and grasped either a light bulb or a tennis ball of similar diameter. Three-dimensional analyses of the movement trajectories showed that peak velocity occurred sooner for the light bulb, so that longer was spent in movement deceleration. This was attributed to knowledge of the relative fragility of the two objects. As discussed by Marteniuk *et al.*, the ecological theorists might attribute this finding to perceptual qualities of the object which 'afford' a faster or slower approach, but this is an unlikely explanation because a young child would undoubtedly grasp the two objects in the same way (or else why should parents go to so much trouble to ensure that fragile objects are kept out of reach). In a second experiment subjects had to reach for and grasp a wooden disk, then either throw it into a cardboard box or place it in a tight-fitting well. Again the movement trajectories for grasping the disk differed in the two cases, this time according to the eventual intention of the subject. More time was spent decelerating when a more exact later movement was required to place the disk in the well. The subjects were planning ahead for the next part of the movement sequence. This seems a fairly obvious finding, but it is not easy to explain without proposing that some processing is intervening between perception and movement planning. Requin (1980) has examined the organization of the motor system from a neurobiological perspective and, based upon a number of reviews in the physiological and neurological literature, has identified routes within the system which bear a close relationship to cognitive notions of serial processing stages which deal respectively with defining the nature of an action, selecting and assembling a motor programme and movement execution.

The role of intention is best illustrated in movements to which the performer adds expression. In musical performance, variations are applied to a written or memorized score in order to provide a performer's own interpretation. Sloboda (1982) distinguishes between context-free variation, in which a tune is played or sung faster or slower, or in a different key. For these variations the same transformation is applied to every note, altering either timing or pitch. Expressive variations are context-sensitive and are selectively applied to obtain a particular effect which may vary with the context of the performance or the inclination of the performer. These variations include rubato, pitch fluctuations and variations in timbre. In order to be able to apply such variations without destroying the structure of the piece, the performer must be able to access detailed knowledge of the musical structure, and must be using an abstract plan for performance.

Van Wieringen (1988) distinguishes between natural (phylogenetic) skills, such as locomotion, and cultural (ontogenetic) skills such as dancing (he points out that this distinction may not be absolute). Cultural skills employ a symbolic code, and are referred to elsewhere in this chapter as cognitive motor skills. Van Wieringen suggests that natural skills may exploit existing coordinative structures and thus have little reliance on cognitive involvement, while cultural skills may require coordinative structures to be overruled. He gives as an example the movements made by actors in a Polish theatre school which relies very heavily on movement and posture as expressive technique. Considerable practice is required in attending to and varying movements in different parts of the body in order that relaxation and movement can occur appropriately and spontaneously during performance.

This notion that under certain circumstances we need to dismantle existing patterns of movement organization has been observed elsewhere. One illustration comes from Shaffer's (1982) observations of keyboard playing, where different rhythms must be produced by the two hands. Swinnen and Walter (1988) describe kinematic and electromyographic analyses of the acquisition of two differing upper limb movements (Swinnen, Walter, and Shapiro, in press). In bimanual coordination there is a strong tendency for entrainment to occur: that is, the spatiotemporal characteristics of movement in one limb are reflected in the other limb. This has been used as evidence for coordinative structures in bimanual control which reduce the degrees of freedom. When two different rhythms are required of the two limbs, this entrainment needs to be uncoupled and the coordinative structure broken down. Swinnen, Walter and Shapiro found evidence of this uncoupling, but also found considerable individual differences between subjects in the time during practice when this occurred. Delaying one movement in relation to the other appears to facilitate the uncoupling. This presumably could reflect a strategic decision on the part of the subject, which would explain why individual differences occur.

Procedural learning and strategy may form the basis for uncoupling coordinative structures so that new structures can be constructed. The discovery of new coordinative structures may also be mediated by high-level strategies. To explain learned skills or the modification of old skills we need to be able to explain how coordinate structures can be constructed and modified. Frohlich (1988) describes how knowledge of a control system (controlling a cursor on a CRT using two knobs) is acquired and apparently organizes bimanual coordination in the early stages of learning. He found evidence for the use of different initial strategies by subjects. Frohlich and Luff (1987) successfully conducted a computer simulation of task performance using production rules to describe the relationships between the cursor display and knob movement. This is evidence for a substantial initial role for strategy and planning in the early stages of learning a motor task with apparently little requirement for cognitive processing.

Cognitive processing and movement

Adams (1987) in his historical review of some 100 years of motor skills research bemoans the fact that there is still a 'void in the failure to relate higher processes to action' (p. 66). He then suggests several fruitful lines of research which may go some way to solving this problem: observational learning of movement, investigation of the role of mental imagery in action, and investigation of the relationship between language and action. There is some existing research in all of these areas, but it is difficult to interpret in the broad context of movement control because no satisfactory theoretical framework has been offered, and little attempt has been made to integrate it with the mainstream of ideas in cognitive psychology. Some attempt will be made later in this chapter to lay the foundations for a more integrated approach.

Recent theoretical advances in cognitive psychology, such as the use of production systems models (e.g. Anderson, 1982) and parallel-distributed processing (McClelland and Rumelhart, 1985) have implications for the manner in which cognitive processes in motor skills are conceptualized. For example both features are present in Allport's (1980) specifications for a theory of action. Anderson's theory is described in some detail in the first chapter of this book, so will not be repeated here, however, the early stages of the learning of many motor skills can be put into his theoretical framework in much the same way as the learning of more purely cognitive skills. In the early stages of learning, facts from declarative memory may be assembled in working memory, proceduralized and used to guide an approximation to a required movement or movement sequence. How these procedures access action routines which produce the movement is far from clear, but could presumably be via condition-action or production rules in the same way as procedures outlining cognitive 'steps' are acessed. Allport (1980) suggests this rather direct linkage. One can assume that a basic repertoire of action routines (or GMPs) is available, in much the same way as general problem-solving procedures are available to proceduralize new information at an earlier stage in the system (Anderson, 1982). This basic repertoire of routines may be based on reflexive movements found in neonatal infants and decerebrate animals. Easton (1972) describes reflexes as 'the raw material from which the central nervous system may build volitional movements' (p. 591). There are a number of these, and they include reflexes which are similar to volitional grasping and locomotory movements, and postural reflexes, which resemble positions adopted for balance or exertion of force in sports (Fukuda, 1961). Turvey (1977) sees these reflexes or combinations thereof as a partial evolutionary answer to the degrees of freedom problem in movement.

One of the tenets of the ecological position is that movement control is not mediated by representations in the form of traces or schemata. This raises the question of how we remember movements and reproduce them.

Memory for movement

In the 1970s a significant amount of research effort was directed at attempting to discover movement cues which might be stored and used to recall movements from motor short-term memory (see Laabs and Simmons, 1982, for a review). The standard paradigm was one in which the subject made a criterion movement, then reproduced the movement immediately, or after a filled or unfilled retention interval. By manipulating the conditions for reproduction, subjects were (supposedly) forced to rely on certain cues rather than others. The accuracy of their recall attempts could then be examined, and inferences drawn concerning the primacy of certain cues. The most widely studied cues were location, or the end-point of a movement, and movement distance (e.g. Laabs, 1973; Marteniuk, 1973). A number of serious methodological problems gradually emerged and research in the area declined. Two of the general conclusions that can be drawn from the corpus of work are: first, that location does seem to have a significant role to play in movement recall (Laabs, 1973; Marteniuk, 1973; Posner, 1967; Roy, 1977), and second, that subjects can use different strategies to facilitate movement recall. For example, in the study by Laabs (1973), distance recall was facilitated in some subjects by a strategy of counting which provided a timing measure of distance. These strategic differences found among subjects were called 'encoding flexibility' by Diewert and Roy (1978).

An explanation of the relatively good recall of movement end location in a number of experiments has been given in terms of the internal spatial representation of movement in abstract space coordinate form (Russell, 1976). This representation is thought to be independent of modality, developing from all available sources of movement information, although vision does seem to play a particularly important role in adding precision to judgements based upon it. Colley and Colley (1981) found that blind subjects with some previous visual experience reproduced movement end location and distance more accurately than congenitally blind subjects, although both groups were more accurate for end location than for distance. The blind subjects who had some visual experience also reported using strategies based on some form of visual representation to facilitate reproduction.

Is motor memory simply based upon an integrated sensory store of some kind, possibly a schema or schemata defining the relationship between different sources of movement information? This is possibly part of the answer. It seems very unlikely, however, that movement commands are stored in the short term for repetition of a given movement. It is much more likely that successive movements are generated using a schema rule to set parameters for an appropriate GMP which itself may be schematic. The notion that cues are represented in memory has been rejected by the ecological theorists. Saltzman and Kelso (1983) describe this approach as a 'first order isomorphism fallacy' because it involves taking an observable aspect of a movement and assuming that there is a corresponding representation in the nervous system. Saltzman and Kelso suggest that we should look instead at the action units that are functionally defined to enact a certain skill.

Another problem arises from trying to generalize from the laboratory to movement control in general. The experimental tasks used in this area have been found to have a number of methodological problems (e.g. Kerr, 1978; Walsh, Russell, Imanaka, and James, 1979) and are not always easy to interpret. In the rather artificial conditions of a standard motor short-term memory experiment, subjects may use working memory strategically to aid retention by methods such as counting. The motor short-term memory literature has a very limited scope: it deals only with the short-term retention of relatively simple movements and therefore looks at only one aspect of movement reproduction. Little or no procedural memory is necessary for the simple linear positioning tasks used. What the tasks do require is the setting of appropriate parameters for the execution of a fairly stereotyped simple movement. Location may be a more useful cue in this respect than distance, for reasons that the motor short-term memory literature has outlined: that it is more readily codable in terms of a spatial representation.

So far motor memory has been discussed, but what about memory for movements? Wilberg (1983) discusses the clear distinction which can be drawn between motor memory and memory for movements. Motor memory refers to *how* a particular movement is implemented, whereas memory for movements refers to knowing *what* to do to execute a movement, i.e. its procedural details. Information about *what* to do is not necessarily accessible to consciousness. The illustration given by Wilberg is that of correcting a stumble on a kerb. This is normally accomplished successfully without awareness of the sequence of corrective movements involved, or indeed of the error in movement that causes the stumble in the first place. If an actor attempts to simulate this it is extremely difficult to do so in a convincing manner without considerable practice. In order to be able to reproduce the appropriate sequence of movements, it is presumably necessary to be able to access procedures containing details of successive parts of the sequence via working memory. This appears to be difficult because the sequence is normally run off automatically.

Being able to access the *what* of a movement sequence is insufficient, on its own, to generate a successful movement. Turvey, Fitch, and Tuller (1982) rightly conclude that any explanation of movement control which does not consider the interplay of forces along a chain of effectors is describing the miming of movement, not movement itself. Memory for movements is the representation of this mime.

What form might this memory for movements take? The notion of passive stores located somewhere or other in the central nervous system does not find much favour in contemporary cognitive psychology. Allport (1980) and Neisser (1976), among others, have pointed out that memory and processing mechanisms are one and the same thing: patterns for action are patterns of action. Memory for movements is procedural memory which in current theories is usually described in terms of production rules. In well-learned movements the procedures may be accessed directly rather than via working memory.

MOTOR SKILL ACQUISITION

From the arguments reviewed so far, three major processes of motor skill acquisition can be identified. First, abstract procedures for action must be acquired—the action concept (Turvey, 1977) or GMPs. These define the necessary subcomponents of a given action but do not specify in detail how the movement is to be enacted. Second, the kinetic characteristics of movement must be discovered so that the coordinative structures to be used by the action plan can be identified, and its differentiation through lower centres can proceed. Third, the performer must become attuned to lawful perceptual properties of the environment which inform action. Motor skills vary in their kinetic complexity, in their relationship with affordances in the environment, and in their requirement for computation prior to enactment. The contribution of the three processes outlined above will therefore vary with the skill in question.

Fitts (1964) identified three major stages of skill acquisition, and his description has been taken up and used both in the training literature (see Annett, this volume) and by Anderson (1982) in his ACT* theory of skill acquisition (see Chapter 1). The first, early or cognitive stage is when the learner is trying to understand the task using information from a variety of sources, including instruction. Because of the heavy reliance on verbal instruction, this stage has been called the verbal-motor stage by Adams (1971). Fitts and Posner (1967) describe this stage as 'the first step in the development of an executive program' (p. 12). More recent terminology would stress the acquisition of procedural information concerning a skill. But this stage must be more complex than this. As outlined above, in early attempts to learn a movement skill the learner is also discovering the kinetic properties of movements and becoming attuned to information in the environment. Learning is therefore proceeding at a number of levels in the nervous system, although verbal-motor learning is particularly prominent. The second, intermediate or associative stage, involves practice, error correction and integration of task components. There is an implicit assumption that verbal mediation has largely ceased, so that the learner is focusing on discovering how different parts of the movement interrelate and on the motor performance itself. The third, final or autonomous stage, occurs when the learner has reached a reasonable level of competence with the task, and improvement in performance slows down quite considerably. The task or some of its components may appear to be automatic in the sense that there is spare capacity to attend to other tasks or to strategic aspects of the task in question. As Schmidt (1982) concludes, there has been relatively little research on performance at this level. Shaffer's work on typing and especially on piano-playing (1978, 1981, 1982) emphasizes the importance of examining performance after many hundreds of hours of practice. Fluency and expressiveness are features of the highly skilled performer which must be acknowledged in any account of skill learning or control.

Of course, it is difficult to identify strict stages in skill acquisition, but Fitts' description serves to illustrate how task performance appears to change over a period of practice. Early accounts of skill acquisition were in terms of the learning and integration of 'subroutines' into a hierarchy of control for a given task (Bryan and Harter, 1899; Fitts and Posner, 1967). At the top of the hierarchy is an executive which provides the basic task structure, the detail of which is then filled in by lower levels (see Figure 7.1). In the case of motor skills, at the bottom of the hierarchy are small, stereotyped movement subroutines, which in some accounts were attributed to reflexes.

Hierarchical descriptions have been used in more recent models of cognitive motor skills such as typing (Rumelhart and Norman, 1982) and speech (Mackay, 1982), although these models do not have an executive in charge of the logical and decisional processes, but are based instead on activation of nodes or schemata and priming for transferring control down the hierarchy. I have argued elsewhere (Colley, 1989) that such models need to be *dynamic* in the sense that they need to account for learning. Mackay's theory does this, which takes it one step further than simple hierarchical descriptions. Also, the removal of the executive as a decision-making entity and its replacement with distributed nodes which function in parallel is in line with current attempts to remove the mysterious 'black box' from models in cognition, and bring them more into line with neurological and neuropsychological evidence.

There is another way of trying to identify what aspects of performance change during skill acquisition, and this takes us back to the three processes outlined earlier: acquisition of procedural detail, discovery of kinetic charac-

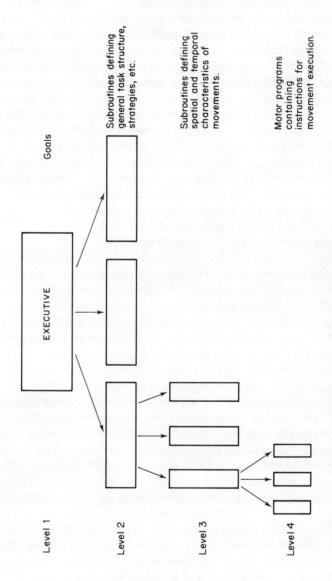

Figure 7.1. A hierarchical description of motor skill organization.

Level 1

Level 2

Level 3

Level 4

EXECUTIVE

Goals

Subroutines defining general task structure, strategies, etc.

Subroutines defining spatial and temporal characteristics of movements.

Motor programs containing instructions for movement execution.

teristics, and attunement to perceptual affordances. One problem outlined earlier with information-processing accounts of motor skill acquisition, which the ecological theorists have correctly identified, is that they have regarded information as that which is processed and which requires interpretation by cognitive mechanisms before it is meaningful for a given task. It is specific to a given task only when interpreted in the context of previous experience. The information-processing approach has tended to ignore or underestimate the role of perception in skill acquisition. A second problem with traditional information-processing accounts is their neglect of the complexity of move-ment kinetics, and the role of lower centres in movement control. Bearing this in mind, this chapter will next examine the ways in which performers learn to make movements, and interpret these in terms of the development of the three processes outlined above.

Learning movements

In the initial stages of learning a new movement, several different strategies are open to the learner: simply try out the movement and 'how it feels' or learning by doing; take instruction from a teacher or coach who will outline a strategy for approximating to the correct movement; watch a skilled perfor-mer undertake the same task. These three methods, and how they relate to the three processes of skill acquisition will be outlined next. These methods are not intended to apply singly to the learning of a given skill. For many skills all three methods may be used to varying degrees.

Learning by doing

One way of uncovering the underlying biomechanical constraints on a given movement is by attempting to perform a crude approximation to the task and, through practice, discovering the kinetic characteristics of the movement and becoming attuned to relevant perceptual cues. Anecdotal evidence suggests that this method of learning is used successfully with movements which require balance and postural adjustment, for example, the majority of children learn to ride bicycles or to roller skate mostly by sitting on a bicycle and trying to balance, or by skating, initially with some support. It is unlikely that this method would, on its own, be very successful for skills which have a procedural component, such as driving a car or learning a musical instrument. In such skills learning normally proceeds by a mixture of methods. The difference between skills for which 'learning by doing' forms the majority of the acquisition process, and those for which it takes a more minor role, at least in the initial stages, is in the requirement for the learning of procedural information.

Learning by watching

Observational learning has been used extensively in the training of sports skills. It is also more generally used in the early stages of learning a wide range of movement skills. Bandura (1977) suggests that observational learning has two roles to play in skill learning: first, it provides a conceptual representation of a movement which acts as a guide to the appropriate behaviour, and second, it imparts a standard of correctness which allows the learner to detect errors in performance. This second role must presumably be limited to correction of procedural detail, since unless a movement is actually performed and sensory feedback received and matched with knowledge of results, correction of parameters which are given to an action concept or GMP cannot take place. As Adams (1984, 1987) points out, observational learning provides only incomplete information for movement. Some aspects of a movement will probably be out of sight, and all internal proprioceptive/ kinaesthetic sensation is missing.

By watching others performing a particular movement or movement sequence the learner is able to generate an internal description of the movement. This can be used in the initial stages of skill acquisition to guide an approximation to the required movement. Later on, it can be used to introduce modifications into a given movement task to make it more efficient. Its major role therefore is to introduce procedural information for an initial approximation to a task, and to update procedural information during later stages of acquisition.

Learning by instruction

Instruction facilitates learning in much the same way as observation. It allows the learner to generate procedures for the enactment of a particular movement or to update existing procedures. For the majority of skills in which instruction is used, it is present during only the very initial stages of acquisition. The exception is in sport, where performance is under constant scrutiny by coaches. As Annett (1985) observes, initial instruction may be particularly effective if it evokes a potent image (Annett's example is of a squash coach who instructs his pupils to receive service by pretending to be a Red Indian waving a tomahawk). This begs the question, raised by Annett in his chapter in this volume and elsewhere (1985), of how verbal instructions access action routines. Allport (1980) has argued that action routines are accessed by the neural equivalent of production rules. Instruction, in turn, accesses production rules via working memory, perhaps using imagery as the access key.

The argument advanced here is that one way of looking at the different ways in which individuals learn movement skills is to look at the aspect of the task they are trying to acquire and the method adopted to do this. Instruction and observation allow the learner to establish procedures for executing the task, while learning by doing allows the learner to experience the interplay of forces which prevail during the movement.

Fitts (1964) and most other skills researchers have observed characteristic changes in performance over skill acquisition. One question which arises from such observations is whether or not at different stages during the acquisition process performance is accomplished in qualitatively different ways. There are a number of examples within the literature (e.g. Pew, 1966; Frohlich, 1988) which suggest that this is the case. The model that follows is a preliminary attempt to describe possible routes for performance of different tasks at different stages of learning. It does not describe the mechanisms by which performance of one kind changes to performance of another kind.

A description of the action system

The description offered here offers three potential routes to action routines. Embedded in it is Anderson's ACT* theory and its subcomponents of procedural memory, declarative memory and working memory. This is in line with the view offered in this chapter, that some motor skills have a substantial procedural component, and most motor skills use procedural memory in their initial stage of acquisition to generate an approximation to the desired movement. The major features of the description are shown diagrammatically in Figure 7.2.

The mediated route involves working and procedural memory, and is used in initial acquisition, or when strategic shifts are necessary. Declarative memory is used only in the initial stages of acquisition to accumulate knowledge about performance. The major difference between this and other routes lies in its use of working memory to proceduralize or change strategy. This route is responsible for mental rehearsal effects, in which procedures are rehearsed in working memory. It also allows for the construction of new coordinative structures or the overruling of old ones, by permitting the learner to strategically alter the manner in which a particular movement is enacted.

In the automatic route, procedural memory is accessed directly from perceptual analysis of the environment. This route is used when procedures are sufficiently task-specific not to require the use of working memory. It is used where skills require procedural detail, such as in the performance of music or writing to dictation, and are well-practised so that the procedures are well-learned. Hunt and Lansman (1986) have produced a production activation model of cognitive processing in which automatic processing occurs by the spread of activation among productions in a cascade-like manner without the intervention of working memory. A similar mechanism is proposed here.

The direct route directly links perceptual affordances with action routines.

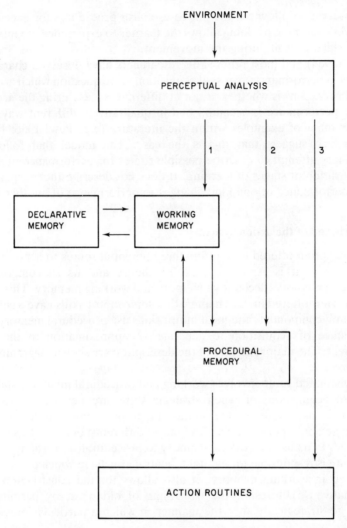

Figure 7.2. Three routes to the action system: 1—mediated route, 2—automatic route, 3—direct route.

It is used where procedural differentiation is unnecessary, as, for example, in the case of locomotion or postural control. One proposal advanced in this chapter is that this direct route can develop as a function of learning. There is anecdotal evidence for this. For example, when I start to drive a new car I have initial difficulty in deciding whether or not I can drive it through a small gap between a parked car and an oncoming car. I err on the side of caution and wait, or negotiate the gap by attending carefully and continuously to the amount of space available on either side. After driving the car for a relatively short time, it becomes easy to estimate whether a given gap is easy to negotiate, risky or impossible. Gibson (1979) suggests that environmental properties are scaled with respect to body size, and Warren's (1984) work on stair-climbing, referred to earlier, illustrates this. There is a scalar relationship between the maximum riser height perceived as climbable and leg length. This scaling is a necessary precursor to determining whether a particular aspect of the environment affords a given activity. In a skill such as driving, the scaling must take place with respect to the car, which can be viewed as a mechanical extension to body size.

Of course we require more than anecdotal evidence for the development of the direct route through learning. Longitudinal studies of skill development are now required which look for the gradual acquisition of sensitivity to lawful perceptual relationships between the environment and action. Also, in practice, it may be difficult to distinguish the direct route from the automatic route, in situations where there is little use of procedural memory. One prediction from this description is that in all cases where the direct route is used, it should be possible lawfully to relate perception and action. No such direct correspondence should be evident for the automatic route, since further extrapolation on environmental information will be necessary prior to the triggering of action routines.

As a final word of caution, no assumptions are being made here concerning the architecture of the central nervous system. It is simply a description of the different ways in which action routines may be accessed which takes into account current views of cognitive processing and the ecological perspective on motor control.

CONCLUSIONS

Accounts of movement control have tended to become polarized in recent debates between action systems and motor systems theorists (see Meijer and Roth, 1988) although compromise viewpoints may provide a better fit to existing data (Sheridan, 1988; Van Wieringen, 1988). This chapter has argued for a substantial role for cognitive processing in movement, while acknowledging the contribution of a direct link between perception and action in some instances. Recent changes in the way in which cognitive processing is conceptualized have altered for the way in which the cognitive input to motor control is described, particularly with respect to the representation of procedural information.

The implications of describing the action system in the way presented in this chapter are twofold: first in terms of research directions, and second in terms of practical issues in skill acquisition. As far as research directions are concerned, we need to know considerably more about the role of working memory in movement control and acquisition. There is a large literature on working memory and verbal tasks (see Baddeley, 1986) but very little on spatial working memory and the involvement of working memory in skill acquisition. We also need more detailed longitudinal studies of the acquisition of different kinds of motor task, and careful documentation of any changes in control that occur. Finally we need to look for lawful relationships between aspects of the perceptual environment and action, as the ecological approach suggests.

By adopting a descriptive framework such as that offered here, the major practical issue in skill acquisition becomes one of classifying the type of task to be acquired in terms of its ultimate reliance on direct or automatic or mediated processing. If we can identify lawful relationships between the environment and action, to which the performer becomes attuned over practice, then perhaps task acquisition might be facilitated through appropriate strategic training. Similarly, if task acquisition requires the uncoupling of coordinative structures, then again appropriate strategic training might assist the performer.

REFERENCES

Adams, J. A. (1971). A closed-loop theory of motor learning, *Journal of Motor Behavior*, **3**, 111–149.

Adams, J. A. (1984). Learning movement sequences, *Psychological Bulletin*, **96**, 3–28.

Adams, J. A. (1987). Historical review and appraisal of research on the learning, retention, and transfer of motor skills, *Psychological Bulletin*, **101**, 41–74.

Allport, D. A. (1980). Patterns and actions: cognitive mechanisms are content-specific, in G. Claxton (ed.), *Cognitive Psychology: New Directions*. London: Routledge & Kegan Paul.

Anderson, J. R. (1982). Acquisition of cognitive skill, *Psychological Review*, **89**, 369–406.

Annett, J. (1985). Motor learning: a review, in H. Heuer, U. Kleinbeck, & K. Schmidt (eds), *Motor Behavior: Programming, Control and Acquisition*. Heidelberg: Springer-Verlag.

Baddeley, A. D. (1986). *Working Memory*. Oxford: Oxford University Press.

Bandura, A. (1977). *Social Learning Theory*. Englewood Cliffs, NJ: Prentice-Hall.

Bernstein, N. (1967). *The Coordination and Regulation of Movements*. London: Pergamon.

Bryan, W. L. & Harter, N. (1899). Studies on the telegraphic language: the acquisition of a hierarchy of habits, *Psychological Review*, **6**, 345–375.

Carson, L. & Wiegand, R. L. (1979). Motor schema formation and retention in young children: a test of Schmidt's schema theory, *Journal of Motor Behavior*, **11**, 247–251.

Colley, A. M. (1989). Cognitive motor skills, in D. H. Holding (ed.), *Human Skills*, 2nd edn. Chichester: Wiley.

Colley, A. & Colley, M. (1981). Reproduction of end location and distance of movement in early and later blinded subjects, *Journal of Motor Behavior*, **13**, 102–109.

Diewert, G. L. & Roy, E. A. (1978). Coding strategy for memory of movement extent information, *Journal of Experimental Psychology: Human Learning and Memory*, **4**, 666–675.

Easton, T. A. (1972). On the normal use of reflexes, *American Scientist*, **60**, 591–699.

Fitts, P. M. (1964). Perceptual-motor skill learning, in A. W. Melton (ed.), *Categories of Human Learning*. New York: Academic Press.

Fitts, P. M. & Posner, M. I. (1967). *Human Performance*. Belmont, CA: Brooks/ Cole.

Frohlich, D. M. (1988). The acquisition of bimanual coordination in an interactive graphics task, in A. M. Colley & J. R. Beech (eds), *Cognition and Action in Skilled Behavior*. Amsterdam: North Holland.

Frohlich, D. M. & Luff, P. (1987). The acquisition of bimanual coordination in an interactive graphics task: a computer simulation. Paper presented to the International Conference on Skilled Behaviour, University of Sussex, Brighton, UK, April.

Fukuda, T. (1961). Studies on human dynamic postures from the viewpoint of postural reflexes, *Acta Oto-Laryngologica, Suppl. 161.*

Gibson, J. J. (1979). *The Ecological Approach to Visual Perception*. Boston: Houghton Mifflin.

Guiard, Y. (1988). The kinematic chain as a model for human asymmetrical bimanual cooperation, in A. M. Colley & J. R. Beech (eds), *Cognition and Action in Skilled Behavior*. Amsterdam: North-Holland.

Hunt, E. & Lansman, M. (1986). Unified model of attention and problem solving, *Psychological Review*, **93**, 446–461.

Keele, S. W. (1968). Movement control in skilled motor performance, *Psychological Bulletin*, **70**, 387–403.

Keele, S. W. (1981). Behavioral analysis of movement, in V. B. Brooks (ed.), *Handbook of Physiology*: Section 1. *The Nervous System*. vol. 2. Bethesda, MD: American Physiological Society.

Kerr, B. (1978). The effect of invalid task parameters on short-term motor memory, *Journal of Motor Behavior*, **10**, 261–273.

Kugler, P. N., Kelso, J. A. S., & Turvey, M. T. (1982). On the control and coordination of naturally developing systems, in J. A. S. Kelso & J. E. Clark (eds), *The Development of Movement Control and Coordination*. New York: Wiley.

Laabs, G. J. (1973). Retention characteristics of different reproduction cues in motor short-term memory, *Journal of Experimental Psychology*, **100**, 168–177.

Laabs, G. J. & Simmons, R. W. (1982). Motor memory, in D. Holding (ed.), *Human Skills*. Chichester: Wiley.

Lee, D. N. (1980). Visuo-motor coordination in space-time, in G. E. Stelmach & J. Requin (eds), *Tutorials in Motor behavior*. Amsterdam: North-Holland.

Lee, D. N. & Reddish, P. E. (1981). Plummeting gannets: A paradigm of ecological optics, *Nature*, **293**, 293–294.

Mackay, D. G. (1982). The problems of flexibility, fluency, and speed-accuracy trade-off in skilled behavior, *Psychological Review*, **89**, 483–506.

Marteniuk, R. G. (1973). Retention characteristics of motor short-term memory cues, *Journal of Motor Behavior*, **5**, 249–259.

Marteniuk, R. G., MacKenzie, C. L., Jeannerod, M., Athenes, S., & Dugas, C. (1987). Constraints on human arm movement trajectories, *Canadian Journal of Psychology*, **41**, 365–378.

Marteniuk, R. G., MacKenzie, C. L., & Leavitt, J. L. (1988). Representational and

physical accounts of motor control and learning: can they account for the data? in
A. M. Colley & J. R. Beech (eds), *Cognition and Action in Skilled Behavior*.
Amsterdam: North-Holland.

McClelland, J. L. & Rumelhart, D. E. (1985). Distributed memory and the representation of general and specific information, *Journal of Experimental Psychology:
General*, **114**, 159–188.

Meijer, O. & Roth, K. (eds) (1988). *Movement Behavior: the Motor-action Con-
troversy*. Amsterdam: North-Holland.

Neisser, U. (1976). *Cognition and Reality*. San Francisco: Freeman.

Newell, K. M. & Barclay, C. R. (1982). Developing knowledge about action, in
J. A. S. Kelso & J. E. Clark (eds), *The Development of Movement Control and
Coordination*. New York: Wiley.

Pew, R. W. (1966). Acquisition of hierarchical control over the temporal organization
of a skill, *Journal of Experimental Psychology*, **71**, 764–771.

Posner, M. I. (1967). Characteristics of visual and kinaesthetic memory codes, *Journal
of Experimental Psychology*, **75**, 103–107.

Reed, E. S. (1982). An outline of a theory of action systems, *Journal of Motor
Behavior*, **14**, 98–134.

Requin, J. (1980). Toward a psychobiology of preparation for action, in G. E.
Stelmach & J. Requin (eds), *Tutorials in Motor Behavior*. Amsterdam: North-
Holland.

Roy, E. A. (1977). Spatial cues in memory for movement, *Journal of Motor Behavior*,
9, 151–156.

Rumelhart, D. E. & Norman, D. A. (1982). Simulating a skilled typist: A study of
skilled cognitive-motor performance, *Cognitive Science*, **6**, 1–36.

Runeson, S. (1977). On the possibility of 'smart' perceptual mechanisms, *Scandina-
vian Journal of Psychology*, **18**, 172–179.

Russell, D. G. (1976). Spatial location cues and movement production, in G. E.
Stelmach (ed.), *Motor Control: Issues and Trends*. New York: Academic Press.

Saltzman, E. L. & Kelso, J. A. S. (1983). Toward a dynamical account of motor
memory and control, in R. A. Magill (ed.), *Memory and Control of Action*.
Amsterdam: North-Holland.

Schmidt, R. A. (1975). A schema theory of discrete motor skill learning, *Psychological Review*, **82**, 225–260.

Schmidt, R. A. (1982). *Motor Control and Learning: a Behavioral Emphasis*. Cham-
paign, Ill.: Human Kinetics.

Shaffer, L. H. (1975). Control processes in typing, *Quarterly Journal of Experimental
Psychology*, **27**, 419–432.

Shaffer, L. H. (1978). Timing in the motor programing of typing. *Quarterly Journal of
Experimental Psychology*, **30**, 333–345.

Shaffer, L. H. (1980). Analysing piano performance: a study of concert pianists, in
G. E. Stelmach & J. Requin (eds), *Tutorials in Motor Behavior*. Amsterdam:
North-Holland.

Shaffer, L. H. (1981). Performances of Chopin, Bach, and Bartok: Studies in motor
programming, *Cognitive Psychology*, **13**, 326–376.

Shaffer, L. H. (1982). Rhythm and timing in skill, *Psychological Review*, **89**, 109–122.

Shapiro, D. C. & Schmidt, R. A. (1982). The schema theory: recent evidence and
developmental implications, in J. A. S. Kelso & J. E. Clark (eds), *The Development
of Movement Control and Coordination*. New York: Wiley.

Sheridan, M. (1988). Movement metaphors, in A. M. Colley & J. R. Beech (eds),
Cognition and Action in Skilled Behavior. Amsterdam: North-Holland.

Sloboda, J. A. (1982). Musical performance, in D. Deutsch (ed.), *The Psychology of Music*. New York: Academic Press.

Swinnen, S. P. & Walter, C. B. (1988). Constraints in coordinating limb movements, in A. M. Colley & J. R. Beech (eds), *Cognition and Action in Skilled Behavior*. Amsterdam: North-Holland.

Swinnen, S. P., Walter, C. B., & Shapiro, D. C. (in press). The coordination of limb movements with different kinematic patterns, *Brain and Cognition*.

Todd, J. T. (1981). Visual information about moving objects. *Journal of Experimental Psychology: Human Perception and Performance*, 7, 795–810.

Turvey, M. T. (1977). Preliminaries to a theory of action with reference to vision, in R. Shaw & J. Bransford (eds), *Perceiving, Acting and Knowing*. Hillsdale, NJ: Erlbaum.

Turvey, M. T. & Carello, C. (1986). The ecological approach to perceiving-acting: a pictorial essay, *Acta Psychologica*, 63, 133–155.

Turvey, M. T. & Carello, C. (1988). Exploring a law-based, ecological approach to skilled action, in A. M. Colley & J. R. Beech (eds), *Cognition and Action in Skilled Behavior*. Amsterdam: North-Holland.

Turvey, M. T., Fitch, H. L., & Tuller, B. (1982). The Bernstein perspective: 1. The problems of degrees of freedom and context-conditioned variability, in J. A. S. Kelso (ed.), *Human Motor Behavior: an Introduction*. Hillsdale, NJ: Erlbaum.

Turvey, M. T. & Kugler, P. N. (1984). An ecological approach to perception and action, in H. T. A. Whiting (ed.), *Human Motor Actions—Bernstein Reassessed*. Amsterdam: North-Holland.

Van Wieringen, P. C. W. (1988). Discussion: self-organization or representation? Let's have both, in A. M. Colley & J. R. Beech (eds), *Cognition and Action in Skilled Behavior*. Amsterdam: North-Holland.

Walsh, W. D., Russell, D. G., Imanaka, K., & James, B. (1979). Memory for constrained and preselected movement location and distance: Effects of starting position and length, *Journal of Motor Behavior*, 11, 201–214.

Warren, W. H. (1984). Perceiving affordances: Visual guidance of stair climbing, *Journal of Experimental Psychology: Human Perception and Performance*, 10, 683–703.

Wilberg, R. B. (1983). Memory for movement: discussion of Adams and Saltzman and Kelso, in R. A. Magill (ed.), *Memory and Control of Action*. Amsterdam: North-Holland.

Wrisberg, C. A. & Ragsdale, M. R. (1979). Further tests of Schmidt's schema theory: development of a schema rule for a coincident timing task, *Journal of Motor Behavior*, 11, 159–166.

VARIATIONS IN PERFORMANCE

Chapter 8

A methodology for assessing the detailed structure of memory skills

K. Anders Ericsson and William L. Oliver

In this chapter we describe an unusual approach to the study of human memory. Our approach involves an intensive analysis of individual subjects' performance over extended periods of time and relies critically on monitoring the subjects' cognitive processes by having them verbally report their thoughts. Traditional memory research, in contrast, tends to study large groups of subjects for short times, like an hour or so, and only rarely probes the subjects' thought processes through verbal reports and post-session interviews. Our approach also differs from the traditional approach in its theoretical framework and aims. We begin by briefly describing the pioneering work of Ebbinghaus and some of the underlying assumptions of his approach.

HISTORICAL BACKGROUND

Ebbinghaus (1885–1964) recognized that previous experiences determined how easily information could be memorized. Because of large individual differences in experience, he realized it would be difficult to identify general laws of memory. People's memory for everyday material, such as poetry or music, depends on their prior experience for that material and not purely on the basic memory processes Ebbinghaus wanted to study. Ebbinghaus dealt with this problem by finding experimental conditions, in which purely basic

Acquisition and Performance of Cognitive Skills. Edited by A. M. Colley and J. R. Beech
© 1989 John Wiley & Sons Ltd

memory processes would be at work. He believed that the formation of simple associations could be studied with experiments that minimized the influence of previous knowledge by studying his memory for quickly presented, unfamiliar nonsense syllables. Because he assumed that the cognitive states remained the same under these conditions, he saw no need to collect information beyond the times needed to memorize the lists successfully. Ebbinghaus's method also relied on statistical analyses of his study times. He formed a frequency distribution for the study times of nonsense syllables aggregated over many experimental sessions, and found the distribution to be remarkably similar to the normal distribution. Ebbinghaus argued that this distribution reflected a uniform process for memorizing each nonsense syllable and that this process took a constant amount of time with some random fluctuation. Such an interpretation discourages a search for more complex cognitive processes.

The view that basic memory processes can be studied under certain experimental conditions has been maintained in the mainstream of experimental psychology, even up to recent times. That such a view has been able to survive a number of attacks is noteworthy and deserves some comment. The first criticisms came from researchers contemporary with Ebbinghaus. Georg Elias Mueller with Schumann and Pilzecker showed conclusively that subjects use a variety of strategies to memorize even the simplest stimuli. For instance, subjects often grouped and mnemonically encoded nonsense syllables in order to remember them better. In his classic book, Woodworth (1938) reviewed this and other research. This research was probably later forgotten or discounted because of the behaviourist movement, which rejected all cognitive theorizing.

Further evidence for important cognitive processes during learning comes from many studies that test memory for the same type of material over several sessions (Ericsson, 1985). These studies show that subjects' ability to memorize material that is varied from trial to trial can dramatically improve with practice. This improvement suggests that additional processes are involved beyond merely forming new associations between the presented items.

Other criticisms came from researchers (e.g. Binet, 1894) who questioned whether the prevailing view of memory processes could account for vastly superior memory performance. Subjects who showed amazing aptitude at memorizing nonsense material, such as Luria's (1968) S and Binet's (1894) Inaudi, were thought to have exceptional memory capacity, i.e. structurally different memories (Wechsler, 1952). The belief that basic memory processes were involved in memorizing meaningless materials forced investigators into biological explanations for exceptional memory performance.

In the late 1960s and early 1970s, some research looked into the mediation of previous knowledge in the learning of nonsense syllables and paired associates. Montague (1972) reviewed several lines of research demonstrating how natural language provided mediators for subjects' memorization of unfamiliar and unrelated information. Subjects' difficulty with memorizing different nonsense syllables could be fairly accurately predicted from other subjects' ability to generate meaningful associations, i.e. words for the corresponding nonsense syllables. A more direct assessment of cognitive processes involved asking subjects after a memory task how they remembered a given nonsense syllable or paired associate. The verbally reported encodings were then analysed and different types of encodings were found to predict different levels of recall. For example, Bower (1972) explored different encoding strategies for lists of words. He found that many subjects spontaneously used imagery to encode words and found that imagery facilitated later recall as compared with mere rehearsal of the words. This, along with more recent research (e.g. Bellezza, 1981, 1982), showed the overwhelming influence of pre-existing knowledge and encoding processes on subsequent memory for briefly presented information. This research also showed that the different knowledge people possess causes them to encode the same material in different ways. If the knowledge and associations found differ dramatically among individuals, one must wonder whether it is possible to discover general principles of memory.

A METHODOLOGY FOR ASSESSING COGNITIVE PROCESSES DURING MEMORIZATION

In the previous section, we observed that subjects draw extensively on pre-existing knowledge during memorization. Furthermore we noted large individual differences in the knowledge used for encoding information. To obtain a more detailed understanding of how subjects use their existing knowledge in memorization, we need to know more about that knowledge and how it is organized. Because of the large individual differences in knowledge, the best opportunity for describing the relevant knowledge would emerge if we restricted our analysis to a single subject. If we are unable to perform an analysis for a single subject, we would have to conclude that the entire effort is misguided.

How would we go about describing the relevant knowledge that a given subject uses in memorizing a certain type of information? A complete description of somebody's vast knowledge would be impossible to obtain. It is reasonable to assume, however, that a subject would use only a fraction of his or her available knowledge to encode information of a specific type. This limited set of relevant information would be best assessed by having the subject memorize information of a specific type and then obtaining verbal reports on the knowledge accessed and used to encode that information. The verbal reports of accessed information provide us with crucial insights, because the traditional data on speed and accuracy of memorization cannot help us identify the knowledge used by the subject. For years, traditional experimental psychologists have doubted that verbal reports provide valid evidence on cognitive processes, and even have shown that verbal reports are misleading in some studies (Nisbett and Wilson, 1977). Ericsson and Simon (1980, 1984), however, have shown that the validity of verbal reports depends on the way they are elicited by the experimenters.

Conditions for valid verbal reports

Ericsson and Simon (1980) started out by examining the situation for which the requested verbalizations would provide the best information about the subject's thoughts. This situation occurs, they argue, when subjects think aloud while they perform a task. Ericsson and Simon (1984) also examined the validity of retrospective verbal reports, which are collected when subjects report their thoughts after they have performed a task.

Information-processing theory views a cognitive process as a sequence of internal states successively transformed by a series of information processes. Moreover, each of these successive states can be described, in large part, in terms of the small number of information structures, or chunks, that are attended to, or are available in the limited-capacity short-term memory (STM). For many tasks that involve extended thinking, only information that is currently in STM can be reliably reported, because these thoughts are quickly supplanted by new thoughts that come into focal attention. Some thoughts may be available to be reported retrospectively, but only if those thoughts are still in STM or if the subject was able to store and later retrieve them from long term memory (LTM). Hence, as a subject thinks aloud during a task, new thoughts may be expressed verbally as they enter attention, whereas many of these same thoughts would not be reported by the subject later on.

Ideally, when verbal reports are gathered, subjects are instructed to verbalize their thoughts as they emerge, without trying to explain, analyse, or interpret those thoughts. This was the conclusion drawn in a recent review by Ericsson and Simon (1984), which surveyed a wide range of different instructions that have been used to elicit verbal reports. The experimenter, not the subject, should play the role of the theoretician who seeks to explain the sequential process of thought. Other instructions that ask subjects to give reasons for their behaviour often yield verbal reports that are inconsistent with other observed behaviour. For example, some cognitive processes, like those used to recognize familiar words or objects, do not use STM for intermediate steps of recognition, but only for the final recognized object. If forced to give reasons for their recognition of a particular stimulus, subjects, lacking direct knowledge of the actual retrieval cues, simply speculate and make the same kinds of inferences about the cues that observers would make (Nisbett and Wilson, 1977).

Subjects are sometimes asked to describe what they are doing in experiments extending over hundreds of trials. Since under these circumstances the subjects cannot recall their thought processes in each trial, they often generalize from individual instances that they do recall. By taking into account the instructions given to subjects and the structure of the task they are to perform, it is often possible to predict the veridicality of the verbal reports. In particular, Ericsson and Simon (1984) found substantial empirical evidence for the validity of the contents of thinking aloud reports and immediate retrospective reports and no empirical evidence that these kinds of reports fail to reflect what the subject attends to.

A framework for verbal reports and performance data

Within current information-processing theory a number of different types of observations can provide information about the sequence of cognitive processes for a task. Examples of different types of observations include observations of subjects' reaction time, response accuracy, eye movements, and verbal reports. In this section we will briefly discuss how these different types of observations can be used in studies of memory.

We showed earlier how concurrent and retrospective verbal reports were assumed to correspond to the sequence of heeded thoughts and thus provide information about sequences of thoughts. The reaction time, which is the duration measured from the beginning of the task to its end, consists of the sum of the durations of individual processing steps. If the generated response or answer is correct, it is likely that one of the sequences of processes specified by a task analysis was used. If the generated answer is incorrect, the subject either lacked some crucial knowledge or made an error in executing one or more of the processing steps. Therefore, both reaction time and response accuracy provide information about the overall performance of a task and we call these observations performance data. Internal processing steps cannot, of course, be directly observed through any of the sources of data one can collect, but within the framework of information-processing theory we can specify hypotheses about the relationship between the internal processing steps and the observable behaviour. For example, when a subject fixes his or her gaze on a specific item in a visually presented table of information, we can infer that the corresponding internal step involves processing of that information. Ericsson and Oliver (1988) provide a survey of these assumptions for different types of observations.

As we have pointed out, verbal reports provide the only source of observations that help identify what knowledge subjects use to encode information. Hence, in several memory studies we first studied individual subjects for extended periods of time to uncover the knowledge the subjects used and how they encoded the presented information through an analysis of the verbal reports. We then were faced with the problem of validating the description of the subjects cognitive processes derived from the verbal reports. One method at our disposal was to relate differences in memory performance to verbal reports of successful or unsuccessful access of mediating knowledge. However, the most powerful method at our disposal involved designing experiments that collected performance data. From our analysis of the subjects' encoding processes we could design new experimental conditions or tasks, in which alternative hypotheses about the subject's cognitive processes could be tested and evaluated.

ANALYSES OF SPECIFIC MEMORY SKILLS

In the remainder of this chapter we will apply the methods we have described to analyse four different memory skills. The first two examples concern studies of extensive practice, in which subjects with initially normal performance on the memory tasks acquired exceptional levels of skill under carefully monitored laboratory conditions. The last two examples concern analyses of existing memory experts.

Acquisition of exceptional digit span through practice

In the digit-span task the subject hears a series of digits and then immediately tries to recall the digits in order. Miller's (1956) classic paper reviewed studies that showed that normal subjects are able to recall between five and nine digits correctly. Many investigators have thought that individual differences in digit span provide a measure of subjects' fixed-capacity short-term memory. But this view of digit span as a fixed measure of memory capacity seems inconsistent with an early study by Martin and Fernberger (1929), which showed clear effects of practice on digit-span performance. Chase and Ericsson (1981, 1982) set out to replicate these improvements by providing subjects with extensive practice on digit span and monitoring any changes in the subjects' cognitive processes by requesting retrospective reports after some of the trials.

We will focus on our first subject (SF), who discovered how to improve his memory performance by himself. SF was an average college student with average memory ability. His original digit span was about seven digits. During each session, SF was read random digits at the rate of one digit per second; he then recalled the sequence. If the sequence was reported correctly, the next sequence was increased by one digit; otherwise it was decreased by one digit. Figure 8.1. shows SF's average digit span as a function of

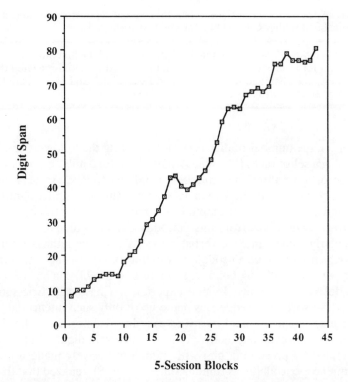

Figure 8.1. Improvement in digit span as a function of practice for SF.

practice for over 200 practice sessions distributed over two years. SF's memory performance is truly exceptional considering that previous subjects alleged to have exceptional memory had digit spans of less than 20 digits (Ericsson, 1985).

SF's retrospective reports indicated that during the first practice session he merely rehearsed the presented digit sequence, which is similar to what most subjects do in the digit-span task. After that session he formed a group of the first three digits of the series, concentrated on that group for a moment, and then rehearsed the remaining digits in the sequence. At recall he retrieved the three-digit group from memory and then reported it followed by the digits in the rehearsal group. An example of his verbal reports from this period are given in Table 8.1.

During Session 5, SF realized that a three-digit sequence could be interpreted as a running time for a mile. For example, 418 could be a 4-minute, 18-second mile time. His average digit span for this session jumped four standard deviations from the previous session. SF was a long-distance runner with extensive knowledge of both specific and general categories of running

Table 8.1. A transcription of the retrospective verbal report for the subject SF after he had recalled the digits '1053144'. See the text for details.

When you said the . . . started saying the digits, I blocked the first three into a little set and, forgot it for a second and then went on to the next five, and repeated those four or five times, and when you raised your hand I came back and remembered the little set of three, and proceeded all the way to the end.

times for a large number of different races. During the following sessions, SF began using a set of races (¼-mile, ½-mile, ¾-mile, 2-mile, etc.) that covered the range of most three-digit numbers from 100 to 959. As SF's digit-span performance improved, he began to segment the list of digits into several groups of digits, which he attempted to encode as running times. An illustrative retrospective report from this period is given in Table 8.2.

Particularly salient in SF's verbal report is his complaint regarding digit groups which cannot be encoded as running times. In fact, no three-digit numbers with a middle digit of 6, 7, 8 or 9 (e.g. 483, 873) can be interpreted as meaningful running times. In one experiment Chase and Ericsson (1981) presented SF with digit sequences made up of only such unencodable three-digit sequences, and his memory span was reduced almost to the level prior to practice. An improvement relative to his then current digit span (27 per cent) was obtained by presenting him with stimuli exclusively made up of three-digit sequences encodable as running times. Later, SF realized that three-digit and four-digit sequences uninterpretable as times could be encoded as ages (for example, 592 to 59.2 years old and 4976 is 49 and 76 years old). Clearly, rapid access to knowledge in semantic memory from which meaningful encodings could be formed was critical for SF's ability rapidly to encode and store digit groups in memory.

With further practice SF was able to encode several three-digit or four-digit groups before turning to rehearsal of the remaining digits. In order to recall the order of these three-digit groups, SF reported encoding them as 'first,'

Table 8.2. A transcription of the retrospective verbal report for the subject SF after he had recalled the digits '08033806321431'. See the text for details.

I made the 803 in the beginning a 2-mile. I put a zero onto it, so I just remembered the 803 as a 2-mile time then the 380 was difficult, very difficult, to remember because it was not a time. I had to concentrate especially hard, then I made six-thirty-two a mile time, then I made fourteen-thirty-one a 3-mile time. I hope it wasn't fourteen-thirty-two. I think it was fourteen-thirty-one. I should have concentrated a little bit more on the last four, but I didn't because of three-eighty, so had to go back. (Experimenter: Did you rehearse anything?) Yes, fourteen-thirty-one, just a little bit, just a little bit, maybe a few times, then I had to get onto that 380.

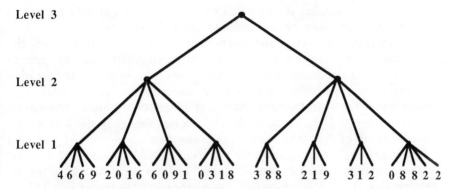

Figure 8.2. A schematic drawing of SF's retrieval structure.

'middle', and 'last'. Further increases in SF's digit span occurred when he began to group digit groups into several supergroups, which are illustrated at the second level of the hierarchy in Figure 8.2.

Before presentation of a digit sequence, SF would report his plans on how he would group and organize the sequence. During the presentation he would encode the corresponding location within the hierarchy for all digit groups. Chase and Ericsson (1982) called the cues associated with the location within the hierarchy *retrieval-structure* cues. During recall SF used these cues to attain complete and accurate serial recall of the stored digit groups.

In one experiment Chase and Ericsson presented SF with digit sequences much shorter than his current memory span, which were encoded as illustrated in Figure 8.2. After successful recall of the sequence, they showed him different *probes* or subsequences of digits selected from the memorized sequence, and asked him to name adjacent digits. SF could name the last digit of groups very rapidly when the first two or three digits of that group were presented. For example, for the digit sequence in Figure 8.2. the visual probe *231* would elicit *9* as a response. Thus retrieval within the lowest level of the hierarchy (the encoded digit groups) was quite fast (1.8 s).

Chase and Ericsson also presented SF with individual digit groups (e.g. 388) and asked him to generate the preceding or following digit group, which would be 0318 and 219 respectively for the example appearing in Figure 8.2. There was a remarkable difference in retrieval time depending on whether or not the retrieved digit group was part of the same supergroup as the probe. When both groups belonged to the same supergroup, the average retrieval time was 4.4 s. When the two groups belonged to different supergroups, the average retrieval time was much longer (10.1 s). Chase and Ericsson asked SF to point out where a presented digit group was located in a schematic drawing similar to Figure 8.2. In a yet another experimental condition, they would point to a location and ask for recall of the corresponding digit group. SF was much faster at pointing to the location of a probe (1.2 s) than he was at recalling the digit group at a specified location (7.5 s).

The immediate access of the location of a probe strongly supports the hypothesis that information about location of a digit group is directly encoded in the retrieval structure. However, the results also show that the location information was not sufficient for directly accessing the corresponding digit group stored at that location. Retrieval based on location information apparently involved mediated retrieval processes similar to those processes used for recall of digit groups adjacent to the probes.

The mnemonic encodings and the retrieval structures were first evidenced in the verbal reports, but two additional findings were derived from the performance data alone. First, SF stored the digit sequences in LTM, as demonstrated by his post-session recall of over 90 per cent of all digit groups presented in a session totalling 200–300 digits. The second finding was observed during SF's performance on a task involving self-paced memorization of sequentially presented digits. In this task SF memorized lists of up to 50 digits at his own pace. He regulated the presentation of individual digits on a CRT by pressing a button. With practice SF was able to memorize digit sequences shorter than his current digit span at rates much faster than the rate of one digit per second used in the regular digit-span task. This reduction of study time for a list of fixed length as a function of practice suggests that practice effects in memory skills are similar to the speedup observed in most other skills (Newell and Rosenbloom, 1981).

From the analysis of this subject Chase and Ericsson (1982) argued that practice enables subjects to use long-term memory with storage and retrieval characteristics similar to short-term memory. This new type of memory was named *skilled memory* and is based on the following three principles (Chase and Ericsson, 1982). First, information is encoded in terms of knowledge structures in semantic memory through meaningful associations (meaningful encoding). Second, during encoding or storage, retrieval cues are explicitly associated with the memory encoding, so that the retrieval cues are sufficient to retrieve the memory encoding at some later time from LTM (retrieval structure). Third, encoding and retrieval operations can be dramatically speeded up by practice, resulting in storage and access speed of the order of a few seconds, speeds that are characteristic of STM.

These principles have been found to characterize the memory performance of several other subjects attaining exceptional digit span through practice (Chase and Ericsson, 1981, 1982; Ericsson, Fendrich, and Faivre, in preparation; Staszewski, 1986) as well as the performance of other mnemonists and memory experts described by Ericsson (1985). More recently Ericsson and Staszewski (in press) have shown that superior memory of other experts in their domain of expertise is consistent with the structure of skilled memory.

Exceptional memory for chess positions

In this classic work on expertise in chess, de Groot (1966, 1978) found no clear differences in the cognitive processes involved in selecting chess moves between grand masters and much less experienced chess players. By having the chess players think aloud while they selected the best move for a chess position, de Groot (1966, 1978) assessed the number of different moves considered. Interestingly, no differenes were found among the players in the number of moves considered, yet the grand masters consistently identified the best moves, whereas the less experienced players did not. It appeared that the grand master, unlike the experienced chess player, could rapidly determine the promising moves through perception. In support of this hypothesis, de Groot (1966, 1978) showed that grand masters had almost perfect recall of briefly presented chess positions. Chase and Simon (1973a,b) extended this finding and showed that the amount of recall of briefly presented chess positions was highly related to one's chess-playing ability. Chase and Simon (1973a,b) also found no differences in recall among the chess players for briefly presented boards of randomly arranged chess pieces, showing that the chess masters' superior recall was restricted to meaningful chess positions. To account for the superior recall of chess masters Chase and Simon (1973b) proposed that the chess masters could recognize many individual patterns of several chess pieces (chunks), and that this recognition of chunks enabled them to encode the chess positions. In contrast, beginners at chess could only encode individual pieces and less experienced players could use patterns involving a smaller number of pieces. Simon and Gilmartin (1973) estimated that a chess master acquires about 50,000 such patterns during the ten years or 10,000 hours of chess playing which appear necessary to acquire the chess-playing strength of a chess master. The question arises as to whether this superior memory pattern occurs in isolation of other aspects of chess skill. Our next case study investigated whether exceptional memory for chess positions could be developed without a corresponding development of chess expertise.

Ericsson and Harris (in preparation) studied the effects of practice on memory for chess positions, each of which was presented once for 5 seconds. The subject (BB) was a female undergraduate with minimal experience of chess. Before the study she knew only the names of the different pieces and their legal moves. Approximately three times a week she received an hour of practice, which consisted of presentation and immediate recall of about ten middle-game chess positions. Each chess position was taken from chess books and displayed between 24 and 28 chess pieces. Before the end of the spring semester 43 training sessions had been completed and the average percentage of correctly recalled pieces for each training session is shown in Figure 8.3. BB's recall performance was 18 per cent on the first training session, which

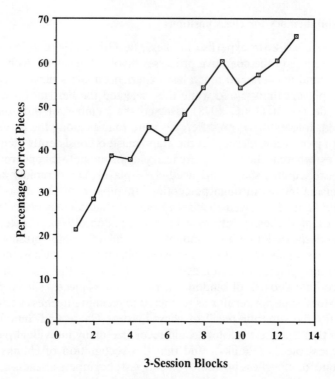

Figure 8.3. Improvement in the recall of chess positions as function of practice for BB.

corresponds to almost 5 correctly placed chess pieces for each chessboard position, almost precisely matching the recall performance obtained by Chase and Simon (1973a) for beginning chess players. At the end of the training phase, BB's recall performance was 67 per cent of the presented pieces, which corresponds to more than 17 correctly placed chess pieces. This recall performance matches the performance of the master-level chess player studied by Chase and Simon (1973a), who recalled about 64 per cent or 16 chess pieces. Evidently, BB attained in less than 50 hours a recall performance comparable to a recall performance requiring several thousands of hours of chess playing! BB continued her practice sessions through the summer and fall, but only on an intermittent basis. During the continued practice her recall performance remained at about 60 per cent correct.

On three occasions at an early, a middle, and a late stage of practice BB's recall of randomly arranged chess positions was tested and her recall was 12.6, 16.3, and 15.2 per cent respectively. Hence, there was no indication that BB's ability to recall random chess positions was improved beyond the initial ability of recalling 4 different chess pieces. These results are remarkably consistent with those obtained by Chase and Simon (1973a,b) for random chessboards with chess players ranging from beginners to chess masters. Furthermore, Ericsson and Harris (in preparation) were able to show that BB's memory of the briefly presented chess position from the 5-second presentation was not stored in STM. In a separate experiment, BB's recall performance was not significantly affected when she had to count backwards by threes immediately after the presentation of a position. Similarly, Charness (1976) has shown that experienced chess players' recall of the chess position is uninfluenced by tasks assumed to eliminate storage in STM.

One might think that BB's encoding processes were the same as those of experienced chess players, because she performed as well as they did on the same tasks. A closer examination of BB's encoding processes, however, shows that they were different. The initial evidence on BB's encoding processes came from spontaneous comments she made during the initial training sessions. During the continued practice period, verbal protocols were obtained more systematically, especially during five special sessions. Retrospective reports of her encoding processes were collected directly after the 5-second exposures of the chess positions. A sample retrospective report from one of the trials is given in Table 8.3. Her reports showed that the chess positions were scanned in an order reflecting the spatial layout of the pieces.

The important function of this scan path was to maximize the rapid detection of familiar patterns of chunks. In BB's retrospective reports there are several types of familiar patterns. One type of pattern occurred when chess pieces were left in their starting positions (e.g. 'There were five pieces in their original positions in the black row. That's how I code it. Then I go back and try to remember which pieces they were'). Another type occurred when the chess positions reflected sequences of commonly occurring moves, as in the case of castled kings and fianchettoed bishops. BB was familiar with the castling procedure but not with terminology for fianchettoed bishops and hence developed her own labels. Figure 8.4 shows several verbal labels she used to encode the pieces at locations on the board where fianchettoed bishops could occur. Several other configurations not shown were encoded as variations on candlesticks, such as a 'backwards candlestick' and 'half cand-

Table 8.3. A transcription of the retrospective verbal report for the subject BB after she had recalled a chessboard position. See the text for details.

Looked back and saw the black castle, counted three pawns. Came to the white and saw the king castled, empty candlestick. Went back to the lefthand corner of the black and saw the queen on her original color, the rook in its original place. And then a black pawn, white bishop, black pawn. Came back to the white line on the left side, saw the queen, bishop rook, in a row and a pawn on the very far left.

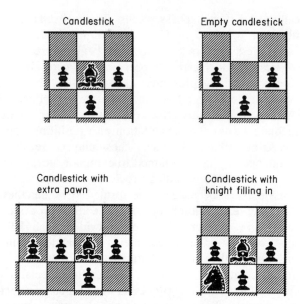

Figure 8.4. Examples of the patterns used by BB to encode chess positions with her verbal labels.

lestick'. Still other types of patterns were due to perceptual configurations, like pawn chains forming diagonals ('saw three pawns in a diagonal'). Finally BB encoded rows of pieces as sequences, like 'three pawns, a queen and a knight', 'one, two, three [pawns], queen'.

The verbal reports suggests that BB searched the chess position to find familiar patterns. During the continued practice period, BB was instructed to identify the pieces belonging to a single pattern or chunk. On average she would identify four patterns for each chessboard position. On the average, these patterns were made up of 4 pieces. The accuracy of recall for pieces that belonged to patterns was 97 per cent compared to 89 per cent for the pieces that did not belong to patterns. Hence, the patterns seemed to serve as units of recall, though recall of these units was hardly all-or-none. An analysis of BB's pattern showed that the patterns she identified were quite similar across memory trials. The patterns reflected arrangements of pieces that were perceptually salient and drew minimally on knowledge of chess-playing. In contrast to a chess expert, BB did not use attack or defend relationships among the pieces to encode the chessboard positions. BB's most frequently reported patterns matched the most frequent configurations of chess pieces in master-level chess games determined by de Groot (1966) from a statistical analysis of a large number of middle game positions. In sum, BB was able to attain a recall performance of briefly presented chess positions, which matched the level of recall of chess players with many years of experience. A close examination of her memory encodings showed the use of perceptual patterns and capitalization of redundancies across chess positions, and no dependence on the more meaningful relationships among the pieces that a chess expert might use.

Analysis of existing memory experts

In the two case studies described above we monitored the acquisition of memory skill and followed the gradual development of new types of memory encodings and the use of retrieval cues. A similar analysis of existing memory experts is more difficult for several reasons. First, the amount of knowledge acquired by an expert may be extensive and virtually impossible to describe. Second, the memory expert has acquired a skill in a specific environment, which may be difficult to reproduce in a laboratory setting. And finally, experts may have automated their skill to the point where they cannot verbally report their mediating thought processes. Below we will discuss two studies with different goals. The first study attempts to assess the memory skill of a waiter, who can memorize many dinner orders without writing anything down. The second study is concerned with uncovering how actors have their parts encoded in memory.

Exceptional memory for dinner orders

A waiter (JC), who could take over 20 dinner orders without writing anything down, participated in an extended laboratory study of his memory skill. The first challenge for Ericsson and Polson (1988a) was to create a laboratory situation, or task, that preserved JC's memory skill for dinner orders. In collaboration with JC, we devised the following experimental procedure. Each dinner order consisted of four items: one of seven possible steak entrées (e.g. filet mignon), one of five temperatures ranging from well-done to rare, one of five possible salad dressings (e.g. bleu cheese), and one of three starches (e.g. fries, baked potato, and rice). A computer program generated dinner orders by sampling one item from each of the four categories. Three different table sizes were simulated corresponding to 3, 5 or 8 customers and are referred to as a 3-top, 6-top, and 8-top, respectively. Each customer was represented by a card with a picture of a face cut out of a newspaper. Before each memory trial the given number of customers were 'seated' by arranging the corresponding number of cards in front of JC.

A fixed procedure was used for presenting the dinner orders. Facing the cards, JC said 'go', and the first dinner order for the first customer was read to him. When JC said 'next', the order for the next customer (proceeding clockwise) was read to him. The study time for each order was measured. JC was allowed to request a repetition of presented items and would signal that he had the dinner orders memorized by saying 'done'.

To what extent was JC able to preserve his skill in memorizing dinner orders under these experimental conditions? In order to compare JC's performance with that of normal subjects, Ericsson and Polson recruited 8 college students to do the same memory task. JC's performance was simply outside the range of the college students' performance (see Ericsson and Polson (1988b), for a detailed comparison). He required less than half the study time used by the college students, and his recall was essentially perfect (less than 3 per cent errors), whereas the college students averaged around 20 per cent errors in recall. In a subsequent study Crutcher and Ericsson (in preparation) identified 5 waiters and waitresses, who regularly memorized dinner orders from tables of 5 or less customers. Somewhat surprisingly these waiters and waitresses required about the same study times as the college students, but their error rates were quite low and comparable to JC. Hence, even compared to waiters and waitresses with experience of memorizing dinner orders, JC's memory performance was exceptional.

During the first study of JC, he was instructed to think aloud during memorization. An example of a think-aloud protocol JC gave while memorizing dinner orders for 5 people is given in Table 8.4. Most of the verbalizations during the actual memorization of dinner orders concern the experimenter's presentation of dinner orders and JC's repetitions of the same information. To highlight the verbalizations reflecting JC's thinking we have italicized them in Table 8.4. The first verbalizations of that type are 'two rices in a row', 'so that's HB'. The first phrase indicates that JC has noticed that the starches are the same for the first two salad dressings. The second phrase refers to an encoding of salad dressings (*o*il and vinegar and *b*leu cheese) by a first-letter mnemonic. After the third dinner order, JC verbalizes his mnemonic encoding of the first three salad dressings and also that all starches so far are rice. In Table 8.4. we find similar encodings for temperatures, as well as attempts to recall entrées across the different dinner orders. When JC recalls the dinner orders he invariably recalls them by category, which is illustrated in Table 8.4. By analysing many other think-aloud protocols, like the one above, Ericsson and Polson (1988a; 1988b) were able to derive a model of JC's cognitive processes during memorization of dinner orders. The different encoding types for the different categories are illustrated in Figure 8.5.

Salad dressings were encoded with the first-letter method described above, and JC reported encoding letter combinations as familiar abbreviations or even words, such as BOOT. Because there are only three different starches, a sequence of four starches invariably contains repetitions, which can be encoded as patterns. JC reported encoding temperatures as spatial patterns as shown in Figure 8.5. JC's encoding methods relied on his simultaneous attention to all of the items in a given category. He required efficient memory access to items presented previously in order to form encodings of an entire

Table 8.4. A verbatim transcripton of JC's think-aloud report of his memorizing dinner orders from 5 customers. The dinner orders were read by the experimenter and his verbalizations appear in the transcripts preceded by E; JC's verbalizations are preceded by S. Verbalizations judged to reflect JC's thinking are underlined.

E: Why don't you start thinking aloud while . . .
S: I'm thinking about 5 tables so I've got slots in my head for 5 people. Now I begin to put them into patterns to see if there might be any patterns and there are. Suddenly, there's 3 blacks and 2 other people at the table and they're all sitting together in one corner. So that's the first pattern I see. Okay. Begin.
E: Steak, oscar, medium, creamy Italian, rice.
S: Oscar, medium, creamy Italian, rice. Okay. Very complex. Next.
E: Teriyaki, well done, bleu cheese, rice.
S: Two rices in a row. Well done. So that's HB, teri, well done, oscar, medium. Next.
E: Rib eye, medium-rare, creamy Italian, rice.
S: Medium-rare, creamy Italian, rice. Three rices in a row. Rib eye, medium-rare, creamy Italian, HBH. Three different steaks. Next.
E: Boulder steak, medium-rare, thousand island, fries.
S: First different starch. HBHT. Steak and temperature again?
E: Boulder steak, rare.
S: Boulder steak, rare. Not medium-rare.
E: Excuse me. Medium-rare. I'm sorry.
S: It is medium-rare. Okay. So that's M, W and then two MRs and that's a Boulder. That's 4 different steaks. Next.
E: Barbecue, rare, bleu cheese, rice.
S: Barebecue, rare, bleu cheese, rice. Four rices at the table. Salad dressing again?
E: Bleu cheese.
S: Okay. So that's two doubles on the dressings and now steaks. Five different steaks at the table. Steak cut again.
E: Rib eye.
S: Steak cut here.
E: Barbecue.
S: Okay. Done. Seems fairly tough for one thing cause there are five different steaks at the table. I think. Temperatures—medium, well, medium-rare, medium rare, rare. Boy, I hope I've got these steaks right. I'll try the steaks because I'm forgetting them fast here it seems like. Steak oscar, and I'm going to leave this guy blank for a minute. Rib eye. Boulder, barbecue, and now it all comes back I think. This guy should be, number 2 should be a teriyaki, and starches are easy. Number 4 is fries and everything else is rice. Right?
E: Right. But we don't have any salad dressings yet.
S: Oh, you don't? Oh, I'm sorry. Salad dressings: Creamy Italian, bleu, creamy Italian, thousand island, bleu.

---

category. JC attained this rapid access by associating the items with retrieval cues about their locations at the time of encoding. He could then later retrieve the items from memory using the retrieval cues in a manner analogous to SF's retrieval of digit groups.

Ericsson and Polson (1988a; 1988b) conducted six different experiments on JC to validate the protocol data and to assess the generalizability of JC's memory skill to information other than dinner orders. Findings

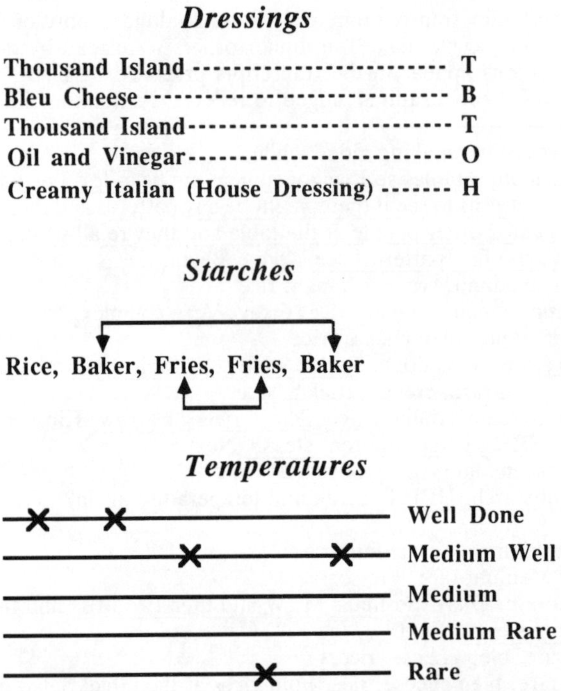

Dressings

Thousand Island ----------------------- T
Bleu Cheese ---------------------------- B
Thousand Island------------------------ T
Oil and Vinegar------------------------- O
Creamy Italian (House Dressing) ------- H

Starches

Rice, Baker, Fries, Fries, Baker

Temperatures

Well Done

Medium Well

Medium

Medium Rare

Rare

Figure 8.5. Examples of JC's encodings for different categories of food.

from these experiments, as well as findings from the experiments we have just described, were consistent with principles of skilled memory. To encode information rapidly, JC consistently used meaningful encodings and identifiable retrieval structures.

Actors' memory for their parts

Because actors must perfectly memorize scripts, it is possible to specify much of their knowledge for a part. Given that we know what is stored in memory we can ask questions about how this information is represented and accessed. Actors' memory is of further interest because we know that a part is studied and practised extensively before it is performed, thus providing a natural situation for studying the effects of practice on retrieval. In this section, we will describe research aimed at identifying the readily accessible units in memory that represent the actor's part.

Our research (Oliver and Ericsson, 1986) has shown that repertory actors have rapid access to parts they are currently performing, even when the memory cues are quite minimal. We found, for instance, that four words taken at random from an actor's part cued retrieval of the corresponding line almost 100 per cent of the time. This result shows that an actor needs only to be aware of a few words from a part to gain access to subsequent words from the part. We had expected a degree of context dependency; that is, we had expected that retrieval would depend on the use of additional cues such as what scene or speech was being probed, the meaning of the lines, positioning on stage, and so on. We knew that this non-verbatim information was an important component of an actor's representation of a part and was probably relied on by the actor to recall a part before extensive practice enabled direct access to its verbatim wording. Impressive as this accessibility is, the question remains of exactly what units in memory are being accessed by the verbatim cues.

The actors' immediate retrospective reports indicated that the verbatim wording of a part was represented as a sequence of phrases or chunks. They reported that, when cued with a word or two from their parts, larger phrases containing the cues immediately came to mind. In several experiments, we collected reaction time data to validate these reports. When selecting probes for these experiments, we assumed that word groupings, or chunks, would invariably be demarcated by sentence boundaries if actors used their well-learned linguistic knowledge to segment the text. It seemed unlikely to us that sensible segmentations of the text would fail to take into account sentence structure. Word groupings that began in one sentence and ended in the middle of another sentence would not stand on their own as a sensible unit of meaning and probably not be focused upon by the actors when they learned their parts.

In the first part of our initial experiments on chunking, the subjects were presented with four-word probes and asked to generate the subsequent words appearing in their parts (forward task). Probes were presented on a computer screen and latencies to respond to the probes were timed with a voice key. The probes were selected such that half of them were the first four words of sentences (within units) and half of them were the last four words of sentences (across units). We expected the subjects to generate the words fastest for the probes beginning sentences since the target words were likely to fall within the same linguistic unit as the probe. On the other hand, we expected probes ending sentences to be responded to the slowest because the subjects would be forced to generate a different linguistic unit than the one that the probe would cause them to access directly. In the second part of the experiments, the subjects were asked to produce the word that preceded the four word probes taken from their parts (backward task). Half of the probes were four words that followed the first words of sentences (within units). We expected these four words to fall within the same linguistic units as the first words and thus to be retrieved rapidly. The remaining probes were all four words in length and began sentences, so that the target words occurred in different

Table 8.5. Examples of probes for the different combinations of the task and boundary variables with the target words underlined.

FORWARD	BACKWARD
Within	Within
Can I refrain from <u>expressing</u> . . .	If doctors prescribe too <u>many</u> . . .
Across	Across
. . . are everything to me. <u>Believe</u> . . .	<u>that.</u> One could celebrate its . . .

sentences than the sentences that the probe occurred in (across units). We expected these probes to be responded to more slowly than the within units probes. Examples of the four probe types appear in Table 8.5.

Subjects were slower on the average responding to the across-units probes (3.4. s) than the within-units probes (1.9 s). Not surprisingly, the subjects were faster in the forward condition (2.3 s) than the backward condition (3.0 s). The task and units variables did not interact. These findings support the idea that the actors' parts are represented as verbatim phrases or chunks. The within-units probes enabled direct and rapid access of the chunks bearing the target words; the across-unit probes enabled access of chunks that were adjacent to the chunks bearing the target words, thus forcing the subjects to go through additional mediating retrieval processes before responding correctly.

We also collected immediate retrospective reports of a subject performing this task. There were several changes in the experimental procedure for the additional protocol subject. First, he performed the backward task prior to performing the forward task, and second, he was asked to give retrospective verbal reports after each trial. He was instructed to say out loud exactly what had gone through his mind during the interval between when he first saw the probe and when he responded. In all other respects, the experiment followed the same procedure described above. The session was recorded and later transcribed.

On the average the protocol subject retrieved the target words across units in 4.5 seconds and the target words within units in 2.2 seconds. There was no significant difference in how fast he performed the two tasks, nor any interaction of task and units. The subject reported on many trials that he had thought of other words from his part prior to retrieving the correct answer. Table 8.6 shows representative examples of his reports. By consulting the transcript of his protocols it was possible to estimate the number of words he consciously scanned from his part for each trial (wscan). Table 8.6 shows that the subject was quite explicit about the words from his part that he consciously scanned. Examination of the protocols revealed that the subject tended to scan entire phrases of words before responding with the target words. As a

Table 8.6. Examples of probes and retrospective verbal reports that the subject gave after responding to those probes. See the text for details.

Forward-Within probe: I fear that scoundrel's __
'Threats. I fear that scoundrel's.' I just started where it starts up there and just kept going.

Backward-Across probe: __ **You've given Valerie your**
'Rot.' I finished out the line 'You've given Valerie your word, will you keep it or not?' And then I went back to 'Come brother, don't talk rot.'

---

rule, he scanned only one phrase before responding to within-units probes, whereas he scanned what appeared to be at least two phrases before responding to the across-units phrases. When included in the analysis of log-transformed reaction time, the variable wscan caused the proportion of variance accounted for by the units effect to fall from 0.40 to 0.09. These results showed that more words were scanned in response to across-units probes than within-units probes and that the time taken to scan these words accounted for much of the difference between the within- and across-units conditions. Hence, the protocol data gave converging evidence for a chunked representation of a part and provided additional insights into the mediating processes required to access the units in this representation that could not be accessed directly.

CONCLUDING REMARKS

The four studies described above have illustrated a methodology for assessing the detailed structure of memory skills. In all four cases, the verbal reports of the subjects' encoding or retrieval processes allowed us to hypothesize about the content and structure of information that the subjects attended to while performing memory tasks. We then tested our hypotheses with analyses of performance data that came from specially designed experiments. The goal for each study was to find an account for the subjects' memory performance that was supported by analyses of all the different types of data we collected. We believe that this approach enables researchers to describe individual subject's memory skills in detail. These detailed accounts inevitably reveal large individual differences among memory experts with respect to the content and structure of memory encodings.

We believe that researchers must accept this diversity in the detailed organization of each subject's skill before they can come to a general understanding of memory skill and expert performance. According to this view, describing the detailed structure of individual subjects' skill is a necessary first step toward finding principles that are generalizable across subjects.

By comparing the structure of several subjects' skill, one can detect regularities and induce theoretical principles, which can be tested in analyses of other subjects and in investigations of other memory skills.

REFERENCES

Bellezza, F. S. (1981). Mnemonic devices: classification, characteristics and criteria, *Review of Educational Research*, **51**, 247–275.

Bellezza, F. S. (1982). Updating memory using mnemonic devices, *Cognitive Psychology*, **14**, 301–327.

Binet, A. (1894). *Psychologie des grands calculateurs et jouers d'échecs*. Paris: Libraire Hachette.

Bower, G. H. (1972). Mental imagery and associative learning, in L. W. Gregg (ed.), *Cognition in Learning and Memory*. New York: Wiley.

Charness, N. (1976). Memory for chess positions: resistance to interference, *Journal of Experimental Psychology: Human Learning and Memory*, **2**, 641–653.

Chase, W. G. & Ericsson, K. A. (1981). Skilled memory, in J. R. Anderson (ed.), *Cognitive Skills and their Acquisition*. Hillsdale, NJ: Erlbaum.

Chase, W. G. & Ericsson, K. A. (1982). Skill and working memory, in G. H. Bower (ed.), *The Psychology of Learning and Motivation* (vol. 16). New York: Academic Press.

Chase, W. G. & Simon, H. A. (1973a). Perception in chess, *Cognitive Psychology*, **4**, 55–81.

Chase, W. G. & Simon, H. A. (1973b). The mind's eye in chess, in W. G. Chase (ed.), *Visual Information Processing*. New York: Academic Press.

Crutcher, R. J. & Ericsson, K. A. (in preparation). *Assessing the structure of skill in memorizing dinner orders in experienced waiters and waitresses*.

de Groot, A. (1966). Perception and memory versus thought: some old ideas and recent findings, in B. Kleinmuntz (ed.), *Problem Solving*. New York: Wiley.

de Groot, A. (1978). *Thought and Choice in Chess* (2nd edn). The Hague: Mouton.

Ebbinghaus, H. (1964). *Memory: a Contribution to Experimental Psychology* (H. A. Ruger and C. E. Bussenius, trans). New York: Dover Publications (original work published, 1885).

Ericsson, K. A. (1985). Memory skill, *Canadian Journal of Psychology*, **39**, 188–231.

Ericsson, K. A., Fendrich, D., & Faivre, I. (in preparation). *A chronometric analysis of the acquisition of exceptional digit-span performance*.

Ericsson, K. A. & Harris, M. (in preparation). *Acquiring expert chess memory without chess-playing skill*.

Ericsson, K. A. & Oliver, W. L. (1988). Methodology for laboratory research on thinking: task selection, collection of observations, and data analysis, in R. J. Sternberg & E. E. Smith (eds), *The Psychology of Human Thought*. New York: Cambridge University Press.

Ericsson, K. A. & Polson, P. G. (1988a). An experimental analysis of the mechanisms of a memory skill, *Journal of Experimental Psychology: Learning, Memory, and Cognition*, **14**, 305–316.

Ericsson, K. A. & Polson, P. G. (1988b). Memory for restaurant orders, in M. T. H. Chi, R. Glaser & M. J. Farr (eds), *The Nature of Expertise*. Hillsdale, NJ: Erlbaum.

Ericsson, K. A. & Simon, H. A. (1980). Verbal reports as data, *Psychological Review*, **87**, 215–251.

Ericsson, K. A. & Simon, H. A. (1984). *Protocol analysis*. Cambridge, MA: MIT Press/Bradford.

Ericsson, K. A. & Staszewski, J. J. (in press). Skilled memory and expertise: mechanisms of exceptional performance, in D. Klahr & K. Kotovsky (eds), *Complex Information Processing Comes of Age*. Hillsdale, NJ: Erlbaum.

Luria, A. R. (1968). *The Mind of a Mnemonist*. New York: Avon.

Martin, P. R. & Fernberger, S. W. (1929). Improvement in memory span, *American Journal of Psychology*, **41**, 91–94.

Montague, W. E. (1972). Elaborative strategies in verbal learning and memory, in G. H. Bower (ed.), *The Psychology of Learning and Motivation* (vol. 6). New York: Academic Press.

Miller, G. A. (1956). The magical number seven, plus or minus two, *Psychological Review*, **68**, 81–97.

Newell, A. & Rosenbloom, P. S. (1981). Mechanisms of skill acquisition and the law of practice, in J. R. Anderson (ed.), *Cognitive Skills and their Acquisition*. Hillsdale, NJ: Erlbaum.

Nisbett, R. E. & Wilson, T. D. (1977). Telling more than we can know: verbal reports on mental processes, *Psychological Review*, **84**, 231–259.

Oliver, W. L. & Ericsson, K. A. (1986). Repertory actors' memory for their parts, *Proceedings of the Eighth Annual Conference of the Cognitive Science Society*, Amherst, MA.

Simon, H. A. & Gilmartin, K. A. (1973). A simulation of memory for chess positions, *Cognitive Psychology*, **5**, 29–46.

Staszewski, J. J. (1986). The psychological reality of retrieval structures: an investigation of expert knowldege. Unpublished PhD dissertation. Ithaca, NY: Cornell University, Department of Psychology.

Wechsler, D. (1952). *The Range of Human Capacities*. Baltimore: Williams & Wilkins.

Woodworth, R. S. (1938). *Experimental Psychology*. New York: Holt.

Chapter 9

Executing two tasks at once

Paul J. Barber

INTRODUCTION

This chapter is about limitations on people's abilities to carry out more than one concurrent activity—described in everyday terms as 'doing two things at once'. Indeed everyday experience contains some useful illustrations of what can and cannot be achieved. People carry on conversations while driving, they knit and watch television, listen to a radio play while ironing, read the newspaper when eating breakfast, make notes as the lecturer is talking, and solve personal problems while walking. These combinations of tasks are feasible, if not always very effective; and when the difficulty of carrying them out together exceeds margins of competence (or safety), one of the tasks may be temporarily abandoned. For example, sensible drivers are prone to allow the conversation to lapse when making a tricky manoeuvre. One job for cognitive psychology is to discover what makes some task combinations easy and some difficult (Kinsbourne, 1981), and how in general to explain dual task performance.

Interest in whether or not people are capable of doing two things at once stems from the question of how many things can be simultaneously present in consciousness, and was discussed by William James (1890) towards the end of the nineteenth century. James was sceptical about the concept of attention, as to whether humans possess such a capability, but he was clear about the unitary indivisible nature of consciousness. On the other hand we do in everyday terms talk about attention as something we can apply selectively to a particular object or activity, and as something we can divide between activities. It can be seen that it would not be difficult to take the further step of

Acquisition and Performance of Cognitive Skills. Edited by A. M. Colley & J. R. Beech interpreting attention as a mental resource, whose allocation to a mental process is generally beneficial.

However we choose to think about the problem, it is apparent that it is difficult to deal with two complex activities at the same time. The first relevant experiments also date from the late nineteenth century (Solomons and Stein, 1896; Welch, 1898). Solomons and Stein were interested in the automatization of skill, and themselves practised two simultaneous tasks— such as reading a story while taking down another to dictation—until they were no longer aware of one of the tasks. It took considerable practice for one of the tasks to (reportedly) drop out of consciousness. Unfortunately there is no record of the actual details of the performance achieved. This is a study which, as we shall see, has been followed up in the recent past. In another classical study, Welch (1898) reported that a physical task, exerting maximum hand grip, interfered with a concurrent mental task such as mental arithmetic or reading. This rather ancient finding seems to be something of an embarrassment to certain contemporary theoretical accounts, although it is not an intuitively surprising result, and does not appear to have been replicated.

SINGLE CHANNEL THEORY

The scale of research into divided attention and dual task performance increased in the 1950s and the issues arising from this research have subsequently continued to be a preoccupation for experimental and applied psychologists. At the outset of this resurgence of interest in attention and human performance, the key theoretical perspective was to treat the human operator as acting in many situations as a single limited capacity communication or information-processing channel; this is the *single channel hypothesis*. There are two principal limitations on performance according to this hypothesis, the first arising from the single channel facility itself, which enables only one batch of information to be dealt with at a time. The second arises from the capacity limitation on the single channel, which restricts how much can be done via the channel in terms of batch size and speed of processing. In fact 'batch size' was never measured (or indeed even expressed in this way) and it is easy to substitute 'task' for 'batch of information' in the expanded statement of the hypothesis, so the limitation becomes one of dealing with one task at a time.

The original account of single channel theory (SCT), however, had a quite restricted view of what the channel could cope with. Welford's (1952) formulation of the single channel hypothesis postulated that the central processes concerned with two separate stimuli could not co-exist. The stimuli were those associated with a simple dual reaction time paradigm, in which two simple signals (such as tones or lights) are presented in rapid succession, each to be responded to (usually by pressing the appropriate one of a set of keys assigned for the purpose) as fast as the subject can manage. This is the 'psychological refractory period' (PRP) paradigm and is one of the classical tools of dual task research, though it has fallen from favour in recent times. Suppose the channel is occupied by a preceding stimulus or the processes needed to organize a response to it. If a second stimulus now arrives which also requires a response, then it will have to wait to be processed until the decision channel is free. Moreover, the sooner the second signal follows the onset of the first, the longer it must wait. Experimental findings generally bore out these predictions (Broadbent, 1958; Welford, 1968). It should be emphasized that PRP delays occur when the responses are not given by the identical anatomical structure (e.g. the same finger) so the limitation on performance is not due to a simple output bottleneck. Moreover the delays also appear when one signal is visual and the other auditory so they are not merely due to an input bottleneck either.

A stronger prediction is that the more difficult the first task and hence the longer the subject takes to make the first response, the longer will be the delay in responding to the second stimulus. This was confirmed by Broadbent and Gregory (1967). They used stimulus-response compatibility to engineer a difference in task difficulty, the 'easy' and 'difficult' versions of Task 1—a two-choice spatial reaction time task—having compatible and incompatible mappings respectively. The reaction time (RT) for Task 2 was delayed more when there was an incompatible mapping on Task 1, by the amount predicted by the single channel hypothesis. Indeed a wide collection of experimental studies, aside from dual task research, may be marshalled in support of the hypothesis (Legge and Barber, 1976).

RELAXING THE ASSUMPTIONS OF SINGLE CHANNEL THEORY

Experimental evidence

Despite this promising start the evidence from the psychological refractory period paradigm does not on the whole favour a strict version of SCT. Another strong prediction of SCT is that within the range of inter-stimulus intervals (ISIs) bounded by RT1, there is a systematic relationship between RT2 and the actual value of ISI. Thus the maximum delay is when S2 follows immediately on the heels of S1, and the size of the delay then decreases millisecond for millisecond with increasing values of the ISI (i.e. S2 is increasingly delayed relative to the onset of S1). No further decline occurs when S2 arrives after R1 is issued, at which time the level of RT2 is its single task baseline value. Thus RT2 falls from its maximum value (actually RT1 +

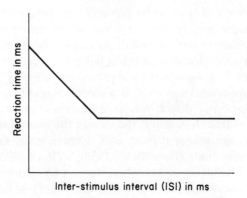

Figure 9.1. Reaction time for the second signal in a psychological refractory period paradigm: Schematic showing the unit negative slope effect. Scales for reaction time and ISI are identical.

baseline value of RT2), with a negative and unit value slope, to its minimum value (baseline value of RT2). One important testable feature is the unit negative slope prediction, but this has been found in only a few studies (e.g. Herman and McCauley, 1969). The key to obtaining a close approximation to a unit negative slope seems to be to place extreme emphasis on the priority of Task 1. One circumstance under which the slope prediction tends to break down is when the two stimuli occur in close temporal sequence, say within 50–100 msec of one another. In this case the phenomenon of 'grouping' may occur, with the two responses appearing to be organized and issued as a unit, though both tending to be delayed. Because of the delay it does not seem appropriate to view this as parallel processing; the performance seems to entail a qualitatively distinctive, integrated chord-like response whose central mediation is unclear.

The test posed by the Broadbent and Gregory (1967) study entailed a comparison of the delays in RT2 associated with two types of Task 1, an easy and a difficult version. A related test is contained in the data reported by Karlin and Kestenbaum (1968), using the number of stimulus-response alternatives (one or two) as the way to vary the difficulty of the *second* task. Task 1 was to press one of two buttons according to which of two digits was displayed. Task 2 was either a simple or a two-choice auditory reaction time task. The RT difference between the two versions of Task 2 was greater in control conditions (single task) than in experimental conditions (dual task). Both versions took longer to do in the dual mode, but the extra difficulty imposed by increasing the demands of Task 2 was not fully reflected in the performance of that task. It appears that the processing activities for Tasks 1 and 2 overlapped in some fashion. It has been concluded (Karlin and

Kestenbaum, 1968; Keele, 1973) that the perceptual processing of S2 can proceed in parallel with Task 1 processes, which is consistent with the alleged 'automatic' nature of much perceptual activity (see Wickens, 1984). In any event the findings are embarrassing for a strict version of SCT.

One rarely noted prediction is that the performance on Task 1 should be impervious to any property of Task 2, such as difficulty level. In particular, RT1 should be independent of RT2, most obviously because S1 has precedence through the processing sequence, while S2 is held in an unprocessed state of limbo. This is cast in doubt by various reports including one finding by Way and Gottsdanker (1968) using a pair of two-choice spatial reaction tasks, both of which required a compatible mapping of stimuli on to the associated responses. The disconcerting finding, from an SCT perspective, is that the *first* response is slower if it has to be made in the opposite direction to the response to the ensuing S2. Evidently on the arrival of the second stimulus the nature of the response it requires is appreciated sufficiently rapidly to influence the ongoing course of the Task 1 processing sequence. This suggests that the processes responsible for response organization are relatively easily disrupted, but it also more strongly suggests that under some circumstances at least, subjects conduct anticipatory processing for Task 2 while still dealing with Task 1. This is reinforced by unpublished studies by Triggs (1968), discussed in Legge and Barber (1976), in which the nature of the second task also affected RT1.

Divisibility of processing sequence

One possible explanation for the preliminary processing of the S1–R1 complex that seems to have occurred in these studies is that the subject momentarily ceases the processing for Task 1 and switches to that for Task 2. This amounts to abandoning the assumption of the indivisibility of the processing sequence for a simple task like making a manual response to one of a pair of tones or lights. Evidently we may need to consider that the sequence is interruptable, that it does not have unbreachable integrity. Once in train, it may become possible on a mandatory or a strategic basis to switch between concurrent processing activities. This is referred to as *time-sharing*.

Divisibility of processing capacity

It should be formally contrasted with an alternative, *capacity-sharing*, in which two activities are handled simultaneously with a shared processing capacity (also referred to as 'resources'), each receiving less than the maximum allocatable to a single activity. The relative amounts of the available capacity assigned to two simultaneous activities may vary over time, and are set according to instructional or subjective priorities.

Variations on these particular formulations are possible, such as specifying limits on the rate at which switching or reallocation between activities can be achieved. For present purposes, however, we shall concentrate on the simple versions of the hypotheses. The term 'time-sharing' will be used in the particular way just described, as an explanatory device, and it should be noted that some authorities use it as a descriptive tag for dual task performance in general (see Wickens, 1984).

Single channel theory, in short, has been challenged in relation to a number of its basic assumptions. The assumption of the indivisibility of the reaction time process needs to be revised, and if this is done the possibility of a time-sharing account becomes apparent. An alternative is to reject the idea of the indivisibility of central capacity, thus abandoning the implicit assumption of SCT that the central capacity of the human information processor has to be applied in a dedicated fashion to one task at a time. This raises the possibility of sharable capacity, but this leaves the question of how the distribution operation is effected, and in relation to what priorities, if any. A similar consideration applies to time-sharing, because one has to account for the switching sequence and its priorities even if the limitation of 'one task at a time' is retained.

Multiple channels and processing resources

Recognizing the possibility of capacity-sharing, we should mention a related possibility, that separate processing mechanisms exist—possibly limited by the same kinds of bounds as the traditional single central channel is considered to have (i.e. as to one batch of information on each channel, and being subject to processing rate limitations). This is the *multiprocessor hypothesis* (or multichannel hypothesis). According to this hypothesis, two activities can be conducted without mutual impairment, when each can be assigned to its own information-processing structure. We thus discard the notion of a unitary general-purpose central processing mechanism (Allport, 1980).

Examination of the PRP literature suggests that most experiments in this tradition use manual responses for both tasks, as well as mainly employing the visual modality to deliver both sets of signals. In such circumstances common processing mechanisms may be involved and PRP delays be a result. The multiprocessor hypothesis would be supported if the PRP delay could be eliminated by a task arrangement avoiding reliance on common mechanisms. Greenwald and Shulman (1973) conducted an experiment which seems to satisfy this requirement. The two tasks were to move a lever in the direction indicated by an arrow, and to repeat aloud a spoken letter. Modalities differed both with respect to the input and the output (and both tasks are highly stimulus-response compatible). The PRP effect was reportedly eliminated in these optimized conditions. The fine grain of the findings does, however, raise doubts about this conclusion, with signs of some trading of overall performance levels between tasks. Moreover the dual mode RTs were slower than single task control RTs, and there was some indication of RT grouping effects. Notwithstanding these aspects of the data, the result has been cited (Allport, 1980) as support for a multiprocessor hypothesis. Further supporting dual task evidence is discussed in a later section.

The idea of capacity-sharing was initially mooted on the assumption that the central resources are sharable and undifferentiated, and hence equally applicable to all processing stages and subprocesses. An alternative that flows from a development of multiprocessor theory is that there are specialized reservoirs of resources each applicable to a limited range of processing activities (e.g. one for visual and another for auditory imputs; one for manual responses and another for vocal responses). This is *multiple resource theory*. The resource distribution issue applies equally to the multiple resource hypothesis as it does to the original proposition that there is a single undifferentiated but sharable capacity. While multiprocessor theory postulates the indivisibility of capacity associated with each structure, even this residual assumption of SCT is relaxed in multiple resource theory.

There is one assumption of SCT which is intact, so far. This is the assumption that capacity is limited. In the modified accounts this capacity limitation applies to component mechanisms or resource reservoirs, but it applies nonetheless. It too has been challenged, as we shall see later in this chapter.

DUAL TASK PERFORMANCE AND RESOURCE SHARING

The concepts of resources and processing capacity are extensively used in discussions of human performance and attention (see Wickens, 1984). Resources may be thought of as a form of mental energy, a reservoir drawn on to improve the speed of reacting, the quality of decisions, the precision of actions selected. Although the exact connotations of the term 'resources' may differ from those of 'capacity', in practice it seems possible to interchange them. A broad selection of studies on capacity and resource concepts as applied to dual task performance is presented in the next sections. In the immediately following section the focus is on some research which has used dual task methodology to illuminate the question of how processing demands may vary during the conduct of a task.

Distribution of processing capacity in dual task performance

Studies of single channel theory often used the psychological refractory period paradigm to chart moment-to-moment changes in the processing of a dual reaction task. The changes in the functions relating RT1 and RT2 with task parameters, in particular the interstimulus interval, are diagnostic with respect to single channel theory. An alternative related explanatory framework interprets the data from the PRP paradigm in terms of the distribution of processing capacity between the two tasks.

The *probe task method* is another methodological variation of the dual task paradigm used to explore how capacity is allocated over time during the course of an activity. This technique involves the presentation of a usually simple probe task (given secondary emphasis in the subject's instructions), interjected on different trials at various points while the subject does the main or primary task (also established as such by instructions). An example is the work of Posner and his colleagues, discussed in the next section. The probe task can also be used to assess processing capacity devoted to the primary task in a global sense, by averaging over all the measures of secondary performance taken during the primary activity; the work of Britton and his co-workers, discussed in the section after the next, illustrates this use of the probe task.

Probe task studies: local effects

In an influential research programme Posner and Boies (1971) used letter-matching as the primary task; the subject pressed one key when two letters presented in sequence were the same, and a second key when they differed. The letter sequence was preceded by a warning signal. For the probe task, the subject pressed a different key whenever an auditory tone was presented; to help tip the priorities in the direction of the primary task, the tone was scheduled for only a proportion of the same-different trials. The purpose of the probe task was to assess the central-processing demands of the letter-matching task. Hence to track the progress of these demands, the tone was presented at any one of eight positions in the event sequence for the matching task. These points covered the period between responses (as a form of single-task control), the warning interval (when the subject is preparing for the primary task), the inter-letter interval (when encoding of the first letter might be going on), and during the half-second following the second letter (while the response is being selected and prepared).

The assumption of the method is that 'any event which requires the central capacity will interfere somewhat with the processing of any other event using that central capacity, even if that event involves another sensory modality' (Posner, 1973). It is apparent from this and similar statements that central capacity is assumed to be undifferentiated and general purpose in character. It turns out that RTs to the probe are relatively stable during the presentation of the first letter, while the response for the matching task is being prepared. Reaction times to the primary matching task are relatively unaffected by the inclusion of the probe task. It has been inferred from this pattern of findings that processes involved in dealing with the first letter (perhaps pattern recognition, and name retrieval) require no central capacity, and that only later processes do (e.g. encoding a letter while maintaining a representation of a preceding one, pattern matching, or response selection).

One critical finding, indicative of the fluctuating central demands of the primary task, is that Posner and Boies (1971) found that at certain positions in the processing sequence the probe RT was especially sensitive to the difficulty of the main task. In one version of the letter-matching task, the subject had to move forward two letters through the alphabet from the first letter in the pair, and report whether the result matched the second letter in the pair (thus when G is the first letter, the matching letter is J, and any other is counted as 'different'). This is harder than the usual same-different task and much more marked increases in the probe RT were noted, with the increase essentially restricted to the interval during which the matching response was being prepared. This seems to open the way to a close examination of the demands of different subprocesses, by suitable design of the primary task.

A problem for the use of the method is that the choice of the response modality for the probe task alters the profile of the probe reaction time function. Posner and Boies (1971) used manual responses for both probe and primary tasks, so a delayed probe RT could be due to a 'structural' form of interference arising from the use of common or similar output processes, not an interference due to joint calls on a more central general purpose capacity. McLeod (1978) demonstrated the importance of response modality in the probe paradigm, finding no delay in the probe reaction if the response was given vocally instead of manually. Evidently data from a probe task cannot be straightforwardly interpreted in terms of the implications for how central capacity is allocated. Indeed Wickens (1984) considered that the auditory probe task makes 'minimal central processing demands'. He argued too that this is a task highly loaded on perceptual-motor factors and thus is very sensitive to competition for input and output modalities (however, this must be contrasted with the research and theoretical analysis of Britton and his associates discussed in the next section).

Probe task studies: global effects

The preceding probe studies assume that the deployment of resources is sufficiently rapid and its consequences for the affected processes immediate enough for the effects to show up in speeded response measures like RT. The evidence is consistent with this idea in so far as there are effects of probe position on RT in the studies cited. Secondary task measures of a more global kind (e.g. tapping speed measures taken over the span of a session on the primary task) presumably reflect the summated consequences of these more molecular effects. Besides these, however, there may be more general effects which result from the allocation of some central resource or capacity for the overall management of the task. They would be slow-acting, subject to instructional modification, and independent of the rapid changes in processing demands within the span of a speeded task (e.g. letter-comparison, or choice-reaction time).

One use of the probe task that illustrates this is the research by Britton and his co-workers on the use of 'cognitive capacity' during text comprehension, which they have sought to measure using an auditory probe task (Britton, Westbrook and Holdredge, 1978; Britton, Holdredge, Curry and Westbrook, 1979). In this research the subject silently reads a passage and makes a simple manual response to each of a series of occasional auditory probes (clicks). Average RT to the click is influenced by certain general characteristics of the comprehension task. For example, a passage was read either with or without a title (Britton *et al.*, 1979). It was written in such a way that without its title, its meaning was hard to grasp (as confirmed by measured comprehension). The probe RT was significantly different for the two versions of the task. However, counterintuitively it was the apparently less demanding task (titled passage) that produced the slower responses to the probe. On the assumption that probe RT is an index of spare capacity, less cognitive capacity appears to be needed when the task is more ambiguous. The investigators argued that working memory is more fully occupied due to the greater coherence of the passage when the title is known. This explanation seems rather *ad hoc* but it is consistent with the finding (Britton *et al.*, 1978) that the click task was executed faster when the subject was reading difficult text as opposed to easy text; the parallel interpretation being that working memory is occupied more fully and continuously by easy text. Difficult material leads to more frequent lapses in the comprehension processes, releasing cognitive capacity for the probe task.

Britton and Tesser (1982) commented that the evidence that more cognitive capacity is recruited to read easy excerpts than difficult ones may still appear paradoxical. A possible resolution is to suppose that prior knowledge occupies cognitive capacity, for instance in working memory. If easy material evokes more prior knowledge than difficult material then more cognitive capacity would be used for the former, leaving less for the processing of the probe. An obvious next step is to manipulate the amount of prior knowledge evoked during a cognitive activity, and to measure the effect on a simultaneous probe task that also makes demands on cognitive capacity. In one experiment Britton and Tesser (1982) asked their subjects to find the best solutions for a series of chess problems, with the click detection task gauging unused cognitive capacity. Novice chess players and relative experts took part in the experiment and the experts took longer to react to the probes than the novices. Their reaction times in control conditions did not differ significantly. An interpretation of this finding is that high prior knowledge increases the amount of cognitive activity during problem-solving. A second experiment, using the same probe task, included a deliberate manipulation of the subjects' level of knowledge during a reading task. Each subject read booklets consisting of three pages of text. In one condition these pages were taken from the same text, the third following in the correct sequence. In the other condition the third page was taken from another unrelated text. In the former condition the first two pages were assumed to supply a large amount of prior knowledge about the topic of the text, while in the latter condition prior knowledge would be low. Reliably longer RTs were recorded when the subjects had high prior knowledge on the reading task. Both longstanding and recently acquired knowledge recruited to deal with a cognitive task seem to occupy cognitive capacity.

An alternative explanation for such findings is loosely expressed in terms of the level of interest subjects have in the material being read, or otherwise in their main task. For example, the expert chess players will be more interested in the chess problems, more absorbed in solving them. How to develop this explanation is not obvious, as Britton and Tesser (1982) observed. A final point about this brand of experimentation is that its findings seem to conflict with some of the studies on concurrent performance reviewed below. In the light of the ability of some subjects to do two complex tasks simultaneously, for a simple and undemanding task such as reacting to a tone to be a sensitive indicator of the demands of a well-honed skill such as silent reading is a little surprising. The slim opportunity for structural interference between the tasks should also be favourable to their independent operation, as should the light central load purportedly imposed by the probe task (Wickens, 1984).

Resource theory and dual task performance

A key idea in resource theory as applied to dual task performance is that the pool of processing resources (attention, mental effort, processing capacity, or however else it is characterized) is strictly limited in amount, and sharable by more than one task or activity. Thus, in general, as more resources are devoted to a task, performance on it improves, and performance on a concurrent task deteriorates since less resources remain to be allocated to it. The relationship between performance on a task and resources supplied is called the 'performance-resource function', and this function varies according to factors like task difficulty and the emphasis to be placed on the task. The joint performance on the two tasks can be derived from their performance-resource functions, and the form of the function relating the two performances is known as the 'performance operating characteristic' (POC). This derived function indicates any trade-off between performance on the two tasks. The interpretation of the performance-performance relationship for two tasks, however, is not as straightforward as this, as we shall see.

The resource concept has been extensively and effectively used in discussions of human performance (see Wickens, 1984), and it is related to concepts of attention and mental effort. It is, however, generally used without motivational connotations, except in so far as they may be implied when task priorities are involved. Task priorities are considered to be reflected in the resources needed to maintain a given level of performance.

Trading relationships between pairs of performances certainly may be consistent with resource theory (Navon and Gopher, 1979; Norman and Bobrow, 1975). But while much relevant evidence has accumulated, there is still doubt about the validity of some of the experimental test methods available. Some evidence will be briefly reviewed, and several of the methodological problems will be outlined. Before doing this, however, two points should be noted about resource theory; one is a particular point about the performance-resource function made by Norman and Bobrow (1975), and the other is a general one about the resource concept (e.g. Allport, 1980).

Norman and Bobrow (1975) observed that there are tasks on which performance is subject to an upper limit, which applies regardless of what extra resources are devoted to them. For instance, however hard one concentrates in a noisy party, one tends to lose some of the conversation attended to. Being affected in this way by the quality of the available sensory information, performance is said to be data-limited. The reader would probably make no mistakes in copying down familiar three-letter words under dictation, and performance would not increase in accuracy despite investing extra effort. This performance is also data-limited. Other tasks do improve as more resources are allocated to them and are said to be resource-limited.

A performance-resource function may reflect both kinds of limitations. An important case is when both tasks are data-limited, and their data-limited regions overlap. This means that in its data-limited region, the performance on one task (T1) is at a limit while that on the other (T2) is improving, while the converse applies in the data-limited region of T2. Performance on T1 can increase and decrease while performance on T2 is at its limit, and vice versa. But this performance-performance relationship is also consistent with the two tasks drawing on independent resource reservoirs. This is only the first of the difficulties in devising satisfactory and unequivocal tests of resource theory.

A fundamental objection to the general approach is that the performance-resource functions are unknown. The difficulty is a radical one because of the problem of measuring resources, which ideally needs to be done independently of the dependent variables used to characterize performance. A temptation is to infer the form of the underlying functions from the shape of the performance-operating characteristic (POC), though this cannot be done without definitional circularity. Allport (1980) was particularly scathing about this problem, arguing that this circularity is fatal for resource theory. Navon (1984) considered that this is not so and that the theory should be assessed as a whole. His own analysis nevertheless seems to leave the theory in tatters on technical grounds, even if, as he concluded, it has merit intuitively and metaphorically, and will survive for these reasons, if no other.

It is certainly difficult to avoid the definitional circle, although psychophysiological measures of brain activity hold some promise in this respect (Isreal, Wickens, Chesney and Donchin, 1980). A relatively proven method involves monitoring the evoked cortical potential associated with a simple secondary task, aspects of which (e.g. the P300 amplitude) may reflect something like peak cognitive activity, shortly after registering the task (300 msec to be precise). The secondary task is kept simple to avoid confounding problems arising from input and response production bottlenecks, and an example is covertly counting stimuli presented in a modality not used by the main task (e.g. manual tracking). Few studies have as yet been reported using this intriguing methodology (see Wickens, 1984). The P300 amplitude is found to co-vary with the load on the *primary task*, and is therefore interpreted as an index of the resources assigned to the secondary task. Its advantages include the fact that it is non-intrusive relative to the primary task.

Testing resource theory

Methods of testing resource theory include variations in task emphasis. Navon and Gopher (1979) reported studies supporting resource theory using this method. A more recent study, which also bears on the research on the auditory probe method discussed above, is chosen to illustrate the method. It will be recalled that the simple auditory probe task has been assumed to tap the same pool of processing resources as certain complex cognitive tasks. Britton and Price (1981) tested this by constructing a POC for reading and the click detection task. The relative emphasis on the two tasks was varied by instruction (e.g. 'devote 90 per cent of your attention to the reading task and 10 per cent to the click task'). Britton and Price found that RT to the click decreased as the priority assigned to the reading task decreased, and in step with this improvement, there was a decline in the proportion of multiple-choice questions on the text being read that subjects answered correctly. The investigators inferred that this co-variation shows the two tasks share a common resource, and demonstrates a systematic redistribution of central cognitive capacity between them.

Unfortunately the task emphasis method was criticized by Navon (1985) as open to 'demand characteristic' effects. This refers to the possibility that subjects are persuaded by the instructions that the tasks do trade-off, and that they adjust their performance accordingly, presumably to confirm the hypothesis implied by the instructions. Hence they might elect to perform better on one task and worse on a second without needing to draw on a common 'resource', but producing a performance profile that matches the requirements implied by the instructions. In divided-attention tasks with an instruction to allocate different amounts of attention to the two tasks (e.g. Britton and Price, 1981), the subject has a more tangible basis for supposing that trade-off is possible, because an apparently distributable commodity—'attention'—is specified. A related technique is to specify minimal requirements for the two tasks, noting performance as the requirements vary. This is open to a similar criticism; if the pairs of minimal requirement values on the tasks are negatively correlated, and the subjects try only to match performance to these demands, then a performance trade-off between the tasks will be evident. This method too seems to invite subjects to produce data mimicking the process assumed by resource theory, ostensibly shifting shared resources from one task to the other according to the task requirements.

A possible critical test is whether or not trade-off occurs when the subject is led to maximize performance. One way of doing this, suggested by Navon (1985), is to set the performance level for only one of the tasks (T1), while asking for that on the second task (T2) to be maximized. The performance-performance relationship is noted for a graded set of T1 target levels under these conditions. Navon's tasks involved letter classification and digit classification, and he contrasted the optimum-maximum method with the minimum requirements method with these task combinations. No trade-off was found when there was a target level on T1 while performance on T2 was to be maximized, but there was a trade-off when minimum levels on both T1 and T2 were set. Moreover performance for the optimum-maximum method was at least as high as that under minimum requirements. So some performance trade-offs at least may be a response to demand characteristics. It remains a possibility that in response to demand characteristics, an allocation rule is being employed, with respect to a reservoir of processing resources. This raises the interesting question of the control mechanism by which this might be regulated. It is notable that dual task performance in task emphasis and minimum requirements regimes is consistently below equivalent single task levels, which suggests that the control of joint performance under such a regime is costly in terms of the common resource reservoir.

Multiple resource theory

Manipulation of task difficulty using a dual task paradigm seems to offer the most straightforward test of resource theory (Navon, 1984, 1985). If two tasks draw on a common resource reservoir, increasing the difficulty of one of the tasks (T1) should impair performance on the other (T2) by depleting the resources available to it. A direct contrast is also supplied with the alternative hypothesis that the tasks tap independent resources, since a difficulty manipulation on one task will be reflected by a performance on it and not the other. However, this attractively simple picture is clouded in various ways, including the possibility—under the single resource hypothesis—that the subject may protect performance on T2 by recruiting extra resources from the common pool. This outcome (no effect of T1 difficulty on T2 performance) therefore can arise on either hypothesis.

Navon and Gopher (1979) proposed that the two positions could be successfully distinguished by jointly manipulating task difficulty and task emphasis, and a test of this kind was implemented by Gopher, Brickner and Navon (1982). They reasoned that on a shared resource account, an interactive effect on performance would result when task emphasis and task difficulty both varied. The interaction effect comes about because for an easy version of a task, the effect on performance of a given change in task emphasis is greater than for a hard version of the same task. This does not follow if T1 performance is protected, in which case the interactive effect is passed to the other task. The scope for intermediate changes in task priorities makes unequivocal predictions impossible for a single resource account, but performance interaction effects are a strong possibility. If on the other hand the difficulty manipulation on T1 affects a resource only used by that task, then the task emphasis factor will be additive with difficulty for T1, and independent of it for T2.

Gopher *et al.* (1982) combined a set of typewriting tasks varying in difficulty with a tracking task, under three levels of task priority (emphasizing an even balance between tasks, or with a 70 : 30 bias in one or other direction). Both tasks were affected by changes in task priority, consistent with their sharing a common resource. Two kinds of 'difficulty' were represented, one relating to motor processes (via easy vs difficult transitions between component keypress actions), and another based on a memory load change (via number of letters). Typing performance was affected in both cases, but the critical interaction with priority was restricted to motor difficulty. This is consistent with both tasks tapping motor-related resources, and only the typing task using memory-load-related resources. A problem for this seemingly critical kind of test is that task emphasis is achieved by instructions and there is no guarantee that their implementation by the subject is the same for different difficulty levels of a given task (Navon, 1985). In other words the task emphasis factor is not under independent control by the investigator, and the results may therefore be misleading or ambiguous.

Especially significant are those studies in which a modality difference (input or output) leads to improved performance when task difficulty has not been manipulated. One striking finding is that of Wickens (1976), who conducted a dual task study with tracking as the main task, comparing performance with two secondary tasks whose subjective difficulty differed. The tracking task involved a manual response. One of the secondary tasks involved vocally reporting when auditory signals were detected, while the other, the easier task according to the subjects, simply required constant pressure on a stick to be maintained. Tracking performance was better when done along with the individually more difficult secondary task of detection. Arguably this was because the tracking and constant pressure tasks make demands on the same output stage (e.g. response control), and otherwise do not tap a common resource. Plainly in light of the evidence an account in terms of a single undifferentiated resource reservoir is not sustainable.

To accommodate as much as possible of the evidence on dual task perform-ance, Wickens (1984) postulated three kinds of resources, each characterized by a two-valued dimension. The first is modality (visual vs auditory), support for which is the evidence of a reduction in dual task interference when inputs are delivered cross-modally rather than intra-modally. The second is proces-sing stage (early vs late) and the third is related to the central processing code used (spatial vs verbal). Early vs late processing (i.e. before vs after a response is selected) is a conventional distinction although there is little specific evidence in the dual task tradition directed at it. To support the distinction it would seem necessary to show resource-sharing effects which are dependent on relevant manipulations, and for instance are distinct from input modality effects. The most direct evidence for resources related to the central processing code employed by a task is from research suggesting two forms of working memory (Baddeley, 1983). Although studies showing interference effects reflecting these central codes have been reported (reviewed by Wick-ens, 1984), to associate them confidently with specialized resource reservoirs will wait on evidence showing resource-sharing effects (for example, in line with an appropriate task-difficulty manipulation).

Multiple resource theory, particularly the comprehensive system proposed by Wickens (1984), has established a role in the explanatory framework needed to characterize and explain dual task performance. Its merits and some of its shortcomings too have been identified by Wickens (1984). It is tempting for a theorist unparsimoniously to attribute each demonstration of a novel dual task interference effect to a new resource pool. One of the chief advantages of Wickens's account is that this temptation is avoided by making separate supportable assumptions about the structures and processes of human information processing.

DUAL TASK PERFORMANCE AND PROCESSING STRUCTURES

One of the earliest and most widely used dual-task paradigms was to employ shadowing (repeating spoken words) as a task to occupy the subject's atten-tion, while he or she also received a second auditory message. Of course this may also place an extra load on the same input mechanism (even if the messages are separated by being delivered one to each ear), and some form of peripheral bottleneck or interference may account for impaired performance. Indeed shadowing a message to one ear at the same time as picking up useful information from a spoken message received on the other ear (e.g. as in remembering a spoken series of unrelated words) is extremely difficult (Moray, 1959). On the other hand this difficulty may be reduced by extensive practice (Underwood, 1974). Moreover shadowing turns out to be quite easy to combine with some other tasks, such as remembering a visually presented series of words or even highly complex skills like sight-reading piano music (Allport, Antonis and Reynolds, 1972) and copy-typing (Shaffer, 1975). Such findings have been taken as evidence for a multiprocessor system, with specialized processors for particular tasks operating in parallel (Allport, 1980). Much of the support for a multiprocessor model has rested on the performance of subjects with a high degree of skill in at least one of the component tasks (e.g. reading music, copy-typing), or who have been given prolonged practice at dual task performance (see pp 235–238). But there is a growing body of evidence, using selected combinations of typical laboratory tasks on which the subjects have been given little or no specialized training or practice, of very little interference between two tasks (McLeod and Posner 1985; Rollins and Hendricks, 1980; Shallice, McLeod and Lewis, 1985).

One objective is to discover more about what is described as the functional architecture of the processing system, by determining which tasks suffer impairment when performed together, and which can be done independently. The rationale is that tasks using separate 'processing structures' can in principle be carried out with minimal interference (Shallice, McLeod and Lewis, 1985). The basic assumption, in the spirit of the classical single channel concept, that specific processing systems are unable to deal with two simultaneous tasks was stated a number of years ago (e.g. by Treisman, 1969) though not using the current terminology. Treisman referred to inputs converging on single 'analysers' as having to be dealt with serially, though inputs arriving at separate analysers could be handled in parallel.

This idea could clearly be generalized to other processing components than input mechanisms. Nevertheless it was reasonable to begin an analysis of the properties of the human processing system as a totality at the point at which processing queues can most obviously be engineered, that is at the point when information is received at the sensory receptors. This, after all, is the last point at which the experimenter controls the flow of information to the subject. Immediately beyond this point are the 'processing structures', the inner mechanisms that bracket the controlled input and the observed output, and they are invisible and only known to us via inference. In support of Treisman's (1969) account, Treisman and Davies (1973) found that monitoring two verbal messages simultaneously was difficult if they were both presented auditorily, but that it was a less severe problem if the messages were presented to different modalities (one visual, the other auditory). In the latter case different input analysers are used and the messages may be treated in parallel. The assumption is that separate structures are more likely to be engaged initially (for stimulus encoding, say) if different input modalities are used. This is not to say that different structures cannot be found within a modality, indeed vision seems to support a degree of parallel processing.

The possibility that processing difficulties may arise because of convergence on common analysing mechanisms at later points in the information-processing flow was considered by Rollins and Hendricks (1980). They noted that, for example, semantic analysis of two simultaneous messages might prove difficult despite the use of separate modalities to deliver the messages, if semantic processing was achieved by a unitary modality-independent system. A task such as naming the category to which each of a series of spoken words belongs would be hard to combine with a visual search task in which the target is, for example, any animal name, since both tasks would require semantic analysis. Similarly, if a single auditory analysing mechanism is available for dealing with the acoustic properties of inputs, processing difficulties would be expected if acoustic analysis is required of simultaneous visual and auditory messages. Visual search for a word rhyming with a target word, or for a word having a certain number of syllables, would be hard to combine with an auditory task like shadowing, since both would depend on the analysis of acoustic information.

Applying similar reasoning in the design of their experiments, Rollins and Hendricks (1980) found that subjects doing various types of shadowing tasks could simultaneously monitor a stream of words presented visually for a specific target, or for a member of a particular category. To minimize problems to do with response organization, the task to be combined with shadowing would run for some time without an explicit response having to be made, with the trial terminated as soon as the critical item for the non-shadowing task was noted. Performance on these task combinations was at a high level. Since the shadowing tasks included versions in which semantic analysis of the auditory material was required (i.e. responding with their antonyms, or stating the category to which they belonged), Rollins and Hendricks concluded that semantic processing of two separate but simultaneous streams of verbal information is possible. But performance was very poor on another combination in which shadowing was combined with visual rhyme monitoring, even for a direct shadowing task (simply repeating each word as it is heard). This suggests the two inputs share a mechanism for analysing speech, the rhyme task first engaging a conversion system for translating the printed word into a phonological form. The capacity of this mechanism seems to be severely limited, possibly reflecting the weight of the computations entailed in speech analysis in the human central nervous system.

Stronger conclusions regarding speech-processing mechanisms are drawn from a similar study by Shallice, McLeod and Lewis (1985) who were interested in the possible functional separateness of mechanisms responsible for speech perception (phonological input) and speech production (phonological output). They studied a range of dual task combinations including reading aloud while monitoring spoken words. This combination was done by unpractised subjects with quite a small decrement relative to single task control conditions. If it is assumed that the first task relies on speech production and the second on speech perception (among other things), then it follows that these two system components can be simultaneously engaged at no great cost to efficiency. On the other hand the task of monitoring a visual stream of words for a name target was hard to combine successfully with shadowing. Both may be assumed to involve phonological analysis, and the inference is that simultaneous loading of the phonological input mechanism leads to performance decrement. A task combination that intended to place simultaneous demands on a common mechanism was reading aloud at the same time as monitoring a series of spoken words for one with a specified number of syllables. Both tasks were considered to entail the use of phonological information necessary to specify the spoken form of each word received in the two input streams, hence imposing a joint load on the phonological output mechanism. Performance on this task arrangement was indeed poor. If simultaneous passage of two streams of information through different processing structures is reflected by the relative absence of processing delays and errors in responding, then the data support the assumption made by Shallice *et al.* that speech input and output mechanisms are functionally separate.

The series of experiments reported by Shallice *et al.* are a model of careful design and include controls dealing with various alternative explanations (e.g. the use of a common mechanism by the judicious means of a time-sharing strategy). There remains a reservation relating to the possible unique status of shadowing, one of the components in the critical task combination (reading aloud + shadowing) that showed minimal interference, and upon which the functional separateness inference rested. It is not clear how important this reservation is, but shadowing may rely on an informational pathway that is a special case, described by McLeod and Posner (1985) as a 'privileged loop' linking perception and action.

DUAL TASK PERFORMANCE AS A SKILL

The *elimination* of peripheral bottlenecks was one of the aims of Spelke, Hirst and Neisser (1976) in a study in which just two subjects took part—very proficient readers at the outset—receiving extensive practice at reading while simultaneously transcribing dictated words. This was a latterday attempt to discover whether these two tasks could be done concurrently, first reported by Solomons and Stein (1896). The input bottleneck is considered to be avoided because reading entails vision and dictation uses hearing. An output conflict also seems to be excluded, since the subjects read silently and comprehension testing was delayed, while the dictation task involved an immediate written response. Initially the subjects read at a slower rate while transcribing single words, and understood less than usual of what they read. But after some weeks of practice they improved considerably and eventually regained their previous levels of reading performance. Evidently two tasks both requiring a degree of linguistic processing may, under optimal conditions, be conducted simultaneously and without impairment.

It is possible, however, that the dictation task was done without recourse to deep linguistic processes. Indeed how superficially the subjects were doing the dictation task is suggested by their failure to notice when constraints were introduced into the dictation sequence, such as when several succeeding words were drawn from the same category, or when they formed a sentence. On the other hand a series of rhyming words embedded in the dictation sequence were noticed spontaneously. To probe the limitations of what could be achieved, more practice at the dual task was given, with the extra requirement to report when the categorical or sentence constraints occurred. Reading performance was again impaired under this new requirement, yet the two subjects regained their old reading levels again after a few more weeks of practice.

Finally, to ensure that a relatively deep level of linguistic analysis was required for each word in the dictation sequence, the subjects were asked to write down for each word not the word itself, but the category to which it belonged. Again reading was initially impaired but with another prolonged bout of practice it returned once more to the pre-experimental level. This seems to clinch the matter; surely both tasks entail a non-trivial degree of linguistic analysis. Silent reading, assessed with the expectation of a comprehension test in due time, depends on many processes, but it presumably includes looking up individual words in the mental lexicon, finding their meanings and coordinating them into the comprehended version of the passage. To report category membership of dictated words presumably also depends on lexical access, and on finding their meanings. The conclusion is that some forms of linguistic processing can be carried out simultaneously, given sufficient practice.

An objection to this inference is that the subjects may not have been continuously devoted to both tasks at all times. Subjects could, by capitalizing on small breaks in one activity, have picked up enough information to support the processes for the other. This is an appeal to the time-sharing hypothesis, with the rider that the coordinating skill involved improves with specific extended practice. While evidence of changes in the microstructure of performance would seem a good way of settling the issue, this might be impossible to obtain since the shuttling between activities might not have any observable manifestation. For instance, if the motor programme for writing a word once initiated can be executed unmonitored, this would allow attention to be switched during the copying response. Similarly switching could occur before a spoken word is fully registered, so long as the recognition process is terminated early.

The opportunity to time-share arguably depends on the predictability of the tasks (Broadbent, 1982). For example, if the passage being read is highly predictable, then the reader may have more opportunities to switch attention to the secondary task. Practice at the reading/copying dual task might be effective by providing conditions for learning how to use the 'redundancy' of the text to facilitate time-sharing. High-redundancy text would be easier to read in a time-sharing mode than text with low redundancy. This was tested by Hirst, Spelke, Reaves, Caharack and Neisser (1980), together with further predictions on the time-sharing hypothesis. Readers trained on the dual task arrangement with passages with high redundancy, such as short stories, will have difficulty if these are replaced by pasages of low redundancy, such as articles taken from an encyclopaedia. The reverse kind of transfer, moving from low- to high-redundancy material, should prove no obstacle. The latter prediction seems less convincing than the first since it is not clear how reading encyclopaedia articles could help the individual to acquire the skill of skipping the redundancies characteristic of short stories.

In any event Hirst et al. gave massive amounts of practice (an hour a day for between 35 and 50 days) to two small groups of subjects, until they could read at their normal rates and levels of comprehension while taking down dictated words. Following the training stage, 5 days were devoted to assessing reading performance with rigorous measures of comprehension. No subject showed a reliable deficit in reading speed or comprehension on the dual task trials relative to the control trials, replicating the findings of Spelke et al. (1976). At the transfer stage subjects switched from one set of materials to the other, and all but one made the transition without a reappearance of a dual vs single condition deficit on the reading task. The suggestion that subjects were time-sharing is weakened because the redundancy factor was not a major influence on the results.

As in many other dual task studies aspects of the methodology used by Hirst et al. (1980) raise doubts about the findings. The dictation task was given to the whole group of subjects, and seems to have been paced by the response of the slowest member of the group, so the quickest dictation-takers may have been able to interleave the two tasks with some success. Performance on the dictation task was not reported so it is not clear whether there were any trade-offs resulting from time-sharing (or forms of resource sharing). It is of interest too that the subjects were all highly proficient readers to being with, yet the level reached in the final reading-only trials was better than pre-experimental levels for all subjects but one. This suggests that the pre-experimental tests underestimated the subjects' abilities, making the interpretation of the results less straightforward.

Having rejected explanations in terms of time-sharing and automaticity, what explanation did Hirst *et al.* offer for their 'divided attention' effects? Their alternative was to characterize the subjects' dual task performance in terms of the acquisition of *divided attention skill*. But since a skill is among other things a product of practice, it seems almost tautologous to characterize their much-practised subjects' performance as a developing skill. The development of a motor skill such as typing, or a perceptual skill such as wine-tasting, leads to quite different ways of carrying out the task. Through practice and training, the basic perceptual and motor processes employed by the novice at any skill are 'changed by becoming embedded in larger schemes and may lose their independent existence entirely'. The question is whether or not this applies in the case of 'divided attention'.

It presumably follows that the definitive features of skill would be apparent as subjects practise two tasks over long periods. One of the principal characteristics of the development of a skill is the changing nature of its organization. Thus higher orders of control increase in importance as a complex tracking skill develops, and typewriting entails a shift from a letter-based transcription technique to one involving letter groups. If divided attention is a skill, presumably analogous changes in its organization will be found, and it will be necessary to specify what they might be. Arguably qualitative changes in performance should be looked for rather than the mere quantitative improvements reported abundantly in the literature; relevant to this, Hirst *et al.* (1980) cite the skill of *segregating* the information flows supporting the two component tasks. Scrutiny of the microstructure of performance would seem essential, and it is ironical that this is precisely the kind of methodology necessary to assess its competitor, the time-sharing hypothesis. It would also be of interest to specify forms of training beneficial to the development of the *run-of-the-mill* instances of this important skill, aside from spectacular versions studied in the laboratory. Although there is a good deal of research into the possibility of a basic attentional ability generalizing across situations (Barber, 1988; Wickens, 1984), there is little on how to enhance a person's attentional skills.

It is obvious that the skill approach has been empirically productive, with extraordinary dual task feats achieved by a band of hugely devoted subjects. On the other hand its theoretical yield is harder to detect. Neisser's (1976) declaration that attention is a skill is intuitively appealing, though what follows from this is not obvious. This insight might profitably be re-examined by considering what it directly implies about attention in general, and dual task performance in particular.

In much of the research reviewed above, the implications for theory are based on the fruits of massive amounts of practice. We should not overlook other aspects of dual task performance which may be interpretable in a skills framework. Arguably the most striking omission in the literature is a discussion of the problems faced by the beginner dealing for the first time with an experimental dual task set up . The reports of subjects include an impression of being overwhelmed by the number of things needing attention. Researchers circumvent this phenomenon by using pre-experimental training, rather than studying it *per se*. However, it is clear that special initial effects do occur that are characteristic of the early stages of skill acquisition, some of which may be 'attributed to initial demands on coordinating mechanisms that disappear with practice' (Gopher *et al.*, 1982).

In contrast to previous research based on the skill approach, Hirst and Kalmar (1987) presented both task inputs auditorily and mapped both on to manual responses. Task combinations which entailed similar message content gave poorer performance than those with dissimilar message content. In one experiment the tasks were detecting spelling errors in a spoken sequence of letters, and detecting errors in short and simple arithmetic sequences (numbers advancing in twos). Performance on the spelling/arithmetic combination was better than performance on either two simultaneous spelling or two simultaneous arithmetic tasks. The same advantage for a different task-pairing over an identical task-pairing was obtained when the tasks were spelling-error detection and word categorization. Again this result was repeated when two category-detection tasks were used, performance was better if the targets for each ear were drawn from different categories (i.e. animals vs body parts) than from identical categories.

Hirst and Kalmar noted that these results may be interpreted by multiple resource theory, by postulating a new reservoir in light of each new finding. However, they argued that this is unparsimonious, and is against the spirit of the traditional resource concept which is less flexible than their findings require, and is typically considered as 'part of the basic architecture of the mind'. A sounder test might, however, be whether or not resource-sharing effects can be obtained relative to each of the putative resource reservoirs. Hirst and Kalmar contrasted the traditional resource interpretation with the skill approach arguing that their findings are better interpreted in terms of cross-talk between parallel processes. On this approach efficient concurrent performance is based on the avoidance of confusions among information flows. One source of interference may be the rich interconnections in semantic memory, with its often but not always advantageous property of spreading activation. Other possible difficulties in segregating messages were discussed by Navon and Miller (1987), in the context of a study using a methodology like that of Hirst and Kalmar (1987), also finding large task-similarity effects.

FURTHER OBSERVATIONS AND THEORETICAL RÉSUMÉ

Difficult data

A complete theory of multiple task performance, and of resource allocation, already has to accommodate a wide variety of findings, as we have seen. The evidence should be included that there is invariably a small deficit in performance of a task when it is done in company with a second task, even in the most propitious of circumstances. This is most clearly demonstrated in a study by Noble, Sanders and Trumbo (1981). In this research, circumstances were contrived, using two reaction time tasks, that on the face of it were a recipe for eliminating the interference from a secondary task. The stimuli were delivered in different modalities (simple auditory and visual signals were used), and the responses were also in different modalities (motor and verbal). In addition the highest priority was placed on the primary task (emphasizing speed of response), and a very low priority on the secondary task (instructing the subject to respond only when the response for the primary task had been made). Thus on a given trial a pair of stimuli were presented, one of which had to be dealt with as fast as possible, while the response to the other could be delayed as long until the first task was completed. The reaction time to the primary signal (RT1) was the critical measure of performance, and this was invariably delayed by a small but consistent amount (20–30 msec) relative to performance in a single task control condition. Most notably RT1 was not affected by any of the variables that influence performance on a reaction time task, such as the difficulty of the primary task. Moreover the delay occurred even when the secondary stimulus was presented as much as one second after the primary stimulus, by which time the primary response had been completed by more than half a second. Noble and his co-workers suggest that the results indicate that the mere addition of a second task to a first consumes some resources. It is the consistent delay in RT1 incurred when this is done that implies that the organization of the performance of two simple tasks involving temporally neighbouring S-R sequences imposes an effectively fixed cost. The signs are that this may be independent of the resources intrinsically demanded by the tasks themselves.

There are a number of studies, reviewed in this chapter, which are interpreted to show that, with careful choice and design, certain task combinations can be done without mutual or even one-sided disruption. The conclusions are of course based on statistical tests. But in the last analysis, the investigators have to base their decisions on the absence of statistically significant differences, for example, between single and dual task trials. While they may also be beset with many other procedural and technical obstacles, this is a kind of methodological bottom-line for them. It is notable that almost invariably the critical contrast between conditions on which the decision is based shows a small residual disadvantage in the dual task condition (see Broadbent, 1982). If the single vs dual difference were truly zero, then we should see a reversal of this disadvantage recorded on an appreciable number of occasions. That we do not suggests that concurrent performance exerts a small but inescapable residual toll on central processing resources.

There is a further study to consider which obtained an effect with a dual task paradigm that seems to reflect an intriguing generalized effect on the use of central capacity. In this study (Luder and Barber, 1984) the effect of colour-enhanced displays for aircraft cockpits was the focus of interest, and a pair of tasks was used which approximated the kinds of tasks done concurrently in the flying environment. The conditions on a static display had to be checked periodically while the subject also engaged in the primary task of tracking (to simulate flying). The principal purpose of the study was to evaluate an hypothesis about redundant colour coding. The finding of interest in the present context, however, is that the subjects who had the use of colour-enhanced displays (and whose performance on the display checking task was generally improved thereby) came to do the tracking task more effectively than subjects using a monochrome display. This applied after a short amount of practice (the two groups had equal tracking skill at the outset). More importantly, it applied to the tracking performance in the absence of the static display and the subjects had only the tracking task to do. In the absence of active competition for common structural resources, this generalized advantage is interpretable as a diffused (i.e. not localized) and prolonged release of central capacity. How general this effect is is not known, nor is its origin, though it may have a parallel in the probe RT literature (see Paap and Ogden, 1981).

An intriguing strand of research that has not been accommodated within the theoretical frameworks described here is that which focuses on controlling and coordinating two concurrent motor actions. Tapping responses to two independent rhythmic inputs becomes more difficult as the rhythms are made perceptually more distinctive (Klapp, Hill, Jagacinski, Tyler, Martin and Jones, 1985). Wickens (1984) has noted that such effects are embarrassing for multiple resource theory since similarity of input rhythms is advantageous to performance. Another piece of evidence that seems to pose an awkward problem for most views of dual task theory is that a tracking response was found to interfere more with a concurrent auditory detection task as the force required to make the response increased (Mastroianni and Schopper, 1986). It is not intuitively surprising, but multiple resource theory, for example, does not seem to account for an interference effect from physical exertion on a mental activity (see also the study by Welch, 1898).

A final observation that needs to be explained is one from the psychological refractory period paradigm. The delay in the second reaction time to a pair of signals requires explanation in itself, and this does not seem to be forthcoming from resource, interference or skill accounts, except on an *ad hoc* basis. There is a nice irony about this, considering the firstcoming position of this basic finding in the dual task literature. The finding seems to be critical for current theories because the delay does not seem to be disposed to disappear with extended practice (Gottsdanker and Stelmach, 1971).

Unresolved issues

The previous section may seem to have a somewhat Luddite intention, putting obstacles in the way of the progressive accounts of dual task performance advanced to counter single channel theory. The point needs to be made that we do not seem to be converging on anything like a satisfactory and comprehensive unitary theoretical account (and this is not to imply that SCT should be viewed as more than a theoretical relic). To be fair, it should be noted that some theorists have noted the shortcomings of their accounts; for example, Wickens (1984) recorded some difficulties for his own powerful multiple resource theory. Arguably we may be best off accepting a multifactor theoretical perspective. In addition there is a residue of seemingly bloody-minded findings that need to be accommodated by our theoretical accounts, and some were reviewed in the previous section.

Unitary accounts of dual task performance (e.g. single channel theory, and simple resource theory) have stubbornly survived while contradictory observations amassed. Multiple resource and multiprocessor theories reflect a retreat from the parsimony of single factor accounts, but a realistic response to the evidence. Moreover various authorities have acknowledged the force of anomalies in the experimental evidence for all efforts which seek to explain dual task performance in terms of a single framework. For example, as we have seen, multiple resource theory, which is the most comprehensive of these efforts, has numerous challenges to it within the existing literature. A resolution may be to accept that dual task performance is subject to several sources of interference effects (Navon and Miller, 1987; Hirst and Kalmar, 1987; Wickens, 1986).

REFERENCES

Allport, D. A. (1980). Attention and performance, in G. Claxton (ed.), *Cognitive Psychology: New Directions*. London: Routledge & Kegan Paul.

Allport, D. A., Antonis, B. & Reynolds, P. (1972). On the division of attention: a disproof of the single channel hypothesis, *Quarterly Journal of Experimental Psychology*, **24**, 225–235.

Baddeley, A. D. (1983). Working memory, *Philosophical Transactions of the Royal Society*, **B302**, 311–324.

Barber, P. J. (1988). *Applied Cognitive Psychology*. London: Methuen.

Britton, B. K., Holdredge, T. S., Curry, C. & Westbrook, R. D. (1979). Use of cognitive capacity in reading identical texts with different amounts of discourse level meaning, *Journal of Experimental Psychology: Human Learning and Memory*, **5**, 262–270.

Britton, B. K. & Price, K. (1981). Use of cognitive capacity in reading: a performance operating characteristic, *Perceptual and Motor Skills*, **52**, 291–298.

Britton, B. K. & Tesser, A. (1982). Effects of prior knowledge on use of cognitive capacity in three complex cognitive tasks, *Journal of Verbal Learning and Verbal Behavior*, **21**, 421–436.

Britton, B. K., Westbrook, R. D. & Holdredge, T. S. (1978). Reading and cognitive capacity usage: effects of text difficulty, *Journal of Experimental Psychology: Human Learning and Memory*. **4**, 582–591.

Broadbent, D. E. (1958). *Perception and Communication*. London: Pergamon Press.

Broadbent, D. E. (1982). Task combination and selective intake of information, *Acta Psychologica*, **50**, 253–290.

Broadbent, D. E. & Gregory, M. (1967). Psychological refractory period and the length of time required to make a decision, *Proceedings of the Royal Society*, **168B**, 181–193.

Gopher, D., Brickner, M. & Navon, D. (1982). Different difficulty manipulations interact differently with task emphasis: evidence for multiple resources, *Journal of Experimental Psychology: Human Perception and Performance*, **8**, 146–158.

Gottsdanker, R. & Stelmach, G. E. (1971). The persistence of psychological refractoriness, *Journal of Motor Behavior*, **3**, 301–312.

Greenwald, A. G. & Shulman, H. G. (1973). On doing two things at once: II. Elimination of the psychological refractory period effect, *Journal of Experimental Psychology*, **101**, 70–76.

Herman, L. G. & McCauley, M. E. (1969). Delay in responding to the first stimulus in the 'psychological refractory period' experiment, *Journal of Experimental Psychology*, **81**, 344–350.

Hirst, W. & Kalmar, D. (1987). Characterizing attentional resources, *Journal of Experimental Psychology: General*, **116**, 68–81.

Hirst, W., Spelke, E. S., Reaves, C. C., Caharack, G. & Neisser, U. (1980). Dividing attention without alternation or automaticity, *Journal of Experimental Psychology: General*, **109**, 98–117.

Isreal, J. B., Wickens, C. D., Chesney, G. L. & Donchin, E. (1980). The event-related brain potential as an index of display-monitoring workload, *Human Factors*, **22**, 211–224.

James, W. (1890). *The Principles of Psychology*. New York: Holt.

Karlin, L. & Kestenbaum, R. (1968). Effects of number of alternatives on the psychological refractory period, *Quarterly Journal of Experimental Psychology*, **20**, 160–178.

Keele, S. W. (1973). *Attention and Human Performance*. Pacific Palisades, CA: Goodyear.

Kinsbourne, M. (1981). Single-channel theory, in D. H. Holding (ed.), *Human Skills*. London: Wiley.

Klapp, S. T., Hill, M. D., Jagacinski, R. J., Tyler, J. G., Martin, Z. E. & Jones, M. R. (1985). On marching to two different drummers: perceptual aspects of the difficulties, *Journal of Experimental Psychology: Human Perception and Performance*, **11**, 814–827.

Legge, D. & Barber, P. J. (1976). *Information and Skill*. London: Methuen.

Luder, C. B. & Barber, P. J. (1984). Redundant colour coding in an airborne CRT display, *Human Factors*, **26**, 18–32.

Mastroianni, G. R. & Shopper, A. W. (1986). Degradation of force-loaded tracking performance in a dual-task paradigm, *Ergonomics*, **29**, 639–647.

McLeod, P. (1977). A dual task response modality effect: support for multiprocess models of attention, *Quarterly Journal of Experimental Psychology*, **29**, 651–667.

McLeod, P. (1978). Does probe RT measure central processing demand? *Quarterly Journal of Experimetnal Psychology*, **30**, 83–89.

McLeod, P. & Posner, M. I. (1985). Privileged loops from percept to act, in H. Bouma & D. G. Bouwhuis (eds), *Attention and Performance X: Control of Language Processes*. London: Erlbaum.

Moray, N. (1959). Attention in dichotic listening, *Quarterly Journal of Experimental Psychology*, **11**, 56–60.

Navon, D. (1984). Resources—a theoretical soup stone? *Psychological Review*, **91**, 216–234.

Navon, D. (1985). Attention division or attention sharing? in M. I. Posner & O. S. M. Marin (eds), *Attention and Performance IX*. Hillsdale, NJ: Erlbaum.

Navon, D. & Gopher, D. (1979). On the economy of the human processing system, *Psychological Review*, **86**, 214–255.

Navon, D. & Miller, J. (1987). Role of outcome confict in dual-task interference, *Journal of Experimental Psychology: Human Perception and Performance*, **13**, 435–448.

Neisser, U. (1976). *Cognition and Reality*. San Francisco: Freeman.

Noble, M. E., Sanders, A. F. & Trumbo, D. A. (1981). Concurrence costs in double stimulation tasks, *Acta Psychologica*, **49**, 141–158.

Norman, D. A. & Bobrow, D. G. (1975). On data-limited and resource-limited processes, *Cognitive Psychology*, **7**, 44–64.

Paap, K. R. & Ogden, W. C. (1981). Letter encoding is an obligatory but capacity-demanding operation, *Journal of Experimental Psychology: Human Perception and Performance*, **7**, 518–527.

Posner, M. I. (1973). *Cognition: an Introduction*. Glenview, Illinois: Scott Foresman.

Posner, M. I. & Boies, S. J. (1971). Components of attention, *Psychological Review*, **78**, 391–408.

Rollins, R. A. & Hendricks, R. (1980). Processing of words presented simultaneously to eye and ear, *Journal of Experimental Psychology: Human Perception and Performance*, **6**, 99–109.

Shaffer, L. H. (1975). Multiple attention in continuous verbal tasks, in P. M. A. Rabbitt & S. Dornic (eds), *Attention and Performance V*. London: Academic Press.

Shallice, T., McLeod, P. & Lewis, K. (1985). Isolating cognitive modules with the dual-task paradigm: are speech perception and production separate processes? *Quarterly Journal of Experimental Psychology*, **37A**, 507–532.

Solomons, L. & Stein, G. (1896). Normal motor automatism, *Psychological Review*, **3**, 492–512.

Spelke, E., Hirst, W. & Neisser, U. (1976). Skills of divided attention, *Cognition*, **4**, 215–230.

Treisman, A. (1969). Strategies and models of attention, *Psychological Review*, **76**, 282–289.

Treisman, A. & Davies, A. (1973). Divided attention to eye and ear. in S. Kornblum (ed.), *Attention and Performance IV*. New York: Academic Press.
Triggs, T. J. (1968). Capacity sharing and speeded reactions to successive signals. Technical Report 9, University of Michigan, Contract No. AF 49(678)-1736, US Department of Defence.
Underwood, G. (1974). Moray vs the rest: the effects of extended shadowing practice, *Quarterly Journal of Experimental Psychology*, **26**, 368–372.
Way, T. C. & Gottsdanker, R. (1968). Psychological refractoriness with varying differences between tasks, *Journal of Experimental Psychology*, **78**, 38–45.
Welch, J. C. (1898). On the measurement of mental activity through muscular activity and the determination of a constant of attention, *American Journal of Physiology*, **1**, 253–306.
Welford, A. T. (1952). The 'psychological refractory period' and the timing of high-speed performance—a review and a theory, *British Journal of Psychology*, **43**, 2–19.
Welford, A. T. (1968). *Fundamentals of Skill*. London: Methuen.
Wickens, C. D. (1976). The effects of divided attention in information processing in tracking, *Journal of Experimental Psychology: Human Perception and Human Performance*, **2**, 1–13.
Wickens, C. D. (1984). *Engineering Psychology*. Columbus, Ohio: Merrill.
Wickens, C. D. (1986). Gain and energetics in information processing, in G. R. J. Hockey, A. W. K. Gaillard & M. G. H. Coles (eds), *Energetics and Human Information Processing*. Dordrecht, The Netherlands: Martinus Nijhoff.

Chapter 10

Ageing and skilled performance

Timothy A. Salthouse

What happens to skilled performance as we age? Are there reasons to expect cognitive skills to deteriorate as a function of increased age, and if so, are these expectations supported by empirical evidence? Is increased age in adulthood associated with reduced efficiency in the learning of new skills, and is age a factor in the ultimate level of proficiency that can be achieved in a cognitive skill? The present chapter addresses these questions, but the reader should be forewarned that few definitive answers are provided because the amount of relevant research is still quite limited. Nevertheless, some tentative conclusions will be offered on the basis of the available evidence, and considerable discussion will be devoted to the research procedures that seem likely to provide the most informative resolution of these issues. Also discussed in the chapter are the mutually beneficial contributions that can be expected from the joint investigation of ageing and skilled performance.

REVIEW OF RELEVANT RESEARCH

The first section of the chapter is devoted to a review of the literature on three topics concerned with the relationship between adult age and skilled performance. The initial topic is the effects of age on the elementary information processes that are often considered to represent the building blocks of cognition. Because the levels of these basic capacities presumably set limits on the ultimate proficiency of skills composed of those capacities, it is important to examine whether they vary systematically as a function of increased age in adulthood. To the extent that increased age is associated with declining levels of efficiency in elementary processes, one might expect that it

Acquisition and Performance of Cognitive Skills. Edited by A. M. Colley and J. R. Beech
© 1989 John Wiley & Sons Ltd

would be difficult for older adults to achieve, or possibly even to maintain, proficient functioning in complex skills.

Examination of results relevant to the ease of acquiring new skills at different ages will be the second focus of this section. Important questions within this topic are whether older people can learn new skills as readily as young adults, and whether, regardless of the efficiency of their learning, they can ultimately achieve the same asymptotic level of proficiency.

The third topic in this section concerns the issue of whether adults of different ages utilize different mechanisms to achieve the same levels of skill. Of particular interest are situations in which one would expect older adults to have lower levels of efficiency in certain relevant component processes, but in which, perhaps because of selective sampling research participants, there is little or no relationship between age and overall degree of skill.

Elementary processes

A basic assumption underlying the information-processing approach to cognition is that there are a limited set of elementary or fundamental cognitive abilities that function as the building blocks of cognition. In fact, prominent cognitive psychologists such as Posner and McLeod (1982) have not only endorsed this position, but have suggested that the primary task of cognitive psychology is to determine how these cognitive primitives are combined to perform complex cognitive activities.

In support of this goal, a number of theorists have attempted to enumerate cognitive psychology's equivalent of chemistry's periodic table, with the elements referred to as elementary information processes (Chase, 1978; Newell and Simon, 1972), as elementary mental operations (Posner and McLeod, 1982), or as cognitive components (Sternberg, 1977; Sternberg and Gardner, 1983). Although certain processes tend to recur in many lists (e.g. discrimination, comparison, association), there is still little consensus on the exact composition of what are postulated to be fundamental cognitive abilities. Despite the lack of unanimity concerning the identity of these elementary processes, however, there seems to have been considerable tacit agreement that complex cognition is composed of, and consequently is at least partially dependent upon, these processes. A reasonable first step in the discussion of ageing and skilled performance is therefore to review the effects of age on the efficiency or effectiveness of processes that might be considered elementary or fundamental.

Comprehensive reviews documenting largely negative effects of ageing on relatively simple cognitive processes are available in numerous recent sources (Birren and Schaie, 1985; Kausler, 1982; Salthouse, 1982, 1985). Because data recently reported by Salthouse, Kausler, and Saults (1986, 1988) seem representative, they will be used to illustrate the major findings concerning the relationship between age and the efficiency or effectiveness of elementary cognitive processes.

The Salthouse *et al*. project involved the administration of similiar batteries of cognitive tests to two groups of 129 and 233 adults, respectively, ranging from 20 to 79 years of age. Most of the tests were designed to assess fairly basic cognitive abilities, and a test-retest procedure ensured that the assessments were all fairly reliable (i.e. estimated reliabilities of at least 0.6). Table 10.1 contains a brief description of several of the measures from the project, and the correlations between each measure and chronological age.

The first two variables are presumed to be indices of the speed with which the individual can execute elementary operations because the tasks were quite simple—involving a binary true/false decision—and most subjects had very high levels of accuracy. The verbal and spatial memory tasks were designed to assess the individual's capacity for temporarily retaining verbal or spatial information. Both tasks involved the presentation of seven target items, and performance averaged 5.35 verbal items correctly recalled and 3.76 spatial items correctly recalled, suggesting that in the average adult the passive storage capacity of verbal information may be somewhat greater than that of spatial information. The measure of paired-associates performance is assumed to reflect the efficiency with which the individual can form an association between two items. Performance in the geometric-analogies and series-completion tasks is hypothesized to reflect the individual's ability to infer or abstract the relationship that exists among familiar items. This is presumed to be a fundamental operation in most tasks involving inferential reasoning (e.g. Sternberg and Gardner, 1983). Finally, accuracy in the paper-folding task was hypothesized to represent the individual's effectiveness in carrying out mental transformations of spatial material. It should be noted that the performance measures reported for the last three tasks are all indices of accuracy; similar trends were also evident in measures of speed of performance despite the use of self-paced procedures and instructions emphasizing accuracy more than speed.

Inspection of the values in the first column of Table 10.1 reveals that increased age was associated ($p < 0.01$) with poorer performance on each of the measures that might be postulated to reflect basic information-processing capacities. As mentioned earlier, this pattern is typical of much of the literature on cognitive ageing. In fact, the median of the correlations reported in Table 10.1, (i.e. $r = -0.37$), is nearly identical to that (i.e. $r = -0.36$) computed from 54 correlations extracted from studies of memory, reasoning, and spatial abilities by Salthouse (1985, Tables 11.1, 12.1, and 13.1).

Given the substantial negative relationships frequently found to exist between age and measures of presumably basic cognitive processes, it seems reasonable to expect that older age would be a disadvantage in most complex skills. That is, if the constituent elements from which skilled performance is

Table 10.1. Summary results of the effects of age on elementary cognitive processes, data from Salthouse, Kausler and Saults (1988).

Age correlation	Measure	Task description
−0.55	Digit symbol speed ($n = 362$)	Rate of determining whether symbols and digits match according to a specified code
−0.36	Number comparison speed ($n = 362$)	Rate of determining whether two strings of digits are identical
−0.38	Verbal memory ($n = 362$)	Accuracy of recalling the identities of target letters from a matrix
−0.43	Spatial memory ($n = 362$)	Accuracy of recalling the locations of target letters from a matrix
−0.34	Paired associates ($n = 362$)	Accuracy of recalling the response word associated with a stimulus word (average of 2 trials)
−0.43	Geometric analogies ($n = 233$)	Accuracy of determining the truth or falsity of geometric analogies
−0.28	Series completion ($n = 233$)	Accuracy of extrapolating a numerical sequence
−0.28	Paper-folding ($n = 129$)	Accuracy of determining the outcome of a sequence of folds of a paper followed by punching of a hole

assembled are disintegrating, then it would presumably be impossible to achieve the same levels of proficiency in that skill at older ages. When evaluating this expectation against empirical evidence, however, it is important to distinguish between the acquisition of skilled performance on the one hand, and its continuation or maintenance on the other hand. These two issues are therefore considered separately in the following sections.

Efficiency of skill acquisition

Although the results summarized above concerning the negative relationship between age and measures of component processes suggest that older adults may be less efficient than young adults in the acquisition of cognitive skills, there is surprisingly little direct evidence in support of (or, it should be added, in opposition to) this expectation. It could be argued that the absence of well-documented increments in cognitive functioning with increased age, despite a generally positive correlation between age and experience, is indirect evidence that acquisition processes decline in efficiency across the adult years. However, this argument is not particularly compelling because alternative interpretations can be proposed to account for the failure to find age-related increases without assuming that there are age-related declines in the effectiveness or efficiency of acquisition processes. For example, although the total amount of experience may be positively correlated with adult age, it is possible that there is a gradual restriction with age in the diversity or variety of those experiences. Age-related improvements might not be expected under circumstances such as these because the additional experiences are primarily repetitions of earlier experiences, and not genuine opportunities for gaining new information. Another possible interpretation of the lack of convincing cases of age-related improvement in cognitive functioning is that the efficiency of acquisition processes might remain unchanged across the adult years, but there could be losses in previously acquired skills or knowledge such that there is no net change in overall proficiency. In other words, if the loss of old information occurs at a rate equal to or greater than the gain of new information, then there may be no net increment in level of cognitive functioning across the adult years despite invariant acquisition processes and the advantages of greater experience on the part of old individuals.

Because of the ambiguities of interpretation associated with this type of indirect argument, it is clearly preferable to base one's conclusions on an examination of the direct evidence concerning the effects of age on the efficiency of acquiring cognitive skills. Unfortunately the relevant literature is impoverished, and flawed in several important respects. For example, many of the studies purportedly investigating age differences in skill acquisition involved very small amounts of experience—rarely exceeding three hours with a given task—and thus cannot be considered as truly addressing the issue of skilled performance. The transition between novice and skilled levels of performance is not yet well defined, but it seems clear that considerably more than three hours is needed to reach interesting levels of skill on any moderately complex cognitive activity.

Another weakness of some studies that might have been considered relevant in the present context is that they examined adults from only a single age group, and thus provided no basis for determining whether or not there were age differences in the efficiency of acquisition processes. Much of the research conducted under the rubric of cognitive training (for reviews see Baltes and Willis, 1982; Willis, 1985) falls within this category in that the primary focus of the research was to demonstrate the existence of substantial cognitive 'plasticity' in older adults. However, the absence of groups of young adults receiving similar training severely restricts the usefulness of these studies for the purpose of evaluating the possibility that there were age differences in responsivity to training.

Several of the age-comparative studies involving moderate (at least 4 hours) amounts of experience have concerned perceptual-motor activities. For example, Salthouse and Somberg (1982) examined the improvements in performance of young and old adults in four perceptual-motor tasks across 50 one-hour experimental sessions. Measurement ceilings in several of the tasks precluded valid comparisons of acquisition efficiency with some performance measures. However, the practice effects in a reaction time task, after the first few sessions in which older adults improved more than young adults, were nearly parallel for young and old adults. This finding seems to suggest that young and old adults may not differ in the efficiency of acquiring, or optimizing, processes relevant to simple perceptual-motor performance. Moreover, because there is little indication in the data that the age differences were being attenuated with further practice, it also seems reasonable to infer that the two groups may never achieve the same asymptotic levels of performance on this type of task.

Some of the earliest, and still among the most impressive, studies of the effects of ageing on skill acquisition were reported by Thorndike, Bregman, Tilton, and Woodyard (1928). Although their volume, *Adult Learning*, summarized the results of many studies, two are particularly relevant in this context. Both studies involved 16 young adults (mean age = 22 years) and 16 middle-aged adults (mean age = 41 years), with one concerned with the activity of learning to write with their left hands (all individuals were right-handed), and the other with learning the artificial language Esperanto.

In the writing experiment the two groups started at nearly equivalent levels of speed and quality. Both groups improved a similar amount in the rated quality of their left-handed handwriting after 15 hours of practice, but the young adults made greater speed gains than did the middle-aged adults.

Esperanto was selected for the learning material in the other Thorndike *et al.* (1928) experiment because it represented a novel and complex intellectual task, and yet consisted of coherent and systematic material. The two groups of research participants were similar at the beginning of the study in measures of vocabulary, following printed directions, following oral directions, and paragraph comprehension. Both groups improved on all measures with 10 hours of classroom instruction and 10 hours of individual study. However, the magnitude of the performance improvement on the oral directions test was substantially smaller for the middle-aged adults than for the young adults.

Two recent, as yet unpublished, studies have also examined age effects in the acquisition of clearly cognitive tasks. One study, by Charness and Campbell (1987), compared 16 young (mean age = 24 years), 16 middle-aged (mean age = 41 years), and 16 old (mean age = 67 years) adults in the acquisition of a mental procedure to compute the squares of two-digit numbers. Although there were the expected age differences favouring young adults in most speeded measures, the three groups improved their speeds by nearly comparable amounts across four training sessions, and exhibited similar transfer to new problems. A particularly interesting aspect of this study was that measures of the speed of performing the components of the mental squaring procedure were obtained at both the beginning and the end of training. These measures allowed analyses of the ratios of the sum of the durations of the components in isolation to the mean time for the complete problems. To the extent that these ratios are less than 1.0, they can serve as an estimate of the amount of 'overhead', or added time needed to coordinate the components, required in the task. All groups increased their ratios with practice on the task, but the older adults had smaller ratios both before and after practice, suggesting that increased age may be associated with greater difficulty in the integration or coordination of component processes, independent of the efficiency of those processes.

The skill investigated in the second recent project, by Smith, Kliegl, and Baltes (1987), was serial word recall as mediated by a specially-trained mnemonic procedure. Four young adults (mean age 22.8 years) and 20 older adults (mean age 71.7 years) received mnemonic training either until they correctly recalled 32 out of 40 nouns, or until they had completed 26 individually-administered 90-minute training sessions. In virtually all measures of acquisition efficiency the young adults proved to be superior to the older adults. They achieved the criterion level of accuracy in fewer sessions (8.8 vs 17.0), with a smaller number of practice lists (19.3 vs 30.8), and with a smaller amount of total study time (188.0 minutes vs 381.8 minutes). The young adults also performed significantly better than the older adults in the final post-criterion assessment (39.8 vs 32.4 correct words out of 40) when the participants could determine the rate of item presentation.

The preceding summary suggests that the results from the existing studies of age effects in skill acquisition are somewhat contradictory. That is, with perceptual-motor skills, Salthouse and Somberg (1982) found nearly parallel improvements for young and old adults, while the young adults improved more than the middle-aged adults in the Thorndike et al. (1928) study of wrong-hand writing. In the case of cognitive skills, Charness and Campbell (1987) reported similar improvements in the speed of mental computation for adults of different ages, Smith et al. (1987) described results suggesting an advantage for young adults in the ease of acquiring a mnemonic skill, and Thorndike et al. (1928) reported a mixed pattern with middle-aged adults improving as much as young adults on three or four measures of Esperanto language proficiency. Because the amount of data is still so small, and because the activities that have been investigated are so different, it is probably premature to attempt a determination of the reasons for these discrepancies at this time. It is nevertheless interesting to note that the studies do seem consistent with respect to the absence of age differences in the amount of forgetting after a period without practice. That is, the performance declines across post-training intervals of 30 days (Charness and Campbell, 1987; Salthouse and Somberg, 1982) and 77 days (both Thorndike et al., 1928 experiments) were found to be similar for all age groups investigated.

Mechanisms of skill maintenance

Because of the complex interrelations possible when one is attempting to examine the effects of age on both the efficiency of component processes and on the proficiency of a more global skill, it is frequently advantageous to investigate age effects on certain variables only after the age relations on other variables have been controlled in some manner. Depending upon which variables are controlled, one of two research strategies will result that can be used to address somewhat different questions related to the general issue of skill maintenance.

One strategy, termed Molar Equivalence–Molecular Decomposition by Salthouse (1984), consists of selecting individuals of different ages who are nearly equivalent in the proficiency of the molar skill, and then analysing the effects of age on the efficiency of the component processes presumed to contribute to that skill. This strategy therefore focuses on the question of whether people of different ages, when performing at comparable levels in a complex skill, place the same reliance on the efficiency of various component processes.

An alternative strategy results when people of different ages are equated in the efficiency of certain relevant component processes, and then age effects are examined in the proficiency of the molar skill. This strategy, which might be termed the Molar Analysis–Molecular Equivalence strategy, would presumably allow one to investigate the possibility that there are influences of age or experience in the effectiveness of integrating or coordinating one's cognitive processes. For example, the Charness and Campbell (1987) findings suggest that increased experience may result in greater optimization of the capacities one possesses, and that there is a loss with age in the ability efficiently to coordinate or utilize processing components, independent of the level of those components. This intriguing outcome could be subjected to verification and extension by systematic application of the Molar analysis–Molecular Equivalence strategy.

Unfortunately, while both analytic strategies seem likely to yield useful information, there has thus far been research only with the former strategy, and even that has been quite limited. This research will be reviewed, but it is first useful to examine how specific outcomes from the Molar Equivalence–Molecular Decomposition strategy might be interpreted. Of course, one cannot anticipate all outcomes that could possibly be observed, nor is it feasible to predict how individual investigators might choose to interpret their findings. It is nevertheless desirable to consider how specific outcome patterns from the Molar Equivalence–Molecular Decomposition strategy could provide insight into the mechanisms of skill maintenance across the adult years.

Perhaps the simplest outcome from equating adults on level of proficiency in a molar skill is that there will no longer be age-related declines on the measures of component efficiency. That is, adults of all ages may rely upon the same combination of component processes to achieve the molar skill such that different-aged individuals can be matched on molar proficiency only if they possess nearly identical levels of the relevant component processes. This would obviously be an interesting result, but it is likely to be ambiguous without further information about the reasons for the absence of expected age-related declines in the measures of component efficiency. That is, if the research literature suggests that there should be negative effects of increased age on the measures of component efficiency and yet there are no age-related effects on those measures in this sample, then the question naturally arises as to why this might be the case. One possibility is that the participants in the research sample were not representative of their age groups, with either the young individuals less select, or the older individuals more select, than their counterparts who have participated in the studies revealing that age is typically negatively related to efficiency of component processes. Obviously if the molar equivalence is achieved only by employing a biased sample of research participants in one or more age groups then the results from the procedure will not be very informative about the mechanisms responsible for the maintenance of skilled performance across adulthood.

An alternative, and in many respects much more interesting, possibility is that because of their extensive experience the older adults in the sample had maintained high levels of competency in relevant processes that normally decline in the absence of this experience. That is, while efficiency of component processes may typically decline with increased age in the general population, the greater experience on the part of the older individuals in the research sample may have been responsible both for the ability to equate individuals of different ages on molar proficiency, and for the maintenance of high competence levels on component processes that would have otherwise declined with age.

The preceding discussion reveals that a finding of no age-related declines in component processes when one is utilizing the Molar Equivalence–Molecular Decomposition procedure can be subject to substantially different interpretations. Unless there is a means of distinguishing between the biased-sample and the experience-mediated maintenance possibilities, therefore, a discovery that there are no age effects in measures of component efficiency, after ensuring that there is no relationship between age and proficiency of the molar skill, may remain ambiguous.

There also seem to be two distinctly different ways in which a Molar Equivalence–Molecular Decomposition outcome of age-related declines in component processes might be interpreted. One possibility is that as adults grow older they alter the manner in which they perform the molar activity such that decreases in the effectiveness of certain processes might be compensated for by increases in the effectiveness of other processes. Compensation of this type should be evident by the discovery that in at least some processes there are actually age-related increases that serve to offset or counteract the age-related decreases occurring in other relevant processes. Another somewhat technical implication of this view is that adults of different ages should have different regression weights in multiple regression equations attempting to predict molar performance from measures of molecular (and compensatory) processes. More specifically, as age increases among equally skilled adults the importance (weighting) of molecular processes should decrease, and that of compensatory processes should increase.

A second way in which declines in component efficiency without concomitant declines in molar competence might be interpreted is in terms of the encapsulation (e.g. Rybash, Hoyer, and Roodin, 1986) or compilation (e.g. Anderson, 1982) of the molar skill such that it is no longer dependent upon the efficiency of the molecular processes. This view can be elaborated by contrasting two metaphors of the molar skill. One metaphor is that of a building in which the structure will collapse if the materials from which it is constructed deteriorate. This is the perspective implied in the preceding discussion in that the skill would be expected to decline as the components lose their effectiveness because proficiency of the skill is always assumed to be dependent upon the current integrity of the constituent elements.

A second metaphor of the nature of skill is that of a computer program which is first assembled from subroutines, and then compiled into an efficient operational form. Because once in a compiled form the efficiency of the program will be independent of later changes in the efficiency of the subroutines, the program can be considered to have encapsulated an earlier level of functioning. In other words, variations in the effectiveness of what were once constituent parts of a program or skill may no longer influence the proficiency of the overall activity after it has been automated or compiled. From this perspective, therefore, compensation processes may not be necessary to achieve molar equivalence when molecular processes are declining because the important molecular-molar relation is not the current one, but rather that which existed at the time the skill became fully automated (or compiled, or encapsulated).

At least in principle, it seems possible to distinguish between the compensation and compilation interpretations on the basis of two criteria. One criterion is the presence or absence of a compensatory mechanism. That is, the existence of a process correlated with performance of the molar activity, but which increases rather than decreases with advancing age, is predicted from the compensation view but is not easily reconciled with the compilation interpretation. On the other hand, the compilation view seems to imply that the correlations between molecular efficiency and molar competence should decrease with increased skill because the important relationship occurs rather early in skill acquisition when the component processes are compiled to produce the automated version of the activity. A discovery that highly skilled individuals had smaller correlations between measures of component processes and proficiency of the molar skill than less skilled individuals might therefore be considered more consistent with the compilation interpretation than with the compensation interpretation.

Three activity domains have been investigated with the Molar Equivalence–Molecular Decomposition research strategy—bridge, chess, and typing. Unfortunately, research in the domain of bridge has been somewhat hampered by the lack of a valid measure of current level of skill. Charness (1979, 1983) has primarily relied upon an index derived from the total number of master points achieved by the player, and has also considered the player's score on a short bridge quiz. However, the former measure is based on the cumulative master points acquired throughout one's lifetime, and hence may not be an accurate reflection of current level of functioning. The psychometric properties of the bridge quiz are unknown, and it would be of dubious value if it is not reliable or has low validity for prediction of actual bridge performance. Moreover, the two measures do not always yield the same age patterns as the age correlations in the 1983 study were -0.06 with the (log transformed) master points index, and -0.40 with the measure of performance on the bridge quiz.

Although not viewed as such in these studies, it is possible to consider accuracy or quality of bridge bids as the measure of proficiency in the molar skill. There were no significant effects of age on these variables in either the Charness (1979) or Charness (1983) studies, and thus it can apparently be inferred that there was molar equivalence in bridge skill across age of the participants in these studies despite the ambiguous status of the other measures of molar skill.

The major finding in the 1979 study was that the older bridge players performed less accurately than the young bridge players in a task of recalling bridge hands. This memory process is presumably relevant to bridge because it was also reported that more skilled bridge players (i.e. those with more master points) were more accurate in the task than less skilled bridge players (i.e. those with fewer master points). Because the individuals in this sample exhibited fairly typical age-related declines in a relevant memory process, it can apparently be inferred that they did not achieve the same level of proficiency in the molar skill of bridge by maintaining high degrees of efficiency in all relevant components. It is not yet clear, however, whether the same level of bridge skill was achieved by age-related increases in one or more compensatory mechanisms, or by a decreased dependence upon the efficiency of component processes with increased skill.

Somewhat contradictory results were obtained with another suspected component of bridge skill concerned with the time to decide which bid to make in a given situation. In the Charness (1979) study this measure was negatively correlated with an index of skill (log master points), suggesting that it was relevant to the molar activity of bridge, but there were no effects of age, implying that the older players had maintained efficient (i.e. rapid) levels of performance. However, in the Charness (1983) study there were weak or non-existent relations between bidding time and skill, but highly significant positive relations between age and bidding time. In this latter study, therefore, the older players were slower in bidding time than the young players, but there was little evidence that this measure bears any relationship to overall skill in bridge. Different procedures in the two studies may have contributed to these discrepancies in results, but whether one concludes that bidding time is relevant to bridge skill and negatively related to age (1983 study), the results appear to be of only marginal interest to the issue of how adults of different ages are able to achieve nearly comparable levels of functioning in the molar activity of bridge.

Charness (1981a) was also responsible for utilizing, and first describing, the Molar Equivalence–Molecular Decomposition research strategy in the domain of chess. The criterion measure of skill in chess was the player's competitive rating, which is a non-cumulative index that increases or decreases as a function of one's performance against opponents of different skill levels. Molar equivalence was established by selecting the participants such that there was a very low correlation (i.e. $r = 0.085$) between age and chess rating, and this equivalence was confirmed by the absence of age effects on measures of the quality of move selected and the accuracy of evaluating game outcomes.

As was found in the bridge domain, older chess players were less accurate than young chess players in recalling meaningful configurations (in this case, positions of chess pieces during mid-game), even though skilled players were generally better than less skilled players in this task. Further analyses revealed that these memory differences were also evident in measures of recall organization in that older players utilized a greater number of smaller-sized chunks than did younger players.

Another finding in this study was that the older players were faster than the young players in selecting an appropriate move from a displayed configuration. Charness (1981a) initially interpreted this result as suggesting that the older players engaged in a more efficient search than the young players, perhaps by greater selectivity of evaluations. However, later analyses (Charness 1981b) of the verbal protocols of the players produced when they were deciding which move to select suggested that the older players considered significantly fewer alternative moves than the young players. It is therefore not yet clear whether the faster move selection on the part of older players represents search that is more efficient, search that is less extensive, or as Charness (1985) recently suggested, merely reflected a strategy difference in the sense that older players responded as soon as they found an acceptable move while younger players continued to search for better alternatives until the time limit was reached.

To summarize, the Charness studies suggest that, in the domains of both bridge and chess, older individuals are apparently able to achieve the same overall level of skill as young individuals despite experiencing typical age-related declines in skill-relevant aspects of memory functioning. While this pattern is inconsistent with both the maintained-abilities and the biased-sample interpretations, it is not yet possible to distinguish between the compensation and the compilation interpretations of these findings. No convincing evidence for an age-related increase in a compensatory mechanism was available in either domain, and the relatively small sample sizes precluded analyses of the magnitude of the molecular-molar correlations as a function of skill to determine whether, as expected from the compilation view, the relationship between component efficiency and level of molar performance declines with increasing skill.

Somewhat more definitive results were obtained in an application of the Molar Equivalence–Molecular Decomposition strategy in the domain of transcription typing by Salthouse (1984) and Salthouse and Saults (1987). (Also see Salthouse, 1987, in press, for further discussion of these studies.) Skill in typing was assessed by determining the individual's net (adjusted for errors) typing speed, and the samples of participants in each study were selected such that there were near-zero correlations between age and net typing speed.

Several measures of perceptual-motor speed were initially examined as potential molecular components in typing, and for each it was found that faster typists performed better than slower typists, but that older typists performed worse than younger typists. In other words, although there were no effects of age in overall typing speed, the older typists exhibited typical age-related declines in the speed of relevant perceptual-motor processes (e.g. finger tapping, choice reaction time, visual-manual transcription).

Investigation of several possible compensatory mechanisms eventually revealed that older typists appeared to have larger anticipation spans of to-be-typed characters than young typists. The span difference was most clearly demonstrated by determining the number of characters a typist needed to have visible in order to type at his or her normal rate (Salthouse, 1984), but it was also evident when the display was altered to determine when the typist no longer responded to switched characters (Salthouse and Saults, 1987). Because the older adults were actually superior to the young adults in the size of these measures of anticipatory processing, and because a greater span obviously minimizes the consequences of slower perceptual-motor processes in typing, these results seem to support the compensation interpretation of the maintenance of skill across adulthood.

Although there has not yet been much research examining how adults of different ages are able to achieve comparable levels of skill on cognitive tasks, the question has considerable theoretical significance, and the limited results that are available appear quite intriguing. It is thus desirable that more research of this type be conducted, examining a variety of different cognitive tasks and employing both the Molar Equivalence–Molecular Decomposition strategy and its converse, the Molar Analysis–Molecular Equivalence strategy.

INTERRELATIONS OF AGEING AND SKILL

This final section of the chapter consists of a discussion of how the joint study of ageing and skilled performance might result in improved understanding of each topic. For ease of communication the discussion is organized in terms of uni-directional relationships, but it should be recognized that this is simply for expository convenience and that the knowledge benefits are likely to be bi-directional, and highly interactive in nature.

Contributions of the study of ageing to the understanding of skill

Perhaps the major benefit of examining the joint effects of age and skill is that it might allow one to determine the minimum requirements needed to achieve skilled performance. That is, because older adults typically have lower levels of many relevant abilities than young adults, investigation of how older adults are able to achieve and maintain high levels of proficiency in different activities can be expected to yield valuable information about the basic nature of skill in those activities. Three specific examples of this type of contribution will be described, based on possible outcomes of studies designed to explore how age and experience interact in the production of skilled performance.

One potentially informative outcome would be a finding that young and old adults matched on the efficiency of all relevant component processes (i.e. the Molar Analysis–Molecular Equivalence Strategy) differed significantly in overall proficiency of the molar skill. Because the research participants were matched on the degree to which they performed on the components thought to be the elements of the molar skill, a finding of this type would imply that skilled performance is something more than the sum of its parts, and, in addition, that the something more was related to adult age. (It should be noted that the existence of age differences in the ratio of sum of component durations to complete problem time in the Charness and Campbell, 1987, study is also consistent with this interpretation.) The possibility that skilled performance consists of the efficient control and integration of processes, and not just the processes themselves, has been frequently discussed, but using the variable of age as a means of establishing the existence of this control or integration mechanism has apparently not yet been explored.

A second possible outcome from the simultaneous study of ageing and skilled performance that would probably contribute to greater knowledge about process of skill acquisition and skill maintenance is a result that adults of different ages who are matched on level of molar skill (i.e. the Molar Equivalence–Molecular Decomposition Strategy), also do not differ in the efficiency of relevant component processes. If such a finding were observed under circumstances where a selection bias in the sample could be ruled out, it might reasonably be inferred that practice or experience in the molar activity either remediates or maintains proficiency in the constituent processes of that activity. That is, because increased age is typically found to be associated with lower levels of functioning on the component processes, a discovery that otherwise representative adults matched on level of molar skill do not exhibit age effects on the relevant molecular measures would suggest that experience may retard or prevent age-related declines that would otherwise occur. Of course, the importance of this outcome is obviously related to how similar the assessment of molecular proficiency is to the molar skill. However, it would be interesting, and surprising from the perspective that capacities are relatively stable characteristics of an individual's information-processing system, to discover that continued performance of a complex activity leads to alterations in the efficiency or effectiveness of presumably fundamental information processes.

The third outcome from research on ageing and skill that could prove informative about the nature and composition of skilled performance is the compensation pattern discussed earlier in which age-related declines in certain molecular components are apparently compensated for by age-related improvements in other components. This type of exchange, in which decreases in the efficiency of some processes seem to be offset by increases in other processes in order to maintain the same overall level of molar skill, would indicate that there is considerable flexibility in how a given degree of molar proficiency can be achieved. Determination of the limits of component substitutability and the conditions leading to particular patterns of compensation would obviously require systematic investigation, but this might be most feasible in the study of adults who are striving to maintain their high levels of performance in activities where they are experiencing declines in the efficiency of component processes.

Contributions of the study of skilled performance to the understanding of ageing

There seem to be at least two ways in which knowledge about the nature of skill might lead to improved understanding of processes of ageing. One concerns possible parallels between skill or expertise and ageing because the tendency for age and experience to be positively correlated suggests that older adults are likely to be more skilled than young adults in the ability domains in which they have specialized. Of course, experience is only a necessary and not a sufficient condition for the development of extreme skill or expertise, but it nevertheless seems reasonable to expect that highly skilled individuals and very experienced older individuals will have numerous characteristics in common. In particular, the study of skill may indicate the breadth of the specialized competence acquired as one develops expertise. Information of this type should be very helpful in understanding the range of abilities in which one might anticipate that high levels of competence could be maintained with continued experience in later adulthood.

Knowledge about skill, and specifically the consequences for skill of prolonged periods without practice, would also be very relevant for one of the dominant theoretical perspectives in the area of cognitive ageing. This position, sometimes referred to as the disuse theory, postulates that age-related declines in many types of cognitive functioning are attributable to older adults having less current experience than young adults with activities similar to those being tested. Empirical evidence for this interpretation is currently mixed (e.g. for reviews see Salthouse, 1985, in press), but the study of skilled performance may provide some of the most directly relevent evidence. That is, if age-related differences in cognitive functioning are attributable to the same mechanisms responsible for proficiency losses in a skill that has not been exercised, then the differences between young and old adults in a given activity should be qualitatively similar to those between performers in that domain who were once equally skilled but now differ with respect to whether or not the skill has been recently exercised.

SUMMARY

Perhaps the major conclusion to be reached from this chapter is that substantial gaps exist between what we would like to know and what we do know about the interrelationships of ageing and skilled performance. For example, despite frequent speculation, there is still little evidence establishing whether skilled activities that are continuously exercised are less susceptible to negative ageing effects than are unfamiliar or novel activities. Furthermore, even if the evidence were consistent in suggesting that there were smaller effects of ageing on skilled activities, it would still not be known whether this is attributable to the influence of ageing being restricted to novel activities, or to increased age being associated with greater amounts of experience with the relevant activities. It is clear, however, that there are substantial age-related decreases in the efficiency or effectiveness of measures that might be considered to reflect the building blocks of cognition. By capitalizing on this fact in the designs of one's research it appears possible to determine not only the answers to the questions posed above, but also to obtain much additional information about the nature of both ageing and skill, and how they interrelate with one another.

ACKNOWLEDGEMENTS

I should like to acknowledge the helpful comments of Neil Charness and Reinhold Kliegl on an earlier version of this chapter.

REFERENCES

Anderson, J. R. (1982). Acquisition of cognitive skill, *Psychological Review*, **89**, 369–406.
Baltes, P. B. & Willis, S. L. (1982). Plasticity and enhancement of intellectual functioning in old age: Penn State's Adult Development and Enrichment Project (ADEPT), in F. I. M. Craik & S. Trehub (eds), *Aging and Cognitive Processes*. New York: Plenum.
Birren, J. E. & Schaie, K. W. (1985). *Handbook of the Psychology of Aging* (2nd edn). New York: Van Nostrand Reinhold.
Charness, N. (1979). Components of skill in bridge, *Canadian Journal of Psychology*, **33**, 1–16.
Charness, N. (1981a). Aging and skilled problem solving, *Journal of Experimental Psychology: General*, **110**, 21–38.

Charness, N. (1981b). Search in chess: age and skill differences, *Journal of Experimental Psychology: Human Perception and Performance*, 7, 467–476.
Charness, N. (1983). Age, skill, and bridge bidding: a chronometric analysis, *Journal of Verbal Learning and Verbal Behavior*, 22, 406–416.
Charness, N. (1985). Aging and problem-solving performance, in N. Charness (ed.), *Aging and Human Performance*. Chichester: Wiley.
Charness, N. & Campbell, J. I. D. (1987). Acquiring skill at mental calculation in adulthood: A task decomposition. Unpublished manuscript. Waterloo, Ontario: Department of Psychology, University of Waterloo.
Chase, W. G. (1978). Elementary information processes, in W. K. Estes (ed.), *Handbook of Learning and Cognitive Processes*, vol. 5. Hillsdale, NJ: Erlbaum.
Kausler, D. H. (1982). *Experimental Psychology and Human Aging*. New York: Wiley.
Newell, A. & Simon, H. A. (1972). *Human Problem Solving*. Englewood Cliffs, NJ: Prentice-Hall.
Posner, M. I. & McLeod, P. (1982). Information processing models—in search of elementary operations, *Annual Review of Psychology*, 33, 477–514.
Rybash, J. M., Hoyer, W. J., & Roodin, P. A. (1986). *Adult Cognition and Aging*. New York: Pergamon.
Salthouse, T. A. (1982). *Adult Cognition*. New York: Springer-Verlag.
Salthouse, T. A. (1984). Effects of age and skill in typing, *Journal of Experimental Psychology: General*, 113, 345–371.
Salthouse, T. A. (1985). *A Theory of Cognitive Aging*. Amsterdam: North-Holland.
Salthouse, T. A. (1987). Age, experience, and compensation, in C. Schooler & K. W. Schaie (eds), *Cognitive Functioning and Social Structures over the Life Course*. Norwood, NJ: Ablex.
Salthouse, T. A. (1988). The role of experience in cognitive aging, in K. W. Schaie (ed.), *Annual Review of Gerontology and Geriatrics*, vol. 7. New York: Springer.
Salthouse, T. A., Kausler, D. H., & Saults, J. S. (1986). Groups versus individuals as the comparison unit in cognitive aging research, *Developmental Neuropsychology*, 2, 363–372.
Salthouse, T. A., Kausler, D. H., & Saults, J. S. (1988). Investigation of student status, background variables, and the feasibility of standard tasks in cognitive aging research. *Psychology and Aging*, 3, 29–37.
Salthouse, T. A. & Saults, J. S. (1987). Multiple spans in transcription typing, *Journal of Applied Psychology*, 72, 187–196.
Salthouse, T. A. & Somberg, B. L. (1982). Skilled performance: effects of adult age and experience on elementary processes, *Journal of Experimental Psychology: General*, 111, 176–207.
Smith, J., Kliegl, R., & Baltes, P. B. (1987). Testing-the-limits and the study of age differences in cognitive plasticity: the sample case of expert memory. Unpublished manuscript. Berlin: Max Planck Institute for Human Development and Education.
Sternberg, R. J. (1977). *Intelligence, Information Processing, and Analogical Reasoning: the Componential Analysis of Human Abilities*. Hillsdale NJ: Erlbaum.
Sternberg, R. J. & Gardner, M. K. (1983). Unities in inductive reasoning, *Journal of Experimental Psychology: General*, 112, 80–116.
Thorndike, E. L., Bregman, E. O., Tilton, J. W., & Woodyard, E. (1928). *Adult Learning*. New York: Macmillan.
Willis, S. L. (1985). Towards an educational psychology of the older adult learner: intellectual and cognitive bases, in J. E. Birren & K. W. Schaie (eds), *Handbook of the Psychology of Aging* (2nd edn). New York: Van Nostrand Reinhold.

Chapter 11

Stress and skill

L. R. Hartley, D. Morrison and P. Arnold

INTRODUCTION

Human beings have a remarkable ability to respond to the demands of a wide range of complex situations. In drawing relationships between skill and stress it is important to consider, first, how we as adaptive systems can successfully control our actions, and second, how human capacity limitations and environmental conditions interact to produce failures of control. If stress is viewed as a process, then it reflects a psychological and physiological attempt by the human system to compensate for unusual acute or chronic demands by mobilizing its resources. If stress is viewed as a product, then it is synonymous with the subjective effect of resource depletion. This short review, while being necessarily selective and introductory, examines the most important empirical findings on the effects of stress upon skilled performance and interprets these results within a broad conceptual framework. It first reviews the action of several stressors, including noise, heat, cold and sleep-loss, upon laboratory tasks. Performance during the circadian cycle is considered in Chapter 12. The second section considers the role of individual differences and drugs in stress. The third section examines the effect of stress on performance of complex tasks, such as industrial processes control.

Four empirical generalizations about the effects of stressors emerge in this review. First, some studies show that stress causes changes to the early, input, processes of attention. Some tests carried out under stress are not influenced by the subjects' preparedness or task instructions. In these instances stress may be affecting the passive or automatic processes of attention. These changes can be seen in experimental studies of the perception of large letters

Acquisition and Performance of Cognitive Skills. Edited by A. M. Colley and J. R. Beech

made up from small ones (Smith, 1985b), vigilance performance and matching judgements of sequential stimuli. Second, other studies show that stress can affect active or control processes of attention. This occurs when stress affects tasks in which the subject's preparedness and instructions play a role, such as in the processing of stimuli differing in probability, the processing of stimuli of temporal uncertainty and tasks in which responses must be prepared and executed. It is helpful to refer to Navon (1977) to clarify this distinction. He has proposed that perception proceeds in two stages. First there is a passive, bottom-up, process involving a global analysis of information. This is followed by an active, top-down, process when local detail is examined in the light of current attentional strategies.

The third generalization is that motivation can influence the way in which stress affects performance. Some effects of stress on tasks are influenced by incentive, and in others, strategies of problem-solving are changed by the subjects' expectation. Fourth, the duration of exposure to a stressor is an important determinant of its effect. Almost all studies show that long exposure to noise, sleep-loss or heat is more detrimental than, or qualitatively different from, brief exposure.

Although it is useful to make these generalizations, the different stressors have rather different profiles of effect on performance. Indeed, some workers have questioned whether a coherent theory of stress can be proposed. However, one of the most interesting findings has been that different stressors have similar or opposing effects on some tasks. Thus, noise and sleep-loss, when applied together, may be less detrimental than either alone. To a degree stressors can be usefully grouped according to their similarities and differences. This is of importance in the practical context. Gopher and Sanders (1984) propose a model for the interpretation of these differing effects of stressors. They suggest that there is a pool of energy or effort which separately supplies input mechanisms, to carry out stimulus processing, and output mechanisms to prepare and execute attentional and control responses. This distinction is similar to the first two generalizations above. Changes in either or both mechanisms occur under stress and arise from changes in the amount or distribution of resource energy. The third generalization above, concerning motivational effects and strategy shifts, parallels the executive or evaluation mechanism proposed by Gopher and Sanders. This monitors the distribution of resources and the output of the system to determine its optimal state. Gopher and Sanders' model is akin to Broadbent's (1971) proposal of two arousal systems and to the distinction Humphreys and Revelle (1984) draw between arousal and effort. Gopher and Sanders' executive or evaluation system is similar to Broadbent's upper arousal system. The pool of resource energy is similar to the lower arousal system. Their more recent approach differs by proposing separate distribution of resources to input and output processors.

NOISE AND SKILL

Studies of the immediate and delayed effects of noise on skill are of practical importance, not only because noise is a contemporary and widespread problem in industrial and domestic environments but also because these studies have shed light on the mechanisms by which other stressors affect people. Four types of task have been studied: vigilance performance, performance on dual or concurrent tasks, studies of choice reaction time, and immediate memory or retrieval from long-term memory under noisy conditions. These tasks have been studied under conditions of concurrent noise, and sometimes after-effects of noise have been observed.

Most reaction-time and vigilance studies have employed continuous white noise at about 95–100 dBA, but recent memory studies have tended to use noise levels of 85 dBA. The control condition has usually been the same noise spectrum presented at 70 dBA. Recent experiments have therefore been less stressful than the earlier ones and may not be so useful for understanding stress. In these recent experiments the effects of the subjects' strategy in the task are certainly more in evidence in comparison to the earlier experiments in which localized impairment in processing was observed.

Vigilance and maintenance of attention in noise

In vigilance studies, attention is directed for long periods to one or more signal sources. The normal deterioration in detection rate over the watch is exaggerated by noise. This deterioration is greater with more sources of information (Broadbent, 1971). Clear changes occur when false alarms and confidence in report are required in a signal-detection analysis. Noise reduces reports of intermediate confidence and the decision criteria the operator uses move closer together (Broadbent and Gregory, 1963). This has implications for the type of task affected by noise. Movement of criteria together has its greatest detrimental effect when performance is risky in the first place for it causes a fall in correct responses. This occurs when multiple sources, or many signals, are monitored. It would also occur if the subject were more aroused by the presence of other stressors, such as high incentive, in demanding settings (Broadbent, 1971). Correspondingly, noise can have a beneficial effect on performance where the operator is underloaded because events are infrequent or the task easy. Although performance in noise on these tasks may reflect changes in passive perceptual mechanisms, it clearly affects the active processes of attention and response preparation discussed above. This is shown by the way in which stimulus probability and incentive influence performance in noise.

Concurrent or dual task performance in noise

In this setting subjects are required to deal with two or more sources of stimuli which require different responses. Hockey (1973) required subjects to examine a display to see if a signal had been presented on one of three sources, each of which presented signals with differing probability. Noise made uncertain responses rarer and the subjects' examination of the display reflected increasing attention to the most probable source of signals. This is referred to as 'narrowing of attention'. Similar effects have also been found in other work, especially that which uses the dual task paradigm (Hockey, 1970; Hartley, 1980). In dual tasks, the operator is typically required to track a target, at the same time as visually monitoring events in the field ahead. This research found that tracking was improved by noise, and increased attention was paid to the most likely source of information in the secondary monitoring task. Noise again can be seen to affect active processes involved in attention distribution or allocation.

Smith (1985b) examined the effect of noise in a dual perceptual task involving processing large letters made up of small ones. Processing of small letters was improved by noise, but that of large letters impaired. These effects were immune to instructions. Thus in some settings noise causes changes in passive attentional processes.

Serial reaction and selection of information

These studies have required subjects to cancel signals as quickly as possible, by tapping a key or pressing a button. In noise, there is an increase in errors of commission (responding to the wrong signal) and omission (missing a response) over half-an-hour of work (Hartley 1973a). In a field study of a related task by Broadbent and Little (1960) noise increased errors made by workers threading film spools. Performance on this task is sensitive to a number of factors. Instructions or feedback to the subject cause more deterioration in noise. Furthermore individual differences and environmental factors that are stressful interact with noise. Sleep-loss, for example, may antagonize the adverse effect of noise (Broadbent, 1971). Furthermore Smith (1985a) has shown that noise speeds serial reactions to the stimuli of higher probability. These results indicate that although noise can affect automatic perceptual processes, its main effect is upon the active processes involved in narrowing of attention to the dominant or most probable sources of information.

Teichner, Arees and Reilly (1963) examined search speed in a visual task which was accompanied by bursts of noise of differing duration. Search speed increased early in the task but decreased later. This is the first study to suggest two effects of noise: an initial distraction effect impairing the intake of information, and a later factor affecting alertness. Other studies distinguish between an effect of the loudness and intermittency of noise on commisions and a later effect of the perceptual isolation noise causes on omissions. For example, Hartley (1974) and Hartley and Carpenter (1974) found ear protection, although reducing the intensity of noise, only reduced the number of omissions in the first half of the test. Free field noise is more variable and subjectively louder than headphone noise, and was found mainly to impair commissions. Studies of noise bursts also point to two different mechanisms mediating the adverse effects. Woodhead (1964) found bursts during the intake of information, but not during the execution of a response, were disruptive and this was a function of intensity. Fisher (1972) found a slowing of responses when bursts arrived during their execution. These studies show that noise has separate effects on the intake of information and preparation of responses.

Effects of noise on verbal memory and performance

There are many recent reviews of the several effects of noise on memory (e.g. Jones, 1983). These effects are briefly discussed here. First, noise improves memory for the order in which words are presented. Second, noise increases confusions between words that sound alike, but not between synonyms. Dornic (1975) suggests noise increases the 'parroting-back' of words learned. Third, noise favours recall of items recently presented at the expense of recall of those first presented in a list. Fourth, when Hockey and Hamilton (1970) presented words in several locations on a screen, noise improved memory for the words and their order, but impaired memory for their location. Smith (1982) has confirmed that although order information is better remembered in noise, this effect is greater when it is the higher priority task. Wilding, Modhindra and Breen-Lewis (1982) suggest that these results can be explained if noise slowed down the rate of rehearsal and thereby encouraged maintenance rehearsal of words at the expense of elaborative rehearsal. M. W. Eysenck (1975) has found that retrieval from long-term memory is biased by noise towards recalling the most likely members of verbal categories. Taken together, the results of these studies show that noise has effects on the active processes of attention given to material to be learnt or remembered. More prioritizing of the components of the task takes place, accompanied by shifts in strategy or rehearsal and recall. Smith summarizes this by suggesting that noise changes performance because the subject seeks to optimize it to repay his or her efforts better.

Although the majority of verbal experiments have shown effects of noise on retrieval there are also instances in verbal tasks when noise may affect the intake of the stimulus. This is discussed in the following experiment which is also interesting because it demonstrates an after-effect of prior noise exposure on a later test. Hartley and Adams (1976) found ten minutes of noise exposure increased interference and twenty minutes decreased interference in a brief Stroop colour interference test carried out later. Although reduced colour name interference may have enhanced maintenance rehearsal the reversal of this pattern with a longer exposure shows that maintenance rehearsal is only one of several factors affected by noise. Furthermore Smith and Broadbent (1985) found, on a Stroop task, that reading of colour names, but not naming colours, was affected by noise. They conclude that their findings reflect that noise induced changes in the intake of information, rather than on memory.

Changes in cognitive strategies in noise

Hartley, Dunne, Schwartz and Brown (1986) used a sentence verification task similar to MacLeod, Hunt and Mathews (1978) to look at the effects of noise on the active processes of attention. They tested the idea that noise encourages operators to adopt their preferred strategy. Two groups of twelve subjects were found who preferred either a spatial or verbal strategy on the task. Noise did not assist their preferred strategy. Instead it assisted the group with the verbal strategy and hindered subjects using the spatial approach. Hartley, Boultwood and Dunn (1987) also confirmed this conclusion in a practical situation, using problems from Rubic's Cube. In this type of task noise seems to affect the allocation of active attentional effort to different strategies, some of which are then more successfully employed than are others. The findings may have implications for the presentation of instructional information in noise and perhaps for the selection and training of operators who have to use the instructions. If information is to be understood in noise, it is better written than pictured and the operators should be selected and trained for verbal abilities if they are to work in noise.

After-effects of noise

Hartley (1973b) found that adverse effects of noise on a serial reaction task continued after the noise ceased, and performance recovered only slowly. Glass and Singer (1972) also found after-effects of intermittent noise on cognitive tasks. Subjects made fewer attempts on insoluble puzzles and detected fewer proof-reading errors. In addition they found that, if the subjects felt that they had controlled the noise, impairment was reduced. Fisher (1972) suggests that the perception of control reduces the adverse effect of stresses.

After-effects of noise occur outside the laboratory in occupational, educational and domestic environments. A. Cohen (1973) showed that workers in noisy environments have more illness and job-related accidents than do comparable employees in quiet environments. This effect is reduced by wearing hearing protection. S. Cohen (1980) has found that intermittent aircraft noise reduces persistence, causes distraction and impairs performance in schoolchildren. These problems increase with more overflights. Smith and Stansfield (1986) have shown that people who are exposed to noisy overflights and also those who are noise-sensitive, independently forget more facts when tested later. On the latter point, there is evidence that noise sensitivity is linked to neuroticism. After-effects of noise, and the personality factor of neuroticism, may have similarities in their effects.

The studies summarized here agree that recovery occurs slowly after a noise exposure. The findings suggest two accounts of the after-effects. First, chronic effects of noise exposure may occur because inappropriate strategies for learning are permanently adopted. Some studies show that this does take place in noise, as subjects strive to compensate for its detrimental effects on the processes discussed above. On the other hand, Gopher and Sanders' model would suggest that depletion of the energy pool might take place as subjects compensate for stress. A period of recovery might then be required to replenish diminished resources.

It is of considerable interest that studies of one of the most prolonged stresses, several days of sleep-loss, suggest similar conclusions. This is discussed in the following section.

EFFECTS OF LOSS OF SLEEP ON SKILL

People can lose sleep in varying amounts and for varying reasons. Sometimes a person may have to work during the day following a sleepless night. Sometimes a person may have to work when they would normally sleep, if they have changed their time zone or working shift. Therefore studies of skilled performance following sleep-loss have important implications.

Several tasks have been found to be sensitive to lack of sleep. One result, which many studies have confirmed, is that long tests are more sensitive to sleep-loss. For example, Webb and Levy (1984) compared the effect of partial and full sleep-loss on vigilance and shorter cognitive tasks. They concluded that shorter tests are less affected by sleep-loss than are long vigilance tasks. Furthermore, impairment increases with repeated testing on these tasks when sleep-loss is held constant. In many tests individuals may try to compensate temporarily for lack of sleep just as they try to do in the presence of noise. For example Poulton, Hunt, Carpenter and Edwards (1978) showed that doctors working with three hours sleep debt were much less affected in a reasoning test if they received feedback of their performance on another test than if they did not. Together these findings show the importance of motivational resources in combating sleep-loss. This suggests that the subjects' motivation is of importance during sleep-loss in maintaining their active processes of attention.

Sleep, vigilance and detection performance

Many studies show monitoring ability declines following sleep-loss. Investigators have tried to find out why this occurs and what mechanism is affected by sleep-loss. Wilkinson (1969) studied vigilance under partial and complete sleep-loss. Reducing sleep to less than two hours for one night or five hours for two nights impaired performance. A signal detection analysis of the data showed this was due to a decline in d'. During 60 hours of continuous wakefulness, Horne, Anderson and Wilkinson, (1983) also found that d' declined during the normal sleep period. This decline did not occur during the day and beta was unaffected. Hartley and Shirley (1977) confirmed this and found that brief naps elevated d' in the first part of the test, but this measure declined steeply in the latter part. Horne and Pettitt (1985) showed that monetary incentive for good performance partly, and temporarily, reduced the decline in d'. These results suggest that a limited loss of sleep seriously affects vigilance performance. However, this decline can, to some extent, be compensated for by motivation and this indicates the importance of the active processes of attention following a short loss of sleep. Some studies also show that, if the sleep deficit is severe enough, compensation is ineffective in combating this decline in performance. Presumably the pool of resources has been depleted by chronic sleep-loss and therefore is unable to maintain the active processes of attention.

In a related study, Hockey required subjects to monitor six sources of visual signals arranged across the visual field. Sources in the centre of the field were more likely to deliver signals than those in the periphery. Sleep-loss reduced the normal focusing of attention on the sources of higher probability. However, Sanders (1983) found, in a related task, adverse effects of sleep-loss on sources of low probability that were in peripheral view. Although the two experiments do not show the same pattern of results, they do agree in again revealing a decline in the active processes of attention following sleep-loss. Sanders suggests that this is due to a reduction in the volume of attentional resources during sleep-loss. The precise pattern of results this produced would depend on the strategy that the subjects thought might best repay their efforts.

Sleep-loss and reaction time

Simple and choice reaction time tasks have also been found to be impaired by sleep-loss. Tilley and Wilkinson (1984) found that in comparison with normal sleep, restricting sleep to the first or second half of the night equally impaired simple reaction time. This is of interest because rapid eye movement (REM sleep) or dreaming sleep, in contrast to non-REM sleep, occurs mainly in the latter part of the night. This shows that performance is impaired by whichever type of sleep is lost. In choice reaction tasks there is normally an increase in omissions, or lapses of attention, over a half-hour test. Wilkinson (1969) found that this increase is augmented following a night without sleep. Again these results show the reduction in the active preparation of attention following sleep-loss. However, sufficient motivation, provided by feedback of results to subjects, was found to be sufficient to overcome the impairment of one night of lost sleep.

Recent experiments by Sanders (Sanders and Reitsma, 1982a,b; Sanders, Wijnen and van Arkel, 1982) suggest that sleep-loss affects two mechanisms. Their proposal is related to the distinction Pribram and McGuiness (1975) draw between phasic arousal and tonic activation mechanisms. Phasic arousal is though to control perceptual orientation. Activation influences the subjects' readiness or preparedness to respond and may control processes of active attention. Both systems draw separately on the pool of effort resources. Sanders and his co-workers suggest that the first mechanism, which is supposed to be passive or automatic, influences perceptual integration. In both of Sanders' experiments subjects were sleep-deprived. First, they were required to match a central and peripheral light source. Second, they were required to carry out an additive factor task involving degraded stimuli and stimulus response compatibility. Two effects of sleep-loss were found. The first was impaired perceptual integration of successive signals. Sanders suggests that sleep-loss prevents the development of a clear stimulus code. This effect of sleep-loss would be seen in perceptual tasks in which the role of the active process of attention is very small or can be excluded. The second effect observed was impairment of the preparation and execution of responses. Tasks requiring active preparation of attention would reveal this effect of sleep-loss. These include vigilance tasks with stimuli of temporal or spatial uncertainty and tracking tasks requiring discrete responses.

In the Gopher and Sanders' model sleep-loss might be viewed as depleting the pool of energy resources available to support the separate perceptual input and response processes. Effects of sleep-loss might occur when the evaluation or executive system could not maintain an adequate distribution of resources to these mechanisms. Correspondingly sleep would replenish the pool and provide better active and passive attentional processes.

Sleep-loss and memory

Many studies have found that some aspects of memory are also impaired by sleep-loss. In one of the first experiments Jenkins and Dallenbach (1924) found that subjects remembered material better if they slept immediately after learning it as compared to remaining awake for an equal interval. Other studies have confirmed this result and found that part of the detrimental effect of sleep-loss on memory is due to fluctuations in the daytime performance of the sleep-deprived. Recent studies show that a waking interval between the learning episode and later sleep reduces the beneficial effect of sleep on memory for the material. These results may indicate that sleep either prevents interference with the material already learnt, or that sleep-loss detrimentally affects strategies for its recall.

Some studies have found that the time at which sleep occurs is important for retention. Sleep at night is more beneficial than during the day, and this may be related either to the quality or to the type of sleep obtained, or to a disturbance of the circadian cycle in a daytime sleep. In an attempt to find out what contribution type of sleep makes to retention, Empson and Clarke (1970) tried to deprive subjects of only REM sleep as compared to yoked controls deprived of non-REM sleep. Prose material learned the previous day was more poorly recalled by the REM-deprived group. However, they found, in some other studies, which varied the amount of REM obtained during sleep, that REM sleep reduced memory for words. Differences in the processing resources required by different types of material may be important because these latter experiments did not use prose. Differences in the type of material learned are important, for Ryman, Naitoh and Englund (1985) found that sleep-loss impaired retention of sentences in the active voice but not in the passive. Perhaps the greater attentional effort required for processing passive sentences compensated for the effect of sleep-loss.

Chapter 12 describes the important effect on learning and retention of the point on the diurnal cycle at which learning and testing occur. Following sleep-loss Tilley and Warren (1984) examined the interaction between the type of material learned and the point on the circadian cycle at which learning took place. They studied the semantic categorization of words during a night without sleep. There was an increasing difference in classification speed between probable and improbable members of the categories during the descending phase of the circadian cycle to 4 a.m. It was followed by a decreasing difference during the ascending phase until the point when the person normally woke. The result may be due to a scarcity of processing resources at the low point of the circadian cycle which differently affected the processing of the probable and improbable category members.

On balance both sleep-loss and any attendant effects on circadian cycle can influence learning and retention, but these effects are mediated by the demands of the material on attentional resources.

HEAT AND SKILL

Investigations of the effect of the thermal environment on skilled performance are important for several reasons. Many people work in tropical climates without air conditioning and are subject to much radiant heat. This may raise whole body temperature. Industrial or military operations often involve high temperatures. These may cause elevated temperatures of parts of the body, such as the head, or they may raise the temperature of the whole body in more severe settings. Finally, metabolic processes, such as muscular work during manual handling and athletics, will produce heat and this will raise whole body temperature. When body temperature is raised, compensatory heat-loss takes place through sweating, convection, radiation and behaviour. As long as this occurs in a relatively cool environment, heat-loss will exceed the heat-gain and body temperature will not rise, although performance may be inconvenienced. Thus studies of the effect of raised body temperature on performance have used two measures of heating: core temperature derived from the rectum, mouth or ear canal, and Effective Temperature (ET) which is a psychophysical judgement by moderately energetic people in known temperature and humidity. Meaningful ETs depend on the climate and task but as a rule body temperatures rise when people are exposed to ET in excess of 29°C for long periods.

The methodology to study the effect of temperature on performance is complex. Rapid, brief, heating may not initiate compensatory heat-loss, especially if it is selective heating. A short exposure to high ET may have a different effect on skill from a long exposure, when compensation for the rise in core temperature will occur.

Studies of the acclimatization of skilled performance by repeated exposure to high ET are rare. Curley and Hawkins (1983) found no evidence of psychological acclimatization although physiological adaptation occurred over ten days' exposure to heat. This suggests that psychological adaptation to raised body temperatures does not occur to any great extent.

Mackworth (1961) exposed men to hot conditions for several hours and then tested them. Normal rectal temperature is 36°C. His three cognitive tasks, including vigilance, coding and problem-solving, all suffered when the rectal temperature rose by a degree to 37°C. A task familiar to the subjects, morse-coding, was only affected when the rectal temperature reached about 38°C. A fifth, heavy manual task was less severely affected. Mackworth also found that inexperienced subjects deteriorated more than experienced ones above ET of 33°C.

Wilkinson, Fox, Goldsmith, Hampton and Lewis (1964) recorded sublingual temperature during arithmetic and vigilance tasks. Their results show that a slight rise affects performance differently from a substantial rise. Vigilance response time was impaired as temperature rose slightly. As temperature rose further to 38.5°C, vigilance response time improved and arithmetic speed deteriorated. Other studies found that a rise in core temperature to 38.5°C improved verbal and non-verbal reasoning and speed of calculations, without impairing accuracy or other memory measures.

In order to examine the effect of raised temperature on the brain the head can be heated rapidly and transiently while leaving the rectal temperature unaffected. Studies show that under these circumstances subjects can withstand higher temperatures before impairment occurs. Nunneley, Reader and Maldonado (1982) found that head heating through 2°C improved choice reaction time but diminished accuracy and Hancock (1983) found that a head temperature rise of 1°C increased the number of arithmetic additions without affecting accuracy. However, a large rise of 3.5°C increased reaction time latency (Hancock and Dirkin, 1982).

On the basis of these results and recent studies of tracking performance, Hancock (1982) concludes that a small rise in core temperature or initial exposure to high ET may benefit speed of skill but at the expense of accuracy. Furthermore the temperature at which performance is impaired is generally related to task complexity. The limit for simple tasks is a rise of about 1.5°C, and for complex tasks 0.3°C. Although experience of the task may reduce the impairment caused by high temperatures, segments of performance requiring complex control suffer severely. This suggests that if performance is sufficiently automatic, so as to be relatively attention-free, then it is more resistant to raised core temperatures. The unskilled operator, or one placed in novel situation, may be impaired because of the demand on the active processes of attention which seem sensitive to the stress of raised body temperature.

COLD AND SKILL

The effect of low environmental temperature on skilled performance is also important for industrial and service personnel. Those people who operate in unusual settings, such as divers, may also experience lowered body temperature. The effects of cold may be local, when the temperature of a part of the body cannot be maintained, or general when the environment is so severe that heat generated in the body cannot compensate for heat lost to the environment. Usually cold first affects limb and joint movements as circulation fails to maintain their temperature. Some acclimatization is apparent in people used to cold. They show a smaller fall in skin temperature and their manual dexterity is not so impaired as in unacclimatized people. Kay (1949) demonstrated that handgrip and nut-screwing ability fell as skin temperature dropped below 15°C. This impairment is due to loss of skin sensation as its temperature drops below normal. Presumably loss of strength is also due to reduced blood flow.

A fall in whole body temperature has been found to impair cognitive skills. Poulton, Hitchings and Brooke (1965) examined vigilance performance when sublingual temperature fell to 35.6°C. When compared to normal this fall increased the number of long responses to signals although manual dexterity was not required in responding. Recent informal studies reveal that divers who core temperatures fell to 34–35°C suffered amnesia for part of their dives. Baddeley, Cuccaro, Egstrom, Weltman and Willis (1975) have shown that the longer the diver is in cold water the slower the cognitive skill. An important question in these studies is the contribution that the severe peripheral effects of cold make to the impairment of cognitive skill. Attempts to solve it try to reduce the peripheral sensations of cold. Lockhart (1966) varied hand and body surface temperatures independently and examined manual dexterity. When the body was cold, and the hands warm, performance was impaired. Coleshaw, Van Someren, Wolf, Davis and Kreatinge (1983) excluded peripheral sensations of cold discomfort by warming the surface of the body, following cooling the body core down to 36°C. If material was learned when the surface was warm, but core temperature below 36.7°C, recall was impaired up to 70 per cent. When learning was at normal temperature, but recall took place with a warm surface and cold core, memory was unimpaired. These studies show that consolidation but not retrieval processes of memory, and speed of mental calculation are impaired by reduced core temperature. Even when the peripheral sensations of cold are removed low body temperature seriously impairs several forms of cognitive skill. Whether this impairment is in the passive or active processes of attention is unclear.

ANXIETY AND SKILL

Just as arousal theories have dominated theories of the effects of environmental stress, so they have dominated theories about individual differences and stress. Research has taken two approaches: first, examining the process of stress by studying the way in which the performance of individuals differs in response to stress; and second, examining the outcome of stress, by studying reactions, such as anxiety and worry, that stressors cause in individuals. These reactions are often regarded themselves as stresses that have to be coped with and which may modify an individual's response to the stressor. Most laboratory research has focused on acute stress where the individual's resources can compensate for the stressor. By contrast there is little research into settings where resources may be depleted and inadequate, such as performance under chronic stress.

Much of the research which is reviewed below can, for convenience, be summarized in two empirical generalizations. These are dealt with separately. First, a number of studies show some individuals are more sensitive to stressors. For example, we have seen that noise affects some people more than others, and anxious people are often more affected by task variables than are the non-anxious. Second, there are studies which show that individuals can use and learn a variety of strategies for coping with the adverse effects that stressors, including anxiety, may have on them and their perform-ance. For example, under stress some people may work faster and others may change the way stimuli are encoded.

Individual differences in anxiety and stress

An important idea, which has guided research into the effects of anxiety and drugs upon skill, was advanced by Easterbrook (1959). He proposed that the range of cues utilized in the execution of a task narrows as anxiety or arousal increases. Task-irrelevant information is discarded at lower arousal levels than task-relevant information. With increasing arousal, task-irrelevant in-formation is discarded resulting in improvements as fewer distractions impede performance. However, as arousal becomes high and all task-irrelevant information has been excluded, task-relevant information is than discarded and performance declines.

Although this theory has often proved to be very useful, recent authors have applied the idea, referred to earlier, that there is a pool of resources which can be allocated to different cognitive skills. Effort or motivation may influence the allocation policy or even determine the availability of resources. Humphreys and Revelle (1984) propose that anxiety increases arousal, as other stresses do, and is therefore potentially beneficial. However, anxiety may also cause task avoidance, because it produces worry or self-concern (M.W. Eysenck, 1984). The latter suggests that anxiety may degrade per-formance because it is a self-concern which competes with task-relevant information for resources allocated to working memory. When irrelevant concerns utilize some of these resources, there is reduced capacity for the processing of task-relevant information and impaired performance follows. M. W. Eysenck (1984, p. 357) summarizes his view of the several effects anxiety has on performance by concluding that it 'typically increases atten-tional selectivity, reduces short-term storage, reduces accuracy without in-creasing speed, impairs long-term memory, and often reduces attentional control. This suggestion is supported by the finding that failure on an initial task changes subsequent performance on other tasks in the direction of greater reflectivity, rigidity and stereotyped responding (Geen, 1985). Thus the effects that are attributed to preoccupation with failure are possibly the result of a further allocation of resources away from task-relevant factors to task-irrelevant factors.

Although some researchers also distinguish between worry and emotional-ity, the two major components of anxiety, M. W. Eysenck (1983) postulates that anxiety impairs tasks mainly because it produces the self-concern of worry. Indeed Spielberger, Gonzalez, Taylor, Algaze and Anton (1978) found that worry was negatively correlated with a measure of academic achievement but emotionality was not.

Explanations of individual differences in performance under stress further distinguish between trait and state anxiety. Trait anxiety is an individual's more or less permanent susceptibility to being anxious. State anxiety refers to the transient anxiety experienced in different situations. The level of state anxiety interacts with the level of trait anxiety under some circumstances. No matter what their level of trait anxiety, all people respond to physical danger with similar high levels of state anxiety. However, people with high levels of trait anxiety are likely to report greater anxiety in the presence of an ego threat (for example failure feedback) than are people low in trait anxiety (M. W. Eysenck, 1984).

Many experiments find that, when under stress, subjects high on trait anxiety perform more poorly than those low on trait anxiety. For example, Leon and Revelle (1985) assessed performance on geometric analogies under either relaxed or time-constrained conditions. When relaxed, the high-anxiety subjects were both slower and less accurate than the low-anxiety subjects. In the stressed condition, while anxious subjects were faster, they made more errors than less anxious subjects. Thus performance under stress demonstrated differences in speed–accuracy trade-off strategies rather than differences in processing abilities. Leon and Revelle (1985) suggest that anxious subjects, not knowing how quickly they needed to respond to avoid losing the stimulus from view, attempted to gain control by responding more quickly. They adopted a strategy which minimized the additional anxiety resulting from an unpredictable and uncontrollable situation. Conversely, the less anxious subjects did not have the same motivation to adopt a coping strategy to minimize additional sources of anxiety. This reflects a lower demand on the resources of the less anxious. So the less anxious subjects could allow themselves more time in which to consider their response, with resulting higher accuracy.

Hammerton and Tichner (1968) observed that while there is a widely held commonsense belief that performance of skilled tasks declines under fear or stress, there are few real-life data to support this belief. For ethical and technical reasons it is usually impossible to expose people to alarming situations in which subjects are deceived into supposing they are in genuine danger. An avenue in which people under chronic stress may be observed has been utilized by several experimenters. Scott (1983) observed the level of stress of women admitted for breast biopsy immediately before the procedure and six weeks later. All women included in the sample were those whose biopsies showed benign conditions. Prior to the procedure the mean state anxiety level was comparable to norms for patients with acute anxiety reaction. Post-crisis scores were comparable to each woman's trait score and the distribution was normal. A group of highly anxious patients demonstrated that critical thinking ability was depressed as a function of this high anxiety. Scott concluded that general reasoning ability was substantially reduced during hospitalization, a phase when decisions were demanded in relation to treatment and authorization.

Strategy differences in response to anxiety

Several studies show that anxiety may not always be detrimental, especially if useful coping strategies are provided for people to use in the task. Edmundson and Nelson (1976) required high- and low-anxiety subjects to learn a paired-associate list of physically dissimilar words. In addition subjects were given either an effective encoding strategy or an ineffective one. Low-anxiety subjects performed considerably better than high-anxiety subjects when performance was unaided by the effective strategy. The use of an effective strategy slightly improved the performance of low-anxiety subjects but improved the performance of high-anxiety subjects considerably, so much so that it was comparable to that of the low-anxiety group. They concluded that without a task-assisting strategy, the high arousal resulting from the anxiety caused a narrowing of attention and underutilization of task-relevant information. With an encoding strategy, the additive effects of task demands and anxiety on arousal were lower, and better utilization of task-relevant information was possible.

Scott and Nelson (1979) repeated the experiment, selecting subjects who scored either high or low on both trait and test anxiety. They also added a time constraint by shortening learning and response times. In the unpaced conditions of the Edmundson and Nelson study, high-anxiety subjects had time to reinstate their study-trial encoding and were able to perform at the same level as low-anxiety subjects. Yet under the paced conditions of the Scott and Nelson study, the high-anxiety subjects performed worse with the encoding strategy than without it because the test was too fast. In the paced condition high-anxiety subjects were unable to take advantage of the encoding strategy presumably because their anxiety diminished the resources available to do so. Without a coping strategy the performance of the low-anxiety subjects was worse than that of the high-anxiety subjects. Scott and Nelson report that some of the low-anxiety subjects exhibited very poor performance and appeared uninvolved and untouched by the task and its requirements. Anomalously, with the aid of the encoding strategy, which it has been suggested should lower anxiety, the performance of all the low-anxiety group improved greatly. For these people providing heuristics for problem-solving appeared to facilitate performance, perhaps because it improved the utilization of attentional resources.

In another study illustrating the diminished processing resources of the anxious, M. W. Eysenck and M. C. Eysenck (1980) tested retention of words paired with either strongly or weakly associated words. High anxiety had little effect on recall when the paired associate was strong. It lowered recall, however, when there was a weak association with the cued word. As more extensive processing is required to recall words linked with weak associates, it might be concluded that anxiety reduced elaborative processing. M. W. Eysenck (1982) reviewed the effect of the diminished processing resources of the anxious in dual task experiments. In 16 out of 20 studies, anxiety did not impair processing efficiency on the main task, but 11 of those studies found detrimental effects on a subsidiary task. Eysenck suggests that the absence of an effect on the main task masks a processing inefficiency that only becomes apparent when an additional task is included. The subsidiary task places demands on the resources of the subject for which he cannot compensate. Anxiety may cause decrements in performance when resources are strained and compensatory mechanisms can no longer overcome its adverse effects.

The individual's anxiety level is clearly an important determinant of successful performance. Although the raised arousal of the anxious may facilitate some aspects of performance the reduction of processing resources will impair many cognitive skills. Providing coping strategies during execution of a skill is only partly successful in preventing this impairment, for anxiety may often diminish the resources available to employ the strategy.

DRUGS AND SKILL

Drug research may be divided into studies of the process or product of drug action. Thus the effect of drugs on performance may be either (i) used as a tool to aid the understanding of cognitive processes, or (ii) used in a clinical context to benefit those cognitive operations. Sanders and his co-workers have carried out an important series of experiments investigating the first question (Sanders, 1983). They used the stimulant amphetamine, and a drug with generally opposite effects, a barbiturate, to investigate the resource pool model discussed previously. Sanders (1983) summarizes their findings of the effect of these drugs on the additive factor method. He suggests that barbiturates have their main impact upon the operation of the stimulus input processor of Gopher and Sanders (1984). Such drugs would impair the acquisition and development of stimulus codes. By contrast, amphetamines affect the output processor or activation mechanism. These drugs would therefore impair the preparation and execution of attentional and motor responses.

On the second question, there have been a large number of studies which have investigated the use of drugs, such as the anxiolytics and recreational drugs, in clinical or other applied contexts. Most of the findings with these drugs point to their effect on arousal or effort mechanisms and therefore, perhaps to an effect on the allocation of resources. Some individuals appear to dislike trying to sustain an adaptive response to stress and therefore take psychoactive substances that ameliorate their response to stress. These are often on prescription but sometimes may be recreational drugs. Although a drug may reduce the immediate experience of stress, it can also impair cognitive performance (Cox, 1978). Alcohol highlights this point.

Alcohol and skill

Alcohol taken in relatively small doses may reduce feelings of tension and self-consciousness, and increase conviviality and pleasant feelings. These effects antagonize the response to stress both physiologically and in self-report measures (Baum-Baicker, 1985). Indeed low alcohol doses have been found to improve some types of cognitive performance including problem-solving and short-term memory. Moderate doses, however, can cause significant changes in the accuracy of judgement and in the speed of reactions. Larger doses result in more obvious and gross changes in performance. Epidemiological data highlight the part played by perception and cognition in traffic accidents. There is an increased probability of accidents associated with perceptual failure when alcohol is present in the blood. Accident investigation teams have found that many driver-related errors result from information failures which are frequently related to attention errors precipitated by alcohol (Moskowitz, 1984). This has led to the examination of sensory functions such as visual acuity, glare recovery and peripheral vision in the presence of alcohol. It has been found that these simple sensory functions are resistant to alcohol impairment except when it is present in high concentrations (Moskowitz, 1984). Findings that alcohol does not impair central visual acuity or peripheral vision are incongruent with reports from alcohol-related accidents that drivers failed to see vehicles, traffic signs or pedestrians. Moskowitz (1984) suggests that perceptual performance deteriorates only when attention is divided amongst several subtasks, a condition common to many vehicle- and equipment-operating situations.

Two experimental paradigms are of special interest when considering the perceptual and cognitive processes underlying driver errors. These are the focused attention or vigilance tasks and the divided-attention or dual tasks discussed previously. Single task measures of driving behaviour have failed to reveal significant impairment even when blood alcohol levels are 0.08 mg/100ml. Moskowitz (1984) reports that alcohol had no effect on peripheral signal detection in a vigilance task. This is consistent with other studies which have failed to find that alcohol impairs peripheral vision. However, impairment has been demonstrated at blood alcohol levels of 0.063 mg/100ml when complex decisions underlying driving are assessed (Collins and Chiles, 1980).

Moskowitz and his co-workers demonstrated that a divided-attention task, measuring cognitive decision-making rather than simple performance, is sensitive to the effect of alcohol even at low doses. In a divided-attention task, performance became progressively worse, both as the concentration of blood alcohol increased and as demands on central visual information processing increased.

In a related study, Beirness and Vogel-Sprott (1982) found that alcohol impaired the rate of performance rather than accuracy. They also demonstrated that alcohol-induced impairment is independent of pre-test level of skill on a motor task. That is, whether skilled or not, subjects suffered the same absolute decrements in performance. R. M. Williams, Goldman and D. L. Williams (1981) found that level of performance was related to the subject's expectation of alcohol-induced deficits; subjects compensated for deterioration if they were aware that they had consumed alcohol. The effectiveness of compensation was, however, related to the complexity of the task, with least compensation possible on complex cognitive tasks. These interesting results from alcohol point to it impairing the allocation of resources.

Caffeine and skill

In low to moderate doses, caffeine is considered to be a mild stimulant, relieving minor fatigue. Robertson *et al.* (1978) reported significant increases among non-coffee drinkers in plasma and urinary excretion of adrenaline and noradrenaline following the ingestion of 250 mg/100ml of caffeine. Only a few regular coffee drinkers show increases of the same magnitude (Jung *et al.*, 1981), Sawyer, Julia and Turin (1982) suggest caffeine is a sympathomimetic agent in some, if not all, individuals. Such individuals may interpret elevated catecholamine levels and increased arousal states as normal. Increases in both physical and emotional consequences in the form of increased stress and anxiety would be expected.

Studies demonstrate that coffee provides a prolonged and slightly increased ability to perform exhausting work. However, it interferes with hand steadiness and eye–hand coordination and has effects on simple and complex tasks involving choice and discrimination (Sawyer *et al.*, 1982). Anderson and Revelle (1983) found that caffeine facilitated a low-memory-load, visual search task but hindered a similar high-memory-load task. Several experiments have found that personality factors interact with caffeine in performance. Keister and McLaughlin (1972) found that auditory vigilance improved for extraverts but not introverts after the ingestion of caffeine. Gilliland (1980) found similar results in which extraverts showed increasing accuracy with increased dosages of caffeine. The speed and accuracy of introverts, however, first increased and then fell as the dosage increased. Other studies by Anderson and his co-workers have also found interactions between caffeine, time of day and the personality dimension of impulsivity; the latter is a factor in extraversion.

An interpretation proposed for these studies relies on Easterbrook's hypothesis and assumes caffeine is an arouser and that introverts have higher levels of arousal than do extraverts. On a task with low demands, those low in arousal (extraverts) perform poorly because they attend to task-irrelevant information. Introverts utilize only task-relevant information. On this theory, caffeine ingestion would lead to improvements in performance only for the extraverts by increasing their arousal to a point when they can discard task-irrelevant information. Humphreys and Revelle (1984) have suggested a comprehensive theory of arousal, effort and personality. They proposed that the curvilinear relationship between arousal and performance, which Easterbrook (1959) tried to explain, is due to two opposing effects of arousal. Arousal and effort improve the allocation of resources and thus information transfer. However, the same changes impair immediate memory. In low-memory-load tasks the underaroused extraverts benefit from the arousal caffeine causes and allocate their resources better. In higher memory load tasks the normal introvert and the coffee-drinking extravert would show impairment. In the morning extraverts are especially underaroused and therefore benefit more from caffeine.

Nicotine and skill

Smokers' self-reports identify stress reduction, tranquillization and relaxation as major reasons for smoking (Wesnes and Warburton, 1983). These reports are supported by observations that people in highly stressful situations are more likely to smoke heavily and relapse more under stress. Smoking produces an increase in plasma corticosteroids, proportional to the nicotine content of the cigarette (Hill and Wynder, 1974), and increases electrocortical arousal. Other physiological, neurochemical, endocrinological and electrophysiological evidence suggests that nicotine produces changes characteristic of increasing arousal which could benefit performance. Indeed it has been found that smokers performing rapid information-processing tasks detect targets more quickly and accurately when smoking high-nicotine cigarettes. They also perform more efficiently in visual and auditory vigilance tasks while smoking (Hartley, 1973a). An interpretation of these findings is that nicotine maintains the effort required by active attentional mechanisms and thus facilitates the allocation of resources.

Why then do smokers emphasize the stress-reducing property of smoking? An explanation of this anomaly might be because stressful situations may result in the intrusion of anxious or worrisome thoughts about the outcome, perhaps because of doubts about competence. These intrusions require resources and therefore make it more difficult to maintain performance or may even interfere with it as anxiety is supposed to do. If nicotine maintains effort, it could improve resource allocation to the task at the expense of intrusions. This form of narrowed attention would enable the individual to ignore these distractions, thereby facilitating performance.

STRESS AND COMPLEX MENTAL SKILLS

Most of the research work on the effects of stress on skilled performance has been conducted on laboratory tasks that are relatively simple when compared to most decision-making problems encountered in the real world. Some authors (e.g. Jenkins, 1980) consider this to be a lamentable state of affairs and argue that major theoretical advances will only be made through the study of human behaviour outside the laboratory. In the real world it is much more difficult to identify the specific effects of exposure to stressors on different stages in the execution of mental skills. Nevertheless it is the more complex and elaborate forms of human behaviour that occur outside the laboratory that we urgently need to understand, predict and control. Unless progress can be made in reliably estimating the magnitude of the main effects and interactions of different stressors on performance of complex tasks, then major industrial accidents caused by 'human failure' such as Flixborough, Chernobyl and Three Mile Island, will remain as interesting case studies.

From a survey of the literature, we have found very few studies which looked at stress and complex problem-solving performance. This is an area in which it might have been expected that there would have been a good deal of research activity, especially from workers involved in selection, training and allocation of function between humans and machines. This state of affairs simply reflects the lack of current knowledge about problem-solving be- haviour and the absence of a theory of problem-solving. There are many metaphorical descriptions of how problem-solving is performed (e.g. Minsky, 1975; Schank and Abelson, 1977) and even a sizeable literature on the natural heuristics biases and traps that befall problem-solvers (e.g. Kahneman and Tversky, 1982). There is, however, little published experimental research dealing with problem-solvers under stress. What literature there is deals with the effects of stress on performance of mental skills resulting from *post hoc* analyses of error data e.g. (Reason, 1984).

In the preceding sections of this chapter a fluid dynamic model of informa- tion processing during stress was referred to. Such an approach is certainly not new and a number of variants on the same theme have been described elsewhere (see M. W. Eysenck, 1982, for a review). It is not the purpose of this chapter to discuss these specific variations. Instead, the idea that informa- tion-processing capability is dependent upon a fluctuating pool of processing resources is seen as a useful metaphor with which to try to understand how diverse sets of stressors might affect human problem-solving capabilities as demonstrated in 'real world' tasks.

Unlike the previous sections of this chapter that have considered the impact that stress has on performance, we shall now look at the problem in reverse. In other words, at what can be done to make the execution of cognitive skills less stressful and make it more likely that human operators will maintain effective high levels of performance in controlling automated systems. Before describing the factors that need to be considered the scene is set by briefly describing the events that occurred at Three Mile Island.

The events at Three Mile Island

The Three Mile Island (TMI) incident is of interest for a number of reasons, including the fact that a series of totally independent problems conspired to produce the unique set of events that led to the near melt-down of the nuclear reactor. This fact is not unique to TMI, but is a feature of many reported accidents (see Perrow, 1984). Since the fine details of the TMI incident have been documented elsewhere (e.g. Rubinstein and Mason, 1976) we will not present anything other than the sketchiest detail here.

No one single event led to the near melt-down at TMI. Prior to the accident the operators had been trying to transfer spent material from that part of the system where steam is generated. The pipes used in the transfer process became clogged, which caused a series of pumps to trip. As designed, the automatic safety system acted to shut down the turbine. In order to stop the secondary cooling system from boiling dry a set of auxiliary feedwater pumps were activated. Unfortunately, these were prevented from operating due to being incorrectly set after routine maintenance work. As a result the water in the secondary cooling system became less effective in maintaining the temperature and pressure of the core coolant surrounding the nuclear fuel. The rising temperature and pressure in the core cooling system opened a pressurizer relief valve. Perhaps the major contributor to the severity of the accident was the fact that the relief valve failed to re-seat but this was not indicated on the console. As a result of the open valve massive coolant loss from the primary core cooling system occurred.

Despite information to the contrary, the operators became convinced that there was too much water in the system rather than too little. Consequently, when a final fail-safe high-pressure emergency core cooling system came into operation the operators closed it off. To all intents and purposes, the operators had become 'locked' into believing that their interpretation of events was the correct one and they discounted information that was not consistent with their hypothesis. They had, to use Sheridan's (1981) description, developed 'cognitive tunnel vision'. With hindsight, it is not surprising that the operators made these errors. The environment had overwhelmed them with information. The visible alarms were so numerous and were activated so quickly that it was impossible for the operators to understand their significance. The additional audible alarms interfered with information processing and, in all probability, increased the operators' arousal above and beyond a level at which optimal performance could be maintained. Some two and a half hours after the initial incident an additional operator, from another shift, came to the stricken control room and diagnosed the system failure within about five minutes. It is possible to speculate that the new operator, with a reduced level of arousal, was able to attend to a wider variety of cues relevant to accurate diagnosis and was, therefore, not biased in his judgement by a preconceived hypothesis.

In the remainder of the chapter we consider the consequences, in psychological terms, of being required to deal with an emergency like that at TMI. Then we consider three ways in which the stress of trying to control a hazardous situation may be reduced.

The impact of the immediate environment on the operator

Once a failure had been detected at TMI, a plethora of alarms and annunciators were activated on the instrument console. Ironically, the techniques that are used in most of today's automated environments to alert operators that something is amiss may serve to hinder efficient processing of information. As discussed in an earlier section, experimental work has shown that exposure to even moderate levels of noise can interfere with both the selection and processing of information from the environment. In order to overcome these effects the operator must divert some processing capacity to deal with the intrusive effects of noise (Kahneman, 1973). The narrowing of the focus of attention may be considered to be one way in which this might be done. Such a strategy may, however, be particularly dangerous under some circumstances since it is possible, as occurred at TMI, that important relevant information may be overlooked or ignored. The increased effort required to overcome the effects of noise may act to inhibit information processing in two possible ways. First the operators may, for strategic reasons, filter out task-relevant information or secondly, they may be unable to deal with extra information because of reduced capacity.

Although the onset of many alarms almost certainly degrades information-processing efficiency the noise can, in most control rooms, be turned off. Even so, arousal will still be high and performance impaired because the operator is under time pressure to diagnose the failure. In addition, as discussed earlier, subsequent performance is certainly impaired by the after-effects of exposure to stressors such as noise.

There are at least three ways in which the debilitating effects of exposure to stress on complex mental skills might be moderated: (i) changing the method of information display; (ii) developing appropriate methods of training personnel; (iii) selecting personnel who have the best chance of performing effectively under stress. Each of these options is discussed in more detail below.

Minimizing the stressors

Information display

One of the defining features of skilled performance is that a number of behaviours are executed in a manner that is smooth and seemingly effortless. It is also a characteristic of skilled performance that little attentional control is used, compared with the effort required by the novice to achieve the same end. This economy of effort is achieved by employing open, rather than closed, loop control of performance, Open loop control may be employed when the decisions are routine for the operators. This situation occurs when the operator is sufficiently familiar with the system to predict events and recognize patterns of symptoms. The performance of any open loop skill, mental or physical, is disrupted, however, when the unexpected occurs. Coping with the unexpected event demands an increased level of attentional control which impairs the efficiency of the information-processing system in dealing with large amounts of information. The mental overload experienced by operators when literally hundreds of alarms are activated on the console of a control room inevitably taxes the diagnosticians' processing resources.

To date, the design philosophy of many consoles is one of an alarm for each sensor. A functional unit of a power production plant will more than likely have several alarms and displays associated with it. In many instances much of the information they present will be redundant. A number of suggestions have been made as to how this burden on the information-processing system, especially working memory (Baddeley and Hitch, 1974) may be reduced. Unfortunately many suggestions remain to be evaluated, or at least the results of the evaluations remain to be published in accessible journals.

A criterion of good display design is that the amount of information it presents does not prevent the operator from attending to the conceptual component of the task to solve the system's problem. Displays that meet this criterion should be especially effective when operators are required to deal with unexpected system failures. Problems of this sort are particularly demanding of the operator's processing resources since it is unlikely that operators will be able to use pre-rehearsed problem-solving routines. Often, the application of abstract logic is required for unexpected system failures.

Presenting information in the manner most easily handled by the human information-processing system will help to maintain good performance. The following suggestions would reduce the load imposed on working memory by poor display designs:

(1) Sequencing and prioritizing of information prevented to the operator (Hopkins et al., 1982).
(2) Integrating correlated information from several sources into one display (Wickens, 1984). In this way the total number of alarms would be reduced without necessarily decreasing the amount of information conveyed to the operator should a failure occur.
(3) Relieving the operator of secondary tasks such as memorizing tests of component status, or memory for functional or geographical information (Morrison and Duncan, 1988).

With regard to the last suggestion, the development of computer systems has meant that innovative displays can now be designed. Included among problems of display design is how large amounts of information, too much to be displayed in a single screen, should be represented. Two obvious alternatives that might be considered are hierarchical and scrolling displays. With hierarchical displays the system might be represented at several different levels, each level containing an abstracted or exploded display of the levels above and below the representation that is currently displayed on the computer screen. Scrolling displays, on the other hand, operate by allowing the operator to move across (or up and down) a representation of the system held in the computer's memory. A good analogy of this type of display would be that of a moveable slide underneath the biologist's microscope. The advantage of the scrolling method is that with each successive move a certain amount of continuity is maintained from the preceding frame.

A small number of studies (e.g. Brooke and Duncan, 1983; Morrison and Duncan, 1988) have shown that hierarchical displays are superior to scrolling displays. Interestingly, these studies showed that it is subjects with lower initial fault-finding ability who benefit most from the hierarchical displays. One explanation for the superiority of the hierarchical displays is that they require less information to be held in working memory because an abstraction is displayed on an overview page to provide a summary of the system structure in the lower levels. When using scrolling displays, unless operators have an accurate mental model of the system structure they must develop one while searching for the failure. Thus with scrolling displays, the diagnostician has two tasks to perform: building a mental model and identifying the failed component. By using hierarchical displays some resource limitations are overcome since the user does not have to attempt to maintain a detailed model of the system while evaluating new information about the problem at hand.

It follows from the above interpretation that the difference between subjects of high and low ability is probably in the pool of processing resources available for information processing. It is interesting to note that, in both of the studies described above (Brooke and Duncan,1983; Morrison and Duncan, 1988), subjects of higher initial ability performed well irrespective of display type. This finding has interesting practical consequences in that if the information format is fixed then the only remaining options for improving performance are through training or selection methods.

More radical suggestions for display design have been made by Rasmussen and his co-workers from the Riso Laboratories in Denmark (Rasmussen, 1986). They suggest that operators at different stages in problem-solving (e.g. symptom interpretation or when identifying the potentially faulty set of failed components) and when dealing with different classes of problems (e.g. familiar or novel), require different types of information. The Riso group suggest that three types of information might be provided that correspond to three forms of problem-solving activity. The three forms of problem-solving behaviour are: skill-based (primarily signal detection), rule-based (primarily responding to patterns of signals that have been observed previously) and knowledge-based (primarily involving complex mental skills). The corresponding forms of display designs are: signals (for skilled performance), signs (for rule activities) and symbols (for conceptual thought). As yet there are no published evaluations of these ideas although the notion of display designs that are flexibly tied to the operator's mode of problem-solving is currently attracting a good deal of favourable attention (e.g. Reason, 1987).

The effects of practice and training

Highly automated systems are very reliable. As a consequence operators rarely have the opportunity to practise the skills that are required when failures occur. Some system failures can be those which operators expect, or are familiar with, while others are those which they could not predict and are therefore unexpected. The incident at TMI was of the latter type. Unexpected failures are the most difficult to cope with since the operator is often required to use abstract knowledge, and not a previously learned procedure or algorithm, that can be applied to the problem. One major difficulty in enabling operators to deal with novel failures is that of knowing what information or skills should be taught and how assessment of competence should be undertaken. Additionally, it is also important to investigate the levels of skill retention that can be expected over time. The benefit of training is that more skilled operators use fewer resources and therefore have greater capacity for coping with difficult aspects of diagnosis tasks.

Norman and Bobrow (1975) argue that level of practice affects the efficiency with which processing resources are allocated. M. W. Eysenck (1982) summarizes the implication of their work in the following way:

> The learning that results from practice means that there is enhanced perform-
> ance for a given resource allocation and also that a given level of performance
> requires fewer resources. (p. 33)

When the task comprises several components, practice in one aspect releases resources to deal with other parts of the task. This suggestion will not be a new one to those who have been involved in training physical skills. One form of training that capitalizes on this effect of practice is known as part-task training (see Stammers and Patrick, 1975, for a more detailed description). A problem in training operators to cope in these highly automated environments is, therefore, to know what should be practised and how that practice should be provided. As yet there are few empirical studies that have tackled the problem directly. Conventional wisdom is that training in theory, or simply giving operators practice in diagnosis, is unlikely to encourage the right sort of skills (Wallis, Duncan and Knight, 1967).

One technique, that has proved to be useful in the process industries, has been to train heuristics, or rules of thumb, to diagnostic personnel. Marshall, Scanlon, Shepherd and Duncan (1981) report that accuracy of novel diagnosis was raised from 33 per cent to around 90 per cent after operators had been trained to use a set of heuristics. Exactly why training of this sort should be effective is not entirely clear. One possibility is that the rules provide a top-down method of structuring the vast array of bottom-up information with which the operator is confronted when a failure occurs. This approach may prevent the operators from making a premature diagnosis. It is important that operators make diagnoses based on sufficient information, for if they do not it is unlikely that they will find it easy to abandon their initial, incorrect, diagnosis and begin searching afresh for another one. This is precisely what occurred at TMI. The reason for this phenomenon is that operators, and other problem-solvers in general, have a natural bias towards confirming their decisions and avoiding information or tests whose outcome might cause them to reconsider. The tendency to behave in this manner is known as the 'confirmation bias' and has been well documented elsewhere (Einhorn and Hogarth, 1981). This effect may be exaggerated under stressful conditions through narrowing of attention as described above.

There is, however, another possible explanation as to why training in heuristics is of benefit to problem-solving. By requiring operators to run through the heuristic rules when a fault occurs, they will feel that they are making progress towards attaining a solution. This will delay the onset of high levels of anxiety. In turn the scope of attention is narrowed and cognitive tunnel vision ensues (Sheridan, 1981).

The question of whether all personnel currently in employment can learn to develop effective strategies for diagnosis is a question that we have not addressed and to which we now turn.

Individual differences and performance

The major activities of human operators in automated systems are those of system monitor and diagnostician. In both of these tasks, large individual differences in performance have been noted. Landeweerd (1979), for example, reports that operators with good visual-spatial images of a chemical distillation process were better at detection and diagnosis of system failures than those with good verbal-causal models of the system. The latter group were, however, better system monitors. The diversity of fault diagnosis abilities and strategies demonstrated in operators' diagnoses is especially noteworthy (Rasmussen and Jensen, 1974). What the difference is between individuals of high and low ability is not entirely clear. One obvious suggestion, from the discussion above, is that people differ in the amount of spare processing capacity that they possess.

Studies that have attempted to demonstrate a relationship between fault-finding ability and measures of intelligence have not been consistently successful. Some studies have found positive relationships (e.g. Dale, 1958) whereas others (e.g. Henneman and Rouse, 1984) have failed to do so. The inconsistencies in these results are probably due to the range of ability levels sampled and differences in statistical power as a function of sample size.

Recently, measures of cognitive style have been found consistently to correlate with fault-diagnosis performance (e.g. Ensor and Morrison, 1986; Henneman and Rouse, 1984). Individuals with different cognitive styles are said to differ in the route taken to attain the solution to a problem rather than in levels of correctness. Morrison (1985) has provided some data which suggest that the relationship between focusing and scanning cognitive styles and fault-diagnosis performance is unaffected by either training or practice. These data are in agreement with the suggestion of Bruner, Goodnow and Austin (1956) that capability determines the strategy that is adopted during problem-solving. In Morrison's study, subjects who might be thought of as possessing more processing resources, by virtue of their preferred cognitive style, were capable of developing the most sophisticated and elaborated strategies for diagnosis performance. Bruner, Goodnow and Austin (1956) have also suggested that problem difficulty will also influence the technique employed by problem-solvers. Only subjects with a large processing capability would be expected to use strategies that impose large amounts of cognitive strain when the level of problem difficulty increases. The implication of this suggestion is that for difficult problems even the most capable subjects should probably resort to adopting strategies for which there is an adequate supply of processing resources. This suggestion has, however, to be investigated empirically in diagnosis performance.

Additionally it is important to remember that motivation, anxiety and arousal levels will also influence the type of strategies and the way that they are used by the subjects. It might, for example, be expected that when a subject attempts to use a strategy for which there are insufficient resources, he or she will resort to using techniques that are less resource-demanding. A suggestion such as this assumes that subjects are aware of a workable alternative strategy; if not we would expect their performance to contain a number of errors since they would be unable to employ a workable strategy. Perhaps only the most able or optimally aroused subjects can be expected to perform in this way.

In stressful environments it is probably safe to assume that all operators will be highly motivated. However, under stressful conditions arousal levels are likely to be affected by factors such as trait anxiety, neuroticism and introversion-extraversion as reviewed above. Introverts or those high in trait anxiety, for example, are more likely than extraverts and those low in trait anxiety to become rapidly over-aroused. The resource-consuming effects of over-arousal will, in all probability, make it harder to deal with more difficult problems (e.g. novel system-failures). The combined effects, on diagnosis performance, of intellectual capability and sensitivity to the effects of stress await future empirical investigation.

CONCLUSIONS

This chapter has, rather selectively, covered a range of research findings of the way stress affects skilled performance. It was deliberately written to take the reader from fairly detailed laboratory experiments and models of stress, to the process of trying to apply some of those findings in applied areas. On the latter point two areas of contemporary interest were considered. The first of these looked at anxiety and the effects of common drugs on skill. The second examined the occupational environment where human factors specialists try to apply the results of laboratory work. In particular we focused on how exposure to stress might affect the way in which operators control complex, highly automated systems.

It is clear that we have gained a great deal of insight from laboratory tasks and models into the mechanisms and processes affected by exposure to stress in various forms. There is, however, a long way to go in the quantification and explanation of the way stress affects real-life skill. This information is needed in order to influence the ways in which selection, training and legislation for occupational health and safety procedures are implemented. The current lack of knowledge concerning the influence of stressors on skilled performance was most clearly revealed in the last section of the chapter. The influence of stress on complex decision-making remains largely unknown. Nevertheless, laboratory studies do provide a framework for understanding variations in human problem-solving performance under stress. The scale of the problem, its social and material importance and the tragedy following failure, are enormous. Unfortunately, there is often a great reluctance to seek and apply knowledge of psychological human factors. One of the reasons for this may be that the utility of sound human factors advice, in monetary terms, is not always apparent to system designers. Future psychologists must correct this, perhaps by following the lead of Hunter and Schmidt (1982). Another reason for the reluctance may be that we have, as yet, failed to come up with any but the most general statements concerning human behaviour. This latter point is apparent in the summary of this chapter which follows.

From the laboratory setting it is discouraging to find such a cocktail of tasks and procedures and mixture of results. Many of the conclusions that might have been drawn are overwhelmed because of inter-experimental differences. In the early studies that examined the effects of prolonged exposure to stress at high noise levels, and in contemporary heat- and sleep-loss experiments, substantial effects of stress occur. More contemporary studies, using lower levels of stress, show that the human information-processing system is very robust. It is responsive to motivational factors and can employ a variety of strategies to compensate for the effects of stress on the input and output processes. This is very apparent in the recent studies of noise and memory. In the Gopher and Sanders' model, compensation is carried out by an evaluation mechanism which monitors and redistributes resources to the separate input and output processors for optimal performance.

The strategic reallocation of resources seems to be very successful when humans are exposed to environments that are found to be only mildly stressful. The subjects' strategies may alter but the effects of stress are minimized. Of course this interpretation begs the question of how one measures the environment in terms of its potential to generate stress. When effects of stress are reported, impairment occurs because of either a failure of the evaluation system or an inadequate replenishment of energy resources.

In work settings, where prolonged exposure to stressors is the norm, some impairment will be inevitable. Those aspects of performance that will be affected detrimentally include: a failure to develop a clear stimulus code, poor preparation or execution of responses and an after-effect during the recovery of the energy resource and evaluation systems. The data from studies that have considered the effects of anxiety and drugs on performance have shown many similar results to those using environmental stressors. Resource models of information processing, developed from laboratory research, have helped us to understand the influence of certain drugs and their effect on cognitive skill.

In the last section we have identified many of the same factors studied in the laboratory that influence the execution of skill in a real-world context. Each of the factors reviewed earlier exerts a substantial effect on mental skills. The task of predicting success in performance or the level of human reliability is difficult when one considers that each of the factors might conceivably interact with each other.

At present those seeking advice from engineering psychologists are likely to become disillusioned and frustrated with the lack of precision and specificity about our knowledge of the level of performance one can expect from human operators under stress. If the single most crucial factor in determining success on the job is the size of the pool of resources that each operator possesses, then the question of how much processing capacity is enough, must be asked. At present, we have no answer to that. Success in the future will depend on our ability to measure unequivocally how large the resource pool is and by how much it will vary. Recent research (e.g. Carswell and Wickens, 1985) has asked whether there are many resource pools for different functions, as opposed to a single all-purpose pool. If there is more than one resource pool, which tasks mutually compete for resources, and which do not will have to be identified. Answers to these questions will have some impact on how the man–machine interface is developed.

If ability is indeed primarily determined by the pool of resources each individual has at their disposal, how much of the variability in performance can be attributed to the other factors that we have discussed? Furthermore, before investigating the interactions between the other factors, which will co-vary uniquely in different contexts, we should determine the size of their main effects with a view to rank-ordering their order of importance for system design purposes.

REFERENCES

Anderson, K. J. & Revelle, W. (1983). The interactive effects of caffeine, impulsivity and task demands on a visual search task, *Personality and Individual Differences*, **4**, 127–134.
Baddeley, A. D., Cuccaro, W. J., Egstrom, G. H., Weltman, G. & Willis, M. A. (1975). Cognitive efficiency of divers working in cold water, *Human Factors*, **17**, 446–454.
Baddeley, A. D. & Hitch, G. (1974). Working memory, in G. H. Bower (ed.), *The Psychology of Learning and Motivation*, vol. 8. London: Academic Press.
Baum-Baicker, C. (1985). The psychological benefits of moderate alcohol comsumption: a review of the literature, *Drug and Alcohol Dependence*, **15**, 305–322.
Beirness, D. J. & Vogel-Sprott, M. D. (1982). Does prior skill reduce alcohol-induced impairment? *Journal of Studies on Alcohol*, **43**, 1149–1156.
Broadbent, D. E. (1971). *Decision and Stress*. London: Academic Press.
Broadbent, D. E. & Gregory, M. (1963). Vigilance considered as a statistical decision, *British Journal of Psychology*, **54**, 309–323.
Broadbent, D. E. & Little, E. A. J. (1960). Effects of noise reduction in a work situation, *Occupational Psychology*, **34**, 133–140.
Brooke, J. B. & Duncan, K. D. (1983). A comparison of hierarchically paged and scrolling displays for fault-finding, *Ergonomics*, **26**, 465–477.

Bruner, J., Goodnow, J. & Austin, G. A., (1956). *A Study of Thinking*. New York: Wiley.

Carswell, C. M. & Wickens, C. D. (1985). Lateral task segregation, and the task-hemispheric integrity effect, *Human Factors*, **27**, 695–700.

Cohen, A. (1973). Industrial noise and medical absence and accident record data on exposed workers, in W. Dixon-Ward (ed.), *Proceedings of the International Congress on Noise as a Public Health Problem*. Washington DC: US Environmental Protection Agency.

Cohen, S. (1980). After-effects of stress on human performance and social behaviour: A review of research and theory, *Psychological Bulletin*, **88**, 82–108.

Coleshaw, S. R. K., Van Someren, R. N. M., Wolf, A. H., Davis, H. M. & Kreatinge, W. R. (1983). Impaired memory registration and speed of reasoning caused by low body temperature, *Journal of Applied Physiology*, **55**, 27–31.

Collins, W. E. & Chiles, W. D. (1980). Laboratory performance during acute alcohol intoxication and hangover, *Human Factors*, **22**, 445–462.

Cox, T. (1978). *Stress*. London: Macmillan.

Curley, M. D. & Hawkins, R. N. (1983). Cognitive performance during a heat acclimatization regimen, *Aviation, Space and Environmental Medicine*, **54**, 709–713.

Dale, H. C. A. (1958). Fault-finding in electronic equipment, *Ergonomics*, **1**, 356–385.

Dornic, S. (1975). Some studies on the retention of order information, in P. M. A. Rabbit & S. Dornic (eds), *Attention and Performance*. London: Academic Press.

Easterbrook, J. A. (1959). The effect of emotion on cue utilisation and the organisation of behaviour, *Psychological Review*, **66**, 183–210.

Edmundson, E. D. & Nelson, D. L. (1976). Anxiety, imagery, and sensory interference, *Bulletin of the Psychonomic Society*, **8**, 319–322.

Einhorn H. J. & Hogarth, R. M. (1981). Behavioural decision theory, *Annual Review of Psychology*, **32**, 53–88.

Empson, J. A. C. & Clarke, P. R. F. (1970). Rapid eye movements and remembering, *Nature*, **227**, 287–288.

Ensor, A. A. & Morrison, D. L. (1986). Individual differences in fault diagnosis behaviour, in D. L. Morrison, L. Hartley & D. Kemp (eds), *Trends in the Ergonomics of Working Life: Proceedings of the 23rd Annual Conference of the Ergonomics Society of Australia and New Zealand*. Melbourne: Ergonomic Society of Australia and New Zealand.

Eysenck, M. W. (1975). Effects of noise, activation level and response dominance on retrieval from semantic memory, *Journal of Experimental Psychology*, **1**, 143–148.

Eysenck, M. W. (1982). *Attention and Arousal: Cognition and Performance*. Berlin: Springer.

Eysenck, M. W. (1983). Anxiety and individual differences, in R. Hockey (ed.), *Stress and Fatigue in Human Performance*. Chichester: Wiley.

Eysenck, M. W. (1984). *A Handbook of Cognitive Psychology*. London: Erlbaum.

Eysenck, M. W. & Eysenck, M. C. (1980). Effects of processing depth, distinctiveness, and word frequency on retention, *British Journal of Psychology*, **71**, 263–274.

Fisher, S. (1972). A distraction effect of noise bursts, *Perception*, **1**, 233–236.

Geen, R. G. (1985). Test anxiety and visual vigilance. *Journal of Personality and Social Psychology*, **49**, 963–970.

Gilliland, K. (1980). The interactive effect of introversion-extroversion with caffeine induced arousal on verbal performance, *Journal of Research in Personality*, **14**, 482–492.

Glass, D. C. & Singer, J. (1972). *Urban Stress*. New York: Academic Press.

Gopher, D. & Sanders, A. F. (1984). S-Oh-R: Oh Stages! Oh Resources, in D. Prinz & A. F. Sanders (eds), *Cognition and Motor Processes*. Berlin: Springer.

Hammerton, M. & Tichner, A. H. (1968). An investigation into the effects of stress upon skilled performance, *Ergonomics*, 12, 851–855.

Hancock, P. A. (1982). Task categorization and the limits of human performance in extreme heat, *Aviation, Space and Environmental Medecine*, 53, 778–784.

Hancock, P. A. (1983). The effect of an induced selective increase in head temperature upon performance of a simple mental task, *Human Factors*, 25, 441–448.

Hancock, P. A. & Dirkin, G. R. (1982). Central and peripheral visual choice reaction time under conditions of induced cortical hyperthemia, *Perceptual and Motor Skills*, 54, 395–402.

Hartley, L. R. (1973a). Cigarette smoking and stimulus selection, *British Journal of Psychology*, 64, 593–599.

Hartley, L. R. (1973b). Effect of prior noise or prior performance on serial reaction, *Journal of Experimental Psychology*, 101, 255–261.

Hartley, L. R. (1974). Performance during continuous and intermittent noise and wearing ear protection, *Journal of Experimental Psychology*, 102, 512–517.

Hartley, L. R. (1980). Noise, attentional selectivity and the need for experimental power, *British Journal of Psychology*, 72, 101–107.

Hartley, L. R. & Adams, R. (1976). Effect of noise on the Stroop test, *Journal of Experimental Psychology*, 102, 62–67.

Hartley, L. R., Boultwood, B. & Dunne, M. (1987). Noise and verbal or spatial solutions to Rubic's Cube, *Ergonomics*, 30, 503–511.

Hartley, L. R. & Carpenter, A. (1974). Comparison of performance with headphone and free field noise, *Journal of Experimental Psychology*, 103, 377–380.

Hartley, L. R., Dunne, M., Schwartz, S. & Brown, J. (1986). Effect of noise on cognitive strategies in sentence verification task, *Ergonomics*, 29, 607 617.

Hartley, L. & Shirley, E. (1977). Sleep, noise and decisions, *Ergonomics*, 20, 481–489.

Henneman, R. L. & Rouse, W. B., (1984). Measures of human performance in fault diagnosis tasks, *IEEE Trans. on Systems Man and Cybernetics*, vol. SMC 14, 99–112.

Hill, P. & Wynder, E. L. (1974). Smoking and cardiovascular disease—effect of nicotine on the serum epinephrine and corticoids, *American Heart Journal*, 87, 491–496.

Hockey, G. R. J. (1970). Signal probability and spatial location as possible bases for increased selectivity in noise, *Quarterly Journal of Experimental Psychology*, 22, 37–42.

Hockey, G. R. J. (1973). Changes in information selection patterns in multisource monitoring as a function of induced arousal shifts, *Journal of Experimental Psychology*, 101, 35–42.

Hockey, G. R. J. & Hamilton, P. (1970). Arousal and information selection in short term memory, *Nature*, 226, 866–867.

Hopkins, C. D., Snyder, H., Price, H. E., Hornick, R., Mackie, R., Smillie, R. & Sugarman, R. C. (1982). *Critical human factor issues in nuclear power regualtion and a recommended comprehensive human factors long range plan (NUREG)* CR-28 33, vols 1–3. Washington, DC: US Nuclear Regulatory Committee.

Horne, J. A., Anderson, N. R. & Wilkinson, R. T. (1983). Effects of sleep deprivation on signal detection measures of vigilance: implications for sleep function, *Sleep*, 6, 347–358.

Horne, J. A. & Pettitt, A. N. (1985). High incentive effects on vigilance performance during 72 hours of total sleep deprivation, *Acta Psychologica*, **58**, 123–139.

Humphreys, M. S. & Revelle, W. (1984). Personality, motivation and performance: a theory of the relationship between individual differences and information processing, *Psychological Review*, **91**, 153–184.

Hunter, J. E. & Schmidt, F. L. (1982). Fitting people to jobs, in E. A. Fleishman (ed.), *Human Capability Assessed*. Hillsdale NJ: Erlbaum.

Jenkins, D. (1980). Can we ever have a fruitful cognitive psychology? in J. H. Flowers (ed.), *Nebraska Symposium on Motivation: Cognitive Processes*. Nebraska: University of Nebraska Press.

Jenkins, J. G. & Dallenbach, K. M. (1924). Oblivescence during sleep and waking, *American Journal of Psychology*, **35**, 605–612.

Jones, D. M. J. (1983). Noise, in G. R. J. Hockey (ed.), *Stress and Fatigue in Human Performance*. Chichester: Wiley.

Jung, R. T., Shetty, P. S., James, W. P. T., Barrand, M. A. & Callingham, B. A. (1981). Caffeine—its effects on catecholamines and metabolism in lean and obese humans, *Clinical Science*, **60**, 527–535.

Kahneman, D. (1973). *Attention and Effort*. Englewood Cliffs NJ: Prentice-Hall.

Kahneman, D. & Tversky, A. (eds) (1982). *Judgement under Uncertainty: Heuristics and Biases*. Cambridge: Cambridge University Press.

Kay, H. (1949). Report on arctic trials on board H. M. S. Vengeance, February–March 1949. *Royal Naval Personnel Research Committee*, Report Number 534. London: Medical Research Council.

Keister, M. & McLaughlin, R. (1972). Vigilance performance related to extraversion-introversion and caffeine, *Journal of Experimental Research in Personality*, **6**, 5–11.

Landeweerd, J. A. (1979). Internal representation of a process fault diagnosis and fault correction, *Ergonomics*, **27**, 1342–1351.

Leon, M. R. & Revelle, W. (1985). Effects of anxiety on analogical reasoning: A test of three theoretical models, *Journal of Personality and Social Psychology*, **49**, 1302–1315.

Lockhart, J. M. (1966). Effects of body and hand cooling on complex manual performance, *Journal of Applied Psychology*, **50**, 57–59.

Mackworth, N. H. (1961). Researches on the measurement of human performance, in H. W. Sinaiko (ed.), *Selected Papers on Human Factors in the Design and Use of Control Systems*. New York: Dover.

MacLeod, C. M., Hunt, E. B. & Mathews, N. N. (1978). Individual differences in the verification of sentence-picture relationships, *Journal of Verbal Learning and Verbal Behavior*, **17**, 439–507.

Marshall, E. C., Scanlon, K. E., Shepherd, A. & Duncan K. D. (1981). Panel diagnosis training for major hazard continuous process installations, *Chemical Engineer*, **36**, 345–356.

Minsky, M. (1975). Framework for representing knowledge, in P. Winston (ed.), *The Psychology of Computer Vision*. New York: McGraw Hill.

Morrison, D. L. (1985). The effect of cognitive style and training on fault diagnosis performance, *Programmed Learning and Educational Technology*, **72**, 132–139.

Morrison, D. L. & Duncan K. D. (1988). The effect of scrolling, hierarchically paged displays and ability on fault diagnosis performance, *Ergonomics*, **31**, 889–904.

Moskowitz, H. (1984). Attention tasks as skills performance measures of drug effects, *British Journal of Clinical Pharmacology*, **18**, 515–615.

Navon, D. (1977). Forest before trees: The precedence of global features in visual perception, *Cognitive Psychology*, **9**, 353–383.

Norman, D. A. & Bobrow, D. G. (1975). On data limited and resource limited processes, *Cognitive Psychology*, **7**, 44–64.

Nunneley, S. A., Reader, D. C. & Maldonado, R. J. (1982). Head temperature effects on physiology, comfort, and performance during hyperthermia, *Aviation, Space and Environmental Medicine*, **53**, 623–628.

Perrow, C., (1984). *Normal Accidents: Living with High Risk Technologies*. New York: Basic Books.

Poulton, E. C., Hitchings, N. B. & Brooke, R. B. (1965). Effect of cold and rain on the vigilance of lookouts, *Ergonomics*, **8**, 163–168.

Poulton, E. C., Hunt, G. M., Carpenter, A. & Edwards, R. S. (1978). The performance of junior hospital doctors following reduced sleep and long hours of work, *Ergonomics*, **21**, 279–295.

Pribram, K. H. & McGuinness, D. (1975). Arousal, activation and effort in the control of attention, *Psychological Review*, **82**, 116–149.

Rasmussen, J., (1986). *Information Processing and Human-machine Interaction: an Approach to Cognitive Engineering*. Amsterdam: North Holland.

Rasmussen, J. & Jenson, A., (1974). Mental procedures in real life tasks: a case study of electronic troubleshooting, *Ergonomics*, **17**, 293–307.

Peason, J., (1984). Lapses of attention, in R. Parasuraman & D. Davies (eds), *Varieties of Attention*. New York: Academic Press.

Reason, J. (1987). Generic error-modelling system (GEMS): a cognitive framework for locating common human error forms, in J. Reason, K. Duncan & J. Leplat (eds), *New Technology and Human Error*. New York: Wiley.

Robertson, D., Frolich, J. C., Carr, R. K., Watson, J. T., Hollifield, J. W., Shand, D. G. & Oats, J. A. (1978). Effects of caffeine on plasma renin activity, catecholamines and blood pressure, *New England Journal of Medicine*, **298**, 181–186.

Rubinstein, T. & Mason, A. F. (1979, November). The accident that shouldn't have happened: an analysis of three mile island, *IEEE Spectrum*, 33–57.

Ryman, D. H., Naitoh, P. & Englund, C. E. (1985). Decrements in logical reasoning performance under conditions of sleep loss and physical exercise: the factor of sentence complexity, *Perceptual and Motor Skills*, **61**, 1179–1188.

Sanders, A. F. (1983). Towards a model of stress and performance, *Acta Psychologica*, **53**, 61–97.

Sanders, A. F. & Reitsma W. D. (1982a). Lack of sleep and covert orienting of attention, *Acta Psychologica*, **52**, 137–145.

Sanders, A. F. & Reitsma W. D. (1982b). The effect of sleep loss on processing information in the functional visual field, *Acta Psychologica*, **51**, 149–162.

Sanders, A. F., Wijnen, J. L. C. & van Arkel, A. E. (1982). An additive factor analysis of the effects of sleep loss on reaction processes, *Acta Psychologica*, **51**, 41–59.

Sawyer, D. A., Julia, H. L. & Turin, A. C. (1982). Caffeine and human behavior: Arousal, anxiety, and performance effects, *Journal of Behavioral Medicine*, **5**, 415–439.

Schank, R. C. & Abelson, R. P. (1977). *Scripts, Plans, Goals and Understanding*. Hillsdale, NJ: Erlbaum.

Scott, D. W. (1983). Anxiety, critical thinking and information processing during and after breast biopsy, *Nursing Research*, **32**, 24–28.

Scott, J. C. & Nelson, D. L. (1979). Anxiety and encoding strategy, *Bulletin of the Psychonomic Society*, **13**, 297–299.

Sheridan, T. (1981). Understanding human error and aiding diagnostic behaviour in nuclear power plants, in J. Rasmussen & W. B. Rouse (eds), *Human Detection and Diagnosis of System Failures*. New York: Plenum Press.

Smith, A. P. (1982). The effects of noise and task priority on recall of order and location, *Acta Psychologica*, **51**, 245–255.

Smith, A. P. (1985a). Noise, biassed probability and serial reaction, *British Journal of Psychology*, **76**, 89–95.

Smith, A. P. (1985b). The effects of noise on the processing of global shape and local detail, *Psychological Research*, **47**, 103–108.

Smith, A. P. & Broadbent, D. E. (1985). The effect of noise on the naming of colours and reading of colour names, *Acta Psychologica*, **58**, 275–285.

Smith, A. & Stansfield, S. (1986). Aircraft noise, noise sensitivity and everyday errors, *Environment and Behaviour*, **18**, 214–226.

Spielberger, C. D., Gonzalez, H. P., Taylor, C. J., Algaze, B. & Anton, W. D. (1978). Examination stress and test anxiety, in C. D. Spielberger & I. G. Sarason (eds), *Stress and Anxiety*, vol. 5. Hillsdale, NJ: Erlbaum.

Stammers, R. & Patrick, J., (1975). *The Psychology of Training*. London: Methuen.

Teichner, W. H., Arees, E. & Reilly, R. (1963). Noise and human performance, a psychophysiological approach, *Ergonomics*, **6**, 83–97.

Tilley, A. J & Warren, P. (1984). Retrieval from semantic memory during a night without sleep, *Quarterly Journal of Experimental Psychology*, **36**, 281–289.

Tilley, A. J. & Wilkinson, R. T. (1984). The effects of a restricted sleep regime on the composition of sleep and performance, *Psychophysiology*, **21**, 406–412.

Walliss, D., Duncan, K. D. & Knight, M. A. (1967). A review of electronic training research in the U.S. Armed Forces. Report No. 5/67.

Webb, W. B. & Levy, C. M. (1984). Effects of spaced and repeated total sleep deprivation, *Ergonomics*, **27**, 45–58.

Wesnes, K. & Warburton, D. M. (1983). Stress and drugs, in R. Hockey (ed.), *Stress and Fatigue in Human Performance*. Chichester: Wiley.

Wickens, C. D. (1984). *Engineering Psychology and Human Performance*. Ohio: Merrill Publishing Company.

Wilding, J., Mohindra, N. & Breen-Lewis, K. (1982). Noise effects in pre-recall with different orienting tasks, *British Journal of Psychology*, **73**, 479–486.

Wilkinson, R. T. (1969). Sleep deprivation: performance tests for partial and selective sleep deprivation, in *Progress in Clinical Psychology* New York: Grune & Stratton.

Wilkinson, R. T., Fox, R. H., Goldsmith, R., Hampton, I. F. G. & Lewis, H. E. (1964). Psychological and physiological responses to raised body temperature, *Journal of Applied Physiology*, **19**, 287–291.

Williams, R. M., Goldman, M. S. & Williams, D. L. (1981). Expectancy and pharmacological effects of alcohol on human cognitive and motor performance: The compensation for alcohol effect, *Journal of Abnormal Psychology*, **90**, 267–270

Woodhead, M. M. (1964). The effects of bursts of noise on an arithmetic task, *American Journal of Psychology*, **77**, 627–633.

Chapter 12

Diurnal variations in performance

Andrew Smith

INTRODUCTION

There have been several recent reviews of this topic (e.g. Colquhoun, 1981; Folkard, 1983; Folkard and Monk, 1985) and it is clear from these that there is evidence of diurnal variation in the efficiency of human performance. The first aim of this chapter is to present a brief historical account of time-of-day research up to about 1980. This will be followed by a profile of time-of-day effects in cognitive performance, with an emphasis on recent results and approaches which have not been covered by other reviews. The term 'cognitive' is used very loosely here and there is discussion of certain simple tasks which would not always be thought to involve cognitive skills. This has been done for three reasons. First, comparison of time-of-day effects in different types of task highlights the importance of considering the nature of the activity being carried out and the dangers of making general statements about performance at different times of day. Second, it is often difficult to separate cognitive processes from other types of function, and many cognitive tasks clearly also involve sensory processes and motor responses. The third reason is that even performance on simple tasks, such as choice reaction time, involves control processes. Indeed, in order to follow the instruction to 'respond as quickly and as accurately as possible' the subject must be able to adjust the speed of responding and detect errors (see Rabbitt, 1979).

Diurnal variation in human performance may reflect endogenous rhythms, and these have been detected in most physiological processes (Aschoff and Wever, 1981). Alternatively, time-of-day effects in performance may be produced by external factors which are associated with particular times, such

Acquisition and Performance of Cognitive Skills. Edited by A. M. Colley and J. R. Beech
© 1989 John Wiley & Sons Ltd

as the consumption of a meal. The third section of the chapter describes recent studies of the effects of meals on performance. These studies are important because they demonstrate the complex nature of time-of-day effects, and illustrate the role of both endogenous and exogenous factors.

Most laboratory studies of time-of-day effects have been confined to the 'normal' day (08.00 to 23.00). There have, of course, been applied studies of the effects of abnormal living routines produced by shiftwork or time-zone transitions. In between these two types of study are experimental studies of nightwork, which will be described in the fourth section of the chapter. Such studies are important because they again demonstrate that it is essential to consider the nature of the task and characteristics of the person performing it. Furthermore, recent studies of the combined effects of environmental stress and nightwork show that researchers are aware that it is a mistake to consider time-of-day effects in isolation, and that from a practical point of view one must study effects of irregular working hours together with other occupational health hazards.

The final part of the chapter will describe important new approaches, such as temporal isolation studies, which could provide further insight into diurnal variation in cognitive performance. It will also include a discussion of the implications and possible explanations of the effects described earlier.

Early research

Much of the early work on time-of-day effects was concerned with applied problems such as which time of day was best for the various subjects taught at school. Freeman and Hovland (1934) have reviewed these studies which, in fact, show little agreement about the effects of time of day on mental performance. Indeed, conclusions were often based on the average performance of many tasks, with the individual tasks often showing a pattern quite different from the average trend. Where the observations suggested better performance later in the day the researchers (e.g. Gates, 1916) argued that this reflected a progressive recovery from the effects of sleep, whereas when performance was worse later in the day this was attributed to increased fatigue (Laird, 1925).

The parallelism between temperature and performance

Kleitman (1963) reported research on time-of-day effects in simple tasks with little cognitive involvement. He suggested that there was strong evidence for a parallelism between time-of-day effects in performance and the circadian rhythm in body temperature (body temperature shows a consistent 24-hour periodicity with a peak around 21.00 and a trough at 04.00). An excellent example of this is shown in Figure 12.1, which gives the results from four

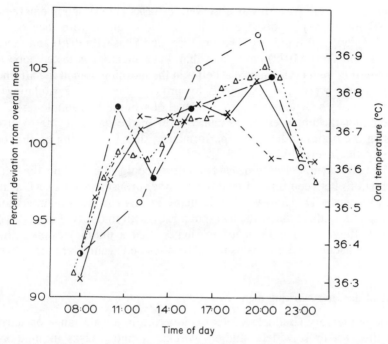

Figure 12.1. The trend over the day in serial visual search speed after Blake, 1967 (●–·–●); Klein *et al*, 1977 (×–––×); Fort and Mills, 1976 (×————×); and Hughes and Folkard, 1976 (○–––○). Also shown is the trend in oral temperature after Colquhoun *et al.*, 1968 (△–––△).

studies of time-of-day effects in speed of visual search. Kleitman even argued that there was a causal relationship between temperature and performance, although this was based solely on correlations between the two on selected tasks. Research in the 1960s continued to examine time-of-day effects in simple repetitive tasks and to investigate the parallelism between temperature and performance. A causal relationship between the two was rejected and a basal arousal rhythm (the inverse of sleepiness) was postulated as the mediating factor.

Arousal theory and time of day

The Yerkes–Dodson law (1908) postulated that there was an optimal level of arousal. This varied depending on the complexity of the task, with more complex tasks having lower optimal arousal. Arousal was assumed to increase over the waking day to reach a maximum in the evening, and simple tasks, which were thought to have a high optimal arousal level, showed the same trend. A different pattern was observed for tasks involving immediate memory. Blake (1967) reported a decline in digit-span performance over the working day, and Baddeley, Hatter, Scott and Snashall (1970) and Hockey, Davies and Gray (1972) confirmed that when memory is tested soon after presentation then performance is better in the morning than in the afternoon. Such results were also explained by arousal theory by postulating that memory tasks have a lower optimum level of arousal than simple tasks. This meant that the impaired performance later in the day was due to arousal passing the optimum level and performance, therefore, being on the 'down turn' of the inverted-U.

The arousal model of time-of-day effects could also explain the various interactions between time of testing and other arousing agents such as noise (see Blake, 1971). However, while many results can be accounted for by arousal theory this reflects the fact that it is difficult to falsify (Folkard, 1983). Indeed, there is other evidence to suggest that a uni-dimensional arousal theory is inadequate and this issue will be discussed again later in the chapter.

Time of day and working memory tasks

Working memory (Baddeley, 1986) is involved in a wide range of activities and the two most widely studied working memory tasks in time-of-day research have been mental arithmetic tasks and verbal reasoning tasks. Laird (1925) and Folkard (1975) found that performance on such tasks reached a maximum about midday. This is shown in Figure 12.2. However, other researchers have shown that performance on such tasks shows different trends depending on the ability or level of practice of the subject. For example, Rutenfranz and Helbruegge (1957) found that schoolchildrens' performance on mental arithmetic tasks peaked earlier in the day, whereas Blake found that sailors who were highly practised at the tasks showed a later peak.

These studies are important, therefore, because they confirm that the diurnal trend depends on the type of task. They also suggest that the trend will depend on the abilities of the subject, with low-ability subjects peaking earlier in the day.

Time of day and recall of prose

Laird (1925) and Folkard and Monk (1980) found that immediate recall of information presented in prose showed a general decline over the day. This is shown in Figure 12.3.

Folkard, Monk, Bradbury and Rosenthall (1977) examined schoolchildrens' immediate and delayed recall (one week after presentation) for a story

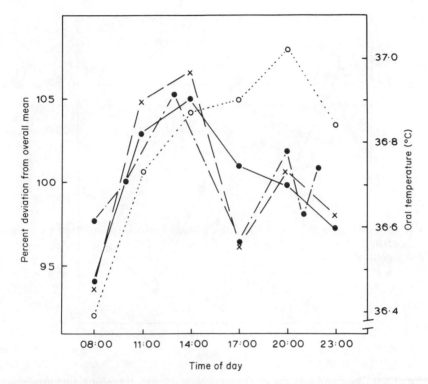

Figure 12.2. The trend over the day in working memory performance speed after Folkard, 1975 (×---× and ●————●), and Laird, 1925 (●–·–●); and in oral temperature after Folkard, 1975 (○····○).

presented at 9.00 or 15.00. The immediate recall results confirmed the above findings, with recall being better at 9.00 than 15.00. However, delayed recall was better when the story was presented at 15.00. This superior delayed recall following afternoon presentation was unaffected by the time at which the delayed memory test was given.

This brief review of time-of-day studies carried out before 1980 has shown that the speed of performing perceptual motor tasks is quicker later in the day, whereas immediate memory tasks show the opposite trend. Working memory tasks often peak in the middle of the day, and delayed recall is better when initial learning occurs in the afternoon rather than the morning. In other words, the diurnal trend clearly depends on the nature of the task being performed. The next section reviews more recent studies of time of day and performance, provides information on other types of task, and discusses the new approaches which have developed from the research described in the previous section.

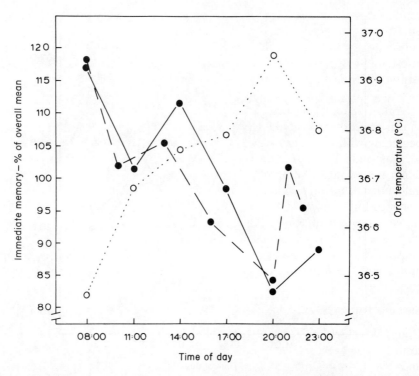

Figure 12.3. The trend over the day in immediate memory for information presented in prose after Folkard and Monk, 1980 (●————●), and Laird, 1925 (● – – ●); and in oral temperature after Folkard and Monk, 1980 (○ · · · · ○).

A PROFILE OF THE EFFECTS OF TIME OF DAY ON PERFORMANCE

The first aim of this section is to describe time-of-day effects in some tasks not examined by the earlier researchers.

Semantic memory tasks

Millar, Styles and Wastell (1980) used a task in which the subject was presented with a category name and a word and had to respond 'yes' if the word was an instance of the category. Some of the words used were 'good' instances of the categories whereas others were 'weak' instances. The tendency was for response latencies to be quicker later in the day, although the main effect of time of day failed to achieve significance. However, there was a significant interaction between time of day and dominance of instances, with subjects tested in the evening responding to low-dominance items more quickly than subjects tested in the morning, but there was little difference between the two times for high-dominance items. Tilley and Warren (1983) also found that retrieval efficiency was better later in the day, and again the largest difference between the morning and evening groups was found with low-dominance items.

Smith (1987a) used a category instance retrieval task where the subject was shown the category name and a letter and had to produce an instance beginning with that letter. The category–letter combinations were arranged so that some produced dominant instances, whereas others led to non-dominant instances. Smith found that performance was better later in the day but obtained no interaction between time of day and dominance. Further evidence for semantic processing being quicker later in the day comes from studies using semantic verification tasks (Smith, 1987a, in press). In this task the subject is shown a statement and has to decide on the basis of general knowledge whether it is true or false. This task was performed more quickly in the late afternoon than in the early morning.

Sustained attention

Craig, Wilkinson and Colquhoun (1981) examined the influence of time of testing on auditory vigilance. Results from five studies showed that both hits and false alarms exhibited a fairly consistent tendency to be lowest at the first test in the morning and then increased in parallel over the day. However, the time-of-day effect was small and significant in only a minority of the analyses. The effects which were present were attributable to shifts in the response criterion rather than to altered levels of signal detection. Other studies (e.g. Craig, 1979; Craig and Condon, 1985) suggest that later in the day detection performance is faster, more confident, but less accurate.

Recently, there has been considerable interest in memory-loaded detection tasks or 'cognitive vigilance' tasks as they are sometimes known (see Davies and Parasuraman, 1982). Gale, Bull, Penfold, Coles and Barraclough (1972) found no time-of-day effects on the Bakan vigilance task which, considering there is diurnal variation in memory tasks, is rather surprising. Davies, Parasuraman and Toh (1984) showed that performance on a memory-loaded vigilance task was worse in the afternoon than in morning, but Smith (1987b) reported no difference between 8.00 and 17.00 for performance on the Bakan vigilance task. This negative result can be explained in the following way. If working memory peaks in the late morning then 17.00 testing would be on the down-turn of the time-of-day function, which means that one would not necessarily expect it to be different from earlier times. The topic of sustained attention will be returned to in the sections on the effects of meals and of nightwork.

Selective attention

Time-of-day effects were for a long time thought to reflect changes in arousal. Easterbrook (1959) explained the inverted-U relationship between arousal and performance in terms of changes in selectivity. When arousal is low the person is unselective and task-irrelevant cues may also be processed, which results in imparied performance. As arousal increases so does selectivity, and there is an optimum level where task-relevant information is processed and task-irrelevant information rejected. However, as arousal gets higher selectivity continues to increase which means that some task-relevant cues are not attended to, and this produces impaired performance. On the basis of Easterbrook's theory one would expect selectivity to be greater later in the day.

Selectivity in memory and attention can be examined in several ways, and those discussed here were concerned with whether testing later in the day biases performance towards dominant, salient, high-priority or high-probability sources and away from non-dominant ones. One task used to study this has been the Stroop colour-word test. In one condition of this test the subject has to name the colour of the ink in which an irrelevant colour word is printed. Hartley and Shirley (1976) showed that interference increased over the day to peak at 20.00. On the basis of an arousal theory of time-of-day effects one would have expected a reduction in interference later in the day. Smith (in preparation, a) found no difference in the amount of interference at 9.00 and 18.00. He did, however, find changes in the control conditions of the Stroop task, with colours being named more rapidly in the morning and colour names read more quickly in the afternoon.

Another task which has been used to examine selective processing is a dual task where one component has a higher priority than the other (see Smith, 1982, Experiment 1 for specific features of the task). Smith (in preparation, a) had subjects recall the order of a list of words (the high-priority task), and then recall which of four possible locations the words had been presented in (the low-priority task). There was no evidence of any interaction between time of day and task priority. Another technique used to examine selectivity involves making one signal source more probable than the others. Smith (in preparation, a) examined time-of-day effects in performance of a biased probability choice reaction time task (see Smith, 1985a, for specific details of the task), and found that time of day did not interact with signal probability.

The studies of Millar, Styles and Wastell (1980) and Tilley and Warren (1983), which showed interactions between time of day and retrieval of dominant/non-dominant lists, have already been described. These results were in the opposite direction to those predicted by an arousal theory of time-of-day effects, and other studies (e.g. Smith, 1987a) have failed to find any interaction between time of day and dominance.

The general conclusion from the above studies is that selectivity in memory and attention does not differ in the early morning and early evening. Furthermore, where there have been differences they have often been in the opposite direction to that predicted by an arousal theory of time-of-day effects. One should point out, however, that reliable time-of-day effects have been observed with serial search tasks, which surely must be regarded as selective attention tasks. The faster search speed later in the day could reflect two things. First, there is evidence from several different areas that there is a change in the speed/error trade-off function over the day, with performance being faster but less accurate later in the day. Second, reliable time-of-day effects are not found in free-search tasks where the subject can scan the material in any way (Monk and Leng, 1982). This suggests that there may be a change in the focusing of attention over the day, with information being sampled from a wider visual angle later in the day. This could explain why colour patches are named more quickly in the morning, whereas reading words, which involves the established techniques of reading and where the eyes are focused on material ahead of the word being uttered, is better later in the day.

Motor tasks

Early work on simple motor tasks (e.g. card sorting) suggested that this type of performance shows a similar trend to that of serial search. However, other studies (reviewed by Monk and Leng, 1982) suggest that motor tasks peak about midday. Monk and Leng (1982) argue that time-of-day effects in motor tasks reflect a change in strategy over the day. They suggest that performance is faster but less accurate later in the day. If one is performing a manual dexterity task, such as transferring pegs from one solitaire set to another, there will be a point where poor accuracy also reduces speed (i.e. the pegs are fumbled). This would explain why performance on such tasks slows down later in the day. This suggests that time-of-day effects in performance may reflect differences in the way tasks are performed rather than changes in the efficiency of processes, and this view is expanded in the next section.

Strategies of performance at different times of day

It has already been shown that performance on perceptual motor tasks often becomes faster but less accurate later in the day (see Blake, 1971; Craig and Condon, 1984, 1985; Monk and Leng, 1982 for specific examples). There is also evidence from cognitive tasks which shows that different strategies are used at different times. Folkard (1979) presents evidence that subjects carry out more 'maintenance processing' in the morning but more 'elaborative encoding' in the afternoon. Indeed, the decrease in digit span over the day may reflect a decline in the use of subvocal rehearsal. Folkard (1980) reanalysed the data from Folkard, Monk, Bradbury and Rosenthall (1977) and found that the better recall in the morning was due to greater recall of unimportant information at this time. Oakhill (1988) has recently shown that the superior immediate recall of text in the morning can be attributed to better verbatim memory at this time. Similarly, Mackenberg, Broverman, Vogel and Klaiber (1974) found that tasks requiring repetitive drill were learned more effectively in the morning, while those requiring restructuring and complex thought were learned better in the afternoon.

There is also other evidence to support the notion that more elaborative processing occurs in the afternoon. Oakhill (1986a) found that subjects presented with a story in the afternoon remembered more important information after a delay of a week than did morning subjects. Marks and Folkard (1988) examined the effects of time of day on recall of information from lectures. There was no effect of time of day on the amount of information recalled, but presentation in the early evening was associated with better delayed recall of important information than was morning presentation. This effect appeared to be related to an improvement later in the day in the subjects' ability to construct a representation of text which incorporates the text's hierarchical structure. Similarly, Oakhill (1988) found that afternoon subjects integrated the text as they were reading it, so that they had an enduring memory for the gist of the text but not for the exact meaning.

If some time-of-day effects depend on the task being performed in a certain way, then it should be possible to alter the effects by eliminating that strategy. This has been demonstrated by Folkard and Monk (1979), who showed that articulatory suppression reduced immediate recall of pre-recency items in the morning but not in the afternoon. Similarly, Folkard (unpublished, cited by Folkard and Monk, 1985) found that neither an acoustically confusable verbal reasoning task nor a visuo-spatial reasoning task showed a reliable trend over the day. This suggests that diurnal variations in working memory performance may be limited to tasks that normally benefit from the use of the articulatory loop.

Another example of the removal of time-of-day effects by changing the way of doing the task has been shown with a semantic memory task. Smith (1987a) found that performance on a category instance task was quicker later in the day when subjects were given separate lists of dominant and non-dominant instances. However, when the two types of instance were mixed in the same list, and the subjects had constantly to change retrieval strategies, then the time-of-day effect was abolished.

Other time-of-day effects are not modified by voluntary changes in strategy. Smith (in preparation, b) examined the effects of time of testing on a serial reaction-time task. Each subject carried out three conditions. The instruction in the first condition was the usual one to 'respond as quickly and as accurately as possible'. In the other conditions either speed or accuracy was emphasized. Performance was faster but less accurate in the early evening compared to the early morning and this was observed in all conditions (even though the instructions changed performance in the desired way).

All of these results show that many time-of-day effects are not due to changes in the efficiency or capacity of the fundamental cognitive processes, but reflect differences in the way tasks are performed at different times of day. The next section examines the effects of consumption of meals on performance.

EFFECTS OF MEALS ON PERFORMANCE

The post-lunch dip

It is obviously of prime importance to identify those diurnal variations in performance which are produced by external agents such as meals. Post-lunch impairments have been found both in real-life jobs (Bjerner and Swensson, 1953; Hildebrandt, Rohmert and Rutenfranz, 1974) and in the laboratory (e.g. Blake, 1971; Craig, Baer and Diekmann, 1981). The following section reviews this topic.

Food-related impairments

It has been suggested that post-lunch impairments are due to endogenous rhythms rather than to the consumption of the meal. However, recent studies have shown that certain changes in performance do depend on eating lunch. For example, Craig, Baer and Diekmann (1981) found that perceptual sensitivity declined following lunch, but they observed no change in performance in subjects who abstained from eating. Similarly, Smith and Miles (1986a, 1987a) showed that subjects detected fewer targets in a cognitive vigilance task and had longer response latencies in a serial reaction-time task after eating lunch. These results are of major interest because, unlike other time-of-day effects, comsumption of lunch reduces the efficiency of performance of sustained attention tasks.

One must now ask what types of task are impaired after lunch. Craig (1986) has suggested that short-duration tasks rarely show an effect of lunch (Christie and McBrearty, 1979). However, Smith and Miles (1986b) used an attention task with a high memory load and rapid presentation rate (a version of the Bakan vigilance task), and found that the post-lunch impairment was apparent in the first minute of the task. This is shown in Figure 12.4. Similarly, Smith and Miles (1987b) found post-lunch impairments with a short search task which had a high memory load, although they failed to demons-

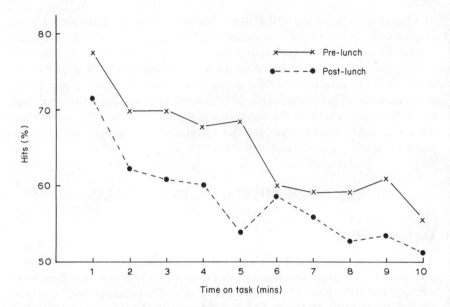

Figure 12.4. Percentage of hits in the pre- and post-meal tests during each minute of the task (after Smith and Miles, 1986b).

trate any impairment with a short, low memory-loaded version. Spring, Maller, Wurtman, Digman and Cozolino (1983) found that consumption of lunch had no effect on performance on a dichotic listening task. Further evidence that lunch has little effect on selective attention was obtained by Smith and Miles (1987a), who showed that it did not change the amount of interference found in the Stroop test.

In many studies it is difficult to tell whether differences between late morning and early afternoon are due to the meal or reflect endogenous factors (because of the absence of a 'no meal' condition). However, many of these studies do show that the local lunchtime effect is different from that observed in studies comparing early morning and evening. For example, Smith (1988) showed that delayed recall of text was worse after lunch than before. However, he found no interaction between pre/post-lunch testing and the importance of the information recalled, whereas Oakhill (1986a), comparing early morning and evening, found an interaction between time of day and the important/unimportant information. Similarly, Smith (1987a) found no difference between early morning and late afternoon in the number of targets detected in the Bakan task, but Smith and Miles (1986b) showed a very clear post-lunch impairment on this task.

Effects which do not depend upon the consumption of lunch

It should be pointed out that there are differences between late morning and early afternoon which do not depend on food intake. For example, Smith and Miles (1987a) found that movement time in the serial reaction task was slower in the afternoon both for subjects who had eaten lunch and for those who had not. Several pre/post-lunch differences were also observable for both groups in performance of the Stroop test. Here the trend was similar to that seen in studies comparing early morning and late afternoon, with colours being named more quickly in the morning and words being read more quickly in the afternoon. Folkard and Monk (1985) argue that the strongest evidence for an endogenous component in the post-lunch dip comes from isolation studies. Here a dip in performance resembling the post-lunch dip is observed even though the performance rhythm is often running with a different period from that of food ingestion, which is normally associated with the sleep-wake cycle.

Individual differences

The effects of lunch on performance have been shown to depend on the type of meal (Spring, Maller, Wurtman, Digman and Cozolino, 1983) and on the characteristics of the person eating it. Craig, Baer and Diekmann (1981) found that the extent of the post-lunch impairment correlated with scores on the Eysenck Personality Inventory, with stable extraverts showing the biggest drop. Smith and Miles (1986b) confirmed this result and found that state anxiety was an even better predictor of individual differences in the extent of the dip, with subjects who showed the biggest post-lunch drop in anxiety also having the greatest decline in performance. Craig and Richardson (cited by Craig, 1986) examined the influence of eating habits on the size of the post-lunch dip. They found that when the meal consisted of a large lunch, then it was the subjects who normally had a small lunch who showed the largest impairment. When the meal consisted of a light snack it was those who regularly had a large meal at this time who showed the impairment.

Importance of the timing of the meal

Both Craig, Baer and Diekmann (1981) and Smith and Miles (1986a, 1987a) examined whether the time at which lunch was eaten modified the extent of the post-lunch dip, and both failed to find any differential effects of 'early' and 'late' lunches. However, there is evidence that the time of day at which the meal is eaten is important in determining its effect on performance. For example, there is little evidence of a post-breakfast dip in performance (although this may reflect the lack of data on the effects of breakfast). Smith

(1988) found that subjects who ate breakfast showed a more rapid increase in alertness than those who had no breakfast. There was, however, no evidence of significant performance differences between the two groups.

One reason why there may be a lack of effects of breakfast is that this meal is typically much smaller than lunch. Smith and Miles (1986b, 1987b) were able to compare the effects of identical meals eaten in the middle of day and night shifts. A post-meal impairment in the detection of targets in the Bakan vigilance test was found both during the day and night. However, there were three reasons for suspecting that the day and night effects were produced in different ways. First, the post-lunch dip is often considered to involve a decrease in efficiency after the meal followed by a subsequent improvement. This was observed during the day but, in contrast to this, performance at night continued to decline. Second, analysis of response latencies revealed differences between the effects of meals in the day and night, with reaction times being slower after the meal in the day but unaffected by the meal at night. Finally, the correlation between changes in anxiety and the size of post-meal dip was much smaller at night than in the day. Smith and Miles (1986b) have suggested that the post-meal impairment has both a food-related and an endogenous component and the correlation between performance changes and anxiety changes may reflect the contribution of the meal. The above results suggest that the food-dependent effect is greater during the day than at night.

The post-lunch dip and other factors which alter alertness

Smith (1985b) has shown that subjects who have eaten lunch report lower levels of alertness and anxiety than they did in the pre-lunch period. It is of major interest, therefore, to examine whether other factors known to change altertness, such as noise, alter the extent of the post-lunch dip. Smith and Miles (1986b) found a 16 per cent drop in hits after the meal for subjects tested in quiet, whereas those tested in 75 dBA noise showed only a 3 per cent drop. A similar interaction between noise and pre/post-meal tests is reported by Smith and Miles (1987b) with noise reducing the extent of the post-meal decline in speed of performance of a memory-loaded search task. Furthermore, Smith and Miles (1986b) have suggested that noise influences the food-related component of the post-meal dip, because it reduces the correlation between anxiety and performance changes.

It has already been shown that post-lunch effects are often quite different from results found in experiments comparing performance in the early morning and late afternoon. Other evidence for this comes from studies of the interaction of noise and time of day. Smith (in press) found no evidence of moderate-intensity noise interacting with time of testing when subjects were tested at 9.00, 12.00 and 18.00, while the above results show that noise modifies the post-lunch dip. This suggests that there are at least two distinct time-of-day effects, and while both involve changes in alertness, it is the effect produced by the exogenous component which is modified by noise.

The following section considers the effects of nightwork on performance to see whether results from a wider range of times are consistent with the view of time-of-day effects based on studies carried out within the normal day.

EXPERIMENTAL STUDIES OF NIGHTWORK

Kleitman and Jackson (1950) and Colquhoun, Blake and Edwards (1968) assessed performance efficiency under the rapidly rotating watch-keeping systems with the four-hour duty spells which are commonly found on warships. The results from the night watches (either before a delayed sleep or after a reduced sleep) showed that perceptual motor tasks are impaired at

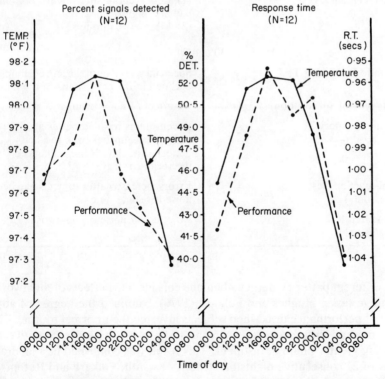

Figure 12.5. The trend over the day for signal detection efficiency and time to detect signals in a simulated sonar task. Body temperature is also shown (after Colquhoun, Blake and Edwards, 1986).

Table 1. A summary of the performance tests used in the study of noise and nightwork, the times at which they are performed, and the overall results (after Smith and Miles, 1985; 1986b; 1987).

Battery 1. Times—09.00, 10.00, 12.00, 13.30, 14.30, 16.30, 22.00, 23.00, 01.00, 02.30, 03.30, 05.30	
Pegboard test	Performed more slowly at night
Logical Reasoning Test	No effect of noise or nightwork
Low-memory-load Search Test	Performed more slowly in the second half of the night
High-memory-load Search Test	(1) Performed more slowly after meals, both in the day and night (2) More errors in noise
Battery 2. Times—09.30, 11.40, 14.00, 16.30, 22.30, 00.40, 03.00, 05.10	
Simple reaction-time Test	Reaction times slower at night
Bakan Vigilance Test	(1) Less accurate after meals, both in the day and night (2) More errors in noise
Battery 3. Times—10.30, 15.00, 23.30 and 04.00	
Semantic Processing Test	Speed increased until the late evening, then declined in the early hours of the morning
Digit–symbol Substitution	No effect of noise or nightwork
Running-memory Test	Recent items recalled better at night, items further back recalled better in the day. Noise influenced the recall strategy
Serial-reaction Test (males only)	Errors increased after subjects had been in noise for some time
Free-search test (females only)	No effect of noise or nightwork

A different pattern emerges when one considers the effects of nightwork on cognitive tasks. Hughes and Folkard (1976) examined the degree of adjustment of performance tests when subjects inverted their normal routine. There were marked differences between the tasks, with the more cognitive tests showing greater phase adjustment. This result was confirmed in a laboratory study of 21 consecutive nightshifts (Monk, Knauth, Folkard and Rutenfranz, 1978). Folkard, Knauth, Monk and Rutenfranz (1976) examined the effects of a rapidly rotating shift system on performance of low-, medium- and high-memory-load search tasks. The results showed that the more complex version was performed better at night.

Smith and Miles (1985; 1986c) examined the effects of nightwork on a range of tasks. These results are summarized in Table 12.1. Generally, the results confirm those from previous studies, with performance of perceptual motor tasks being impaired at night (or at least in the latter part of the night shift) whereas performance on working-memory tasks was not. Additionally, the study demonstrated that semantic memory tasks show a similar trend to the perceptual motor tasks, and are performed more slowly at night. The overall performance level on some tasks was the same at night as in the day but a more detailed analysis revealed selective effects of nightwork, with some parts of the task being impaired at night and others being better at that time. This was found in a running-memory task, with recent items being recalled better at night than during the day, and items further back in the list being recalled better in the day (Miles and Smith, 1988).

One of the main aims of the Smith and Miles study was to examine the combined effects of noise and nightwork. The results showed that both factors influenced performance but that their effects were independent. This confirms results from studies within the normal day and argues against interpreting the effects of these factors in terms of a uni-dimensional theory of arousal. One must now ask which framework should be used to interpret diurnal variation in performance. A recent approach has been to apply circadian rhythm models to changes in performance and these are described in the next section.

TEMPORAL ISOLATION STUDIES

These studies involve placing subjects in isolation so that the influence of external time cues ('Zeitgebers') is eliminated. The various rhythms are allowed to 'free run' or are influenced by artificially induced time cues with a periodicity different from the normal 24-hour day. Such techniques have provided important information about the circadian system, but until recently the research has examined physiological rather than performance variations. On the basis of temporal isolation studies Wever (1979) proposed that there are two (or at least two) 'clocks' or 'oscillators' controlling the circadian system. One is associated with temperature variations, the other with the sleep-wake cycle. Any rhythm may be controlled by both oscillators, but the effect of one will usually dominate.

Folkard and Monk (1982) examined changes in the performance rhythms of low- and high-memory-load tasks during temporal isolation where normal sleep was replaced with four hours sleep at night and a further four hours sleep at times which would have been in the normal working day. This routine led to a dissociation of rhythms, with the low-memory-load task adopting a period of 24.6 hours while the high-memory-load task followed a period of 22.7 hours. Other studies (e.g. Folkard, Wever and Wildgruber, 1983) have provided further evidence for the notion that there must be more than one 'clock' responsible for circadian variations in performance.

One of the major problems with these studies is that the researchers have been looking for rhythms associated with particular types of task. Research using the traditional time-of-day paradigm has shown that many diurnal variations reflect differences in the way the task is performed. It may be misleading, therefore, to examine rhythms for a task without knowing, or manipulating, the way in which it is performed. Another problem is that tasks like logical reasoning often consist of items of varying difficulty, which may mean that there are distinct rhythms for different types of items. The average rhythm for logical reasoning may, therefore, be no more representative of these separate rhythms than the average time-of-day effect observed by early researchers was of the individual tasks carried out.

The above criticisms are not meant to imply that the approach should be abandoned. However, time-of-day effects in performance may reflect many different things and it is unclear exactly which phenomena will be explained by studies of endogenous rhythms. Indeed, some evidence has already been presented to show that time-of-day effects in performance are easily modified and further evidence for this view is presented in the next section.

TIME OF DAY AND MOTIVATION

Colquhoun (1981) has suggested that some time-of-day effects may be produced by diurnal variation in motivation rather than by passive changes in the efficiency of psychological processes. Indeed, the late peak in performance observed by Blake (1967) may reflect a 'last test' or 'end effect'. What evidence is there that task-related motivation changes over the day? Smith (1985b) found that state anxiety was significantly higher in the afternoon than in the morning. A more detailed description of diurnal changes in motivational profiles is reported by Smith (1987b). These results showed that the early-morning state is characterized by high levels of aspiration and low fear of failure, whereas in the late afternoon subjects put more effort into performing tasks, but only into operations which are likely to repay this investment of effort. This view is consistent with results obtained by Oakhill (1986b), which showed that subjects engaged in more effortful processing later in the day, but only when such processing enabled them to answer a subsequent question more rapidly. Breen-Lewis and Wilding (1984) manipulated the amount of effortful processing in a memory task by leading subjects to expect either recall (active, effortful encoding) or recognition. All subjects were, in fact, given a recall test and in the morning there was no difference between subjects given different test expectations. However, in the afternoon those expecting recall performed better than those expecting recognition, suggesting that subjects may adopt effortful processing strategies more readily at this time.

An alternative way of examining the role of motivation is to investigate whether changes in motivation alter time-of-day effects in performance. Blake (1971) showed that diurnal variations in performing a letter-cancellation task could be removed by announcing each subject's score to the group being tested. Similarly, Chiles, Alluisi and Adams (1968) found that raised levels of motivation removed the circadian variation found in a number of performance measures. These results show that time-of-day effects can be removed by changing motivation. Smith (1987b) has shown that time-of-day effects can actually be created by manipulating motivation. In this experiment subjects carried out a version of the Bakan task in the early morning and late afternoon. The control group showed no difference in performance at these times. Another group of subjects were informed that their results would be made public. This manipulation increased anxiety, especially in the afternoon. The greater change in anxiety in the afternoon was associated with a greater improvement in performance. In other words, the 'results made public' group showed a time-of-day effect, presumably because the instruction produced different changes in anxiety at the two times. This result has important implications for the treatment of anxiety. If time of day influences the extent to which anxiety can be increased it also seems likely that methods of reducing anxiety will be more effective at certain times of day.

These studies show that one must take account of the 'whole test situation' when considering diurnal variation in performance. One crucial part of this situation is the personality of the subject and some individual differences in time-of-day effects are described in the next section.

INDIVIDUAL DIFFERENCES

Introversion–extraversion

Colquhoun (1960) and Colquhoun and Corcoran (1964) found that introverts performed better than extraverts in the morning, whereas there was little difference between the two groups in the afternoon. Blake (1971) was able to confirm the superiority of introverts in the morning and he also showed the reverse effect in the afternoon. However, Colquhoun and Corcoran (1964) found that introverts were only better than extraverts in the morning when the subjects were tested in isolation, and the presence of other subjects improved extraverts in the morning. Once again this demonstrates the importance of situational factors in determining time-of-day effects in performance.

The above studies used simple performance tests. Revelle, Humphreys, Simon and Gilliland (1980) used a cognitive task and found that it was the impulsivity component of the extraversion scale that was responsible for the time-of-day effects.

Morning/evening types

It has been recognized that some people prefer to work in the morning whereas others prefer the evening. Horne, Brass and Pettit (1980) found that morning types detected more targets in the morning, while evening types were better later in the day. One of the important features of this study was that while there were large individual differences in performance, the morning and evening types had very similar temperature rhythms. This clearly demonstrates that time-of-day effects in performance do not always show the same trend as the temperature rhythm.

It would appear, therefore, that both inter-individual differences and inter-task ones are important determinants of time-of-day effects. Monk and Leng (1986) examined time-of-day effects for morning and evening types using a simple search task and a logical reasoning task. Only the logical reasoning test showed a significant interaction between time of day and morningness, with the 'larks' being best at 8.00 and the 'owls' showing a later (11.00) peak. This shows that the differences between the performance rhythms of morning and evening tasks are much greater for cognitive tasks than for perceptual motor tasks.

CONCLUSIONS

The first conclusion one can draw from the evidence presented in this chapter is that performance of a wide range of tasks changes over the day. These diurnal variations are often large, with efficiency changing by ± 15 per cent of the daily average. Where a person has only one task to perform over the day it may be beneficial to advance or delay the hours of work to take into account the time-of-day effects associated with that task. There are also individual differences in the time-of-day effects found with cognitive tasks, which means that efficiency may be improved by matching people with times most suited to their circadian typologies. The second conclusion is that the exact pattern of diurnal variation depends on the nature of the task being performed. If a person has to carry out different activities over the day efficiency may be improved by scheduling certain tasks for the morning and others in the afternoon.

Time-of-day effects depend not only upon the nature of the task but also on the way it is carried out. Indeed, results from recent studies suggest that many time-of-day effects do not reflect automatic changes arising from processing limitations, but are produced by the adoption of different strategies over the course of the day. This in turn means that time-of-day effects can easily be modified by changing the way the person does the task. At the moment it is unclear whether the strategy changes observed over the day are due to voluntary, goal-directed activities aimed at maintaining competent performance, or whether they are the result of passive shifts in the use of processing resources.

The area is advancing because researchers are becoming interested in examining changes in the way tasks are performed rather than looking at gross measures of performance efficiency. Most studies have only examined qualitative differences in performance in cases where there is also a quantitative difference. However, it is also possible that methods of doing tasks change over the day but do not always result in significant differences in the level of performance. It is, therefore, very dangerous to say performance is equivalent at two times of day without having a very detailed profile of the microstructure of responding.

One must ask why some strategies are used more readily at certain times. The first possible explanation is that this directly reflects changes in the physiological state of the individual. Alternatively, the individual's appraisal of the whole situation may lead to the adoption of certain strategies rather than others. What is apparent is that diurnal variations are produced in many different ways. The roles of endogenous rhythms, exogenous factors and motivational changes have all been discussed. However, it is the combination of these factors, and the individual's interpretation of them, which determines the nature of the observed diurnal variations in performance. This suggests that future studies should collect as much information as possible about all factors relevant to task performance rather than considering just the time of testing and examining changes in general indices of performance such as average speed and accuracy.

REFERENCES

Aschoff, J. & Wever, R. (1981). The circadian system in man, in J. Aschoff (ed.), *Handbook of Behavioural Neurobiology*, vol. 4. New York: Plenum Press.
Baddeley, A. D. (1986). *Working Memory*. Oxford: Oxford University Press.
Baddeley, A. D., Hatter, J. E., Scott, D. & Snashall, A. (1970). Memory and time of day, *Quarterly Journal of Experimental Psychology*, **22**, 605–609.

Bjerner, B. & Swensson, A. (1953). Shiftwork and rhythm, *Acta Medica Scandinavica*, **278**, 102–107.

Blake, M. J. F. (1967). Time of day effects on performance in a range of tasks, *Psychonomic Science*, **9**, 345–350.

Blake, M. J. F. (1971). Temperament and time of day, in W. P. Colquhoun (ed.), *Biological Rhythms and Human Performance*. London & New York: Academic Press.

Breen-Lewis, K. & Wilding, J. (1984). Noise, time of day and test expectations in recall and recognition, *British Journal of Psychology*, **75**, 51–63.

Chiles, W. D., Alluisi, E. A. & Adams, O. (1968). Work schedules and performance during confinement, *Human Factors*, **10**, 143–196.

Christie, M. J. & McBrearty, E. M. T. (1979). Psychophysical investigations of post-lunch state in male and female subjects, *Ergonomics*, **22**, 307–323.

Colquhoun, W. P. (1960). Temperament, inspection efficiency and time of day, *Ergonomics*, **3**, 377–378.

Colquhoun, W. P. (1981). Rhythms in performance, in J. Aschoff (ed.), *Handbook of Behavioural Neurobiology*, vol. 4. New York: Plenum Press.

Colquhoun, W. P., Blake, M. J. F. & Edwards, R. S (1968). Experimental studies of shift work. I: A comparison of 'rotating' and 'stabilized' 4-hour systems, *Ergonomics*, **11**, 437–453.

Colquhoun, W. P. & Corcoran, D. W. J. (1964). The effects of time of day and social isolation on the relationship between temperament and performance, *British Journal of Social and Clinical Psychology*, **3**, 226–231.

Craig, A. (1979). Discrimination, temperature and time of day, *Human Factors*, **21**, 61–68.

Craig, A. (1986). Acute effects of meals on perceptual and cognitive efficiency. *Diet and behavior: A multidisciplinary evaluation*, *Nutrition Reviews*, **44**, Supplement, 163–171.

Craig, A., Baer, K. & Diekmann, A. (1981). The effects of lunch on sensory-perceptual functioning in man, *International Archives of Occupational and Environmental Health*, **49**, 105–114.

Craig, A. & Condon, R. (1984). Operational efficiency and time of day, *Human Factors*, **26**, 197–205.

Craig, A. & Condon, R. (1985). Speed-accuracy trade-off and time of day, *Acta Psychologica*, **58**, 115–122.

Craig, A., Wilkinson, R. T. & Colquhoun, W. P. (1981). Diurnal variation in vigilance efficiency, *Ergonomics*, **24**, 641–651.

Davies, D. R. & Parasuraman, R. (1982). *The Psychology of Vigilance*. London: Academic Press.

Davies, D. R., Parasuraman, R. & Toh, M.-Y. (1984). Time of day, memory load and vigilance performance, in A. Mital (ed.), *Trends in Ergonomics/Human Factors*, 1. North Holland: Elsevier.

Easterbrook, J. A. (1959). The effect of emotion on cue utilization and the organization of behaviour, *Psychological Review*, **66**, 183–201.

Folkard, S. (1975). Diurnal variation in logical reasoning, *British Journal of Psychology*, **66**, 1–8.

Folkard, S. (1979). Time of day and level of processing, *Memory and Cognition*, **7**, 247–252.

Folkard, S. (1980). A note on 'Time of day effects in school children's immediate and delayed recall of meaningful material'—the influence of the importance of the information tested, *British Journal of Psychology*, **71**, 95–97.

Folkard, S. (1983). Diurnal variation, in G. R. J. Hockey (ed.), *Stress and Fatigue in Human Performance*. Chichester: Wiley.

Folkard, S., Knauth, P., Monk, T. H. & Rutenfranz, J. (1976). The effect of memory load on the circadian variation in performance efficiency under a rapidly rotating shift system, *Ergonomics*, **19**, 479–488.

Folkard, S. & Monk, T. H. (1979). Time of day and processing strategy in free recall, *Quarterly Journal of Experimental Psychology*, **31**, 461–475.

Folkard, S. & Monk, T. H. (1980). Circadian rhythms in human memory, *British Journal of Psychology*, **71**, 295–307.

Folkard, S. & Monk, T. H. (1982). Circadian rhythms in performance—one or more oscillators? in R. Sinz & M. R. Rosenzweig (eds), *Psychophysiology 1980— Memory, Motivation and Event-related Potentials in Mental Operations*, Amsterdam: Elsevier.

Folkard, S. & Monk, T. H. (1985). Circadian performance rhythms, in S. Folkard & T. H. Monk (eds), *Hours of Work: Temporal Factors in Work Scheduling*. Chichester: Wiley.

Folkard, S., Monk, T. H., Bradbury, R. & Rosenthall, J. (1977). Time of day effects in school children's immediate and delayed recall of meaningful material, *British Journal of Psychology*, **68**, 45–50.

Folkard, S., Wever, R. A. & Wildgruber, C. M. (1983). Multioscillatory control of circadian rhythms in human performance, *Nature*, **305**, 223–226.

Fort, A. & Mills, J. N. (1976). Der Einfluss der Tageszeit und des vorhergehenden Schlaf-Wach-Musters auf die Leistungsfahigkeit unmittelbar nach dem Aufsteren, in G. Hildebrandt (ed.), *Biologische Rhythmen und Arbeit*, Heidelberg: Springer Verlag.

Freeman, G. L. & Hovland, C. I. (1934). Diurnal variations in performance and related physiological processes, *Psychological Bulletin*, **31**, 777–799.

Gale, A. Bull, R., Penfold, V., Coles, M. & Barraclough, R. (1972). Extraversion, time of day, vigilance performance and physiological arousal: failure to replicate traditional findings, *Psychonomic Science*, **29**, 1–5.

Gates, A. I. (1916). Variations in efficiency during the day, together with practice effects, sex differences, and correlations, *University of California Publications in Psychology*, **2**, 1–156.

Hartley, L. R. & Shirley, E. (1976). Color-name interference at different times of day, *Journal of Applied Psychology*, **61**, 119–122.

Hildebrandt, G., Rohmert, W. & Rutenfranz, J. (1974). Twelve and 24 hour rhythms in error frequency of locomotive drivers and the influence of tiredness, *International Journal of Chronobiology*, **2**, 97–110.

Hockey, G. R. J., Davies, S. & Gray, M. M. (1972). Forgetting as a function of sleep at different times of day, *Quarterly Journal of Experimental Psychology*, **24**, 386–393.

Horne, J. A., Brass, C. G. & Pettit, A. N. (1980). Circadian performance differences between morning and evening 'types', *Ergonomics*, **23**, 129–136.

Hughes, D. G. & Folkard, S. (1976). Adaptation to an 8-h shift in living routine by members of a socially isolated community, *Nature*, **264**, 232–234.

Klein, K. E., Herrmann, R., Kuklinski, P. & Wegmann, H. M. (1977). Circadian performance rhythms: experimental studies in air operations, in R. R. Mackie (ed.), *Vigilance: Theory, Operational Performance and Physiological Correlates*. New York: Plenum.

Kleitman, N. (1963). *Sleep and Wakefulness*. University of Chicago Press.

Kleitman, N. & Jackson, D. P. (1950). Body temperature and performance under different routines, *Journal of Applied Physiology*, **3**, 309–328.

Laird, D. A. (1925). Relative performance of college students as conditioned by time of day and day of week, *Journal of Experimental Psychology*, **8**, 50–63.

Mackenberg, E. J., Broverman, D. M., Vogel, W. & Klaiber, E. L. (1974). Morning-to-afternoon changes in cognitive performances and in the electroencephalogram, *Journal of Educational Psychology*, **66**, 238–246.

Marks, M. & Folkard, S. (1988). The effects of time of day on recall from expository text, in M. Gruneberg, P. Morris & R. Sykes. (eds), *Practical Aspects of Memory: Current Research and Issues*, vol. 2. Chichester: Wiley.

Millar, K., Styles, B. C. & Wastell, D. G. (1980). Time of day and retrieval from long-term memory, *British Journal of Psychology*, **71**, 407–414.

Miles, C. & Smith, A. P. (1988). The combined effects of noise and nightwork on running memory, in M. Gruneberg, P. Morris & R. Sykes (eds), *Practical Aspects of Memory: Current Research and Issues*, vol. 2, Chichester: Wiley.

Monk, T. H., Knauth, P., Folkard, S. & Rutenfranz, J. (1978). Memory based performance measures in studies of shiftwork, *Ergonomics*, **21**, 819–826.

Monk, T. H. & Leng, V. C. (1982). Time of day effects in simple repetitive tasks: some possible mechanisms, *Acta Psychologica*, **51**, 207–221.

Monk, T. H. & Leng, V. C. (1986). Interactions between inter-individual and inter-task differences in the diurnal variation of human performance, *Chronobiology International*, **3**, 171–177.

Oakhill, J. V. (1986a). Effects of time of day and information importance on adults' memory for a short story, *Quarterly Journal of Experimental Psychology*, **38A**, 419–430.

Oakhill, J. V. (1986b). Effects of time of day on the integration of information in text, *British Journal of Psychology*, **77**, 481–488.

Oakhill, J. V. (1988). Effects of time of day on text memory and inference, in M. Gruneberg, P. Morris & R. Sykes (eds)., *Practical Aspects of Memory: Current Research and Issues*, vol. 2. Chichester: Wiley.

Rabbitt, P. M. A. (1979). Current paradigms and models in human information processing, in V. Hamilton & D. M. Warburton (eds), *Human Stress and Cognition*. Chichester: Wiley.

Revelle, W., Humphrey, M. S., Simon, L. & Gilliland, K. (1980). The interactive effect of personality, time of day and caffeine: a test of the arousal model, *Journal of Experimental Psychology: General*, **109**, 1–31.

Rutenfranz, J. & Helbruegge, T. (1957). Under Tageschwankungen de Rechenges-chwindigkeit bei 11-jahrigen kinder, *Zeitschrift Kinderheilk*, **80**, 65–82.

Smith, A. P. (1982). The effects of noise and task priority on recall of order and location, *Acta Psychologica*, **51**, 245–255.

Smith, A. P. (1985a). Noise, biased probability and serial reaction, *British Journal of Psychology*, **76**, 89–95.

Smith, A. P. (1985b). Diurnal variation in test anxiety and effort, in H. van der Ploeg, R. Schwarzer & C. Spielberger (eds), *Advances in Test Anxiety Research*, vol. 4. Lisse: Swets & Zeitlinger.

Smith, A. P. (1987a). Activation states and semantic processing: a comparison of the effects of noise and time of day, *Acta Psychologica*, **54**, 271–288.

Smith, A. P. (1987b). Task-related motivation and time of testing, in R. Schwarzer, H. van der Ploeg & C. Spielberger (eds), *Advances in Test Anxiety Research*, vol. 5. Lisse: Swets & Zeitlinger.

Smith, A. P. (1988). Effects of meals on memory and attention, in M. Gruneberg, P.

Morris & R. Sykes (eds), *Practical Aspects of Memory: Current Research and Issues*. vol 2. Chichester: Wiley.

Smith, A. P. (in press). Circadian variation in stress: the effects of noise at different times of day, in C. D. Spielberger & J. Strelau (eds), *Stress and Anxiety*, vol. 12. New York: McGraw-Hill.

Smith, A. P. (in preparation, a). Effects of time of day on selectivity in memory and attention.

Smith, A. P. (in preparation, b). Speed and accuracy at different times of day.

Smith. A. P. & Miles, C. (1985). The combined effects of noise and nightwork on human function, in D. Oborne (ed.), *Contemporary Ergonomics 1985*. London: Taylor & Francis.

Smith, A. P. & Miles, C. (1986a). Effects of lunch on cognitive vigilance tasks, *Ergonomics*, **29**, 1251–1261.

Smith, A. P. & Miles, C. (1986b). Acute effects of meals, noise and nightwork, *British Journal of Psychology*, **77**, 377–389.

Smith, A. P. & Miles, C. (1986c). The combined effects of nightwork and noise on human function, in M. Haider, M. Koller & R. Cervinka (eds), *Studies in Industrial and Organizational Psychology 3: Night and Shiftwork: Long-term Effects and their Prevention*. Frankfurt: Peter Lang.

Smith, A. P. & Miles, C. (1987a). Effects of lunch on selective and sustained attention, *Neuropsychobiology*, **16**, 117–120.

Smith, A. P. & Miles, C. (1987b). The combined effects of occupational health hazards: an experimental investigation of the effects of noise, nightwork and meals, *International Archives of Occupational and Environmental Health*, **59**, 83–89.

Spring, B., Maller, O., Wurtman, J., Digman, L. & Cozolino, L. (1983). Effects of protein and carbohydrate meals on mood and performance: interactions with sex and age, *Journal of Psychiatric Research*, **17**, 155–167.

Tilley, A. & Warren, P. (1983). Retrieval from semantic memory at different times of day, *Journal of Experimental Psychology: Learning, Memory and Cognition*, **9**, 718–724.

Wever, R. (1979). *The Circadian System of Man: Results of Experiments under Temporal Isolation*. New York: Springer-Verlag.

Yerkes, R. M. & Dodson, J. D. (1908). The relation to the strength of stimulus to the rapidity of habit formation, *Journal of Comparative Neurology and Psychology*, **18**, 459–482.

Epilogue

Ann Colley and John Beech

The chapters in this book have dealt with the applied as well as the theoretical issues which have emerged from research on cognitive skill learning and performance. It is not possible to provide a neat summary of what has gone before: the breadth of topics covered by the authors is too great. We shall confine ourselves here to outlining some themes which have emerged with some consistency across a number of chapters in this book. These can be regarded as pointers for the direction of future research.

Metacognitive processes

The importance of metacognitive processes in the development of expertise and in expert performance becomes clear in several chapters. In Sincoff and Sternberg's review of theories of the dynamic process of cognitive skill development during childhood we find the suggestion that metacognition, or metacomponential processing, becomes increasingly important for older children. They suggest that further research is necessary to clarify its role in early childhood.

There are individual differences in the ability to monitor one's own performance and to plan ahead, and the strategies used to do this. These individual differences must be taken into account in training, as Annett makes clear in his chapter. The application of metacognitive knowledge is most obvious at the early stages of learning a new skill when there is executive control of decisions which will be later embodied in procedural memory and inaccessible to awareness. Colley's chapter advances the view that the initial stages of motor skill learning are heavily reliant on verbalizable strategies to control the approximation to a desired movement which may later be linked more directly to information perceived in the environment. Annett refers to Fitts' work in the 1960s which gave some prominence to the role of planning and strategic processes early in skill learning. He then goes on to discuss in some detail how individuals can learn what is required of them in a particular task, and use this knowledge to guide their performance. Annett also briefly discusses the literature on learning deficiencies, in which it has been found that poor learners lack metacognitive skills. There is some evidence that such skills can be trained; however, this evidence is not particularly strong, and given the importance of this issue for training, further research is badly needed.

Ericsson and Oliver's chapter details the strategies used by individuals with exceptional memory skills. The value of such observations for our knowledge of human memory lies in the rich and detailed descriptions provided by their subjects of the ways in which they encoded and recalled large amounts of information. The methodology of using protocol data, then validating this with performance data, highlights the importance of individual differences. This has several advantages, some of which are discussed below. Too little attention has probably been paid to the differences between experts in their performance at a given task, and more naturalistic studies of skilled performance can provide data on these differences which are overlooked by standard cross-sectional designs with one or more dependent variables.

Developing expertise

One gap in our current knowledge of the development of expertise in most fields, which is made apparent in Gilhooly and Green's chapter on problem solving is that there is much still to be discovered about how experts acquire and structure their knowledge. The traditional paradigm of comparing expert and novice performance, while valuable in elucidating what the novice needs to learn, can throw little light on how this is to be acquired. Gilhooly and Green suggest that training programmes which attempt to teach novices the knowledge structures and strategies of the expert may not be using the most effective method. A different approach would be to conduct longitudinal studies of skill acquisition over a long time span. Intensive studies of individuals are becoming a more acceptable and popular methodology in this area. The validity of this kind of research has been increased by the use of artificial intelligence methods to embody the conclusions drawn by the experimenters in computer simulations of the learning process. Elsom-Cook's chapter on the acquisition of computing skills emphasizes the value of such methods.

The resource pool

An area of cognition which seems to us to be particularly problematic from the point of view of trying to find a comprehensive framework for diverse findings concerns the deployment of processing resources. The phenomenon of selective attention has had a somewhat turbulent history from the early 1950s onwards in the generation of explanatory theories. Barber's chapter on dual task performance catalogues some of this history and concludes that many of the findings in the area reviewed are task-dependent. The recent distinction between controlled and automatic processing has run into difficulties of definition, as we point out in our introduction. It might be yet another theoretical distinction which only functions within restricted settings.

Understanding how we allocate resources to tasks is fundamental to the application of cognitive psychology in the real world. The chapter by Hartley, Morrison and Arnold on the effects of stressors of different kinds on performance illustrates this point. Stressors affect the way in which we direct attention and utilize processing resources. It is difficult to draw a more specific conclusion than this when we do not know whether we referring to a single pool of resources or different, more specialized pools, as they point out. Taking the parallel distributed processes view currently in vogue, we assume that multiple specialized pools are involved. Indeed, Allport (1980) has similarly argued that interference between tasks and apparent limitations are imposed by structural factors. However, as Barber's assessment of the situation shows, there are 'bloody-minded findings' which defeat every theoretical account so far offered.

Individual differences

Individual differences are inconvenient for the researcher who is looking for general rules of behaviour and for this reason have received less attention from cognitive psychologists than they merit. In fact, they have attracted very little interest until relatively recently. Nevertheless, they are very evident in all skills and therefore for obvious practical reasons it is important to understand, for example, the way in which a teaching programme for backward readers should be structured, to accommodate to idiosyncratic learning patterns of different subgroups of beginning readers. Similarly, comparison of experts within a field will show that they do not all structure the same task in the same way, and such variations in performance must be of interest and relevance in trying to understand the nature of their expertise.

One source of individual differences in cognitive function considered at some length in this book is ageing, the topic of Salthouse's chapter. Older and younger subjects are compared in order to find out whether particular skills or components thereof show effects of age on their acquisition and performance. Salthouse explains how the study of ageing, and more particularly the questions asked by researchers in this area about the relationship between performance of a total skill and levels of relevant abilities, will have more general implications for our understanding of the skill-constituent ability relationship.

At the other end of the lifespan, Sincoff and Sternberg conclude that, in the interests of accuracy, models of cognitive growth must specify how individual differences among children arise. Various theoretical standpoints argue for differences in rate of growth or differences in the course of growth. Biological, motivational, and environmental/exposure influences are variously proposed. Sternberg's theory in particular places some emphasis on the importance of motivational influences in the context of seeking and learning novel tasks. Preferences for novel tasks encourage learning across a wide variety of situations. Motivation in general has been rather overlooked by cognitive psychologists as a determinant of skill acquisition and performance, partly because it has been viewed as outside of their domain of study. Colleagues in educational and other applied settings have not doubted its key role.

Understanding individual strategies goes some way to clarifying inconsistencies in the way in which individuals perform tasks. Smith's conclusion, that many time-of-day effects could be produced by the use of different strategies over the course of the day, and Hartley et al.'s conclusion that individuals appear to be able to overcome some effects of stress by the appropriate use of strategies suggest that more research effort directed at individual differences would be timely, particularly for the application of research to performance in different environments outside of the laboratory.

So where does all this leave us? There are a number of simple and well-replicated findings, and useful general theories in the area of cognitive skills. For instance, the simple learning curve emerges from the acquisition of a wide range of tasks, Fitts' three stages of acquisition provide a rough approximation of learning changes, and Anderson's theory has proved its usefulness in several areas. Thus, at one level it seems that there are simple phenomena and theories. However, there are also some gaps in our knowledge and phenomena not covered by or difficult for existing theories. The contributors to this book have indicated some of these. As a theoretical structure, neural network modelling, or connectionism, may produce some promising accounts of some apparently contradictory phenomena. The only way to fill gaps in our knowledge is by further study, and it is apparent from the chapters in this book, that we are in a position to be able to identify what needs to be done.

One general point which emerges is that methatheories of skill acquisition are not necessarily useful in answering specific problems in an applied context. This is hardly surprising, but nevertheless the point should be made that since expertise is domain-specific, detailed knowledge of individual skills requires study within their domain and the consideration of individual differences. Individual case studies present problems for the researcher because they are difficult, if not impossible, to treat statistically, although they can be supported by computer simulation or by performance data. A more conventional methodology is to study sub-groups of individuals who appear to have the same characteristics, perhaps in the use of strategies or in cognitive ability. This methodology has been used with some success, particularly in reading research, as Beech's chapter makes clear.

As the editors of the first book in this new Series, we look forward to those to follow, which hopefully will address some of the issues we have outlined.

Author index

338   AUTHOR INDEX

Subject index